The photographs of
following page 1

Injurious to Public Morals

Writers and the Meiji State

Injurious to Public Morals

Writers and the Meiji State

Jay Rubin

University of Washington Press
Seattle and London

This book is published with the assistance of grants from the National Endowment for the Humanities and the Japan Foundation.

Library of Congress Cataloging in Publication Data

Rubin, Jay, 1941–
   Injurious to public morals.

   Bibliography: p.
   1. Japanese literature—Meiji period, 1868–1912—
History and criticism. 2. Japanese literature—20th
century—History and criticism. 3. Censorship—Japan—
History. 4. Literature and state—Japan—History.
I. Title.
PL726.63.C37R8   1983   895.6'4'09   83-47976
         ISBN 0-295-96043-4

To the memory of my father, Milton Rubin

(1909–1963)

Contents

Illustrations

Preface

This book devotes several chapters to the approach of the Pacific War. It also refers to events as early as 1673. Why, then, writers and the *Meiji* state, which lasted only from 1868 to 1912? There are three reasons:

(1) On the one hand, the book is primarily concerned with literary developments falling between the Russo-Japanese War of 1904–1905 and the end of Meiji, a revolutionary period in Japanese literature, when naturalism established the novelist as a detached observer of society, an observer whose insights were often abhorred as "injurious to public morals" and threatening to the sanctity of traditional values.

(2) On the other hand, the state structure established in the Meiji period survived past the end of the Pacific War. The Meiji state perfected the censorship apparatus in the 1880s, and the Meiji state evolved the pervasive thought-control system of the 1930s which led to the disastrous clash of Japanese spirit and Western technology in the 1940s.

(3) And finally, those chapters that do survey the Pacific War years tend to concentrate on writers whose careers began in Meiji and who cannot be taken as truly representative of the majority of writers active at the time. I am interested in the Meiji writers' distinctively modern attitude of critical detachment and in the friction between them and government policies intended to encourage the kind of ideological conformity that supported the prosecution of a suicidal war.

The single most important official policy vis-à-vis writers was the establishment and maintenance of censorship, and much of this book is devoted to describing the structure and function of that system, which has been all but ignored in scholarly studies both here and Japan. But censorship was not the only weapon employed against writers, and it is not the exclusive focus of this book. As part of its ongoing war against independent thought, the government tried to organize writers into one sort of academy or another that would encourage the production of "wholesome" literature. And, as were all subjects of imperial Japan, writers were targets of the programs of social education and indoctrination which sought to establish a harmonious national family.

In relations between writers (or, more often, publishers) and the Meiji state, we encounter the familiar Japanese pattern of avoiding confrontation, but this is by no means the dominant pattern. While outright bans were often faced with silence or resigned hopes for ultimate vindication by the historical process, there were also organized protests, bursts of outrage, and long and impassioned arguments for artistic freedom. Attempts to win writers over with official honors were mostly greeted with contempt in refreshing—often sarcastic—displays of professional pride and independence. The rise of this professional attitude and its conflict with state policy between 1906 and 1913 forms the core of this study. Viewed not in terms of abstract debates between art and life but of crass professional reality—sales, editorial decisions, law courts, official secrets, lurid headlines, commercial exploitation, committee meetings, parties, paper shortages, and police threats—the contribution of modern Japanese writers to their society, to literature, and to humane values that transcend national boundaries becomes all the more impressive.

The writers are impressive as a group and as individuals. One of the most exciting aspects of my research has been the discovery of individuals and their differences. I have tried to convey this sense of variety by avoiding a statistical or summary approach and allowing writers (and editors and censors) to speak in their own voices as much as possible. Where I have found anger and cynicism and irony, I have not been content merely to call them opposition. The demonstration of variety itself may be said to be one of my central theses.

In showing how writers related to official policy, it has been necessary to pursue matters of political and legal history. The most frustrating aspect of reading about censorship through piecemeal references is that they never explain how the system works, who is making the decisions, what their criteria are, what degree of punishment the law stipulates, or what effect this may have on the distribution of a work, plus a host of other questions. I have tried to deal with such matters, but it should be kept in mind that this is finally a book about individual writers, their opinions, and the relationship of the literary values of their works to their working environment.

One thing I have not tried to do here on a systematic basis is to draw parallels between Meiji Japan and the late twentieth-century United States, but these will be obvious enough to anyone familiar with recent judicial action threatening the access of the press to pretrial hearings, undermining the confidentiality of reporters' sources, and otherwise chipping away at the integrity of the First Amendment. We hear echoes of the Meiji state whenever citizens ask governments to enforce for them "contemporary community standards" in deciding what books will be allowed to circulate; when we witness attempts by local governments to handle obscenity cases through police action rather than the public forum of the courts; when the federal government establishes secret declassification guidelines for what the public will be allowed to know about nuclear energy (as in the Atomic Energy Act of 1954); or when our smugly "individualistic" society is swept by government-induced military fever, as began again in the autumn of 1980. The Japanese instance is not long ago and far away: it is simply an extreme example of the classic and perennial argument of politicians who urge us to stifle dissent and to unite behind our government in the name of national security; it offers proof that a nation is never more insecure than when it speaks with one voice.

I had much support in working on this project and I am happy to acknowledge it here.

At the University of Washington, Ken Pyle suggested many valuable sources and encouraged me with his continual interest. Roy Miller often succeeded in concealing his impatience at my seminars and provided the link to some valuable materials. Teruko Chin mobilized the resources of the East Asia Library for me, and Suzy Lee provided guidance to the Law Library. Eddie Harrison and Tom Kaasa also contributed their bibliographical talents. Chapter 15 benefited greatly from Richard Torrance's fondness for library stacks and microfilm.

Others who gave advice, opinions, and hints along the way were Martin Collcutt, Etō Jun, John Haley, Hatanaka Shigeo, Howard Hibbett, Imai Yasuko, Marius Jansen, Sumie Jones, Ron Loftus, Phyllis Lyons, Matsuura Sōzō, Masao Miyoshi, Margit Nagy, Odagiri Hideo, Okudaira Yasuhiro, Robin Radin, Wada Kingo, and Kozo Yamamura.

And then there is my family—Raku, Gen, and Hana—without whose constant love and companionship this book would have been finished long ago. Hana, who was particularly effective in this regard, deserves special thanks for having helped me type the manuscript. My mother, Frances (a.k.a. Baba), contributed some much-appreciated enthusiasm, and all my in-laws, the Sakais, provided an invaluable source of psychological calm.

I was enabled to concentrate my full time on this project during several summers thanks to the support of the School of International Studies and the Graduate School Research Fund, University of Washington; and of the Joint Committee on Japanese Studies of the American Council of Learned Societies and the Social Science Research Council. The greater portion of the book was written during 1978–1979 with the aid of a grant from the National Endowment for the Humanities, a government agency of which even Sōseki would have approved.

A few technical matters need explaining.

Japanese words are romanized in accordance with the modified Hepburn system used in the standard Kenkyūsha *New Japanese-English Dictionary*. The only exception is the word for "newspaper," which is written *shimbun* instead of *shinbun* owing to the wide familiarity of the former. Macrons are omitted from well-known place names.

Japanese personal names are given in the normal Japanese order, surname first. Most of the writers treated here, however, replaced their given names with "elegant sobriquets," as Edward Seidensticker has translated the term *gagō* for us. Oguri Fūyō, for example, is known by the sobriquet Fūyō rather than the surname Oguri. Writers who never adopted such *gagō*, however (for example, Tanizaki Jun'ichirō), are designated by their surnames. This customary Japanese usage has been followed throughout, but cross-referencing is provided in the index.

Titles of Japanese periodicals are not translated except in those few instances when the literal meaning of a title is relevant to the discussion at hand.

Annotations are generally restricted to the citation of sources, but notes containing more substantial material or indicating the availability in English translation of works discussed are footnoted within the text.

Injurious to Public Morals

Writers and the Meiji State

1

Introduction

We must choose what is suitable for us and reject what is harmful.
—*Sheik Mahmoud Abu Obayed*
TIME, *April 16, 1979*

Students of Japanese literature and history find much that is familiar in the current rise of Islamic consciousness. Time after time we encounter spokesmen from Iran or Egypt or Saudi Arabia sounding like conservative Japanese of the Meiji period who knew their country needed Western technology but who feared the power of Western ideas to destroy traditional values. There is an ominously familiar ring, also, to Islamic cries for ideological purity to be gained by the suppression of Western influence. For Japan has clearly demonstrated what can happen when a government enforces a xenophobic orthodoxy.

The Japanese government's program to "reject what is harmful" in literature began in earnest following the victory over Russia in 1905, when a sudden wave of "individualism" gave rise to naturalist fiction. From that point to the end of the Pacific War in 1945, literature was under the constant threat of suppression. Everything we have from the pre-Pacific War period was subject to police evaluation, a fact that seems all the more remarkable when we recall the richness and vitality of that literature.

The greater part of this book will be devoted to the rise of the modern Japanese novel and to government attempts to mitigate its subversive influence. These are discussed in Parts Two and Three, which treat the period from naturalism's declared disillusionment with all traditional values in 1906 to the failure of the Ministry of Education's Committee on Literature in 1913. Part One examines the development and deployment of the Meiji censorship system (with a look at its Edo precursors), while Part Four provides a brief survey of the relationship of writers and the state during the years of the approaching Pacific War.

So little has been written on the Japanese censorship system in English (or in Japanese, for that matter) that I have devoted considerable space to describing the mechanisms provided for it in law and in day-to-day practice. Japan's

system was unique both in design and function. In many respects, however, it
fit the classic pattern. McKeon, Merton, and Gellhorn have noted in *The
Freedom to Read* that

> the pressures for censorship arise from the practical problems characteristic of
> periods of crisis and change; but the arguments for censorship normally turn, not
> on inquiry into those problems and into the means of solving them, but on the
> interrelated dangers of immorality, treason, irreligion, and error. . . . The argu-
> ment is circular: it can begin at any point—actual or alleged immorality,
> irreligion, novel and dangerous ideas, or sedition—and move in any direction.
> The crisis that leads to agitation for censorship may be the threat of aggression by
> a despotic power; or subversion of established institutions; or atheism and devia-
> tion from particular religious tenets; or obscenity, immorality, and crime. The
> arguments for censorship are much the same in all crises, for each contributes to
> and is part of all the others.[1]

Each new step in the growth of the Japanese censorship system was a
response to some development perceived by the government as a crisis. The
Meiji government was concerned with the threat of armed overthrow from the
time it took power in 1868 until it successfully quelled the Satsuma Rebellion
of 1877. The ordinances limiting free speech issued at the time of the rebellion
formed the core of all later legislation.

When the threat of the disaffected samurai had been dispelled, the Movement for Liberty and Popular Rights demanded that the rulers share their
power. Although the movement was temporarily defused in 1881 by the
promise of a constitution and parliament, the oligarchs spent the 1880s in
feverish activity preparing for the institution of parliamentary forms by carefully reserving the crucial powers for themselves.

The importance of the 1880s cannot be overemphasized, for during this
time the institutional foundations of imperial Japan were established once and
for all, the relatively liberal era of "Taishō democracy" in the 1920s notwithstanding. As Katō Shūichi has written, "It was not by changing, but by fully
utilizing, the institutions which Taishō democracy had not modified, that the
army gradually rose to power in the 1930's."[2]

During this period of consolidation in the 1880s the "transcendent" cabinet
and the Privy Council were created to function in the name of the emperor,
military independence from civil control was established, and the police force
was strengthened and centralized. In 1882 the decision was made to promote
the development of an emperor cult by emphasizing morals in elementary
education, and in 1887 the Press and Publication Regulations were written to
systematize in the light of experience the various measures that had been taken
on a more or less ad hoc basis until then. The subsequent passage of Diet-made

censorship laws in 1893 and 1909 did nothing substantially to alter the situation. The Censorship Division of the Home Ministry's Police Bureau remained the final arbiter of what could and could not be read, at least until the war years. The code empowered the police censors to strike without the inconvenience of having to set judicial machinery in motion and provided no route of appeal. Not only were the courts unavailable for the redress of unjust administrative action but they too were empowered by law to prosecute offenders, punishing convicts with fines and prison sentences when suppression alone was considered insufficient.

In practical terms, a financial threat stood at the heart of the system, for it stressed the prohibition of sale and distribution of already-printed publications rather than prior assessment of manuscript. This had its roots in the Edo period, when the responsibility for censorship lay with publishers' guilds, the managers of which would be punished if they allowed an undesirable book to find its way to the marketplace.

Because of this approach, the enforcement mechanisms of the Meiji system often seem clumsy. Since periodicals were delivered to the censors as soon as they came off the press but after the distribution process had begun, the police had to act very quickly if they were to confiscate a high percentage of unsold issues. The better they did, the more the publishers lost, but one frequently encountered the anomaly of reading a review of a story that had appeared in a banned magazine.

With regard to books, which had to be submitted to the censors after they were printed and bound but before they were distributed, and which were therefore more easily controlled, the crush of work often made it impossible for the censors to issue a ban until several days after the first edition had been sold out at the bookstores. The ban prevented publication of subsequent editions, however, and thus deprived the publisher of his profit.

What the system lost in terms of absolute suppression it made up for in terms of nurturing a self-policing mentality among publishers, who increasingly sought—and were granted—the privilege of informal "consultations" with censors before committing themselves to a press run.

This cooperative aspect of censorship in Japan may have had ancient roots, but it was not without parallel to the heyday of censorship in the United States; namely, the period from 1872 to World War I when Anthony Comstock's Society for the Prevention of Vice became the arbiter of American literary morals. After Comstock's lobbyists had pressured the federal government into enacting the 1873 law that still governs obscenity in the mails, and after the states had written their own "Comstock laws," even "distinguished editors and publishers timidly presented to the society manuscripts on which they asked a reading opinion, or they bowed to the society's edicts and withdrew books that had already been printed." H. L. Mencken, for example, ap-

proached the society for its approval on the manuscript of Theodore Dreiser's
Sister Carrie.[3]

None of this would have been possible without a widely held orthodox view
corresponding to the religious values that Comstock and his YMCA associates
sought to establish as law. With the breakdown of the orthodoxy and a
concomitant growth in tolerance for a multiplicity of views came Judge
Learned Hand's recognition of contemporary community standards, and there
followed a series of legal battles that have led to the relatively open situation
prevailing today.[4]

Trends favoring censorship in the United States can be seen as aberrations
from the constitutional norm, wherein the inviolability of individual conscience is established as the fundamental purpose of the nation. The Japanese
state, however, was not conceived of as an artificial creation with a pragmatic
purpose but as an organic entity of divine origin. Japan was said to have its
own unique "national polity," or *kokutai*—a suitably vague and ancient term
imbued with mythic resonance. The *kokutai* was one and indissoluble, and it
implied a warm and loving union between the sovereign/father and his children, the people.

The Meiji constitution proclaimed: "The Empire of Japan shall be reigned
over and governed by a line of Emperors unbroken for ages eternal" (Article I);
"The Emperor is sacred and inviolable" (Article III); "The Emperor exercises
the legislative power with the consent of the Imperial Diet" (Article V); and
"Japanese subjects shall, *within the limits of the law*, enjoy the liberty of speech,
writing, publication, public meetings and association" (Article XXIX, emphasis added).[5] According to Maruyama Masao,

> the Japanese state, being a moral entity, monopolized the right to determine
> values. . . . It was . . . the sanctity of . . . an interior, subjective sphere that the
> Japanese law failed to recognize. . . . Accordingly, until the day in 1946 when
> the divinity of the Emperor was formally denied in an Imperial Rescript, there
> was in principle no basis in Japan for freedom of belief. Since the nation includes
> in its "national polity" [*kokutai*] all the internal values of truth, morality, and
> beauty, neither scholarship nor art could exist apart from these national values.[6]

The function of the individualistic writer, then, lay entirely outside the
established system of values. It cannot be said, however, that he was politically
irrelevant. He may have lacked the support of the *law*, but he did have
tangible proof of the support of a significant portion of *society*: namely, his
ability to sell his work to commercial journals and newspapers without com-
promising his artistic principles. The success of naturalism and its establishment of the modern novel in Japan demonstrated that a writer could approach

a sizable audience as kindred intellects and not as a mass to be pandered to and entertained.

In Part One of this book we shall meet the critic who documented the emergence of the modern writer in Japan. An early victim of censorship, Uchida Roan was also a gadfly to the novelists of his day, whom he saw as frivolous traditional entertainers with no idea of what was going on around them in the real world. This criticism was an important one, primarily because it was still true at the time, and because the man who made it would continue to hold writers to his high standards. When they came to meet those standards just a few years later, Roan would attest to the social and political significance of the new literature.

The early years of Meiji censorship are of interest, too, for the parallel they show between the slow maturation of realistic fiction and the growing interest of the censors in nonpolitical writing. Concerned almost exclusively with politically subversive material during the first two decades of Meiji, the authorities ignored much salacious popular writing that adopted the traditional Confucian camouflage of Encouraging Virtue and Chastising Vice (*kanzen chōaku*) after titillating readers. Serious writers began to emerge and experience suppression only toward the turn of the century. Because of this, discussion of development of the censorship system in Part One tends to concentrate on press censorship rather than on strictly literary events.

After the Russo-Japanese War, naturalist theoreticians proclaimed the writer a detached observer, an impersonal scientific instrument. The writers themselves, however, had no such narrow, prescriptive program in mind. Far from clinging to any single aesthetic or social doctrine, they contributed to Japanese fiction a tentative, open-minded approach to the description of the world. For these young, Western-educated writers, there was no established truth. They questioned the sanctity of the family. They portrayed the destruction of Confucian moralism by irresistible sexual urges. And so the older leaders of the establishment were aghast. The moral fabric of the nation was being torn to shreds by shameless pornographers, they said. The police began to crack down, employing the censorship mechanism that had heretofore been utilized almost exclusively against politically sensitive writing.

The great year of triumph and misunderstanding for naturalism was 1908. So well had the new writers done during the previous months that the commercial journals' New Year's issues were bursting with naturalist stories and criticism. The young writers were no longer publishing exclusively for one another, and the day was approaching when they could support themselves by their writing. Then in March the police banned a story by one of the very few new writers whose work did have a salacious streak. In addition, he was put on trial. The newspapers were suddenly reporting "literary" matters at great length, and for a while every scandal that erupted in the press seemed to have the "naturalist" label attached to it. The censors became increasingly vigilant, and writers began to protest.

One new note that emerged as censorship cases increased in number throughout 1908 was a call by some critics for understanding between writers and censors. The Minister of Education responded with a tentative move toward forming a literary academy, but his first contacts with literary men were not encouraging. The writers did not attempt to flatter him, as might have been expected of old-fashioned scribblers. They spoke their minds— some for, some against government involvement in literary matters—and similarly diverse and independent criticism appeared in the periodicals. No academy was instituted at this stage, and, as if to confirm the more skeptical writers' doubts, a reactionary new Press Law was maneuvered through the Diet by the second cabinet of Katsura Tarō (July 1908–August 1911), one of the most repressive governments of the Meiji era.

Naturalism as a movement was all but played out by mid-1910, but individual writers who had been identified with the school were entering their prime, and several new schools and writers that would dominate the coming Taishō era (1912–1926) were establishing journals and beginning to publish. It was a year of unprecedented literary vitality. It also became the year of a shocking event that would place constraints on the political and intellectual climate for years to come. This was the so-called High Treason case (or Kōtoku Incident), which began with mass arrests in June and ended with a mass execution in January.

Only since the dismantling of the censorship system by the Occupation army in 1945 has a clear picture of the government's partially fabricated case against twenty-six "anarchists" come to light. At the time, little more was known than that some very frightening and desperate people had been planning to blow up the emperor, and even this much took months to emerge. The larger issues behind the case were far from clear, even to the government. The censors were sent on a witch-hunt for anything that smacked of the twin subversive elements of socialism and individualism, which, incredibly enough, were thought to be nearly synonymous with each other and with naturalism and anarchism (not to mention free love). The government was widely and bitterly criticized for this and for creating the kind of repressive atmosphere that produces anarchist assassins, but few doubted that all the convicts *were* part of an assassination plot. And though the hasty execution of twelve of them shocked many people, relief was also expressed that the country had been rid of such desperate practitioners of a dangerous foreign ideology.

During this chaotic, terror-filled time, Uchida Roan registered his verdict on the importance of the new literature. He had long accused writers of being cheap storytellers whose lack of self-respect came from their writing of irrele-vant confections. Now, however, he became convinced that the reactionary policymakers instead were living in Shangri-La as they attempted to resusci-tate obsolete Confucian moralisms. The literature of the new generation, declared Roan, provided authentic images of contemporary Japanese society and contemporary ideas filtered through the individuality of each writer. It was an important element in Japan's gradual move toward democracy.

The High Treason case was not a major intellectual dilemma for writers, but it was an important watershed in official policy. Many steps were taken at this time that led directly to the evolution of the thought-control system of the 1930s. The first moves in popular education, which would be another indis-pensable element of the militarists' propaganda machine, were made shortly after the trial and executions. At this time, also, the Minister of Education, Komatsubara Eitarō, obtained funds from the Diet to establish a committee to carry out what he called "the reform of literature."

The announcement of the establishment of the Committee on Literature in May 1911 aroused widespread criticism. Those writers who were not positively hostile either expected nothing from the committee or warned that vigilance would be required to prevent it from controlling literature. Once the committee began to function, the press carried detailed reports of unseemly squabbling between its liberal and probureaucratic factions, neither of which could gain the upper hand. Public enthusiasm eventually turned to disgust and disinterest. When a fiscal retrenchment was announced in June 1913, the demise of the two-year-old Committee on Literature went all but unnoticed. The writers had failed to exploit the committee to counter censorship, but neither had the government been able to use it to control literature. There would be later attempts to make writers behave, but only in the thick of war would such efforts meet with notable success.

Thus writers and the government were locked in stalemate as the Meiji period drew to a close. The emotional upheavals surrounding the grandly orchestrated funeral of the Meiji emperor, however, symbolized the psycho-logical struggle that most sophisticated Japanese would continue to experi-ence as the government sought to preserve the aura of a united national family against the influx of cosmopolitan culture.

The Taishō period, especially after World War I, was a time of genuinely expanded liberties. The growth of the modern Japanese drama into a relatively mature art form was also a Taishō phenomenon. Gradually, however, as the preservers of late-Meiji xenophobia insinuated their influence into govern-ment policy, incidents of literary and intellectual suppression became more frequent, with the theater an increasingly prominent victim.

The Tanaka cabinet of 1927–1929 marked a clear-cut swing in the direction of increased censorship as part of the overall policy of tightening social and thought control. Once the Manchurian Incident of 1931 gave the militarists the old "national emergency" rationale, the process became very rapid until, by 1937, the government was intruding into virtually all areas of daily life.

The difference between Meiji-Taishō and Shōwa (after 1926) was primarily one of scale, both in the upsurge of mass culture and the development of larger bureaucratic and police mechanisms to deal with it. But the roots had been planted in Meiji, and the relationship between writers and the latter-day Meiji state remained essentially unchanged.

After 1936 the military services' propaganda bureaus began to encroach upon the censorship activities of the Home Ministry. Their fanaticism made them far more difficult to deal with than the ministry. They saw Communists behind every hint of unorthodox thought and insisted on complete cooperation with the war effort. Journals such as *Chūō Kōron* and *Kaizō*, with their "foreign" tradition of "libertarianism," came under intense pressure to stop printing fiction concerned with "mere personal problems." Especially after Pearl Harbor, fiction did not have to be either leftist-oriented or erotic to be unacceptable: the military did not want to see anything in print that did not actively support the war. Soon the Allies' trade blockade helped enforce this policy. So limited were stocks of paper through 1944–1945 that the censors became almost irrelevant. Anything that could qualify for a paper ration would have had to be acceptable to the military.

In 1910 one particularly eloquent critic of censorship had accused the government of attempting an "intellectual coup d'etat" and had sardonically suggested governmental measures that could be taken to control the entire mental life of the people. He would have been shocked to see how close the military government came to implementing his modest proposal just a few decades later. Slowly at first, but with increasing rapidity through the Shōwa years, the government fashioned a remarkably effective system of thought control.

Considering the intensity of the onslaught, the writers maintained their independence remarkably well. They neatly subverted one attempted replay of the Committee on Literature between 1934 and 1937. This was to be the last such concerted effort, however. When the Cabinet Information Bureau founded the Japanese Literature Patriotic Association in 1942, virtually all writers joined it.

The Patriotic Association was, by far, the most successful attempt to bring writers in line with the orthodoxy. The government accomplished this, however, only as one small phase of a massive, ongoing program of social control costing millions of yen and requiring years of effort by thousands of bureaucrats, policemen, and military officers. And even then, wartime hysteria was needed to complete the job. When it finally succeeded in bringing the writers into the fold, the military government at last had what it wanted: an entire nation united in spirit and eager to smash the sterile material culture of the West with the aid of the Sun Goddess and her Divine Wind.

Part One

SIMPLER YEARS

2

The Law

THE PRESS AND PUBLICATION REGULATIONS OF 1887

The Meiji government became seriously interested in controlling the content of literature only when the literature itself had become a serious art form after some four decades of experimentation. Long before those decades had run their course, the government had perfected its censorship system, primarily for the control of political criticism. Successive regimes contributed to an increasingly detailed and sophisticated series of regulations which evolved into a relatively mature system as early as 1883. The press regulations produced that year were further polished and expanded and were promulgated by imperial edict on December 28, 1887, as the Press Regulations (Shimbunshi Jōrei) along with a separate document called the Publication Regulations (Shuppan Jōrei).[1] The two documents were very similar, but the former applied only to periodicals (both magazines and newspapers) while the latter concerned books.

As with other political innovations of the 1880s, the government was anxious to establish its publications policy before the new constitution could be promulgated and Japan's first representative assembly, the Imperial Diet, could begin making laws.[2] These regulations must be counted a success, for though they were eventually superseded by Diet-made law (Publication Law in 1893, Press Law in 1909), their provisions remained virtually unchanged until they were nullified by the Occupation government on September 29, 1945.[3]

The 1887 Regulations drew both from solutions to immediate political crises and from traditional legal attitudes going back to the Edo period and even earlier. Although the text maintained a facade of establishing no prior restraint upon the printed word, the practical impact of the law was to encourage the traditional self-policing of the publishing industry. Japan could point to her publication code as the institutionalization of a modern free press, but in fact, with its emphasis on police confiscation of *finished* publications, the law was designed to subvert itself. By concentrating on the financial threat to publishers, it encouraged the development of extralegal arrangements whereby publishers could test the acceptability of their self-censorship through consultations with the police. And should the administrative threat of suppression prove insufficient to achieve control, the law had also established judicial mechanisms for punishment backed by fines and imprisonment.

Articles 12, 19, and 20 were central to the functioning of the Press Regulations.[4] Article 12 required that, as soon as an issue of a periodical came off the press, the publisher submit two copies to the Home Ministry (to be read by the Book Section—later Censorship Section—of the ministry's national Police Bureau),[5] plus one copy each to the local police (in Tokyo, the Metropolitan Police Headquarters)[6] and the local prosecuting agency.[7] Any one of these agencies could initiate a ban, but the chief power of enforcement lay with the Home Minister. Article 19 stated: "The Home Minister may prohibit or suspend the publication of any newspaper [or magazine] which he deems to be disruptive of public peace and order or injurious to public morals."[8] And Article 20 added: "At such time as the Home Minister has prohibited or suspended the publication of a newspaper, he may prohibit its sale or distribution and seize its printed sheets."

Articles 3 and 16 of the Publication Regulations were most crucial. According to Article 3, three finished copies of a book had to reach the Home Ministry ten days prior to its planned date of issue. Then, under the terms of Article 16: "The Home Minister [could] prohibit the sale or distribution of a printed book or picture which he deem[ed] to be disruptive of public peace and order or injurious to public morals, and he [could] seize its plates and printed copies."

The police wanted to see no periodicals or books until the publisher had incurred the expense of setting type and running presses. Because books did not have to be distributed immediately, as newspapers did, the Publication Regulations required the publisher to hold his breath for a while. Even though Article 1 defined "publication" as printing *and* sale or distribution, Article 3 gave the police ten days (later shortened to three days) to decide if the books were to be released to the marketplace. Merely by resorting to a slight inconsistency in the law, the government could have the advantages of both Edo-style self-censorship and prior censorship while maintaining the appearance of modern enlightenment.

As is well known, the key to social control during the Tokugawa period lay in nurturing a self-policing mentality among the populace by holding the group responsible for infractions by any one of its members. (The principle of joint responsibility had been firmly established in Japanese law by the feudal house codes of the fifteenth century.)[9] At the lowest level of the hierarchy came the "five-man group" (*gonin-gumi*), whose "obligations included mutual aid and mutual surveillance of all public and private activities in the group."[10] The Tokugawa rulers employed a similar pattern in controlling publishers by requiring the establishment of a system of self-censorship which held certain members of the publishers' guilds responsible whenever an undesirable book was released for sale.

The earliest known move to control commercial publishing was made by an Edo city commissioner (*machi-bugyō*) some time before the middle of 1673. The commissioner ordered a woodblock carver named Jinshirō to form a professional guild and to report to him whenever "suspicious" documents were brought in for printing. Apparently Jinshirō did not comply with the order. In consequence, a general edict that year required submission and prior approval on any publication involving "public matters, matters that might prove embarrassing to anyone, or any other unusual matters."[11]

The great flowering of popular literature and culture during the Genroku era (1680–1740)[12] met with some resistance from the shogunate, which primarily objected to journalistic elements in literature. As early as 1644, playwrights had been forbidden to use the names of actual people,[13] and edicts against the treatment of current events in books or the selling of news broadsheets (*yomiuri* or *kawaraban*) were issued in 1684, only to be reissued at surprisingly frequent intervals as they were disobeyed.*

When it came to the organizing of publishers, the shogunate had some difficulty making up its mind, as it did with the whole guild question, preferring at first to discourage guild monopolies and later realizing that guilds could be exploited for control purposes. The enforcement of censorship edicts also paralleled the later Tokugawa period's well-known broad swings between periods of relative openness and Confucian reform. It was as part of the first such period of moralistic reaction—the shogun Yoshimune's Kyōhō Reform (1716–1744)—that the shogunate ordered publishers to form guilds (*nakama*) in 1721. An edict issued the following year clearly made the guilds responsible for censorship.

This Tiger Year Interdict, as it was known, comprised the foundation of all subsequent Tokugawa publication law and even influenced modern legislation. Making an exception of books on religion, medicine, and poetry, it

---

*According to James L. Huffman, "as many as three thousand" of these newssheets were issued during the two and one-half centuries of Tokugawa rule, but "all on a one-time-only basis." *Politics of the Meiji Press*, p. 48. The authorities were especially harsh in suppressing news of approaches by foreign vessels in the early 1800s, though after about 1820 *yomiuri* on fires and natural disasters were given tacit approval. See Konta, *Edo no hon'yasan*, pp. 140, 195–96.

denounced as "strictly unnecessary" any new books containing extreme or heterodoxical opinion. Erotic books (kōshokubon) of the kind that had flourished since Saikaku wrote the first one in 1682 were to be investigated and allowed to go out of print, "because they are not good for public morality." All new books without exception were to carry a colophon listing the true names of the author and publisher, a practice that survives today in the form of the rectangular slip pasted to (or, more recently, the box printed upon) the back flyleaf of all books. (The colophon became an especially important control device during the Pacific War.) Writing that reflected badly on the pedigree of any samurai or that mentioned anything about the Tokugawa family was forbidden. The guilds were responsible for evaluating all books prior to sale.[14]

This edict was supplemented later that year and in the following year by prohibitions against the publishing of anything concerning current rumors or love suicides. Although the latter had been an especially important source for the great Genroku dramatist Chikamatsu, further writing and performing of plays dealing with such materials was strictly forbidden.[15] Chikamatsu died in 1724, and the writing of domestic tragedies was never to be the same.

The Kansei Reform of Matsudaira Sadanobu (1787–1793) brought forth four new publications edicts in 1790, but these were primarily reiterations of the Tiger Year Interdict and the earlier broadsheet prohibitions. "The rules laid down in the past are to be observed more strictly," said the most important regulatory document. "There have been books since times long past and no more are necessary, so there ought to be no more new books. If the necessity does arise, inquiries must be made at the City Commissioner's office and his instructions followed. . . . Booksellers are henceforward to take part in the investigations and to inform the City Commissioner's office at once should any books be put on sale in contravention of the law. It is to be regarded as the fault both of the person responsible and of the guild if anything is overlooked or not investigated." A slightly later edict against "depravity and anything injurious to public morality" stipulated that "in the case of an inspection carried out without due care, or of someone's having avoided an inspection, the guild-representatives are to take the blame."[16]

Writers and publishers had little idea that these rehashed old rules were now to be strictly enforced. They soon learned. The popular writer Santō Kyōden, who had been ignoring the prohibitions against the use of contemporary material, suddenly produced three comic sharebon works with transparently phony historical settings. He added some unprecedented postscripts "claiming that his purpose was strictly a didactic one and that his tales of lust were intended solely to warn readers against vice and to encourage them toward virtue." There is evidence that he cut certain passages, and he was also careful to insist that his publisher have the guild representatives (gyōji) approve his work before releasing it. None of this did any good. His three books were banned; his publisher was heavily fined; his father was reprimanded; the guild representatives who had given their approval were banished from Edo;[17] and Kyōden himself was placed in manacles for fifty days. This was apparently a lightened punishment for Kyōden: the authorities deemed it a mitigating factor that in the meantime he had written only didactic works.[18] (It is also known that the publisher gave the banished guild representatives money as they left: they were unsuccessful publishers who had agreed to take their vulnerable posts precisely for this purpose.)[19]

Although Matsudaira Sadanobu resigned in 1793, the Kansei Reform's pressure on publications remained heavy for another two decades. With the assignment of four new civilian censors in 1807, Kyōden and his disciple, the almost unimpeachably respectable novelist Takizawa Bakin (who had written several pieces for Kyōden while the master was in manacles), were required to submit an affidavit promising to eschew current events or rumors, to follow the principle of Encouraging Virtue and Chastising Vice, to concentrate on good characters such as filial children and loyal retainers, and to do their utmost to write books instructive for women and children. They swore also to correct offensive sections of their works in manuscript or even in the woodblock stage if necessary, and to refuse to sell to publishers whose desire for profit made them turn a deaf ear to writers' wishes for revision. Finally, they requested that the new censors summon recalcitrant writers and lecture them sternly.[20]

This abject document demonstrates that, even at its inception, the doctrine of Encouraging Virtue and Chastising Vice was primarily a device to mollify the censors. Nonetheless, the authorities continued to evoke it, even during the liberal 1920s. Indeed, it remained a cardinal principle of theater censorship at least through the end of the Pacific War. The pressures encouraging its prominence in Edo fiction were apparently lost on Tsubouchi Shōyō, whose call for modern realism, *The Essence of the Novel* (*Shōsetsu shinzui*, 1885), rejected the work of the Edo writers largely on the grounds of their preoccupation with this artificial moralistic formula.[21]

According to Peter F. Kornicki, from whose study much of this information is derived, Kyōden's punishment was "almost unprecedented."[22] It was, however, only the beginning. Shikitei Sanba was also sentenced to fifty days in handcuffs in 1799, as was Tamenaga Shunsui in 1842, during Mizuno Tadakuni's Tenpō Reform. Another Tenpō victim seems to have been Ryūtei Tanehiko, whose frail constitution apparently could not stand the shock when he was summoned by the authorities.[23] (See below, pp. 190–91, for a fictional interpretation of this incident by Nagai Kafū.)

The Tokugawa authorities succeeded overall in obtaining the cooperation of the publishing industry and in neutralizing the critical content of literature. The core articles of the 1887 Press and Publication Regulations owed much to that accumulated wisdom. The more immediate causes for the emphasis on an administrative threat can be found in the emergency conditions under which the frail new Meiji government struggled to stabilize its political control.

Regarding problems of publication control, the single greatest difference between Tokugawa and Meiji was the newspaper's sudden appearance on the scene. For over two centuries, the Tokugawa authorities had simply prohibited the circulation of news in any form, thus effectively preventing the illegal broadsheets from developing into newspapers. The Meiji government had inherited a body of book-control legislation, but newspapers were a wholly new phenomenon and called forth a separate set of edicts.[24] This gave rise to a legislative tradition of entirely separate documents governing press and book publication.

The first Meiji edict concerning books (released in the fourth intercalary month of 1868, even before the era name had been changed from Keiō to Meiji!) merely required "official permission" to publish. Within two months, however, this was clarified to mean submission of manuscript to the newly instituted educational authorities. The more detailed regulations of 1869 required that the application include a summary of contents. If this provided an insufficient basis for official decision, the manuscript itself was to be submitted before a properly stamped license could be issued. These regulations contained the first Meiji "morals" clause, a prohibition against books that would "promote lewdness and debauchery," with the severity of the punishment to be determined according to the gravity of the offense.[25] The 1875 version, which transferred jurisdiction from the Ministry of Education to the Home Ministry, required "occasional" submission of manuscript prior to publication. Another twelve years of revising and adjusting resulted in the mature system of submission of finished books seen in the Publication Regulations of 1887.[26]

The first items of journalism banned by the new government were handbills and woodblock color prints (*nishikie*) that evinced a pro-Tokugawa bias in depicting military skirmishes against the Bakufu forces. This was in May of 1868. In that same month, the demand for military news led to the establishment of some of Japan's first newspapers, a half-dozen irregularly issued publications printed from wood blocks on a few sheets of rice paper. One of these, Fukuchi Gen'ichirō's *Kōko Shimbun*, became the first newspaper to be prohibited from publishing, also for its pro-Tokugawa (or rather, anti-Satsuma-Chōshū) bias. Its final issue, the twenty-second, appeared on July 11, 1868. When it was banned, Fukuchi was jailed for eight days and his woodblocks were confiscated. On July 27 the government temporarily wiped out all newspapers by requiring them to obtain the same "official permission" to publish required of books.[27]

As early as 1873, in trying to suppress the call for an invasion of Korea raised by Saigō Takamori and other disaffected samurai, the government set a precedent for most subsequent press regulations by forbidding publication of anything that might tend to "agitate the hearts of the people or incite lewdness."[28] From this would develop the virtually inseparable pairing of public peace and public morals.[29] Tensions were building that would ultimately erupt in Saigō's Satsuma Rebellion of 1877. The government issued increasingly stronger and more detailed press regulations and libel ordinances, shifting control of the press from the Ministry of Education to the Home Ministry in 1875. The libel and press regulations of June 1875 made it nearly impossible to criticize the government or government officials—or the regulations themselves—without fear of prosecution.[30] The most shocking change was specification of prison terms for offenders, replacing the earlier vague prohibitions. With these new regulations began the so-called Newspapers' Reign of Terror.[31]

In the 1875 press code, the editors and writers were made responsible for content, not the publication itself. A newspaper had only to set up dummy editors and keep replacing them as they were jailed to continue printing subversive material. Nine such arrests occurred in 1875, followed by forty in 1876 as the government became increasingly frightened of Saigō, Etō Shinpei, and their expanding troops.*

In this tense military atmosphere, on July 5, 1876, an ordinance was issued supplementary to the previous year's revised press regulations. This ordinance became the cornerstone of all subsequent press laws through the end of the Pacific War: "When a previously licensed newspaper or periodical is deemed to be disruptive to the national peace, the Home Ministry shall prohibit or suspend its publication."[32] In essence, the entire prewar Japanese system of publication control was the extended application of an emergency wartime measure formulated when the fledgling Meiji government was undergoing one of its most crucial struggles for survival. Okudaira Yasuhiro has noted that "the whole history of Japan from the time of Perry's visit until the end of the last war reflected an extraordinary, emergency atmosphere. Indeed, the governmental scheme to restrain free speech, which reached an extreme point during World War II, was no different essentially from that established immediately after the Restoration in 1868."[33]

So exclusively political had been government fears that the writers of the 1875 regulations had not troubled to include an obscenity clause. But when the 1876 ordinance was written into the revised press regulations of 1883, it

---

*These men were usually given a monthly salary in the neighborhood of five yen, which would be converted to daily pay of thirty to fifty sen (i.e., nine to fifteen yen per month!) while they sat in jail. See MBHS, p. 17. For further statistics on the "Reign of Terror," see MGH, pp. 73–77, 86–87.

incorporated a transitional ordinance (October 12, 1880) on peace and morals, emerging nearly word-for-word as the precursor to Article 19 of the 1887 Press Regulations: "The Home Minister may prohibit or suspend the publication of any newspaper which he deems to be disruptive of public peace and order or injurious to public morals."[34] Revision or rescission of Articles 19 and 20 (prohibition of sale or distribution) became the rallying cry for attempts during the next decade to loosen the administrative grip on the press.

Almost as soon as the ordinance was issued on July 5, 1876, empowering the Home Ministry to institute bans as an administrative action without reference to the courts, a test case demonstrated the undiluted power now accorded the ministry. Appealing the prohibition of its publication to the Tokyo Superior Court, one magazine that had been particularly critical of the government, *Sōmō Zasshi*, pointed out that it had been banned on July 11, six days after the ordinance was issued. Because it had not printed a single issue in that time, it could not legally be banned under the ordinance. Both the Superior Court and the Great Court of Cassation* rejected this argument on the grounds that the ordinance had not *created* the ministry's power to ban: this was held as a "unique right" by the ministry in accordance with customary law (*shūkanhō*) and irrespective of the ordinance, which had merely set down in writing a power that already existed.[35]

This arbitrary power of the Home Minister was reinforced throughout the prewar period by the government's steadfast refusal to compromise, either by clarifying standards or by opening avenues of appeal. Despite frequent complaints that the phrases "disruptive of public peace and order" and "injurious to public morals" were too vague and all-inclusive, no specific standards were ever issued for publishers to adhere to. In fact, standards did exist, but they may not have been committed to writing until the late 1920s. Even then they were recorded only in the Police Bureau's periodic secret reports compiled for the Home Minister. The preface to one such in-house list of standards issued annually from at least 1930 ingenuously pointed out that since the usual phrases were "all" one found in the laws, "the standards for invoking a ban are not always clear." (In fact, the government presented a bill to the 1926 Diet which was designed to replace the two separate Meiji publication codes with a single uniform law that would have contained a list of standards, but it was thrown out as being too restrictive overall.)[36]

And concerning the question of appeals, the Home Ministry's power to ban any published material was "absolute and unlimited."[37] The law provided no mechanism by which a publisher could appeal the censor's judgment. No court could overturn the censor's decision. And in contrast to other admin-

---

*Prewar Japan's Supreme Court, modeled on the French system. Dan Fenno Henderson, "Law and Political Modernization in Japan," p. 424.

istrative measures, this measure could not be appealed to the Court of Administrative Litigation (Gyōsei Saibansho), which had been instituted to handle cases of illegal administrative action.[38]

Such were the fruits of the Meiji government's struggle against the last samurai holdouts and the subsequent Movement for Liberty and Popular Rights (*Jiyū minken undō*). Thus, when the constitution was promulgated in 1889 with its guarantee of free speech "within the limits of the law" (Article 29), those limits had been clearly set.[39]

Before reviewing the Diet's feeble attempts to remedy the situation, let us look at other important components of the 1887 Press and Publication Regulations. Because it was both more controversial and more relevant to literature, so much of which appeared in magazines and newspapers, we will concentrate on the Press Regulations.

The first five articles of the Press Regulations concerned registration of all periodicals with the Home Ministry via the local police. Article 5 was especially useful for suppressing publications. It specified that any paper failing to print an issue for a period of fifty days would lose its registered status. Of course, the most likely reason a newspaper might not appear would be that the Home Minister had suspended its publication.

Article 8 required the posting of a bond at the time of registration. This was returnable upon cessation of publication, whether voluntary or mandatory. In Tokyo, the publisher had to put up a "staggering" ¥1000, in other large cities ¥700, in the provinces ¥350. When first instituted in 1883, the bond-posting system had immediately closed down forty-seven newspapers unable to raise the money, including sixteen in Tokyo, four in Osaka, and twenty-seven in the provinces.[40] (Such arrangements had been recognized as a "tax on knowledge" in the West and were being discontinued.)[41]

Certain limited-circulation magazines that could not afford the bond could request handling under the Publication Regulations instead of the Press Regulations. In return for this financial advantage, however, they had to limit themselves strictly to innocuous scholarly or artistic fare (rather like the Tokugawa prohibition on current events). And, of course, copies had to be submitted in advance of distribution, as with books. (These were handled under Article 2 of both the 1887 and 1893 publication codes.)

Legal responsibility for content, under Article 11, was shared equally by the publisher, editor, printer, and writer of each signed article, whatever his formal connection with the paper. Some restrictions on content were specified in Articles 16–18. According to Article 16, no reports were allowed of the proceedings of any preliminary court hearing (*yoshin*), whether for a misdemeanor or a felony, nor of any lawsuit closed to the public. Because the preliminary hearings usually decided a defendant's case in the Japanese system, this effectively blocked press coverage of trials.[42] Article 17 forbade printing of editorials excusing an infraction of the criminal code or articles defending a convicted criminal. Article 18 ruled that the contents of secret government documents and the proceedings of closed official meetings could neither be quoted nor summarized without permission.

Article 21 extended the Home Minister's power of forbidding sale and distribution to include any foreign newspapers that he "deemed" objectionable under the usual terms. Article 22 empowered the Ministers of the Army and Navy to issue news embargoes placing prior restraint on the publishing of any information concerning military operations. (This point was often taken to legitimize embargoes issued by the Home Minister, which developed as an extralegal practice, but the two were in fact quite distinct.)[43]

The first twenty-two articles were thus concerned primarily with relations between periodicals and the police (i.e., instructions for registration with the Home Ministry's Police Bureau and explanations of circumstances under which the police might take direct administrative action against a publication that had printed something it should not have.) By contrast, Articles 23–34 enumerated circumstances under which editors and publishers could be tried and punished in the courts. (Among technical points in the last three articles was a six-months' statute of limitations.) Far from constituting a check on the police powers of the Home Ministry, the judiciary had its own independent power to punish the publication of seditious or obscene items and to enforce compliance with administrative orders. Although the court could not (as yet) summarily order a ban without a hearing, as the Home Ministry could, its punishments could be dealt out in addition to—or instead of—the ministry's ban. Further, even if a not-guilty verdict were reached in the courts, this had no effect on any ban that the Home Ministry may or may not have instituted. The Home Minister *could* lift his ban if he wished, but the law said nothing on this point, the principle being that legal culpability was separate from the administrative need to control morals and ideology. In actual practice, it was the rule for the ban *not* to be lifted and for confiscated items *not* to be returned.[44]

Article 23 empowered the procurator temporarily to impound the copies of a newspaper against which he was issuing an indictment and, depending upon the circumstances of the case, allowed the judge to confiscate the copies.*

Articles 24 and 25 concerned the newspaper's rights and obligations in civil libel suits. These were, of course, no longer as restrictive as the codes that gave rise to the 1875 Reign of Terror, but questions of press responsibility (or

---

*In the prewar judicial system, each court had its own prosecutors, known as procurators (*kenji*). "Procurators were in a strong position. From the Meiji period, procurators dressed like judges, sat on the same level at trials, and identified themselves closely with the bench. . . . Truly, it was often a case of trial and conviction by procurators." MITC, pp. 35–36.

irresponsibility) were to prove troublesome throughout the prewar period and were a major source of difficulty for the Occupation government. Although press-fabricated scandals surface in Japanese fiction with some frequency, the issue lies beyond the scope of this book.

Article 26 stipulated that fines or damage payments not made within a week of the conclusion of a trial would be taken from the bond money posted by the newspaper. This money would have to be replaced by the newspaper within a week, or the police would suspend publication until payment was made. (When the bond was insufficient to cover the amount, it could be recovered through criminal prosecution.)

Article 27 prescribed a fine of not less than five nor more than one hundred yen for publishers who failed to register the newspaper properly, or who operated without having posted the required bond, or who committed some other technical infringement such as failing to deliver the required inspection copies. Willful misrepresentation could be punished by the same fine or by a sentence of one to six months in prison. These punishments also applied to the editor of a journal devoted exclusively to scholarship or the arts which had applied to be treated under the book-publishing law (to avoid the posting of a bond) but which had nevertheless printed material suitable only to periodicals (i.e., political commentary).

According to Article 29, an editor convicted of violating Articles 16–18 (prohibiting the reporting of preliminary hearings, etc.) could be sentenced to one to six months in prison or could be fined twenty to two hundred yen. Article 30 imposed the same punishments on anyone convicted of selling a banned foreign newspaper. Article 31 dealt with violations of Article 22 concerning military affairs. It could bring the publisher and editor from one month to two years in prison or a fine of twenty to three hundred yen.

Article 32 was particularly severe. The publisher, editor, and printer of a newspaper carrying an editorial advocating the "destruction of the political system" * or the "overthrow of the foundations (or constitution) of the state" † could receive two months to two years and, in addition, a fine of fifty to three hundred yen. All machinery used to commit the crime could also be confiscated. Article 33 punished the publisher and editor of an obscene newspaper with one to six months in prison or a fine of twenty to two hundred yen.

These, then, were the major points of the 1887 Press Regulations under

---

*The phrase was *"seitai no henkai,"* employing the nonstandard compound "change-and-destroy."

†This was *"chōken binran"* (or *"bunran"*), an exceedingly diffuse phrase, especially at this time predating a written constitution. Mitchell translates it "subvert the laws of the state," but he points out that its meaning had never been clear to legal scholars, jurists, or legislators since its inception in 1882. MITC, pp. 48–49.

which newspapers and magazines were subject to both administrative and judicial action. The key ingredient, the Home Minister's power to forbid sale and distribution, was unique in world legal history.[45] It was also particularly irksome to liberal members of the new parliament, who tried for nine straight sessions of the Diet to introduce bills that would ease restrictions on the press in general and the Home Minister's absolute power in particular. Each time, however, the legislation died in committee. Finally, in the tenth Diet, the administration agreed not to block a compromise measure that would leave the bond-posting system unchanged. On March 19, 1897, Articles 19 and 20 were struck from the Press Regulations.

This was not the momentous accomplishment one might at first suppose. The Diet was not replacing the pre-constitutional regulations with an entirely new law of its own devising (this would not happen for another twelve years—and then to disastrous effect). In fact, the limited new law changed only the *form* in which the government exercised its police powers over the press, leaving the substance intact and, if anything, strengthened.

Article 22, for example, added the Foreign Minister to the military service ministers, increasing the cabinet members who could suppress news reports dealing with their special fields. Article 32 added "desecration of the dignity of the Imperial House" to the list of severely punishable offenses of advocating "destruction of the political system" and "overthrow of the foundations of the state." This new standard would come to be invoked with increasingly fanatical exactingness as the Pacific War approached.[46]

Article 33 was expanded from a straightforward judicial punishment for obscenity to the usual broad phraseology, making publishers and editors punishable in the courts for articles "injurious to the social order or to public morality."[47] The maximum fine was also raised to three hundred yen.

Further, Article 23 indirectly gave back to the Home Minister what it had taken away from him by abrogating Articles 19 and 20. It empowered him, through complaint to the court, to suspend the sale and distribution of newspapers carrying materials such as described in Articles 22, 32, and 33.[48] He could also temporarily impound the printed newspapers and could suspend the printing of any other editorials or articles dealing with the material in question. In turn, the court could then forbid publication of the offending newspaper. Because no hearing was necessary, this was simply the old administrative ban with an extra step introduced, although final authority was in fact shifted from the Home Ministry to the courts. This "aberration" would be set right in 1909 when the Diet finally produced its own complete Press Law.

The Publication Regulations need not be examined in as much detail as the Press Regulations. Produced as the two documents were for simultaneous release, many of their provisions were nearly identical. Further, as has been suggested, the Publication Regulations and Laws were never as controversial as those governing the press, because far more polemic and literature appeared in media that came under the press codes. The Diet had actually succeeded in producing a new Publication·Law (Shuppanhō) four years before it passed even the limited revision of the Press Regulations of 1897. The new law provoked no major debate and was little more than the old Publication Regulations with a constitutional title.[49] Now, however, instead of submitting three copies ten days prior to release, publishers were only required to submit two copies three days prior to release. Court-imposed punishments for issuing a book despite a ban were also eased somewhat. Where Article 27 of the Publication Regulations specified one month to two years or a fine of twenty to three hundred yen, Article 28 of the Publication Law reduced these to eleven days to one year or ten to two hundred yen.

As in many areas, the imperial government paid a great deal of attention to the legal niceties of its censorship system, partly because it knew the world was watching, and partly because it never was a purely authoritarian government—at least not until the militarist era.* A genuine police state would not have tolerated the kinds of criticism unleashed against the censors—and which, indeed, the militarists of the late 1930s and 1940s did not tolerate. Behind the modern censorship codes, however, lay two centuries of cooperation between censors and publishers which neither side wanted to see abandoned.

BEYOND THE LAW

Nowhere in the Japanese tradition—and certainly not in the Meiji constitution—do we find the sanctification of inalienable individual rights. The absence of an appeal to such rights in criticisms of censorship in Japan should come as no surprise. Perhaps the most frequently heard refrain in the critical chorus was something far more practical; namely, requests from the publishing industry for prior censorship of manuscript to reduce financial risks.

As one advocate of such a system wrote in 1908, "We are free only within limits, and those limits are set subjectively by the Home Minister. It is a truly miserable situation." Starting from this unlikely premise, he noted that first editions of books were often distributed before a ban could be ordered. As a result, the ban itself was ineffective and only imposed a financial burden on the publisher by preventing subsequent, more profitable editions. Suggesting that the financial blow could be minimized by censorship of manuscript rather

*Even such an event as the mass arrest of radicals on March 15, 1928, was orchestrated with extreme attention to legalistic detail and with elaborate precautions against the intrusions of the press. The police did not move until their search warrants were in hand. See MITC, pp. 83–85, 97.

than of finished books, he concluded incredibly, "The government has a clear obligation, in the beautiful and beloved name of liberty, to establish new regulations by which they can respond to the request of authors and publishers for prior censorship of manuscript."[50]

Authors, too, might suffer financial loss with a banned book, because publishers could demand the return of writers' advances.[51] Clearly, however, the publishers pressed the demand for "consultation" with the censors (the term was *naietsu*: private inspection), and for a while they got what they asked for. Officials of the Police Bureau were reading more and more galley proofs (and perhaps even manuscripts), until, in 1927, the bureau announced an end to the system because it simply did not have the budget or manpower to keep up with the explosive growth of the publishing industry.[52] Immediately there was a call for a return to the consultation system. This, according to a pamphlet produced late in 1927, was to be merely a stopgap measure to prevent undue financial losses until a "perfected" system of censorship could be devised. Also part of this supposedly revolutionary program—the last known nationwide call for a reform (not abolition) of the entire censorship system, including the laws governing entertainment forms—was to be prior censorship of dramatic scripts and film scenarios, again to prevent the total loss of production costs.[53] The Police Bureau did provide improved facilities for consultation in 1938 and encouraged publishers to come in if they had "the slightest doubt about any censorship matter," but they revoked this privilege for companies that continued to print undesirable material.[54]

The consultation approach was provided for nowhere in the law, but this did not prevent the development of highly regularized techniques for cooperation between publishers and censors. One secret Police Bureau document (produced annually for the Home Minister) pointed out matter-of-factly: "In addition to" the various prohibitions issued by the bureau in accordance with the statutes, "other administrative measures" existed which were "not carried out in accordance with any statutes but as expedient measures." These included: (1) embargoes (*kiji sashi-tome meirei*) prohibiting publishers from touching on certain forbidden topics; (2) warnings (*chūi*), defined as "stern reprimands," issued when a company had published objectionable material not quite deserving of a ban; (3) deletions (*sakujo*) of entire passages; and (4) the dismemberment and restitution (*bunkatsu kanpu*) of seized publications.[55] Embargoes were designed to *prevent* printing of objectionable material, and warnings were issued *after* publication. Similarly, deletions were cuts ordered by censors at the galley proof stage to prevent printing of sensitive passages, and dismemberment and restitution involved the cutting of already-published material seized by the police before it could be sold.

The embargo system evolved (apparently by about 1920) into a categorized series of increasingly severe notices of prior restraint through which the Home

Ministry could advise publishers not to print news or books on certain subjects.[56] By the late 1920s, it was considered a mark of prestige to be among the companies favored by the Home Ministry with these secret warnings that enabled them to avoid a ban.[57] The National General Mobilization Act of April 1938 elevated this extralegal custom to the status of law and used it to ensure that all war news reaching the public was good news.[58]

The firsthand account of Hatanaka Shigeo, editor-in-chief of *Chūō Kōron* from 1941 to 1947, is of interest. Dating from the militarist era, it nonetheless indicates the kinds of procedures developing during the period that will most concern us. According to Hatanaka, if nothing was heard within ten days after submitting a book to the authorities, all was assumed to be well. Censors' objections were usually expressed within two or three days. When there were problems, the publisher or the editor responsible for the item in question would be called in to receive a stern reprimand, notice of a ban, and/or word that he would be brought to trial.

In the case of an outright ban, the censors could indicate that elimination of certain passages would render the book publishable. Then the publisher could petition for dismemberment and restitution of his publication, and, if this were approved, literally everyone in the company would pile into cars and go around to those Tokyo police stations holding the seized copies (assuming the item had already been distributed to book stores). There, in the presence of Special Higher Police, they would cut out the offensive pages and rubber-stamp the cover "Revised Edition." Their goods would then be restored to them for sale. Hatanaka says this was one of his first jobs when he joined the *Chūō Kōron* publishers as a trainee in May 1931.[59] Even though such techniques as these were practiced outside the legal system, their use was actually recorded in the secret Home Ministry statistics as routine functions of the censors.[60]

One other extralegal method of controlling publications came in itself to symbolize censorship because it left its mark directly on the printed page. Ironically, this technique was not practiced by the Police Bureau but by the publishers themselves. *Fuseji* (marks such as ✕ or ◯) were used to conceal (*fuseru*) objectionable words, with one mark usually substituting for each suppressed character. "Communism," for example, a four-character word in Japanese (*kyō-san-shu-gi*), would appear as "✕✕✕✕." Or, "as I felt her leaning against me, the warmth of her skin seeping through the soft silk of my sleeping robe" (*yawarakai kinu no usuwata no nemaki-goshi ni, motareau onna no hada no atatakasa o kanjinagara*) would appear on the page as "◯◯◯◯◯◯◯◯◯◯◯, ◯◯◯◯◯◯◯◯◯◯◯◯◯◯◯."[61]

These *fuseji* are usually assumed to have been inserted by the censors, but in fact the technique was developed by resourceful publishers as a means of avoiding potentially controversial vocabulary while providing enough of a

hint for most readers. The earliest example is thought to date from 1868, a few
months before the era became Meiji, when the name of the last Tokugawa
shōgun, Keiki, appeared as "✕✕" in a politically sensitive newspaper article.*
The technique probably had not become widespread until about 1885, when
the Home Ministry issued a decree against it.[62] In practice, however, the
prohibition of *fuseji* was not enforced until the Pacific War. Consistent with
the general policy of encouraging self-censorship, the police allowed the publishers to go on substituting ✕s and ○s at the preferred galley proof stage
rather than requiring them to make their editorial decisions in manuscript.
(The publishers themselves preferred to work with galleys. They did not
believe in making arbitrary changes in a writer's manuscript, and pressing
deadlines made it impossible to consult with authors over every questionable
passage.) The magazine *Chūō Kōron*, at least, seems to have maintained the
policy of exercising extreme care with *fuseji* in works of literature, with the
entire editorial staff gathering in some instances to read galley proofs to one
another and to share opinions on which words ought to be suppressed.[63]

The openness with which such self-censorship was practiced could be carried
to amazing extremes, even with official cooperation. One Marxist volume
printed in 1923 was not only filled with *fuseji* but contained large blank spaces
where the typeface had been obliterated so crudely that the scars left in the
metal were printed on the paper. The first page carried an apology from the
author for the wretched state of the book, noting that passages had been
expunged upon the "warning" of the authorities.[64]

To take another example, thirty-seven pages in Morita Sōhei's 1926 novel
Reincarnation (*Rinne*) have *fuseji* of varying lengths, primarily in "erotic" passages. The worst is page 304, which has twelve lines of little circles, all nicely
paragraphed and punctuated with periods, commas, dashes, and quotation
marks, followed by two lines of innocuous narrative. Not even the most gifted
reader could be expected to fill in such blanks, nor were such lengthy examples
of *fuseji* very rare. Sōhei's novel also contains the stub-ends of twenty pages cut
out of the finished volume, indicating that it was probably also subjected to
dismemberment and restitution.[65]

Far from suffering the imposition of *fuseji*, editors continued to think of
them as a countermeasure to censorship and felt severely constrained when
their use was strictly forbidden by the military in the fall of 1941.[66] According
to one former editor of a liberal magazine, the final decision to rid publications
of *fuseji* was reached at a Police Bureau meeting held on September 8, 1936,
after which editors were called together and ordered—orally, not in writing—

*SSDS, p. 178. A distant precursor of this may be seen in the eleventh-century collection of
tales, *Konjaku monogatari shū*, into which copyists seem intentionally to have inserted lacunae
instead of many personal and place names.

to phase out the use of *fuseji* gradually so that readers would not notice their disappearance. By the end of 1938, the use of *fuseji* had been all but eliminated. The authorities were apparently less worried about Japanese than foreign readers, however: the rational for finally doing away with this long-established practice lay in the need for presenting a united front. Publications were "paper bullets" in the "holy war," but their effect would be diminished if *fuseji* remained to suggest to the enemy that there was division within the country.[67]

Had there been no such external threat, the use of *fuseji* might have been a matter of little concern to anyone. In the opinion of Hatanaka Shigeo, authoritarianism was such an accepted part of Japanese life that the censor did not have to hide his presence; it was natural that a higher authority should exist, arrogantly expecting compliance. This remark (made to the author in an interview) does much to explain the openness of the Japanese censorship system.* (Conversely, it may also help to explain why the postwar Occupation authorities, coming as they did from an egalitarian background, insisted on keeping their censorship activities secret.)

The greater part of this book will be concerned with writers who worked during the years when the extralegal methods described here (with the exception of *fuseji*) were still in the formative stage and the Home Ministry was still in control of censorship. Developments pertaining to the late 1920s and into the Pacific War, when agencies practicing censorship proliferated and authority shifted from the Home Ministry to the military-dominated cabinet, will be summarized in Part Four.

In the next two chapters, we shall see the government and writers eyeing each other warily at a time when neither side had perfected the tools of its trade.

---

*Interview, July 9, 1981. Hatanaka insisted that *fuseji* were never inserted by authors or censors but by editors exclusively. For examples of banned passages complete with editors' *fuseji*, see Naimushō Keihokyoku, ed., *Shuppan Keisatsu hō*.

3

Traditional Irony and Old-Fashioned Trash

THE "USELESS" NARUSHIMA RYŪHOKU

The new Meiji government was engaged in a struggle for its own survival and payed little heed to publications of a nonpolitical nature. Even supposedly obscene works, upon closer inspection, turn out to have been suppressed for political reasons. Thus we find that the object of literary suppression generally assumed to have been the first in Meiji Japan was a journalist's discursive essay containing both "immoral" and political elements.* Indeed, we may suppose that the proximity of the two was what most disturbed the authorities. The reputation of the author also must have influenced their decision, for Narushima Ryūhoku (1837–1884), a genuine maverick and one of the more colorful figures of early Meiji, had been an effective critic of the new regime and had only recently emerged from four months in prison as a prominent victim of the Newspapers' Reign of Terror.

Ryūhoku submitted his manuscript in December 1876 during that period (before 1883) when the rules for prior submission of book or manuscript to the Home Ministry were still in flux (see above, p. 20), and was refused a license to publish. This was to have been the third volume of a series that Ryūhoku had begun before the Meiji Restoration entitled *New Chronicle of Yanagibashi* (*Ryūkyō shinshi*) and containing anecdotes on the Yanagibashi pleasure quarter.† Only the preface was published, but it suggests that this volume would

---

*There are no reliable sources for censorship statistics from the Meiji period. Bans were listed in the official gazette, *Kanpō*, from its inception in 1883 until 1910, after which such records were kept secret. All modern commentaries agree that volume 3 of Ryūhoku's *New Chronicle* was refused a publication license in 1876, but volumes 1 and 2 may also have had publication difficulties. See Saitō Shōzō, *Gendai hikka bunken dai-nenpyō*, pp. 2, 3, 6; KBHS, p. 8; OPC, p. 49; MBZ 4:415–16.

†These were slim paperbacks comprising approximately 25–30 pages of material when printed in a modern format.

have detailed the lives of the courtesans much as the earlier ones had done. This material was probably seized upon as obscene. Unfortunately the preface is all that has survived. Considering Ryūhoku's accustomed elevated—not to say pedantic—style of humor, however, it seems unlikely that volume 3 contained anything more suggestive than had volumes 1 and 2, with such occasional phrases as "parting the lush, fragrant grasses beneath her skirts."[1] More objectionable would have been the juxtaposition of episodes such as the following from volume 2, which reflected badly on the upper reaches of the new order:

A geisha with a husband is like watered-down sake: thin and tasteless. A geisha with a child is like sake with sugar in it: heavy and cloying. Long ago, any geisha who became pregnant would be filled with shame. There were those among them who sought medicine with which to asault their wombs, while others would run away and hide themselves. In recent times, however, customs have changed, and geisha now hire wetnurses to raise their children just as ordinary mothers do. Stranger still, they discuss these things openly before their customers without the least embarrassment. There was one woman who had ten regular patrons when she became pregnant, and she had no idea who the father might be. She confided the news to one of her men, but he said, "You have several other patrons: why pick me?" She tried another and his answer was the same. Indeed, the answers she heard from all ten of her men seemed to emerge from a single mouth. Utterly distraught, she went to pray at the shrine of Kiyomasa.[2] "I am with child," she said, "and do not know who the father is. I ask a revelation from the god." The spirit of Kiyomasa appeared in her dream and spoke: "You have ten husbands and all share your bed equally. Not even a god can say which among them is the first. Surely the child in your womb must know his own father. Ask your question of him." The woman awoke and realized what she must do. It was the middle of the night and she was alone. She rinsed her mouth and washed her hands in ritual purification, then lit a stick of incense. Kneeling upon the floor mats, she began to rub her stomach and peered down into her shadowy nether regions. Calmly, she spoke to the child. "The god has commanded me to ask you the name of your father. Relate to me the truth." Immediately a voice within her womb replied, "Mother, how can you not know the truth? You have ten husbands and my flesh is formed as a result of their combined efforts. One made my head, another my abdomen; one made my chest, another my back. My two arms were made by two, and my legs by two others, and likewise my buttocks and penis were formed by the separate efforts of two different men. Thus, I have not one father but ten. The only exception is my ten fingers, which were made by someone else. Have you forgotten, mother, the one who never entered your innermost chamber but would idle away his time merely dipping his fingers into your vessel? He is the father of my fingers."

There was another geisha who was long on talk but short on brains. Everyone
called her "Chatterbox," although another name for her was "Blind Girl." One
day she was among the crowd of geisha serving at the banquet of a certain prince.
The drinking was at its height when she calmly turned to him and said, "I hear
that all the court nobles left in Kyoto make their living by painting pictures for
playing cards and that even you, my lord, used to do this. Can it be true?" * The
prince was thunderstruck and for a moment ventured no reply. "Long ago," he
said at last, "when the nobility had much time on their hands, there may have
been some who would make such cards for their own amusement, but only those
of far lower rank than myself. These days, with so many important national
events to attend to, there could hardly be anyone wasting time on such things."
"Oh, now I see!" exclaimed the geisha, slapping her knee. "The master is always
complaining how few shops have cards to sell these days and how high the prices
are. I never knew why that was until now, thanks to you. Since there are so few
people making them and so many people using them, there is always a shortage
of cards, and so the price has to be high!" All the others listened with fists
clenched in a cold sweat.[3]

Translation can hardly hope to convey the effect of Ryūhoku's mock-heroic
style, with its ponderous Chinese vocabulary. For Ryūhoku was no popular
scribbler (*gesakusha*) but honed his barbs for an educated readership.

When he wrote volume 1 of *New Chronicle* in 1859 at age twenty-two,
Ryūhoku, heir to a line of official Confucian scholars, was still tutor to the
shogun.† He was awarded gold and clothing by the Tokugawa government
the following year for his editorial work on some official histories.[4] In 1863,
however, he was relieved of his post and sentenced to fifty days of domiciliary
confinement for having slandered an important Tokugawa retainer. Apparently he had written some verses parodying the Tokugawas' inability to deal
decisively with the crises raised by foreign demands that Japan end her
seclusion.

Far from withering away in isolation, Ryūhoku exploited his dismissal as an
opportunity to learn more about the enemy. He spent the next two years at
home, studying English and acquainting himself with such students of the
West as Fukuzawa Yukichi.[5] Then, in December 1865, the Bakufu embarked
on a policy of military reorganization along Western lines that made Ryūhoku,

---

*Probably meant to be associated with Sanjō Sanetomi (1837–1891), a minor court noble
who rose to political prominence through his participation in the Meiji Restoration. His father,
Sanetsumu, was said to have painted playing cards for a living. Other courtiers are known to
have carved toothpicks to supplement their meager allowances before the Restoration. NKBT
1:227 n18.

†Ages in this book are calculated in the Western manner from birthday to birthday.

with his newfound expertise, useful to them again. He advanced rapidly to positions of high responsibility, but after the fall of Edo castle in 1868, he no longer had a master to serve, and he decided it was time for him to withdraw from the world.

In 1869, at the age of thirty-three, Ryūhoku retired as official head of his family. Refusing a position that the government offered him the following year, he set up a small academy in a temple on the banks of the Sumida River to teach English and Chinese classics. Comparing his withdrawal to that of China's foremost reclusive poet, T'ao Ch'ien, he declared himself "one of no use to the world," a role he was to play for the rest of his life. He was thus the first of many self-appointed outside observers who would rise to prominence in the history of modern Japanese literature.[6] Volume 2 of *New Chronicle of Yanagibashi* became both the first product of his "useless" existence and a model for the next generation.

Where volume 1 had been a hymn of praise for the Yanagibashi quarter, the second volume was an elegy. Instead of the sophisticate's appreciation for the light makeup and refreshingly uncoquettish style of the Yanagibashi women (who were, he insists, geisha, not mere prostitutes, and so were bedded with great difficulty), there was bitter sarcasm for the country bumpkins who had come to patronize the district and for the women whose urban flare had been lost with such companions. These rustics, of course, were the successful new men in government and business who had come flooding into the capital from Kyushu and western Honshu when the Satsuma and Chōshū clans overthrew the Tokugawa. Ryūhoku would make a career out of observing and jabbing at them, the "only humorist" in the world of Japanese journalism. Unlike certain other prominent newsmen, who came to support the government, Ryūhoku chose to remain outrageous.[7]

Ryūhoku published both volumes of his Yanagibashi work in 1874, after a tour of Europe and America, and accepted an invitation to take charge of the newspaper *Chōya Shimbun*.* It was in *Chōya* that he criticized the new press regulations in 1875, which earned him five days of domiciliary confinement. The following year, he was punished with four months in prison and fined one hundred yen for publishing an attack on the authors of the press and libel regulations, Ozaki Saburō and Inoue Kowashi. Although the article, by *Chōya*'s top writer Suehiro Tetchō, was framed as a criticism of two fictitious Tokugawa officials named Ozaki Kowashi and Inoue Saburō, Ryūhoku and

---

*This would be the primary outlet for Ryūhoku's critiques over the next decade. His more literary works—random essays that, unlike Ryūhoku's *New Chronicle*, were anthologized by other hands—would appear in the company's magazine, *Kagetsu shinshi*, which appeared between January 1, 1877, and October 31, 1884. Ōshima Ryūichi, *Ryūhoku dansō* (Shōwa kankōkai, 1943), p. 367.

Tetchō were induced to confess to an infringement of the libel regulations, reportedly out of gratitude to a fatherly judge who showed them respect after cruel jailers had dragged them to court through the snow. Tetchō got eight months in prison and a fine of two hundred yen![8]

While in prison, Ryūhoku issued an illustrated sheet of comic poetry, and following his release, he serialized a firsthand account of prison life which increased the newspaper's circulation. He also attended a mock prayer meeting led by major newsmen where he offered an address to the "spirit of the newspaper" before an overflow crowd. In his address, he praised the spirit for having come across the sea from the West to awaken the people, who "while born in full possession of the five senses and four limbs, were yet indistinguishable from potato worms, unable to speak a word or to write a line of argument." But the sins of the spirit were great, as well, causing writers to "attack the laws of our wise government" and, "in the gravest cases, to compose texts advocating (heaven forbid!) the destruction of the government and the overthrow of the nation." As heavy as the punishments for such acts instigated by the spirit might seem, they were, "thanks to the benevolence of our wise government, merely three years in prison and a fine of one thousand yen."[9] Unamused, the government gave the Home Minister his notorious absolute power in a special ordinance.

Such were the events immediately preceding the Home Ministry's refusal to license publication of New Chronicle of Yanagibashi. With Ryūhoku directing it until his death at forty-seven in 1884, Chōya Shimbun suffered at least twelve suspensions, some lasting several weeks.[10]

The rambling sarcasms of New Chronicle certainly indicate how far Japan had to go before it could create modern literature, but the book was favorite reading among the first Meiji-educated generation, those men who would become the creators. One of Ryūhoku's best-known latter-day admirers, Nagai Kafū, asserted that it was the rare student indeed who had not read New Chronicle of Yanagibashi.[11]

In yet another influential literary contribution, his preface to the 1878 translation of Bulwer-Lytton's Ernest Maltravers, Ryūhoku pointed out to the Japanese that the West he had seen on his travels was not a monochromatic kingdom of utilitarianism. He emphasized that it had an emotional life and that its literature of the emotions was a vital part of Western civilization.[12] This was not the West that official policy sought to import in order to establish "a rich country and a strong military," as one of the early Meiji slogans would have it. Ryūhoku was hinting at an element in the foreign culture which made room for individuality, an element that, before long, the government would come to recognize as a subversive force.

Writing in 1908 to protest the ban of a work of fiction, the critic Yamaji Aizan would declare, "The novel is history that is truer than history. It tells of man's secrets. It broadens people's view of the world and deepens their sympathy for others." The work that first did this for him, said Aizan, was Narushima Ryūhoku's *New Chronicle of Yanagibashi*.[13]

NEWSPAPERS, POLITICS, AND POISON WOMEN

Ryūhoku's *Chōya* (Universal) was one of the so-called big papers (*dai-* or *ō-shimbun*), which included *Yokohama Mainichi* (Daily) *Shimbun*, *Tokyo Nichinichi* (Daily) *Shimbun*, and *Yūbin Hōchi* (Post-Dispatch) *Shimbun*. These papers concentrated on political editorializing and were written in a style too difficult for any but the educated reader. The men who wrote for these papers did not even mix socially with staff members of the small (*shō* or *ko*) papers,[14] such as *Yomiuri* (Sell-by-Reading Aloud) *Shimbun*, *Hiragana E-iri* (ABC Illustrated) *Shimbun*, and *Kanayomi* (Read in ABC) *Shimbun*. As their titles imply, the latter were more commercialized and were written "making free use of the simple syllabary . . . for the least literate class of reader."[15]

These small papers actually were printed on somewhat narrower sheets than the big papers. They did not editorialize, were all but indifferent to taking political positions, and provided only the most perfunctory reports on political developments. They concentrated instead on those vulgar happenings deliberately excluded from the big papers as degrading to their image. The latest developments in the entertainment districts and the theatrical world were reported, along with other scandalous news and rumors, preferably with a strong sexual interest.[16] These sheets were less expensive than the big ones; they were hawked on street corners.

Beginning in 1877 with the scandalous account of Torioi Omatsu, the first of several "poison women" (*dokufu*) to capture the imagination of the reading public with grotesque killings and sexual adventures, the small papers carried serialized pieces (*tsuzukimono*), often with heavy doses of fiction to spice up the story and always with an illustration. In fact, "the very *raison d'etre* of the small newspapers lay in the *tsuzukimono* with its illustrations."[17] The *tsuzukimono* evolved ultimately into the newspaper novels that have played such an important role in the development of modern Japanese fiction.[18]

The great heyday of the "poison-women pieces," semifictional treatments of Torioi Omatsu and the murderesses Hara Okinu and Takahashi Oden, came in 1878–1880. Although the first, Omatsu, was in part a victim of social injustice—a member of the pariah Eta caste—both Okinu and Oden seem to have gone out of their way to be evil. According to *Nightstorm Okinu: Flower-Frail Dreams of Revenge* (*Yoarashi Okinu hana no adayume*), the popular account of her life, the entertainer Okinu became the concubine of a daimyō (feudal lord) at the age of seventeen. When the daimyō died, his retainer Yūjirō introduced her to a local drug wholesaler named Kikaku. Okinu became Kikaku's legal spouse after she helped him murder his wife. Soon she became involved with Yūjirō and unsuccessfully attempted with him to poison Kikaku. This ended her marriage.

Okinu was living happily with Yūjirō when the Restoration battles broke out. Yūjirō was killed, and Okinu's house was burned to the ground. She made her living after that as a geisha until she reencountered a usurer, Kobayashi Kinpei, whom she had met some years earlier. It was not long before Kinpei found out she was having an affair with a popular actor, but Okinu poisoned Kinpei before he could take action, and she went on to enjoy a period of lustful dissipation with the actor until the truth of the murder came out. She was tried and executed in 1872 at the age of thirty. Okinu's story was serialized in the small paper *Sakigake Shimbun* in 1878. It made such a hit that the fifteen-volume book version began to appear even before the serialization had ended.[19]

The most notorious poison woman was Oden, whose career has been traced briefly by George Sansom.[20] After strangling her leprous husband to death, Oden lured a rich merchant (one of countless men with whom she was involved) to an inn and stabbed him in his sleep. Arrested for this murder, she swore to the judge that she had been avenging a sister who did not, in fact, exist. Oden refused to confess the truth, even after she had been left to languish for more than three years in jail. She was executed in January 1879 at the age of twenty-nine.[21]

Each case (there were five poison women in all), after prominent reportage in the small newspapers, was immediately issued in illustrated book form, known from the Edo period as *kusazōshi*, with a gruesome illustration on every page by the best woodblock print artists of the day. Stage productions did not lag far behind the books; performances in song also recounted the exploits of the poison women. This typical Japanese "boom" could have given the censors a great deal to do had they been interested. All the poison-women pieces gloried in sex and violence while maintaining a properly shocked Confucian attitude, purporting to demonstrate that virtue will be rewarded and evil punished.[22] Some years later the traditional narrative *kōdan* form would also maintain its acceptability by paying lip service to the old morality, while the serious, Western-influenced modern literature of a more iconoclastic sort became the target of widespread moral outrage and administrative suppression.

As the poison-woman boom was beginning to slacken in the small papers, the big papers started serializing a new kind of fiction that would constitute an important stage in the development of the modern Japanese novel. This was the political novel, which flourished as an aspect of the Movement for Liberty and Popular Rights.[23] As with the more popular, poison-women serials, the political novels held surprisingly little interest for the censors. The first of these was *The Stormy Sea of Love: A Drama of Popular Rights* (*Minken engi: jōkai haran*), written in 1880 by Toda Kindō. It was a typically high-minded allegory and offered one of the first demonstrations that fiction could have a serious purpose. The story tells how a man named "National Government Propertext" thwarts the love of a geisha named "Harbinger of Rights" for a young man named "The People of Japan." But in the end he holds a wedding reception for them—that is, the opening of a national assembly.[24]

George Sansom vividly retells the story of the most successful political novel, *Strange Encounters of Elegant Females* (*Kajin no kigū*, 1885, with sequels through 1897). In another context he also mentions a "temporary vogue" for Russian nihilist novels "such as Stepniak's *Underground Russia*, or accounts of the activities of terrorists, political assassinations, treason trials, and so forth."[25] These more extreme offshoots of the political novel finally caught the censor's eye: Nishikawa Tsūtetsu's *Circumstances of the Russian Nihilists* (*Rokoku kyomutō jijō*) in 1882 and Miyazaki Muryū's *True Lives of the Nihilists: The Demon's Sobs* (*Kyomutō jitsudenki: kishushu*) in 1886. Convicted of violating the publication regulations, Muryū spent three months in prison.[26] With the "perfection" of the censorship system in 1887, however, such harsh punishments gave way to an increasing reliance on the Home Minister's power to prohibit sale and distribution.

The distinction between small and big papers broke down in a few short years after 1881, when an Osaka paper called the *Asahi Shimbun* decided to adopt features of both types. The *Asahi* carried news, editorials, and "third-page" scandal reports. It provided pronunciation glosses for less well-educated readers and adopted the small papers' practice of using illustrations, a feature that increased sales when combined with serialized fiction.[27]

Over the next several years, the distinction between highbrow and salacious literature itself began to blur as farmers moved to the cities to work in factories, creating a mass audience with a thirst for third-page articles and for more serious serialized fiction. The huge leap in capitalistic development that turned newspapers into big business was thus an excellent stimulus for the business of novel writing, but it was precisely the effects of a booming economy and dynamically changing society that made the novels themselves so dark. The novel was growing up and edging toward its showdown with the police, but still the 1887 Regulations would be nine years old before "modern" fiction would begin to feel their impact.

4

Developing Realism:
The Censors Begin to Notice

"Serious Fiction": Oguri Fūyō's "Making Up for Bed"

It is generally recognized that Japan's first modern novel appeared as early as 1887–1889. This was *The Drifting Clouds* (*Ukigumo*), by a young student of Russian literature named Futabatei Shimei.[1] At this early point in the development of modern Japanese literature, however, few readers were prepared to respond to such sophisticated Western literary conventions as colloquial language and mundane characters whose simply plotted, ordinary experiences implied an analysis of contemporary society. Far more popular were the works of Ozaki Kōyō and his Ken'yūsha group, who produced what was later recognized to be "Edo fiction in Western disguise."[2]

Kōyō and his disciples employed imported techniques of realistic description to write conventional melodramas without relying on the kind of illustrators who worked with the Edo *gesakusha* and the authors of the poison-women pieces. Commenting on Zola, Kōyō noted that "he uses three pages, four to describe the interior of a room. You can't find anything like that in Japanese literature."[3] But this came later for Kōyō. He initially won his fame—and inspired the next generation of writers to pursue literary careers—with his story "The Erotic Confessions of Two Nuns" ("Ninin bikuni: irozange," 1889), an anachronistic tour de force.[4]

"An avid reader of Saikaku, whose works were then enjoying a revival, Kōyō created in "Erotic Confessions" an elegant style that readers still uneasy with Futabatei's relatively austere prose could immediately recognize as beautiful. With all the bombast and rhythmic majesty of a *jōruri* reciter, Kōyō unfolded his tale of a samurai torn between duty and personal sentiment in a manner that Edo-bred tastes could understand. (It might be mentioned in passing that the title of the story is misleading in two ways. First, the story is not "erotic," nor does it even concern illicit liaisons. Second, it has little to do with the "two nuns" who are supposed to be confessing their pasts to each other. The final point is to have the women, who have spent the long night talking in a mountaintop hermitage, suddenly realize that the husband of one had been the fiancé of the other. "The aim of this story is tears," wrote Kōyō in his preface.)[5]

Kōyō did not continue writing tales of the Edo period, and in fact his style did evolve into something closer to the kind of colloquial medium being fashioned by writers more open to European influence, but he remained an extremely popular creator of intense, convoluted, and skillfully wrought melodramas until his death in 1903.

Kōyō's dominance of the literary scene remained secure until the time of the Sino-Japanese War (1894–1895), when a huge influx of farmers into the cities to man munitions factories gave rise to a new readership with different tastes. The war produced not only a great industrial boom but a sudden, massive undermining of traditional rural life and values that left many feeling anxious and victimized. In response to this darkened atmosphere, there emerged the "idea fiction" (*kannen shōsetsu*) of Kōyō's disciple Izumi Kyōka, which, along with the "serious fiction" (*shinkoku shōsetsu*) or "distressing fiction" (*hisan shōsetsu*) of men like Hirotsu Ryūrō, Kawakami Bizan, and Oguri Fūyō, were naive attempts to transcend Ken'yūsha frivolity through the introduction of "serious" themes.

Ryūrō's version of serious realism is to write about disfigured characters, grotesquely scarred men, or idiot dwarfs with abnormal sexual inclinations. Bizan resorts to gore and necrophilia in some works, but a few of his stories reveal an extraordinarily clear perception of the common people's suffering at the hands of the politicians and businessmen. His "The Ministerial Secretary" ("Shokikan," 1895) is meant to expose the corrupt ties between capital and government by portraying an inexplicably evil ministerial secretary who conspires with a money-mad capitalist, demanding the hand of the capitalist's daughter as his price for privileged information. (The daughter, of course, is in love with someone else, a mild-mannered young philosopher who warns her that it would be "a fate worse than death to fall into that man's clutches.")[6]

Bizan's "Behind the Facade" ("Ura-omote," 1895) opens thus:

> Katsuya awoke to see a suspicious shadow move across the paper door and disappear. . . . Was it a dream? It was not. Was he mistaken? He was not. How could this be? Hatano Jūrō, known to many as a philanthropist, a man of virtue, had stolen into his house late at night and made off with his property. The father of his beloved Shizuko, to whom Katsuya had given—nay, had dedicated himself body and soul, was a low-down, despicable burglar![7]

Thus, in a single, stunning blow, Bizan reveals to us that polite society is not all it seems to be on the surface.

Much of this "serious" and "idea" fiction appeared in the literary magazine *Bungei Kurabu*, which had been launched by the Hakubunkan publishers in January 1895 as part of a large-scale company reorganization in response to the huge demand created by the war. The Ken'yūsha-dominated *Bungei Kurabu* was soon competing with Shun'yōdō's *Shinshōsetsu* for the greatly enlarged readership, and a new era in publishing had begun. Literary magazines until this time had catered to a specialized audience, but these lavish new publications marked the beginning of literary magazines as they are known today, with *Bungei Kurabu* boasting a circulation of over 50,000 in 1895.[8]

When *Bungei Kurabu* printed "Making Up for Bed" ("Ne-oshiroi") by Oguri Fūyō (1875–1926) in September 1896, the censors responded with the first ban issued against the new literary magazines and the only ban of the new "serious fiction." This marked the first time that the Home Minister's power to prohibit the sale of a periodical under the 1887 Press Regulations was exercised against the emerging realism that was eventually to be perceived by the government as a major threat.

Along with these various firsts, "Making Up for Bed" is of interest to us as the first of several pieces by Fūyō that would be banned. Fūyō was not singled out by the censors entirely without cause: his tastes consistently favored the lurid and sensational, and he was criticized by some contemporaries for his superficial manner in treating potentially serious problems.[9] "Making Up for Bed" purports to examine the difficulties faced by the Eta pariahs, and as such it is the first work of fiction to concentrate on this theme (if we except the semifictional tales of the poison woman Omatsu).[10] But ten years would elapse before a Japanese novelist could write a meaningful protest for the Eta cause, capturing the outsider's sense of loneliness.* Fūyō all but smacks his lips over the incestuous relationship that develops between the attractive Okei (she is all of twenty-six but continues to wear bright colors and put on makeup for bed) and her brother Sōtarō when their Eta background consistently thwarts her chances of marriage.

Telling his story in the polished form characteristic of Ken'yūsha, Fūyō writes with the archaic phraseology and the melodramatic intensity he learned from Kōyō. Possibly his description of Okei's delight in finding a man was too intense for the censors: "The delicious sweetness of it penetrated her flesh and marrow. . . . Her feverish excitement was almost indecent."[11] The Official reason for the ban is not known, but modern commentators assume that the

---

*Shimazaki Tōson, *Hakai* (1906), translated by Kenneth Strong as *The Broken Commandment* (University of Tokyo Press, 1974).

themes of incest and Eta alienation were to blame.[12] The story's ending reveals the author's unwholesome attitude. After rumors of their too-close relationship have become even more painful than talk of their lineage, the siblings move their tobacco stand to the outskirts of the city:

> While Sōtarō seemed to grow more downcast with each passing day, all signs of Okei's lingering illness disappeared, a glow came to her cheeks, and a new robustness made her more attractive than ever, like the late-blooming branch of cherry that retains the scent of spring. But the women of the neighborhood who saw her at the baths found one thing difficult to fathom: the color of her nipples and the shape of her belly were slowly beginning to change. Disgraceful! Whose baby could it be?[13]

MYŌJŌ'S FRENCH NUDES

The vogue for "idea fiction" soon ended as authors abandoned their labored search for the melodramatically serious and turned instead to areas more congenial to their talents.[14] The polished Ken'yūsha storytellers had perhaps gone as far as they could with realism. Replacing them in the forefront of literary creativity were men and women whose efforts were expended less on style than on substance. The censors were generally unconcerned with the works of these young romantic poets, although one brief clash did occur in 1900. The November 1900 issue of the literary magazine *Myōjō* was banned— not for the hot-blooded poems of Yosano (then Tōtori) Akiko,[15] as might have been expected, but for two nude line drawings taken from French originals.[16] The case is of some interest as an indication of prevailing standards with regard to nudity and also for the response of the editor, Yosano Hiroshi (Tekkan), leader of the Myōjō school and later Akiko's husband.

Every issue of *Myōjō*—both before and after the banning—carried a cover illustration of Venus (Myōjō), left breast exposed, right breast hidden by the hand holding the lily into which she gazes. The two nude illustrations in the November issue differed from this cover drawing and similar nudes in *Myōjō* by the clear delineation of buttocks in one and a groin (minus pubic hair, rounding of the flesh, or any other distinguishing features) in the other.[17] The eyes of the frontal nude stare straight out at the viewer. The drawings were printed alongside a discussion of nude art by Yosano Hiroshi and the poet/ translator Ueda Bin as part of their commentary on the sixth annual Haku-bakai art exhibit. In the discussion, Ueda notes that nineteenth-century nudes were no longer studies in curvilinear beauty, as classical sculpture had been, but that as part of the new realism associated with naturalism, the artist tended to stress the color and modeling of the flesh to convey the inner spirit of the individual. He also notes that Japanese society is simply not ready for that sort of thing. Its direct appeal to the senses could have a harmful effect on morals.[18]

The government would certainly have agreed with this, for in the next Hakubakai show, the police ordered the exhibitors to cover the lower parts of nudes with maroon curtains. This was the notorious Koshimaki Jiken or Waistcloth Incident of 1901. In 1903 they went so far as to paste fig leaves on paintings and saw the penis off a male sculpture, even after having segregated nudes into a special gallery.[19]

The active debate over nude art in Japan had been sparked by the illustration for an 1889 story by Yamada Bimyō,[20] which prompted a rash of such illustrations and led to a Home Ministry order forbidding them, in November 1889, apparently to no effect. A painting by Kuroda Seiki, founder of the Hakubakai, also caused a scandal when it was exhibited in Kyoto in 1895 (a Tokyo showing the year before had upset no one). Although reproductions of that particular work were forbidden, a resurgence of magazine nudes led to a series of bannings in 1897 in response to the protests of some conservative newspapers. Reproductions of nude Western art had become a commonplace by about 1908, but a 1918 decision by the Great Court of Cassation established the rule that still applies today: the pubic area need not be hidden, but there should be no anatomical details to draw the viewer's attention.[21] Even now, magazines such as *Playboy* are sold only after customs inspectors have carefully scratched out all signs of pubic hair, and even in avowedly pornographic movies, sexual organs are obscured from view by floating black blobs painted on the film.

As Donald Keene has noted, Kuroda Seiki's piece "was the first nude by a Japanese except for those of pornographic intent."[22] Writers, artists, and editors seeking to introduce Western aesthetic standards into Japan were faced with a deep-rooted cultural bias when it came to serious nude art. Yosano Hiroshi, responding to the ban of his magazine in a special issue, saw himself as undertaking an impossibly huge task. His statement, in effect, was as follows: We want to contribute to the development of our nation's poetry; we aim not at the desecration of morals but the cultivation of taste. These are decadent times. The Japanese are devoid of taste and ideals, and although one poet/editor of a small magazine (6,000 copies at best) can only do so much, we hope to lead the ideals of readers to a loftier plane.[23]

Yosano said further that he believed the introduction of famous works of Western art would aid in the cultivation of taste. It was this that the French nudes had been intended to do. He had been certain that no one could be offended by the particularly chaste examples they had chosen and he had been "shocked speechless" by this ban issued "in the name of Baron Dr. Suematsu

Kenchō, Minister of Home Affairs, . . . patron of the arts . . . profound student of Western literature," and translator into English (in 1882) of part of *The Tale of Genji*. As writers, Yosano and his colleagues had hoped for great things from this cultured and powerful politician, but now they could only implore him to explain what "unfathomable reasoning" had prompted this action—not just for the sake of *Myōjō*, but for the future of art in Japan.[24]

Like other writers, Yosano Hiroshi seems to have been rewarded with silence for his cries of pain. Nor is it likely that we shall ever have a rational explanation for the authorities' failure to ban *Myōjō* again, despite its publication of the sensual verse that Yosano Akiko would anthologize in her *Tangled Hair* (*Midaregami*, August 1901) and the powerful antiwar poem that she addressed to her brother in Port Arthur at the height of the Russo-Japanese War (to be discussed in chap. 5). A few years later, these things would not have been missed.

THE WRITER AS SOCIAL CRITIC: UCHIDA ROAN'S "BROKEN FENCE"

Another magazine that, like *Myōjō*, aided in the development of literature characterized by personal commitment rather than stylistic approach was *Kokumin no Tomo*, the influential journal (peak circulation 100,000) that helped create the quasi-religious Emersonian atmosphere common in intellectual circles during the Meiji twenties. As one commentator has remarked, "It can be said that 1887 (Meiji 20), the year *Kokumin no Tomo* was founded, signaled the advent of the age of introspection."[25] Toward the turn of the century, the magazine led a crusade calling for "social fiction" (*shakai shōsetsu*) that would portray the relationship between society and the individual and be otherwise socially relevant. The only writer to respond with a series of works consciously undertaken as social fiction was himself one of the more vocal theoreticians of the movement and one of the most impressive critical minds of the Meiji period, Uchida Roan (1868–1929).[26]

Roan's "Broken Fence" ("Yaregaki"), which appeared in the January 1901 issue of *Bungei Kurabu*, tells the story of a carpenter's daughter, the sixteen-year-old Okyō, who has recently taken a position as a servant in the household of a prominent new baron after having fled from sexual advances in one lowly job after another.* At least in the home of this aristocratic family, she feels, she will be safe from threats to the chastity she has been taught to value so highly

---

*The new peerage was created in July, 1884, "to form the membership of the projected House of Peers." John K. Fairbank et al., *East Asia*, p. 292.

by her former secondary school teacher, an idealistic young man who is working his way through law school. Okyō quickly learns, however, that the baron, founder of the Moral Reform Club, is in reality a beast in human guise who dallies with all the women of his household—this under the silent gaze of his wife, who is a prominent member of several ladies' organizations, especially those devoted to women's rights. The baron and baroness are thought to have a model Western-style household (*hōmu*); there are few who believe the exposés that have appeared in the scandal sheets, particularly since retractions have been printed.

One of those who knows the truth about the baron is Okyō's mother, a heavy drinker given to telling tales of the days when she was the mistress of a priest. As the story opens, she is gushing over Okyō's lavish new surroundings, but soon she is scolding her daughter for having rebuffed the baron's advances. She shocks the girl by revealing that Okyō has been sent here specifically to become the baron's plaything, this being a far quicker road to success than any of the other menial jobs she has held. And besides, "Even if the only thing to come of it is a one-night stand, you'll be paid plenty—at least enough for me to have a good drink and go to the Kabuki theater!"[27]

Needless to say, Okyō's mother is an incredible harridan, as evil as Okyō and her teacher are pure. Another study in depravity is the baron, whom we see drinking with his father-in-law, a prominent count. They have slipped out of the seasonal meeting of the Moral Reform Club, which is being held as a garden party in the baron's suburban villa, and are consoling each other for having to put up with all of the moralistic nonsense. They talk about sleeping with young girls and cackle over their cups like typical dirty old men.

Making his way back to the gathering, the baron overhears Okyō telling a young man who appears to be a student (it is, of course, her teacher, who is one of the sincere members of the club) that she wants to flee from the baron's house as soon as possible. Once, she says, she had to bite him to escape his filthy clutches. "It would be no sin to kill such a scoundrel!" replies the teacher. "You ought to carry a knife. . . . I had no idea he was so immoral. He had me completely fooled!"[28] Suddenly the baron charges in and orders the teacher to go, which—incredibly enough—he does, leaving Okyō alone with the baron but assuring her that he will be back. A brief epilogue informs us that the baron is doing better than ever, while nothing more has been heard of Okyō or the teacher.

"Broken Fence" seethes with righteous indignation, which is augmented by indignation of another sort. Roan portrays the baron as the son of a famous samurai of a certain western domain who has survived the turbulence of the Restoration years as a member of the dominant Satsuma-Chōshū clique government. Like Narushima Ryūhoku, Roan came from a family of Tokugawa retainers. He grew up as an outsider, aware that the new regime was somehow responsible for his family's financial difficulties.

The issue of *Bungei Kurabu* that printed "Broken Fence" was banned.* Apparently a subordinate of the same literate Home Minister to whom Yosano Hiroshi had appealed for an explanation, Suematsu Kenchō, thought he recognized in it a portrait of life at the Suematsu household.† In later years, Roan insisted that he had taken the idea for the story from a foreign pot-boiler and had combined it with rumors concerning another family. Nothing could have been further from his intention than an exposé of the Home Minister, he said, noting with obvious relish that his fictional creation had revealed a kind of "corruption common to all upper-class homes." [29]

At the time of the ban, however, Roan was embarrassed and outraged. He spent all night writing a lengthy critique, which, it turned out, the *Bungei Kurabu* editor was afraid to publish. Nor would the company's intellectual journal, *Taiyō*, risk printing it. It was finally published in the newspaper *Niroku Shinpō* later in the month under the title, "A Notice Concerning the Prohibition of Sale of 'Broken Fence' Directed to the Authorities and the Public" ("'Yaregaki' hatsubai kinshi ni tsuki tōrosha oyobi kōko ni tsugu"), and attached to it was a disclaimer of responsibility by the paper. [30]

Roan's "Notice" merits our attention. He opens by stating that neither he nor the editors of *Bungei Kurabu* have been able to discern what in "Broken Fence" could possibly be injurious to public morals. He has reread the story several times, only to be left with the same questions. Was it the story as a whole? Certain passages? The author's intent? An appeal to prurient interest? Obscene language? Roan raises virtually every issue that has ever been raised in the banning of a supposedly obscene piece of writing, and in no instance does he find his story culpable.

Roan emphasizes several points concerning government censorship, asserting that when the government puts the brand of "pornographer" on a respectable individual who considers himself a contributor to civilization, it owes him an explanation. The all-purpose rubric "injurious to public morals" is so

*The official reason for the ban is not, in fact, known. See MBHS, pp. 145–47.

†Both the fictional baron and Baron Suematsu were from Kyushu and were powerful in the clique government. Suematsu's father-in-law, Prime Minister Itō Hirobumi, was known to have been quite a womanizer. Also censored in 1901 was a particularly hysterical exposé of Itō's tainted sex life, *O Land of Prostitution!* (*Aa baiinkoku*), which contained a photograph of Itō with a Kabuki actor and a prostitute. The preface invited the reader to spit at "the three great shames of Japan." This, claimed author Masaoka Geiyō, an important editor on the board of the influential journal *Shinsei* (predecessor of today's *Shinchō*), was the smartest means for taking revenge on "these embodiments of syphilis and prostitution" for having "demeaned your fatherland." Jō Ichirō, *Hakkinbon hyakunen*, pp. 78–79. See partial text in MBZ 84:173–80.

vague that it is bound to be exploited to suppress works of true value. Further-more, he asserts, only those trained to make aesthetic judgments can evaluate a work of literature, not government functionaries. And no power, whether of the government or the masses, can obliterate an idea. By seeking to prevent the free flow of ideas, the government does injury to civilization itself.

Roan also notes the recent frequent suppression of Edo classics. The banning of the complete works of Saikaku (in 1894) he finds especially objectionable. True, Roan admits, there are lewd sections in works such as *The Life of an Amorous Man* and *The Life of an Amorous Woman*, but no one with the least aesthetic sense would label these works wholly obscene.[31] There is also the question of language: few readers without a thorough knowledge of classical Japanese can read Saikaku with ease; thus, whatever harm they might do is severely limited. "In fact, I cannot help wondering whether the authorities themselves can understand Saikaku well enough to judge him obscene."[32]

Returning to "Broken Fence," Roan notes that he himself does not favor extreme verisimilitude for its own sake. He has avoided portraying bedroom activities, certain that this would reduce the possibility of his story's being offensive. There is not a line or phrase of seduction or other intimate activity, no suggestion of authorial commentary (such as in "Making Up for Bed") that would imply approval of or an attempt to arouse lewd emotions.

Here, perhaps, Roan is on the shakiest legal ground. On October 11, 1900, just three months before "Broken Fence" appeared, the Great Court of Cassa-tion, overturning the ruling of a lower court, established the principle that certain subject matter could be banned as injurious to public morals (and, indeed, to the social order as well) without concern for the degree of detail employed in the author's treatment. The case involved not fiction but a series of articles in the newspaper *Yorozu Chōhō* on the purchasing of actors as male prostitutes by "the wives, mistresses, widows and daughters" of families ranging from that of "a high official down to a shopkeeper." The mere re-portage that such a thing had occurred was judged to be obscene and injurious to public morals, and the editor-publisher was sentenced to five months behind bars.[33]

What ultimately angers Roan is not so much the censorship system as the unjustified suppression of his own highly moralistic work despite what he perceives to be open immorality among the ruling class and elsewhere. In an interview shortly after this incident, he decries the selling of pornographic books, the printing of scandalous third-page reports, and the open advertising for "patent medicines one blushes to mention in a decent home"—an offshoot of legalized prostitution reminiscent of the Victorian era ads both for brothels and for syphilis cures.[34] He also makes some practical suggestions for improv-ing the censorship system, although he would later come to reject such an approach: He says he would like to see the jurisdiction over censorship shifted from the Home Ministry to the Ministry of Education and the job entrusted to "a panel of Imperial University graduates, or University professors, or some scholar who can be trusted as an authority" in "bowdlerizing Bocaccio, say, or rewriting Shakespeare, where their works contain morally objectionable words."[35]

Since such a change cannot be instituted immediately, Roan suggests that several high-ranking, knowledgeable officials be involved when a ban is to be instituted. Another step that might eliminate uncertainty would be for the Home Ministry to issue a set of guidelines such as those circulated to producers of textbooks. (This was only one of countless pleas to the Home Ministry for some rules.) Roan goes on to say that it will do no good to protest that the present unpredictable sanctions might prevent the development of literature, since "the authorities couldn't care less about the development of literature as long as they have morals under control."

"In the end, however," says Roan, "the Home Ministry treats literature with such contempt only because society as a whole does so." The banning of a literary work would arouse protests in England or France that harm was being done to culture or to human rights. Roan finds it "very strange that both writers and publishers have greeted this utterly unexplained command from the government with silence, and that society takes no exception to it." Although he is comforted by the fact that several thousand copies of the magazine were distributed before the police could act, he urges "writers, publishers, and lovers of literature to raise their voices together in response," and "not merely for my sake."[36]

Roan was one of those young, educated Meiji men whose political blood had been stirred by the popular-rights movement, but instead of turning to purely private concerns as so many of them had when they saw the movement frustrated by entrenched powers, Roan vented his anger on the page. The government was not the only target of Roan's trenchant wit, and for our purposes, it was the lesser of his two bêtes noires. Having begun his career as a socially aware critic during the elegant Ken'yūsha school's dominance in the late 1880s, Roan maintained a strong antipathy toward writers without ideas or interest in the world around them. After the profoundly moving experience of reading *Crime and Punishment* in 1889, Dostoevsky became the standard against which he measured the art of his countrymen. He published his own translation of *Crime and Punishment* in 1892–1893 and went on to produce some of the most influential translations of recent literature over the next two decades. Meanwhile, his anti-Ken'yūsha invective crystallized in an entire volume of sardonic advice on *How to Become a Writer* (*Bungakusha to naru hō*, 1894), in which he listed as indispensable qualifications a pretty face and a narrow mind.[37]

An essay published in September 1898 exhibits Roan's contempt for writers who turn away from their society and his hatred for politicians who exploit their power. In "Now Is the Perfect Time to Write Political Novels" ("Seiji shōsetsu o tsukurubeki kōjiki"), he urges novelists to turn from their preoccupation with love stories and to fix their gaze on the upheavals in the contemporary political arena. He ironically cautions writers *not* to fashion the kind of heroic stories that made the first political novels so popular, however: to depict modern-day politics, he says, writers must create farce.

This was not sufficient excuse for turning one's back on politics and society, however, and Roan continued to criticize the "feudal" behavior of writers who did so:

> Europeans, of course, are accustomed to giving the highest priority to their rights in society, but in Japan feudal tradition lingers on. The politicians keep the power for themselves alone, and the other classes follow silently along, provided their own security is not threatened. This is especially true of writers, who tend to shy away from public life, thinking it so very lofty of them to remain aloof from the world. As a result, they become increasingly divorced from the everyday realities of society. They behave like recluses and are treated by others as some sort of otherworldly beings. This is the main reason they know so little about what is happening in society, as a result of which it is often unclear what period their fiction is intended to represent. Of course the root of this is that minds nurtured on *kusazōshi* [comic books] can take no interest in social happenings other than what they read in the scandal sheets. And I suppose one might just as well be distant from social activity if all he writes is love stories. But I believe that anyone who wants to write something more than entertainment for women must be a little more closely in touch with society and a little more knowledgeable with regard to practical activity. . . . When men tell us the world is too trying and pretend they are too cultivated to mingle with the crowd, as today's writers are doing, they simply end up being treated as parasites, more dependent on society than ever. Then they become *truly* alienated and cast away the rights (the human rights, the social rights) they ought to possess, doing nothing to elevate the writer's position.[38]

Roan wrote this in 1899, some seven years before the rise of naturalism made it clear that mainstream fiction had abandoned "love" for the "ugly truth" and that the clash between art and authority had started in earnest. Until then, Roan would go on criticizing writers for the parasitic lack of self-respect that lay behind their unwillingness to stand up to the censors. Ultimately it became clear to him that the ones out of touch with reality were not the writers with their vision of human diversity, but the political and social leaders who were attempting artificially to sustain the life of moribund feudal-era values.

THE EASY PREWAR YEARS

Uchida Roan had provided such a lucid view of the implications of censorship that one might think the issues were now clear, the battle lines drawn. But in fact, censorship continued to be a rather random affair for the next seven years, at least where apolitical writers were concerned. The government gradually increased its pressure on the growing Socialist movement, however. It was a Socialist, for example, who wrote the first collection of poetry to be banned.[39] But while the government was busy suppressing the left-wing peace movement that failed to prevent war from breaking out with Russia in 1904, realistic fiction was allowed to develop without much interference. These were the years in which modern Japanese fiction crystallized. The exaggeration and grotesquerie of serious and distressing fiction gave way to the somewhat more restrained, thematically unified novels of Zolaism in 1901–1902, leading toward the emergence of full-blown Japanese naturalism in 1906–1907.

Two fictional treatments of the theme of adultery published in 1902 illustrate the Police Bureau's haphazard approach during this period. On the one hand, Zolaist Kosugi Tengai's *Popular Song* (*Hayariuta*) was not banned, though it is a glut of steamy, fertile imagery all the way from its opening scene, which has a farmer and a rickshaw man making some remarkably straightforward comments about hereditary nymphomania, to its inevitable conclusion in which the beautiful young wife succumbs to her desires in the family hothouse. No sexual activity is described. The "camera" shifts at the last moment to a wildly flapping butterfly that has been startled by the hot odor of human breath.

The banned work, on the other hand, is a chattily narrated novella. In Shimazaki Tōson's *The Former Master* (*Kyūshujin*), the affair portrayed is probably never consummated, and the whole thing dissolves into farce. In the last scene, there is a knock on the door; the dentist/lover tries to pretend that he has not been kissing the wife but merely pulling her tooth; and crowds of people in a celebration outside are blowing bugles, beating drums, and shouting, "Long live His Majesty the Emperor!" Tōson's graphic description of the kiss—an act considered provocative through the 1940s, at least—might be thought to have attracted the censor's attention. But this is not the whole explanation. The magazine carrying the story was on the stands for a month before an influential acquaintance of Tōson's models complained to the Police Bureau and they went into action.[40]

Arbitrariness, irrationality, and comical inconsistency can be said to characterize censorship in all times and places, including Japan through 1945 and beyond. But compared with the situation that developed after the Russo-Japanese War, when the censors started to bear down on "dangerous thoughts," the period that we have been discussing comes to seem casual, even innocent.

Part Two

AFTER THE WAR WITH RUSSIA

5

The Rise of Naturalism

PROLOGUE: DANGEROUS THOUGHTS OF PEACE

Japan had been preparing for the war against Russia ever since the Triple Intervention had forced upon her the indignity of returning land that she had "rightfully" won in the Sino-Japanese War. The intervening decade had been one of hardship and sacrifice for the people, who supported the nation's increasing military might with taxes on such daily necessities as kerosene and salt.[1] Victory over Russia was to be their revenge. The press had been demanding a fight for months when hostilities were finally declared in February 1904, and after some setbacks, Japan's victory was assured with the destruction of the Baltic Fleet in May 1905. "At the end of the summer of 1905," however, according to Ishikawa Takuboku, "most Japanese seemed to be opposed to ending the war at all. They seemed to believe, in a kind of blind, raging hysteria, that as long as we had started fighting 'the Russian bastards,' we had to cross the Urals, or at least press as far as Lake Baikal."[2]

Japan paid for this hysteria to the tune of 100,000 fighting men's lives, but virtually the only consistent voice of pacifism during the period was *Heimin Shimbun*, a newspaper established in November 1903 by the Socialists Kōtoku Shūsui and Sakai Toshihiko, who took a position of absolute nonviolence in their call for peace and social change. The government attacked with the Press Regulations and with sheer extortion, harassing newsstands and subscribers, but the paper kept alive through a series of valiant court battles. Late in 1904, however, when the seige of Port Arthur seemed as though it were never going to stop chewing up Japan's "human bullets," other newspapers were almost unanimous in condemning the little pacifist weekly with its circulation of under 4,000. "Disappointed by the progress of the war and apprehensive about the future, the Japanese public seems to have turned to witch-hunting at

55

home," F. G. Notehelfer has written. Indeed, by February *Heimin Shimbun* had ceased to exist, Kōtoku was in prison, and the peace movement had effectively ended.[3]

Considering the bloodthirsty atmosphere, one can only marvel that the police did not bother to censor the September 1904 issue of *Myōjō* for the following poem by Yosano Akiko addressed to her brother Chūzaburō, who was fighting with General Nogi Maresuke's Third Army at Port Arthur:

> Oh my little brother, I weep for you
> And beg you: do not die—
> You, last-born and most beloved.
> Did our parents
> Put a blade into your hand
> And teach you to kill men?
> "Kill men and die in battle," did they say
> And raise you so 'til twenty-four?
>
> It is you who are to carry on the name
> You who are to be master of
> This proud, old merchant house.
> I beg you: do not die.
> What concern is it of yours
> If the Russian fortress falls or stands?
> Of this, the merchant household code
> Says nothing.
>
> I beg you: do not die.
> His Imperial Majesty—he himself—
> Enters not the field of battle.
> So vast and deep his sacred heart:
> He cannot wish for you to spill
> Your own blood and another's,
> To die the death of beasts,
> To think such death is glory!
>
> Oh my little brother
> I beg you: do not die in battle.
> To add to mother's grief
> When she lost father this autumn past,
> They took her son
> And left her to protect the house.

I hear of "peace" in this great Emperor's reign,
And yet our mother's hair grows ever whiter.

Your pliant, young bride crouches weeping
In the shadows of the shop curtains.
Do you think of her, or have you forgotten?
Imagine the heart of this sweet girl—
Not ten months were you together!
Who else has she in all the world
To care for her but you?
I beg you, brother: do not die.[4]

The most costly battles of the war were fought over a vantage point over-looking Port Arthur called the 203–Meter Hill, and there were rumors that the Fourth Division of the Third Army was using suicide troops to take it. Chūzaburō was in the Fourth Division, but Akiko could not know that his regiment had not been assigned to this bloody task. She worried that his excitable nature might lead him to volunteer, forgetting his wife and family.[5] Her concern was understandable, but her boldness at the time was nothing less than astonishing.

It can only be a matter of speculation why the censors, who had banned *Myōjō* in 1900 for its French nudes, simply ignored this issue. But *Taiyō* magazine's literary columnist, Ōmachi Keigetsu, responded with a series of angry articles denouncing the poem as "an expression of dangerous thoughts which disparage the idea of the national family," "a vilification that the Japanese people must not allow," and "a case of *lèse majesté*." Yosano Akiko herself he called "a traitorous subject, a rebel, a criminal who deserves the nation's punishment," and he seemed to categorize her with such antiwar activitists as Kōtoku Shūsui. He was particularly rankled by the third stanza, paraphrasing it as follows: "The Emperor himself does not risk the dangers of the battlefield, but from the safety of the palace he heartlessly urges on the sons of others to shed their blood like beasts, assuring them that it is glorious to die."

Shaken by this attack and convinced that Keigetsu had misread her poem, Akiko responded with a letter to her husband Hiroshi which he printed in *Myōjō*. "I am second to none in my love for this country of my birth," she declared. The mere suggestion of the kind of ideas printed in *Heimin Shimbun* were enough to "start me trembling." As a woman, she said, she hated war but recognized that all must do their share to attain victory—and peace—as quickly as possible. In her poem, she had intended to express nothing more than what could be heard at railroad stations every day when families sent their sons off to war: "Take care of yourself, come back unhurt, and Banzai!" Her letter was devoid of irony.[6]

When Keigetsu suggested that Akiko ought to be punished, Yosano Hiroshi decided not to risk the vagaries and delays of a full-scale literary controversy. Such disputants might fire shots at one another in the pages of literary magazines over several months or even years. Instead, he arranged to meet Keigetsu in person, taking two of his *Myōjō* followers along. One of these, Hiraide Shū, was more a critic than poet, more a lawyer than critic, having graduated from law school a year and a half before. Hiraide did most of the talking. He had a reputation as an eloquent speaker, while Keigetsu was apparently a stutterer.

Because their confrontation was reported in *Myōjō*, complete with parenthetical gibes at Keigetsu, Hiraide's victory was a foregone conclusion. Nonetheless, Hiraide's defense of the controversial third stanza offered only the weakest of readings: "Even though the Emperor has no opportunity to see the battle first hand, his compassion is so profound that he must surely bemoan the death of soldiers as a supreme tragedy." Keigetsu agreed that such a reading was possible, but he insisted that no self-respecting poet would write anything so insipid; his major objection was to "dangerous thoughts," to the overall tone of anger directed toward the nation and its ruler. Keigetsu admitted, however, that he had been swept up in his rhetoric when he called Akiko a traitor. She really did not deserve such harsh treatment. In conclusion, Yosano and Hiraide urged Keigetsu to recognize his utter incompetence as a literary critic and "burn his writing brushes."

As Akiko had done, Hiraide argued for the least offensive reading of the poem. But he raised the issue of what a poet should do when his sincere feelings have caused him to write a poem containing what Keigetsu called dangerous thoughts. Keigetsu's answer was that the poet should not publish his work, but in Hiraide's opinion, such a cowardly attitude would put an end to all progress and innovation.[7]

Perhaps the best thing that can be said about this debate is that Yosano saved literary historians a lot of drudgery by getting it over with quickly. It was important, however, for the prominence it gave to Keigetsu's phrase "dangerous thoughts,"[8] which was to become the witch-hunters' favorite cry for the next four decades.* The confrontation with Keigetsu was also important as the first of four cases Hiraide Shū would argue for the "dangerous" side, the other three being major legal battles marking the retreat of intellectual freedom in Japan. We shall see a good deal more of Hiraide Shū.

---

*According to Satō Haruo, *Akiko mandara* 31:451, Keigetsu's critique of Yosano Akiko's poem gave the phrase its start.

We shall also see, in the following passages, the government's increasing awareness of literature and its potential for promoting dangerously private thoughts: not merely a rejection of national values out of "simple expression of attachment to the primary group,"[9] as in Yosano Akiko's poem, but a determination to weigh and test and—in some instances—to discard ideas that seemed to comprise the very fabric of society.

DISILLUSIONMENT AND THE GENERATION GAP

Port Arthur fell on January 1, 1905, and the first tentative steps toward peace were finally taken that June. During the negotiations, the government managed to keep even the most cleverly coded telegraphic reports from reaching the newspapers. Katsura Tarō's administration (Acting Foreign Minister: Katsura Tarō) ignored press demands for open diplomacy, and when abruptly the announcement was made that Japan would be paid no indemnity, disillusionment provoked a storm of protest, much of it violent.[10]

The people had given their best for Meiji's thirty-seven years, and the past decade had been especially burdensome. One could see evidence of the struggle in the emaciated bodies of Japan's aged, said Ishikawa Takuboku, but future generations would grow old in Japan with the good fortune they deserved.[11] Many felt that the time for self-sacrifice had ended, particularly with such a duplicitous administration in power. By January 1, 1906, Katsura was out of office, replaced by Saionji Kinmochi, a man whose liberal tendencies were a matter of concern to Katsura and his mentor, Yamagata Aritomo. Within a few weeks of taking office, Saionji's government granted Socialist petitioners permission to found a party, an act which Yamagata took as a personal affront.[12] As the old oligarch watched, the country seemed to be overrun with dangerous thoughts—not only socialism, but the equally pernicious individualism.

In the "festive" postwar atmosphere,[13] conservative opinion perceived individualism in countless phenomena: No longer were self-improvement and the amassing of personal wealth justified in the name of family or nation as they had been since the beginning of Meiji; young people openly indulged in the pursuit of "sensual pleasure"; everywhere anguished young men sought the meaning of life, spouting philosophies of free love and women's liberation which clashed with the traditional family system. Concurrently, both promoting and giving voice to all these "evil tendencies," naturalism arose as the dominant literary movement.[14]

We have earlier noted the seeds of Japanese naturalism in distressing fiction and in Zolaism, and certainly individualism as an *idea* had been filtering into the Japanese consciousness ever since the opening of the country. But the postwar release from a total devotion to the national mission seems to have combined with the increased importation of foreign literature to turn the naturalist movement into a literary explosion.

Until the turn of the century, most of the literature translated into Japanese had been classics. But when the expanding population of educated young people began to find a seriousness of purpose and an intellectual immediacy in late nineteenth-century European literature, qualities missing from the immature native products (most of which they would have been embarrassed to be caught reading, as one critic put it), the translation of more nearly contemporary thought and literature suddenly took off. Between 1902 and the end of 1908 were introduced works of Pushkin, Turgenev, Tolstoy, Dostoevsky, Gogol, Andreev, Chekhov, Merezhkovski, Kropotkin, Garshin, and Gorki; Balzac, Huysmans, Hugo, France, and Maupassant; Nietzsche, Wagner, Hauptmann, and Sudermann; D'Annuncio and Fogazzaro; Sienkiewicz and Orzeszkowa; Ibsen, Björnsen, Kierkegaard, and Strindberg; Symons, Shaw, Pinero, Meredith, Kipling, Whitman, Twain, and Poe. "One might almost say that the great works of contemporary world literature were all imported together simultaneously," wrote the literary historian who compiled this list in 1909.[15] Donald Keene has remarked on the dramatic difference in milieu experienced by the poets Masaoka Shiki and Ishikawa Takuboku, whose deaths came just a decade apart (1902 and 1912, respectively): "Takuboku lived in a world of incomparably greater sophistication, and the European books he read were not the *Autobiography* of Benjamin Franklin or [*Self-Help* by] Samuel Smiles but Ibsen and Gorki. In literary tastes a century, not ten years, separates the two men."[16]

The skepticism, the loss of belief in traditional certainties, the plainly narrated "blood and sweat of real life"[17] in European fiction that could not be found in the elegantly stylized work of Kōyō (whose death in 1903 and the dissolution of his powerful Ken'yūsha clique provided another kind of release for young writers) found ready receptors in the young. In October 1906 a word was invented that said it all: *genmetsu*, the now-standard Japanese term for "disillusionment."

The creator of the term was Hasegawa Tenkei, chief literary critic for the period's most important journal, *Taiyō*. Tenkei proclaimed that naturalism was the iconoclastic Art for an Age of Disillusionment (*Genmetsu jidai no geijutsu*). The truth sought by the present age is not lofty or abstract, he wrote, but an honest, commonsensical picture of everyday life. The image of woman is no longer framed in stars and flowers; the theory of evolution has shown us that man is an animal and is not fashioned in God's image; we can see now that the upper classes are no different from the rest of us—we all eat, drink, and defecate; the illusions of religion have been destroyed; the sacredness of nature has been reduced to a catalogue of cells, gasses, and elements. Far from being a sad turn of events, however, this advance in human knowledge is cause for celebration. Without the overthrow of the Tokugawa shogunate, veiled as it was in illusion, and without the Restoration's introduction of the scientific world view, the vast developments of the Meiji period would not have been possible and the Russo-Japanese War would not have occurred to demonstrate the illusion of Aryan supremacy. Ibsen, he said, is the one who points the way to the future with his art that does more than reproduce surface realism while it remains free of frivolous embellishment and display.[18]

Had Tenkei merely been contributing to a theoretical call for a new literature, his essay might not have been so influential, but he was writing seven months after the new movement in literature had brought forth its first fruit: Shimazaki Tōson's *The Broken Commandment* (*Hakai*, March 1906). At first glance, the novel seems to be concerned with a social problem, the suffering of the Eta in a prejudiced world. But this social consciousness was not primarily what appealed to its youthful readers. Rather, it was Tōson's portrait of a sensitive young intellectual estranged from the values of his father's society that moved them so profoundly. The novel did not spark a rush of social activism, but it did increase literary activity—and much heated debate along generational lines. "The controversy between the naturalist school and its opponents is, finally, a struggle between the fathers and the sons," Tenkei would later write.[19]

One crucial area of tension between the generations, not surprisingly, was sex. While *The Broken Commandment* was all but indifferent to such matters, it is significant that Tenkei's first example of the new, clear-eyed view of the world was a less romanticized view of woman. Such leading naturalists as Tōson and Tayama Katai had gone through a romantic period of love worship before Zolaism had turned them toward a search for the "ugly truth," an attitude inevitably detrimental to the female image in any case, and consistently so throughout the naturalist revolution.

Having been abandoned by his first wife before the beginning of his literary career, their friend Kunikida Doppo had never committed to fiction his romantic views on love. The down-to-earth stories he had been writing for years were suddenly discovered to be naturalistic, and eager interviewers were not disappointed by his views. "Woman is a beast," said Doppo on his deathbed in 1908. "She is a living imitation of humanity. The ancient zoologists were in error when they assigned her to the human species."[20] Nor was this an entirely idiosyncratic view, as was revealed in one influential critical piece that helped bring Doppo widespread attention in 1906. The writer expressed satisfaction at finding a Meiji writer at last treating love as something less than the whole of life:

Doppo generally looks upon woman with contempt. There has been a tendency in Japan since the beginning of Meiji to admire woman, but of late it seems the tide has been turning and we have begun looking down on her again. There seem to be signs of this new tide in Europe as well. As far as I am concerned, the Japanese have always known woman for what she is and have always taken an extremely natural and proper attitude toward her. The post-Restoration tendency to admire woman was nothing but a brief attempt to imitate Europe. The Europeans have always over-valued woman and worshipped her quite indiscriminately, but I suspect that they, too, have begun to wake up of late. Be that as it may, I for one wish to express my complete agreement with Doppo's view of woman. . . . I fully recognize that there is a beauty in woman to which men can never aspire. But we can never recognize her true beauty until we realize fully that she is a thing to be despised. This may seem irrational, but it is not in the least.[21]

Tayama Katai published his own farewell to youthful illusions of womanhood in May 1907 in the amusing self-parody, "A Morbid Weakness for Young Girls" ("Shōjobyō"), which ends with its incurable protagonist's being run over by a train in mid-longing for a glimpse of the perfect woman. Four months later *The Quilt* (*Futon*) appeared, the short novel for which Katai is best known, an unsparing view of a Katai-like author caught in a pitiful infatuation for a young female disciple. This work was a crystallization of the Zolaist theme that sex was an uncontrollable force, a primitive irrational threat to modern rationality. (See below, chap. 7, pp. 100–102, for a summary and discussion of this work.)

To be sure, one major element of naturalism's disillusioned view was a study of the place of sexuality in modern life. An enthusiastic critic, writing in January 1908, put this into perspective, however, as follows:

The changes in literature since last January, he said, have been more amazing than all the amazing changes we saw in the previous twenty years. Especially since the middle of the year, the commotion over naturalism—both for and against it and spelling out the varieties within it—has been enormous. "Following the Russo-Japanese War, the people came to see the value of self-awareness, which resulted in a recognition of the authority of the individual. Almost before we knew what was happening, we found ourselves looking at the old morality and the old customs with defiance and disgust." The new writers have cast aside the old, unscientific view of man as noble in spirit but base in his physicality. They now depict sex and instinct boldly, as part of human reality. It is just a very small minority of the writers who concentrate solely on sex, however. The new writers see no beauty or ugliness, only truth. The new, liberated atmosphere allows writers to be published for the quality of their work rather than their established credentials as heretofore with Kōyō in control, and this has resulted in an admirable variety. There is room now for both idealism and naturalism. 1907 was an epoch-making year in which a new intensity of debate was achieved along with a whole new level of seriousness: its accomplishments mark a memorable turning point in our literature.[22]

The year 1908 thus opened with a tremendous sense of accomplishment and potential. Of course, not everyone was as happy about naturalism as this particular commentator.

MORALISTIC CRITICISM BEGINS

As early as February of the year before, the rather staid literary journal *Teikoku Bungaku* had mentioned a growing controversy over "unwholesome" ideas in philosophy, religion, and the arts.[23] By January 1908 the editors of *Taiyō* thought the problem important enough to devote a major portion of their New Year's issue to the question of "Education and Fiction: Should We Allow Our Young Men and Women to Read Novels?"

Of the seven prominent men interviewed by *Taiyō*, only Nakajima Tokuzō (1864–1940), an educator and founder of a club for the promotion of morality (and later head of Tōyō University), insisted that "this pimply literature" must be kept out of the hands of the young. Recent fiction, being full of adultery, will do great harm to young minds, he said.

Most of the others, including the head of the First National Higher School, Nitobe Inazō, and the novelists Oguri Fūyō and Iwaya Sazanami, took the position that, as a practical matter, young people could not be prevented from reading fiction (serialized novels having become an indispensable feature in the daily papers, for one thing). But some literary exposure to real life would be far more beneficial than shielding them from any supposed evil influence—which might, in fact, lower their powers of resistance to evil.

Implicit in all the responses, of course, was the fact that a great deal of criticism leveled against the new literature equated it with pornography or at least with "unwholesome" erotic writing. But there was more. One interviewee, Fujii Kenjirō, noted that the Minister of Education, Makino Shinken (a member of the first cabinet of the supposedly liberal Saionji Kinmochi) had issued directives upon taking office which criticized recent literature for three harmful influences: (1) The arousing of base emotions; (2) the spreading of individualistic, liberal ideas; and (3) the cultivation of a pessimistic world view. The problem with today's youth, said Fujii, is that they live in an age of rapid transition that exaggerates the effect of the generation gap. They are caught between the older generation's extreme conservatism, on the one hand, and extremely modern Western views on the other. "To hope for wholesome ideas in a chaotic intellectual climate such as ours is like climbing a tree to catch fish." [24]

Tanaka Kiichi complained that recent literature had no scope, no depth, no nobility because it was written by uneducated, inexperienced youngsters who had nothing to say to mature men and whose views might well be harmful to the young. Nonetheless, he granted, he would rather have young people read this sort of thing in preparation for life than "domestic novels" that pretended the world is a paradise filled with angels.

Oguri Fūyō, author of "Making Up for Bed," assured readers that no official control of literature would be necessary, since the process of natural selection would weed out the works of those few merely exploitative writers—in retrospect, a rather ironic remark coming from him. "We writers of the naturalist school do not depict sex because we like to or because we dare to, but because we *have* to," he added in all sincerity. [25] Sex is too important for the young to ignore, he continued. Indeed, their parents would be horrified if they never learned about sex and spent their lives as celibates. Far better to learn the facts of life from the naturalist writers, he said, with their solemn view of sex, than from the older generation, who maintain the old, sniggering attitude.

As Fūyō implied, there were indeed writers connected with the naturalist movement from whom a great deal could be learned about sexual matters. Fūyō himself was one of these, as were Satō Kōroku and Ikuta Kizan, minor writers who eventually turned to popular fiction and are practically forgotten today. Kōroku in particular had had an enthusiastic critical reception during the previous year. The January 1908 *Chūō Kōron* noted that Kōroku was one of the new writers from whom to expect great things. He was known as—and apparently called himself—a writer of erotic literature (*shunjō bungaku*), it said. The article nonetheless singled out one story for negative comment. "Revenge" ("Fukushū," in the October 1907 *Chūō Kōron*) was held up as an example of a certain staginess from which his fiction suffered. [26] And we might add that the story can be faulted for more than that. It is distinctly sleazy. The "leer of the pornographer" is clearly in evidence when Kōroku describes the woodcarver's oversexed wife enjoying her boyfriend in the mosquito net while the oblivious husband waits for her a few feet away. [27]

Compared with briefly popular writers like Kōroku, the "authentic naturalists" then reaching the mature stage of their careers wrote "relatively few works" that dealt with shocking sexual themes, according to the foremost authority on naturalism, Yoshida Seiichi. [28] And in fact, if we look at the stories of those writers of the day who have not fallen into obscurity, the majority turn out to be quite pristine. The lavish *Chūō Kōron* supplement that carried Kōroku's "Revenge" also contained Tokuda Shūsei's "Sacrifice" ("Gisei"), which focuses on a provincial elementary school teacher in his forties who has sacrificed himself so that his younger siblings could go out into the world. The month before, Shūsei had published "Desperation" (Zetsubō"), a sharp slice of low life set in the back alleys of Tokyo. Its pitiful heroine is presented as having gone from man to man, but that is almost incidental; the local color and the harsh dialogue exchanged by two feuding sisters are the central points of interest in this "representative naturalistic piece."[29] *Chūō Kōron* carried Shūsei's "Two Old Women" ("Nirōba") in April, featuring contrasting portraits of two poor old women on the threshold of death.

The same prestigious New Year's issue that carried the stories by Kōroku and Shūsei contained Kunikida Doppo's "The Bamboo Gate" ("Take no kido"), a grim tale of a gardener's wife who hangs herself when poverty drives her and her husband to steal charcoal.* The New Year's supplement to *Taiyō* had Masamune Hakuchō's "Pool Parlor" ("Tamatsukiya"), a drab little sketch of a sleepy pool parlor boy, while that same month Hakuchō's most important early work, "Where?" ("Doko e") appeared in the pages of *Waseda Bungaku*. The protagonist of this piece sees the family system destroying his life and the lives of his friends. He resists pressure to take a wife and declares that "for me, a woman is nothing but a lump of flesh." † We know that he occasionally sees a prostitute and that he is vaguely attracted to his benefactor's wife, but his attitude leads not to scenes of depravity but rather to a nearly-celibate existence.

Another story in the January *Waseda Bungaku*, Tayama Katai's "One Soldier" ("Ippeisotsu"), was one of that writer's endless experiments in narrative point of view—in this instance, a first-person study of a tubercular soldier's slow death on the Russian front.‡ Katai's "Next Room" ("Rinshitsu," *Shinkō Bunrin*, January 1907) had described the experience of listening to a person die in the next room at an inn, masking his primary interest in the narrative gimmick with suitable profundities on man's animal nature.

Clearly, in addition to sheer technical experimentation, the ugly truth as portrayed by the naturalists included a full measure of oppressive scenes of life among the proletarians and of young men's struggles with the family system and with their own sense of what Hasegawa Tenkei had described as disillusionment. Tenkei himself protested the equation of naturalism with lust, and in this he was entirely justified.[30]

*For a translation, see Jay Rubin, "Five Stories by Kunikida Doppo," MN 27, no. 3 (1972): 325–41.

†GNBZ 30:35. For a translation of another drab early Hakuchō piece, see Robert Rolf, "Dust," MN 25, nos. 3–4 (1970): 407–14.

‡For a translation, see G. W. Sargent in Donald Keene, ed., *Modern Japanese Literature* (New York: Grove Press, 1956), pp. 142–58. Also Kenneth G. Henshall, *The Quilt and Other Stories by Tayama Katai* (University of Tokyo Press, 1981).

Thus far, we have discussed the contributions and misperceptions of naturalism primarily in terms of subject matter. Before turning, in the next section, to the movement's still more fundamental accomplishment of establishing a new professional attitude for writers, I would like to append here two remarkable moralistic denunciations that were aimed at naturalism from very different sources—one journalistic, the other literary.

Hasegawa Tenkei was one of the most influential propagandists in the naturalistic cause. His column reached a large, literate audience through the magazine *Taiyō* (The Sun), which also contained an English-language supplement, the *Sun Trade Journal* (later, *The Taiyo*), offering political and economic—and some cultural and social—news to foreign businessmen stationed in Japan.* The nearly religious fervor that Tenkei brought to his preaching in the Japanese part of the magazine did not deter one "Japonicus" from summarizing the development of naturalism for his foreign audience in the *Sun Trade Journal* as follows, under the title "Literature and Zeit-Geist":

> A change, almost to be called a revolution, is taking place in the current thoughts and ideas, in fact in the entire intellectual life of the Japanese. In religion, in literature, in its principles and aspirations, the nation is about to throw away the whole of old cants and grasp new ones [*sic*]. This is an age of transition and metamorphosis, of revolution and epoch-making, of progress or retrogression,—a crisis or climax in the inner life of the people, in the belief and sentiment of the individuals who constitute the rising nation of the Far East, whose destiny is still an unknown quantity and an enigma to the world in general.
>
> The war with Russia has resulted in a great change in the political status of Japan. She has risen to the position of a power and commands some sort of admiration and dread of other countries. The Western Powers do not now view us in the same light as before the Russo-Japanese War. This change in the external affairs of Japan is so evident to all observers that it hardly needs any further comment.
>
> But as for the internal life of Japan, a change, even more important and more interesting than the political, has been taking place hitherto unnoticed by the West.
>
> The most conspicuous feature of the spiritual transformation of Japan is the rise of the literary school styled *shizenshugi*. This word has been variously translated into English. Literally, it is "natural doctrine"; so it was translated "naturalism." In essence, however, the doctrine is nothing more or less than Zola's

*Along with the title change on January 1, 1910, editorial content was distinctly upgraded, with more translations from *Taiyō*. The English section also provided an advertising medium for American companies such as the Lynn Wood Heel company of Lynn, Massachusetts, and the Monongahela Tube Company of Pittsburgh (read Pittobaraa—after Edinburgh?).

realism. Writers of this school declare that their aim is to depict the human being as it is: to represent the world in its true light; to trample down all false conventions in search of the truth. With such profession of technical aspiration, the literary market for the last one or two years has been flooded with fiction depicting human nature in its most brutal, realistic, sensual aspect. In short, in the name of naturalism, realism, or what other nomenclature that shizenshugi may obtain, extremely fleshly novels, calculated to excite the lower senses of young men and women, were profusely published, and some of these were officially prohibited sale as injurious to public morals. . . .

Shizenshugi has so strongly appealed to the weak points and natural propensities of young people that, if it were untenable as a literary doctrine, it has become a strong factor in the mental life of the Japanese nation. Probed to the bottom, it is nothing but the worship of nudity. Had the worshippers of nudity limited their activities to the sphere of art and literature, the evil would not have been so great. But in Japan, the doctrine was carried a step further and was put into practice by many young people inclined to novel-reading. Shizenshugi writers were bad, but the shizenshugi practitioners are worse. Combined, they brought about a period of moral degeneration and social retrogression in the history of Japan. . . . It is interesting to note that this tendency is essentially the direct result of the war with Russia. . . .

The foreign critics were not entirely mistaken when they said that we had a swelled head on account of the military success. . . . Amid the general hilarity and buoyancy, the young Japanese could not alone remain sober. As the government drew up a rash financial programme, as the businessmen promoted rash enterprises in industry and commerce, the young men and women also committed rash acts of folly. . . . That was an age of the victory for young blood. Shizenshugi literature was born in a responsive mood. . . . The Japanese novelists of the present day, preaching their fond shizenshugi, and driving the youthful blood to moral recklessness, are undermining the national strength and leading the country to ruin and decadence. Do they know why Japan was strong and how she got the position of a first class Power? It was due to the rigorous discipline and militant spirit of the nation. . . .

The statesmen and businessmen have been awakened from the folly of post-bellum financial expansion. I wonder why the literature alone is slow to awake from the rash abuse of its misconceived freedom and strength, and continues to exercise a vicious influence on the rising generation of the country. . . .

The Japanese nation has got a consciousness of strength through the war. The strong spirit cannot be controlled with weak principles of the old days. A voice in the wilderness cries for a new prophet![31]

Perhaps Japonicus thought such a prophet would be able to lead the naked hordes of "shizenshugi practitioners" from the streets of Tokyo into the sea?

One of the strongest critiques of sex in naturalism came from the pen of a man with far more impressive literary credentials than Japonicus. This was Futabatei Shimei, author of the previously mentioned "first modern novel" of Japan, *The Drifting Clouds*, a work far ahead of its time in 1887–1889 (see p. 40 above). Futabatei seems to have been inspired by the new generation's work to try his hand at fiction again after seventeen years, serializing *An Adopted Husband* (*Sono omokage*) in the *Asahi Shimbun* from October to December 1906. In this novel, the new greed and the traditional family system cooperate to crush the uncompromising hero, who had been adopted by his wife's family because he was thought to be "a more profitable investment than government bonds."*

The serialization of Futabatei's *Mediocrity* (*Heibon*) began in October 1907, the month after Katai published *The Quilt* with its shocking ending (having lost the girl he was too indecisive to attempt to seduce, the author/hero buries his face in the soiled collar of her sleeping quilt and inhales her odor as he dissolves in tears). Futabatei seems to have reacted to this like a Japonicus

The middle-aged literary has-been who narrates *Mediocrity* tells us he is adopting the style of the lately popular naturalism, "in which the writer sets down all his experiences, no matter how ridiculous, without the least application of art, just as they happened, drop by drop like the drivel of a cow."† The purpose of fiction, he remarks bitterly, is to "embellish man's depravity."[32] In this, the Meiji novelists surpass their Edo predecessors, he says, because they know how to glamorize their descriptions of sex with phony philosophy. In the book's climactic scene, the hero must choose between fulfilling his long-frustrated sexual (i.e., literary!) desires or rushing home to see his dying father. Returning from the theater near midnight, he finds a letter urging him to come home, but soon the slovenly Oito, the one woman with whom it seems he is finally to be successful, enters the room where he is lying in bed:

> We had been talking about the theatre for a while, when the downstairs clock began grinding away and gave out with a single, convulsive "Bong!" This seemed to make no impression on Oito, who sat there calmly, drinking from my cup. Obviously, she was waiting for me to do something—which again aroused those feelings that had suddenly wilted at the sight of my mother's letter. "This is it!" I said to myself, "Right now! This very moment!" and my heart began to pound.

*GNBZ 1:240. Quoted from the translation by Buhachiro Mitsui and Gregg M. Sinclair (New York: Alfred A. Knopf, 1919–1923), p. 81.

†NKBT 4:255. Quoted from the translation by Glenn W. Shaw (Tokyo: Hokuseido Press, 1927), p. 7. This was more prescient than accurate, for Japan's notorious "I-novel" (*watakushi-shōsetsu*) would not become established for three more years. *The Quilt* was unique in its time.

"Why don't you stay here tonight?" I said playfully.

"I wonder," she said, just as playfully, "Maybe I should. My place is so far away."

There was no doubt about it. I grabbed her hand and pulled her toward me. She did not resist. Through my thick nightclothes, I could feel her leaning against me. She looked straight at me and smiled.

"What are you doing?" she said.

"What *are* you doing? Your father is dying!" said a voice that flitted through my mind like the shadow of a bird, filling me with disgust. I grimaced as though with a chest pain, but Oito probably did not notice because my face was in the shadows.

"You're acting very strangely tonight," she said, smiling, as she withdrew her hand from mine. I lay there with my eyes closed until she said, "I guess I'm just keeping you awake. I ought to go home to bed now. Good night."

She seemed to be getting up. Then I heard her saying "Let me just put the lamp out" and blowing out the flame. But all of a sudden I felt something cover my face and there was her warm breath against my cheek. "I hate you!" she whispered in my ear, but her voice was full of laughter, and she was pinching my arm through the quilt. That was enough to set my head spinning into oblivion. To hell with morality! But oh, how could I, my father was on the brink of death. . . . [Futabatei's punctuation][33]

When the narrator does arrive home the next day to find that his father died still asking for him, he is filled with such remorse that he turns himself into a model filial son, a change of heart that destroys his interest in fiction.

Ahead of his time once again, Futabatei made of *Mediocrity* a parody of novels yet unwritten. The struggle between the hero's individual needs and the demands of the family, however, would emerge as a dominant theme of the modern Japanese novel. The narrator of Natsume Sōseki's 1914 novel, *Kokoro*,* would be torn between two dying fathers, one traditional and biological, the other modern and spiritual, and in choosing the latter he would guarantee his expulsion from the family.

In the above-quoted scene, surely, it was the powerlessness of the familial bonds to resist passion that the publishers of *Mediocrity* in book form were afraid to present to the censors. Although it was the thematic climax of the entire novel and had appeared in the newspaper uncut, it was presented as a blank page in the book with the notice: "What follows is suppressed at the request of the publisher." It was from this edition that Glenn W. Shaw made his translation in 1927.[34]

---

*Translated by Edwin McClellan (Chicago: Henry Regnery, 1957).

FŪYŌ VS. SŌSEKI: WRITING AS A PROFESSION

The excesses of Futabatei and Japonicus notwithstanding, naturalism had an impact far beyond the narrow confines of the study of man's sexual nature—and, indeed, far beyond the walls of the naturalist school itself. A vivid illustration of this can be seen in the contrasting careers of two of the major novelists of the day, Oguri Fūyō (1875–1926) and Natsume Sōseki (1867–1916).

When "Making Up for Bed" appeared in 1896, Fūyō, age twenty-one, had been writing professionally for four years, while Sōseki, already twenty-nine, was just beginning his four-year stint as a teacher of English in provincial Kumamoto Higher School and would not make his amateur literary debut until 1905, following two years of study in England and two more years of scholarship and teaching in Tokyo. A native of Tokyo, Sōseki had graduated from the Imperial University before embarking on an academic career that proved him Japan's most profound and original scholar of English literature.[35] Fūyō had left his provincial home at the age of fifteen determined to pursue a literary career in Tokyo. Failing to graduate from middle school, he had gone through the typical Edo-style initiation into literature—a period of dissipation and writing under the guidance of a major novelist, in this instance, Ozaki Kōyō.[36]

Fūyō was everything that Meiji society expected a novelist to be, a dedicated entertainer closely related to the world of the actor and the prostitute. Thus Sōseki caused a sensation when he abandoned his post in the government's most prestigious university to become staff novelist for the *Asahi Shimbun*. It was a difficult decision for Sōseki. In a letter he wrote at the time (March 1907) we see him clinging to the security of his university post while simultaneously demanding to be treated like the other employees and paid a twice-annual bonus should he make the move.[37] His formal statement in the *Asahi* upon joining the staff is defensive but determined. He does not understand why everyone, both those who applaud and those who decry his decision, should be so amazed. "I did not think it so strange for me to quit the University and become a newspaperman." Here Sōseki is calling himself a *shimbun'ya*, practically equating his new profession with that of a cloth merchant or a noodle seller, and he insists on carrying through his egalitarian logic:

> If being a newspaperman is a trade (*shōbai*), then being a universityman (*daigakuya*) is also a trade. If it were not a trade, there would be no need for anyone to become a professor or a Doctor of Letters. There would be no need to ask for raises. There would be no need for Imperial appointments. The university is as much a business as the newspaper is, and if the newspaper is a vulgar

business, then so is the university. The only difference is that in one you do your job as an individual and in the other you Pursue your Profession on High.[38]

Tsubouchi Shōyō may have caused a sensation in 1885 when he became the first man with a university degree to stoop to writing novels, but the Confucian preconceptions that had until then left only government careers open to ambitious young men were long in dying—if they ever have.[39] Even after Sōseki's death in 1916, the president of Tokyo Imperial University lamented the fact that Sōseki had wasted his talents "writing novels for newspapers" when he could have had a brilliant career writing about Japan in English for foreigners.[40] And undoubtedly some of the psychological strains that led to the suicides of both Akutagawa Ryūnosuke (in 1927) and Mishima Yukio (in 1970) derived from misgivings they felt about the value of devoting their lives to fashioning, Icarus-like, the artificial wings of the artist.[41]

With the rise of naturalism as self-conscious literary art, the question of the value of literature as a profession became a major issue. The journal *Shinchō* carried at least two interview series during 1908: "How I Became a Member of the Literary World" beginning in August; and "Why I Write Novels" beginning in September. The November issue carried yet another related feature, "Is Literature Not Worth a Man's Making It His Life's Work?" which had presumably been inspired by Futabatei's determination that it was *not*. Perhaps the most remarkable quality of these interviews was their overall lack of exaggeration or posturing. Few of the respondents evidenced a need to overcompensate for the public's low opinion of novelists by idealizing the function of the writer. Their remarks reflect a surprising degree of self-confidence and sheer common sense.*

"Everyone has doubts about his profession at some time or other," said the critic Shimamura Hōgetsu. "This is a problem inevitably faced by people who have reached a degree of self-awareness under the influence of modern ideas." The novelists' gadfly, Uchida Roan (see above, pp. 49–51), noted that any intellectual or academic pursuit could be practiced as a pastime and thus trivialized, and that any undertaking not yielding immediate practical benefits could be discounted as useless. Nonetheless, literature, science, and philosophy were all of similar benefit to mankind in their attempts to solve the unanswered questions of the human condition.[42]

Sōseki frustrated the *Shinchō* interviewer on two occasions. In considering "Why I Write Novels," he declared the problem too complicated to handle in an interview. He supposed it could be said that he wrote novels to make a

---

*Shimazaki Tōson was a notable exception. See "Ikin-to hossuru doryoku," *Shinchō* (October 1908): 13–14.

living, but he well might write them even if he were not collecting a salary from the newspaper.[43] And when asked "Is Literature Not Worth a Man's Making It His Life's Work?" he refused—at great length—to commit himself to any stance that would characterize literature as inherently superior or inferior to any profession: it was impossible to say that literature was any less worthy a profession than politics or bean-curd making or carpentry or soldiering.[44]

Oguri Fūyō, however, took a different approach. He complained to *Shinchō* that he was being besieged by interviewers but had almost nothing to say to them, being a man "little acquainted with the world"—that is, a traditional scribbler. Writing fiction had its pleasures and pains, as with any profession, he said, but it seemed that lately the pains were coming to predominate. He spoke more of leaving the profession than of why he wrote novels, as if to presage his departure from Tokyo literary circles the following year.[45]

In a lecture delivered just after joining the *Asahi*, Sōseki expressed his belief in the social validity of his profession with some humor—and with perhaps a bit more idealism than he might have done later:

> Most people think of artists and writers as *himajin* (men of leisure, lazy good-for-nothings), as if they spent their time doing useless things. In fact, there are any number of people doing things far less useful than what an artist or writer does—many of them running around in rickshaws from morning to night. . . .
>
> My friends have all been laughing at me. They say I quit the university to spend my afternoons napping on the veranda. . . . Yes, I nap in the afternoon—and in the morning and the evening, too. . . . But I am not just sleeping, I'm lying there trying to think of something important. Unfortunately, I haven't come up with anything yet, but I am no *himajin*. . . . A *himajin* is someone who can contribute nothing to the world, who cannot provide an interpretation of how we ought to live and teach the common people the meaning of existence. . . . When an artist believes himself to be a *himajin*, he throws his calling out the window and offends Heaven. The artist must decide once and for all that he is no *himajin*. . . .
>
> Finally, what we must have is ideals. . . . And if one person in a hundred—one in a thousand—unites his stream of consciousness with that of the work; if he goes a step farther and joins himself with the truth, the goodness, and the beauty that gleam forth from within the work such that they mark him for all his future life; if, going on still farther, he is able to reach that miraculous state of restorative influence [in which the distinction between reader and writer breaks down in an experience beyond time and space], then the writer's spiritual force will, through intangible contagion, influence the greater consciousness of society, and thus having achieved eternal life in the history of inner man, he will have fulfilled his mission.[46]

At this stage of his career, Sōseki may still have thought he was teaching from a lectern some steps above the head of the common man. But his belief in direct communication from the mind of the writer to that of the reader came to the fore as he soon enough stepped down into the audience. By the following year (1908) he was asserting that the writer and the ordinary person shared a sameness of attitude: both stood midway between the pure objectivity of the scientist and the pure subjectivity of the poet.[47] In his fiction, the confident, self-righteous preaching of Dōya Sensei in *Autumn Wind* (*Nowaki*, 1907) gave way to *The Miner*'s (*Kōfu*, 1908) groping realization that the instability of personality allows for no such certainty among ordinary (i.e., all) men. With his subdued characterization of Hirota Sensei (*Sanshirō*, 1908), the descent of Sōseki the preacher was complete, opening the way for *Kokoro*'s Sensei to assert darkly that "under normal conditions, everybody is more or less good, or, at least, ordinary."*

In his preface to a novel he wrote in 1912, Sōseki said, "I count myself fortunate to be able to present my novels to these ordinary educated men" who have "never peeked into the back alleys of the literary world" but who, "as absolutely ordinary human beings simply live quietly, breathing the air of nature."[48] And it is precisely to this sort of reader that he recommends the reading of novels to counteract the loneliness resulting from the overspecialization of modern society:

> Works of literature are, by their very nature, nonspecialist books. They are written to criticize or depict matters of common concern to all men. They bring people together, stripped naked, regardless of profession or class, and break down all such walls that separate us. Thus I believe them to be the most worthy and least harmful means for binding us together as human beings.[49]

What we find in Sōseki is a mature grasp of the political implications of fiction in the broadest sense. Probably no other writer of his day achieved such a lucid grasp of the relationship of literature and "the greater consciousness of society"—least of all Oguri Fūyō, whose heart remained in the pleasure quarters.

It seems almost incredible in retrospect that Sōseki, still avidly read today and considered by many to be Japan's greatest modern novelist, could have been ranked more or less equally with the anachronistic Fūyō, whose works cannot be found on the paperback shelves of any bookstore in Japan today. Sōseki was the most popular novelist in the area near Tokyo University, while

---

*SZ 6:77; quoted from the translation of *Kokoro* by Edwin McClellan (Chicago: Henry Regnery, 1957), p. 61. See also *Sanshirō* (n.p.) translated by Jay Rubin as *Sanshiro* (Seattle: University of Washington Press, 1977).

Fūyō ranked high in the less cultured parts of Tokyo, but contemporary critics placed them close together. Futabatei was the grand old master of style, with Fūyō and Sōseki tied for second place.[50]

What finally separated Fūyō from Sōseki, sending one into oblivion and the other to lasting international recognition, was the manner in which each reacted to the naturalist revolution. For Fūyō, it was an invitation to write about sex in a new, more realistic style. For Sōseki, it was the catalyst that— for better or worse—turned him from humor and fantasy, and brought forth his deepest doubts about man and society in the modern age.

Yoshida Seiichi has written that there was far more ugly sexuality in Fūyō's turn-of-the-century fiction than in the works of those naturalists coming under so much fire in 1907–1908.[51] A typical example is Fūyō's story "Cold and Flaming" ("Ryōen"), which he wrote in 1902 and thought well enough of to republish in 1908.[52] It bears the marks of Kōyō-style formalism with its "cold" first half and "hot" second half; the first is set in a train moving through the winter night; and the second is in a warm inn to which a man and woman passenger repair for a hot bath and warm sake when a tunnel blockage stops the train.

The man is accompanying his sister-in-law to claim the body of his elder brother—her husband—who has been killed in a hunting accident. In a tearful dialogue on the freezing cold train, the woman vows to become a nurse and serve the fatherland in place of her killed soldier-husband. The man, also a soldier, vows to remain a bachelor rather than risk widowing someone and causing her the kind of grief he sees his sister-in-law experiencing.

These avowals, coupled with the woman's momentary feeling that the younger brother looks exactly like her dead husband, should be hint enough of what is bound to happen between them. But perhaps such subtle deductions were beyond the typical Fūyō reader. The "trained" reader of naturalism just a few years later could be counted upon to respond more flexibly to the conventions of fiction. In any case, it is clear that Fūyō was expecting his reader to be shocked at the end when the innkeeper writes "Wife of above" next to the woman's name in the hotel register and neither attempts to correct the error. "Yes!" he seems to be chuckling, "All those good intentions are as nought in the face of animal instinct!"—in a word: Zolaism.

When the general level of fiction began to rise, however, Fūyō had difficulty keeping up. To him, Katai's novel *The Quilt* was merely a new approach that could help him through a case of writer's block.[53] He serialized *Shattered Love* (*Koizame*), his own story of a novelist in mid-life infatuated with a young girl,[54] but the book version was banned the following year.[55]

Time was running out for Fūyō. Another story, written toward the end of his naturalist career, "Lazy Woman" ("Gūtara onna," *Chūō Kōron*, April 1908), is probably the most poignant example of both his stylistic brilliance and intellectual vacuity. Fūyō sets the scene and time precisely: the fourteen-year-old Matsumura Kenji (i.e., Fūyō) lives in the village of Handa, Fūyō's native place, some two hundred miles west of Tokyo. It is 1889, the year of the promulgation of the Meiji constitution. In Tokyo, commotion over revising the unequal treaties with the Western powers has given way to excitement over the promulgation ceremonies, participation in the representative government which is due to begin functioning next year, and the creative upsurge in literature and journalism. Bringing this excitement with him, a young teacher fresh from Tokyo stirs in the boys of the village elementary school intense longings for life in the capital. Kenji has always expected to carry on the family business, but his new awareness of the world has changed all that. He begs his parents to let him go to Tokyo with an old acquaintance of his mother's who has returned to the village for a short visit after an absence of nineteen years. With her is the pretty daughter she gave birth to the year after she arrived in Tokyo, and Kenji is drawn to the girl. His parents hesitate, but eventually the father takes the boy to Tokyo and leaves him in the woman's care.

The woman, Osaku, has an unsavory past, however. The shady area of her life rather than Kenji's encounter with the big city becomes the center of focus as the story develops. The traditional pattern of life in the village, the boy's hopes, and his excitement at taking the boat trip to Tokyo have been portrayed so vividly that the story's deflection into the morass of infidelity and venereal disease that constitute the world of Osaku and her lazy daughter Oyuki is a great disappointment. There is no shortage of stories of young men swept out of the countryside into Tokyo's maelstrom, but few begin as promisingly as this one.

Aside from all the distracting relationships, Kenji finds that the filthy living quarters given him by Osaku make it nearly impossible for him to study. Finally he moves into a student boarding house and, for reasons that are never made clear, his academic career disintegrates. He does not even graduate from middle school. Instead he becomes dissipated, apprentices himself to a novelist, and begins to write fiction. After seven years, he returns in a rickshaw, stylishly dressed, to visit Osaku's family and to pay a long-outstanding debt. He finds that they have moved into bright, new quarters. Osaku herself is dead. Her disgusting little grandson who used to talk about wanting to buy prostitutes is now in the second year of higher school, far past the point where Kenji dropped out, and is headed for the university. There is a terrible irony in this, for had the family solved its problems before Kenji came to live with them, he might have received the education he thought he wanted.

This irony seems completely lost on Fūyō, however. Instead of being moved to self-reflection, questioning the value of the profession for which his requisite major training has been drink and women, Kenji searches out the lazy Oyuki and ruminates hollowly on her fate. She is twenty-six, a kept woman living in a dark, ramshackle house, sickly and prematurely aged. He sees her—but not himself—as a victim of Osaku. At this point, Fūyō treats us to what he seems to consider the big line of the story: "Alas! When I saw what had become of the beautiful, young Oyuki, I was deeply moved at the fragile evanescence of the beauty of woman." [56]

What this line says most clearly is that Oguri Fūyō has absolutely nothing to say. He was simply unaware how close he came to writing an effective story of mid-life crisis. The local color, the sense of the era conveyed in the first part was probably something he had learned to do from the stories of Kunikida Doppo—and with greater vividness and polish than Doppo. But the man has no sense of the wholeness or uniqueness of his existence. His story tells us of the tragic emptiness of the life of a gifted writer for whom the new literature was nothing but a new style with which to pursue his tired sexual themes.

Emerging from the Kōyō stable, Fūyō had kept pace with distressing fiction and Zolaism, but the demands of naturalism were too much for him. Naturalism was not a style or a formula and certainly not a prescription for a limited area of subject matter. It was, for those with the intellectual apparatus to avoid taking the pronouncements of Tenkei and other theorists as fixed doctrine, an assumption that there were no assumptions. (Actually, despite the simplistic fervor with which Tenkei most often wrote on naturalism as totally devoid of literary embellishment, entirely objective, "scientific," and concerned only with the "truth," etc., he was aware of this crucial aspect of naturalism: variety of theory and form is the sine qua non of the school, he insisted; once a fixed form emerges, it will cease to be naturalism.) [57] With each new novel or story, one started from scratch, bringing to bear one's powers of observation, one's intelligence, and—most crucially—one's sense of self.

To write authentic Japanese naturalism, it was indispensable for the writer to have some conception of individual existence apart from the all-embracing *kokutai*. In general, it was the younger generation that accomplished this, but the break was more along educational than generational lines. Fūyō was four years *younger* than Doppo and Katai, although from our vantage point, he seems to belong to the generation that included his mentor Kōyō, who was born in 1867, as were the scholarly traditionalist Kōda Rohan, the Edo-style scribbler Saitō Ryokuu, and—most anomalously—Natsume Sōseki. With his interrupted education, however, Fūyō did not have the direct access to Western literature and ideas enjoyed by the successful naturalists and Sōseki. Thus, while he was skilled at copying some of the superficial features of the "school," he could not share in its most fundamental breakthrough from literature-as-form to literature-as-personal-vision. It was perfectly natural for him to write a sequel to Kōyō's best-known melodrama, *The Golden Demon* (*Konjiki yasha*), after the master's death, and just as natural for him to farm out work to his own disciples.*

Fūyō was identified with naturalism during its brief heyday as a movement. By 1909, however, when Tōson, Shūsei, Hakuchō, and Iwano Hōmei were developing their own distinctive fiction, Fūyō began to turn away from literary circles.† In May, he left Tokyo for good after depositing a manuscript with *Chūō Kōron* that would cause its June issue to be banned (see below, chap. 9, pp. 126–27). Pursuing his interests in architecture and ornamental gardening, he contributed occasional stories to the magazines, but by late 1910 he could be referred to as "the now-forgotten Fūyō."[58] Popular newspaper fiction constituted the majority of his literary output until his death in 1926.[59]

The year that Fūyō left Tokyo (1909) was the year in which Natsume Sōseki attained his full maturity as a novelist with the serialization of *And Then* (*Sore kara*) in the *Asahi* from June to October.‡ He had made his literary debut in 1905 with "I Am a Cat" ("Wagahai wa neko de aru"), a comic story that grew all through that year and into the next in response to popular demand until it emerged as a long, plotless, very uneven—and often very funny—critique of greed and affectation in Meiji society.§ While serializing this story-turned-novel, Sōseki wrote several short stories and one short novel, the comic *Botchan*, which appeared in April 1906 and won immediate fame for its scathing portrait of petty dishonesty at a provincial middle school. Later that year, Sōseki produced another short novel which ranks among his early classics, *Pillow of Grass* (*Kusamakura*, translated as *The Three-Cornered World*),‖ a unique investigation of the possibilities (and mainly the limits) of transcending mundane reality through a detached Oriental aestheticism. Elegantly

---

*Fujimura Tsukuru, ed., *Nihon bungaku daijiten* 1:389; SK 2:215; Ichiko Teiji et al., eds., *Nihon bungaku zenshi* 5:264. In a *Chūō Kōron* symposium (September 1908), Masamune Hakuchō questioned Fūyō's credentials as a naturalist, pointing out that his use of proxies was a black spot on his career. Tokuda Shūkō said the only thing Fūyō could talk about besides writing was sex. The other pieces combined to portray Fūyō as a sad figure, touchingly aware of a certain something out there that he could not grasp. MBZ 65:395–405 (esp. 396, 398, 401).

† *Taiyō*'s "History of 1908," appended to a remarkable special edition devoted entirely to the history of Meiji literature, lists Tōson, Katai, Hakuchō, Shūsei, Fūyō, and Seika as the most prominent naturalist writers of 1908, implying that all six meet the criterion of possessing a personal vision which distinguishes the authentic new writers from the mere imitators. Only with regard to Fūyō does the anonymous author raise some doubts, suggesting that his mature, inimitable style is accompanied by "an unfortunate tendency for the content of his work to lack any individual distinguishing characteristics." TY (February 20, 1909), pp. 235–37.

‡ Translated by Norma Moore Field (Baton Rouge: Louisiana State University Press, 1978).

§ Translated by Katsue Shibata and Motonari Kai (Tokyo: Kenkyusha, 1961).

‖ Translated by Alan Turney (London: Peter Owen, 1965)

stylized, there could hardly have been a work in starker contrast to Tōson's *The Broken Commandment*, the earnest, rather clumsily written study of Eta suffering that started the naturalist revolution.[60]

In the midst of cries for unvarnished truth and condemnations of sheer stylistic polish, Sōseki struck a most discordant note when he told an interviewer that all he hoped to do in *Pillow of Grass* was to leave the reader with an impression of beauty such as might be obtained from haiku.[61] But beauty does not exist in a vacuum in this novel: it is consciously sought out as therapy for the ills of modern society, and each transcendent flight ends with the artist/ protagonist's fall to earth—in one instance, literally on his rear end! Sōseki was well aware of the importance of *The Broken Commandment*. In an often-quoted letter to a young disciple, he indirectly compared it with *Pillow of Grass*:

> I do not know what percentage of the meaning of life is comprised of living beautifully—that is, like a poet—but I suspect it is an exceedingly tiny part. That is why I don't recommend protagonists like the one in *Pillow of Grass*. . . . Anyone who wants to make literature his life cannot be satisfied exclusively with beauty, [but] I want both at the same time. I want to frequent those detached regions of haiku, but I also want to write with the spiritual intensity of a Restoration hero, as though my very life were at stake. Unless I could do that, I would always feel like some weak-kneed little poetaster who always takes the easy, comfortable way and avoids the dramatic and difficult.
>
> There is not much in *The Broken Commandment* for you to emulate, but where this sort of thing is concerned, Tōson's novel is far superior to everything else.[62]

But this was a private expression of his need for literary engagement. Publicly, Sōseki went on to oppose doctrinaire naturalism and argued that a graceful, detached pursuit of beauty had as much validity as literature locked in a death grip with the real world. His most famous statement to this effect appeared in January 1908, the very month that the naturalist movement seemed to be coalescing in all the major journals.[63] Just a year before, one critic had written that 1906 had been Sōseki's year in the literary world, noting the contrast between his Edo-flavored humor and the "extreme realism" of *The Broken Commandment*.[64] Looking back on 1907, however, another critic noted that Sōseki's popularity had declined drastically, although the critic himself welcomed the variety of a literary scene that produced both the direct view of life of a Doppo and the transcendent view of a Sōseki.[65]

By this time, however, Sōseki had left the realm of haiku far behind, as must have been apparent to the critic who ranked his *Autumn Wind* the best work of

1907.[66] Despite some wonderfully funny scenes in the novel, the protagonist's puerile ranting against the evils of the rich is in dead earnest.

Few critics reacted well to the melodramatic excesses of *The Poppy* (*Gubijinsō*), the first novel Sōseki serialized in the *Asahi* after leaving the university, and initial reaction to *The Miner*, an absurdist allegory of descent into the psyche that had begun to appear on January 1, 1908, was universally negative.* Sōseki was not living up to his early promise, wrote a critic in *Chūō Kōron*,[67] but that same journal demonstrated the continuing broad interest in Sōseki by publishing a feature article the following month (March 1908) in which thirteen prominent writers and intellectuals gave their views of Sōseki. They saw him as an original stylist, a pioneer in humor, a writer attempting to transcend the real world, and a man "incapable of writing tragedy" whose works "are finally not modern fiction."[68]

Among the contributors, Oguri Fūyō himself attempts to view Sōseki according to naturalist dogma. In the process, he reveals the failure of understanding that would soon bring his own career to a halt. Fūyō opens by assenting to his own reputation as a writer who knows nothing about anything but writing—in fact, only his own writing. He has read a lot of Sōseki, has been amused by it, but has never thought about it, he says. He goes on to speak in the first person plural for all naturalists, his awkward phraseology suggesting how uncomfortable he is with ideas:

> The kind of writing that gives us an acute thrill of pleasure may not measure up to the first principles of art, but in it the writer and his work become wholly organic, and the writer's anguish, his doubts, his exertions appear directly in the work. In other words, this is writing extremely lacking in easy detachment [*yoyū*, the word that Sōseki had given currency in his January essay], the kind of piece in which the writer writhes along with the people in his work. Finally, we do not have such fully formed egos that we can stand on a higher plane and criticize, sneer at, or ridicule people; we are still young. . . . [Sōseki's style may be very witty, but] we cannot be satisfied until we write down to the last curtain and draw loud applause from the reader. In order to make a living, we go on writing even if it means groaning with the effort. And as long as we are exerting

---

*Even the most gushily enthusiastic Sōseki fan in the *Chūō Kōron* symposium of March 1908, had grave reservations about *The Miner*. The *Chūō Kōron* editor who compiled the feature had the last word: "Some who think that Sōseki's popularity has declined say that it is merely a reaction to the extreme initial praise and not that his writing has deteriorated, but the inferiority of *The Miner* is undeniable." CK (March 1908): 56. Although *The Miner* remains one of Sōseki's least-appreciated novels, it offers the single most dramatic proof of his modernity. It is a comic tour-de-force belonging in the company of Kafka, Ionesco, and Beckett and anticipating them by decades.

ourselves so, we want to let people know about it, and we look for a commensu-
rate amount of praise. Indeed, it is the desire for praise that keeps us going.[69]

One imagines that serious naturalists cringed at such fawning remarks from
a writer who so openly identified with their movement. And in fact, some of
the new naturalist writers and critics whose opinions were printed with
Fūyō's—Sōma Gyofū and even the exploitative Satō Kōroku—responded to
Sōseki with flexibility and appreciation rather than naturalist cant. Kōroku
went so far as to voice his belief that Sōseki would be changing direction in the
near future and coming closer to naturalism. This was based on a rumor he had
heard that Sōseki was reading Turgenev.[70]

Whether Sōseki was in fact reading Turgenev at this time (he himself
registered amazement at how like *Rudin* some scenes in his *The Poppy* were),*
he definitely *was* reading Japanese naturalism.† When *Sanshiro* and *And Then*
appeared over the next two years, they carried echoes of the new writing.

"The City" ("Tokai"), a story by the now nearly forgotten naturalist writer
Ikuta Kizan, gained a good deal of unwelcome notoriety when it appeared in
February 1908, the reason for which we shall explore shortly. In many ways it
does a creditable job of depicting a country couple's bitter encounter with the
big city. Like Sōseki's *Sanshiro*, which would begin to appear in the *Asahi* in
September, "The City" opens with the principal characters on a Tokyo-bound
train. At one station, the wife looks out of the window and sees a foreign man
and woman walking along the platform. "Foreign couples are very close, aren't
they?" she remarks to her husband. "Look at how they're walking arm-in-arm
in broad daylight."[71] Sanshiro, too, would notice such an exotic pair from the
window of his train and decide that they "were probably husband and wife;
they were holding hands in spite of the hot weather."[72] In "The City," the
husband's first, frightened impression of Tokyo, with its streaming crowds
and thundering streetcars, is remarkably similar to Sanshiro's in the famous
opening passage of the novel's second chapter. Refreshing images of the sub-
urbs with their open blue skies, woods, rivers, and temples, such as found in
"The City," would play a prominent role in most of Sōseki's later novels on the
tragic fate of modern urban man. It seems unlikely that a novelist with Sōseki's

---

*See Sōseki's marginalia in SZ 16:157, where he expresses regret that he had not read *Rudin*
before writing *The Poppy*, if only to avoid the suspicion of his having copied Turgenev.

†Sōseki had found time in April 1908 to catch up on recent fiction, he told an interviewer in
the June 1908 *Shinshōsetsu*, mentioning Shūsei's "Two Old Women," Doppo's "The Bamboo
Gate," and Fūyō's "Lazy Woman" as examples of the uniformly dark tone he seemed to find.
Unfortunately, he had nothing specific to say about any of these stories, but his low opinion of
Fūyō and Fūyō's readers comes through in his letters. SZ 16:584–89; SZ 14:303, 312, 384,
509.

imaginative power needed to do any conscious borrowing from the likes of Ikuta Kizan, but whatever its source, the closeness in perception is remarkable.[73]

Masamune Hakuchō's "Where?," mentioned briefly above (see p. 65), is notable for the clarity with which it formulates themes of disillusionment and alienation that had begun to take shape in Doppo's stories[74] and which would be given their most articulate expression in the novels of Sōseki. In "Where?" we find the unbridgeable gap between people that would torment Sōseki's Ichirō.* We find the descent from youthful romanticism to mature numbness; the conflict—focused on the question of marriage—between an ex-samurai father and his modern-educated son, and the controversy over the inherent value of work, to be seen in *And Then*. We even encounter, in embryo, the theme of the lack of completion in human affairs central to Sōseki's last finished novel, *Grass on the Wayside* (*Michikusa*, 1915).†

Thus we see in their contrasting careers that Fūyō's preoccupation with sexual themes and his avowed membership in the "school" were not enough to qualify him as a part of the naturalist breakthrough to a modern, individualistic world view; conversely, Sōseki's modern mind asked many of the same questions that the naturalists were asking and made his muted, nearly sexless novels far more "naturalistic" than Fūyō's ever had been.

William Sibley has noted that "under the partial misnomer of naturalism, for the first time a whole group of writers succeeded in creating works free of undigested influences. Neither imitations of Western literature nor throwbacks to an eclipsed Japanese tradition, these works stand on their own."[75] Equally important, the publication of the new literature in widely read intellectual journals such as *Taiyō* and *Chūō Kōron* gave incontrovertible proof that an audience of sophisticated readers had come into existence. Serious writers were no longer limited to tiny groups of true believers. The development of a reasonably large audience that could appreciate the naturalists' somber studies must have had an electrifying effect on a man with the artistic potential of Sōseki. This was an audience to be viewed not as mere applauders but as kindred minds. Even before he had decided to write for the *Asahi*, Sōseki knew that he wanted to reach that audience. "What I want to do," he wrote to a friend, "is to stand amidst the raging world and see to what extent I can influence others, to what extent I can become an element of society and survive as part of the flesh and blood of future generations of the young."[76]

In the "struggle between the fathers and the sons" of which Tenkei spoke, it

---

*In *Kōjin* (1912–1913). For a translation see Beongcheon Yu, *The Wayfarer* (Detroit: Wayne State University Press, 1967).

†GNBZ 30:23, 26–28, 32, 35. For a translation of *Michikusa* see Edwin McClellan, *Grass on the Wayside* (Chicago: University of Chicago Press, 1969).

was the sons with whom Sōseki joined. Witnessing his success, the scholar/ poet/translator Mori Ōgai experienced an "itchy" feeling of envy and joined the new upsurge in fiction.[77] Early in his own novelistic renaissance, Ōgai expressed that insight indispensable to the creation of modern fiction which lay at the core of naturalism: novels must be written by individuals who have discarded all formulas and are left with nothing but their open minds—or, as he put it, "one can write a novel about anything one wishes in whatever way one chooses."[78]

Both Sōseki and Ōgai brought philosophical and psychological depth to fiction that was beyond the abilities of the naturalists, and Sōseki proved especially adept as an original creator of a fictive world that transcended the typically reportorial naturalist technique. But the generational tension that infused their writing was something they shared with the naturalists and felt encouraged to express because of the accomplishments of naturalism.

6

Naturalism Explodes in the Press

"The City" on Trial

If there were any doubt as to the expanding public awareness of literature, it was dispelled over a few weeks' time in February and March 1908, when the Lady Chatterley trial of the Meiji period combined with two remotely literary scandals to bring naturalism into the headlines. This was not the sort of publicity that serious writers would have wanted, but it ended any likelihood that they would ever again be writing for themselves alone.

The trial of Ikuta Kizan, author of "The City" (see pp. 80–81), and Ishibashi Shian, editor/publisher of the literary magazine *Bungei Kurabu*, took place in the Tokyo District Court on February 27, 1908. The most remarkable feature of this trial was that it happened at all, since a typical Police Bureau ban had removed the February issue of *Bungei Kurabu* from the marketplace.[1] Apparently, however, Procurator Koyama Matsukichi (who would later rise to the posts of Procurator General and ultimately Minister of Justice, playing a key role in formulating thought-control policies for the Saitō regime of 1932–1934) felt that naturalism posed so grave a threat to the nation that a public example had to be made.[2] In this, it can be said that he succeeded. The papers found the trial far more newsworthy than a routine prohibition of sale, which would at most have merited only a few lines on a back page.

The manner in which the press reported the incident was noteworthy in itself. Neither the *Asahi Shimbun* nor the *Kokumin Shimbun* suggested that journalists shared any interest with the defendants in the issue of freedom of the press. Instead, reporters from both papers made it clear that they maintained the old prejudices against writers as amusing freaks. Their stories were aimed more at eliciting laughs than at chronicling an authentic bid for the freedom of the individual conscience. This was particularly surprising in the *Asahi*, Japan's foremost liberal newspaper. In fact, it was the reporter for the *Kokumin*, a newspaper with strong government ties and a very broad streak of yellow journalism, who gradually seemed to forget his sarcasm and did a creditable job of reporting the news.* The following account draws from both sources.[3]

The *Kokumin* reporter, Matsuzaki Tenmin, remarked at the outset that he had stayed in bed as long as possible when he heard that the trial had been delayed from 9:00 to 10:00 A.M. On a more serious note, he also pointed out that Kizan was wearing a bandage under his left ear and was too ill to speak at length. (Matsuzaki had visited him earlier in the month when the story was banned and noted that he was suffering from several serious infections.)[4] To begin the proceedings, Procurator Koyama requested a closed trial on the grounds that he considered "The City" to be obscene in its entirety. Judge Imamura Kyōtarō refused, saying that he could close the court when discussing specific obscene passages, thus revealing his presumption that the story was indeed obscene, but at least holding out against the procurator. Matsuzaki noted a swell of approval for the judge among the audience, suggesting that despite his flippant comments, his sympathies lay with the defendants.

Questioning Kizan during the morning session, the judge asked whether his story was meant to imply that an adulterous liaison had been accomplished. Absolutely not, replied Kizan, repeating what he had told Matsuzaki Tenmin for the newspaper. Kizan also insisted that he had not had impure thoughts while writing the story. When the judge asked him why he did not write about more pristine matters instead of such unwholesome subjects, Kizan answered that it was the function of the novel to portray life as it is lived. The judge advised him to turn his attention to loftier things.

After a few questions directed to Ishibashi Shian, the procurator said it was his opinion that the story did indeed depict an adulterous affair, was injurious to public morals, and ought to be discussed in closed session. This time the judge complied.

After the noon recess, the proceedings were opened to the public again, and each of the three defense attorneys presented his argument. "Literary Theory in the Courtroom," read the *Asahi* headline. "This trial was nothing but a literary lecture. The lecture hall was the courtroom, the sponsors were the police, and the speakers were the procurator and defense attorneys." This is the first good show we've had in the courts since New Year's, the reporter noted, and he deemed the most bracing performance to be that of Watanabe Terunosuke, also a writer of haiku under the names of Uzan and Shunpū Shūu Koji.†

---

*Hasegawa Tenkei noted that *Kokumin Shimbun* had been carrying so many sensational stories it should change its title to *Zokumin Shimbun*, i.e., from *National* to *Vulgar*. See "Yohakuroku," TY (March 1, 1908), p. 160.

†Watanabe Terunosuke and Miyajima Jirō also defended Tokuda Shūsei when he was

Watanabe announced that since the procurator had declaimed in the German style, he would adopt the French. In fact, said the reporter, the style was all his own, elegant and literate. In support of his argument, Watanabe brought up many of the great Japanese and Chinese classics—the *Kojiki*, the *Man'yōshū*, *The Tale of Genji*, *The Tale of the Heike*, *Essays in Idleness*, *The Dream of the Red Chamber*, Chinese poetry, Nō libretti, Jōruri, even recent drama. "In fact, he brought up so much, it seemed there was nothing else left for him to bring up but his lunch." He hoped this court would take the role of encouraging literature rather than suppressing it, Watanabe said, and noted the change-ability of mores. "But he really seemed to be playing to the gallery when he attacked the Home Ministry and the police for being out of their depth when it came to making literary judgments." According to the *Kokumin* report, Watanabe also accused the authorities of bearing down especially hard on works that concerned the Imperial Household Agency or the army or navy, suggesting that there were some parallels between the story and a recent scandal involving a military man.

The second argument for the defense was presented by another haiku poet/lawyer, Miyajima Jirō (Gojōgen) who sought to refute the charges on the bases of subject matter, the author's purpose, and the language of the story. He said that Kizan was not a writer of mere *nikuyoku shōsetsu* (flesh-lust novels), as was often claimed. Kizan had his own brand of naturalism; naturalism itself was the result of "scientific progress from romanticism to realism and finally naturalism."

Hiraide Shū, the *Myōjō* poet who had defended Yosano Akiko against the charge of spreading "dangerous thoughts," presented a "fine-grained argument" asserting that the writer must be allowed a degree of opposition to the accepted morality if he is to depict real life. Writers will take care to stay within the limits, and the readers and society owe his work a similar degree of care. To attempt to suppress literature that is suited to the age is like trying to dam a flood, Hiraide concluded.

Procurator Koyama rebutted with an assertion of the literary abilities of the Home Ministry and police officials.* This prosecution had been instituted, he insisted, to rescue contemporary literature from its own depravity and to preserve social morality. It was up to the courts, he said, to put a stop to this pernicious development here and now.[5]

---

brought to trial in June 1909 for his story "The Go-Between" ("Baikaisha"), *Tōa bungei* (April 1909). The case was much less widely publicized than the Kizan trial. See AS (June 30, 1909), p. 5.

*Hasegawa Tenkei responded to this in "Zuikan-zuihitsu," TY (April 1, 1908), p. 160: "I'd dearly love to see them write a novel or a critical essay!"

A separate report in the *Asahi* noted that an overflow crowd of young men and women had come to hear the trial, which was in itself proof of the broad acceptance of "flesh-lust novels" among the student population. In the hallways, one heard conversations about naturalism and instinctualism (*honnō-shugi*). The reporter had spotted the naturalist novelist Tokuda Shūsei in the crowd, and he had also overheard a well-dressed gentleman saying that he had no objection to naturalism, but that writers of obscene works ought to be punished. The *Kokumin* reports also stressed the youthful courtroom crowd, and both papers referred to Kizan as a "young novelist" (he was 31, Hiraide, 29), reflecting at least some sense that this was a generational struggle.

The verdict was handed down on March 5. Both men were found guilty of having violated Article 33 of the Press Regulations (see above, p. 25) and were fined twenty yen for each violation. Ishibashi was judged to have committed two violations as both editor and publisher. Since they could have been fined anywhere from twenty to three hundred yen or jailed for from one to six months, it can probably be said that they got off lightly. (An appeal was rejected four months later.)[6] As a result of this case, Kizan claimed, his career was ruined. He went personally to the Home Ministry, seeking an explanation for their ban, and he later gave an angry public lecture, all to no avail. The magazines, fearing a prohibition, would not buy his stories.[7] So little of his writing is available today that an objective evaluation of this view is next to impossible. It does seem, however, that "The City"'s potential for commentary on the modern metropolis was considerably diluted by Kizan's preoccupation with the sexual situation. In any event, Kizan is rarely mentioned now outside the context of the banning of "The City," and Yoshida Seiichi blames him for having helped to give the naturalist school its bad name at the time as a nest of pornographers.[8]

Kizan's story was described in the judge's written opinion as follows:

> In said story, "The City," one Kawamata Hirotarō is shown making provocative advances to Otomo, the wife of Tamura Chūzō. This court deems the passage which graphically portrays a man urging a married woman to commit adultery and which employs highly obscene descriptive techniques to be potentially injurious to public morals. . . . Because such immoral acts as adultery do occur in society, we cannot judge a work to be injurious to public morals simply because it adopts such subject matter. [Here the judge reverses the principle established in 1900 that certain subject matter could be inherently obscene (see above, p. 48). He goes on to establish treatment rather than subject matter as grounds for conviction.][9] In this work, however, the scene which so graphically portrays the man Hirotarō urging the young wife Otomo to commit adultery and which employs such extraordinarily obscene language, is such as

instantly to arouse a sense of shame and disgust in a person of ordinary moral conviction.[10]

The offending story may be summarized as follows: Tamura Chūzō is a middle-aged failure who has brought his voluptuous but obedient and faithful second wife and his child by his first wife to Tokyo in hopes of finding an official position. His hopes are pinned on Kawamata Hirotarō, a successful native of his village now employed in the Imperial Household Agency. Hirotarō gives Chūzō a job, but he takes an immediate fancy to Chūzō's wife, Otomo, and wastes no time in attempting to seduce her. She cannot coldly rebuff her husband's benefactor, and Chūzō himself is too spineless to act on his suspicions at first. When he finally confronts her, she blames him for having made her a human sacrifice. "You are a coward who would eat a dog's leftovers if your superiors told you to!"

Common sense would suggest that by this time she has become Hirotarō's mistress, but the story's time scheme and the characters' conversations are vague enough to allow some room for doubt. If we take Kizan's courtroom denial of consummated adultery at face value, the somewhat upbeat ending makes a bit more sense: after Otomo berates him, Chūzō walks out into the bright, chilly morning and decides that he will quit his job and they will make a new start. "He raised his weary eyes and looked at the sky of Tokyo, where the weak many slave for the strong few, working, bearing children, dying, and never knowing why."[11]

The scene to which Judge Imamura objected shows Hirotarō, red-faced and reeking of sake, in his only direct assault on Otomo's chastity. He tells her that he has seen Chūzō leave the house and has taken advantage of the opportunity to feast his eyes on her. Flustered, she runs out to buy sake at his request. As she begins serving it, the old atmosphere of the country tavern where she was raised comes back to her, and Hirotarō does not disgust her so much any more. She cautions herself to resist his advances and maintain the demeanor of a proper wife. "Then Hirotarō sought to agitate her woman's heart, not hesitating to use vulgar, embarrassing language that he had learned Heaven knows where."[12] Unfortunately, not one word of this disgusting language is quoted for the reader's benefit. Otomo, however, is vulnerable to Hirotarō's temptations. Her head begins to swim, her pulse throbs. She struggles to master her mounting feelings, and suddenly Chūzō comes back and the danger is averted.

If the mere mention of obscene language is what the judge considered to be obscene, some question remains as to the purity of the motives of the court. Several accounts of the incident note that the villain in "The City," like the evil baron in Roan's "Broken Fence," was thought to have been modeled on a certain powerful official.[13] Certainly just as important as the identity of the supposed individual model, however, must have been the author's decision to make Hirotarō an official of the Imperial Household Agency. In fact, Kizan goes so far as to indicate that Hirotarō had reached his high position only because his sister was the mistress—and is now the wife—of à baron in the top echelons of the agency.[14]

Also working against Kizan in the eyes of the court, no doubt, was the fact that the Police Bureau had already banned two earlier works of his, *Princess Fumiko* (*Fumiko-hime*) in 1906 and *Vanity* (*Kyoei*) in 1907. These were typical administrative bans, the reason for which can only be speculated upon,* but it is clear that by 1908 Kizan had earned enough of a reputation to be referred to in *Kokumin Shimbun* as something like "the super-star of injury to public morals."[15]

One important point that emerged from this case, almost incidentally, had to do with extralegal practices that were being engaged in by the censors. Angry and hurt at this third ban, Kizan told a reporter that he had revised the questionable parts of *Princess Fumiko* several times and had checked with the authorities beforehand, but that it was banned nevertheless.[16] The law of course did not provide for such cozy arrangements between the producers and the censors of literature, but they would come to take on increasing importance.

The trial may have had an adverse effect on the career of Ikuta Kizan, but it propelled Judge Imamura to new prominence as a spokesman for censorship. Two similar interviews that he gave to *Waseda Bungaku* and *Taiyō* became, in effect, the only official response to the increasingly insistent call for publication of the censors' guidelines. In *Waseda Bungaku*, Imamura defined literature injurious to public morals as "that which arouses a sense of disgust, which depicts ugly, vulgar matters—especially fornication or adultery—too concretely or in such a way as to provoke or encourage them, or to express sympathy or admiration for them." The "jurist's standard of judgment" lies in "that which would naturally seem to arouse a sense of defilement when viewed in the light of the moral concepts of the general populace." This standard is not to be determined in accordance with the tastes of the most vulgar members of society nor of the most saintly and fastidious. Nor is it the jurist's own, personal moral sense. When considering a case, the judge must raise or lower his own standards until they arrive at "just the right level" to be in accord with the "general" values of contemporary society. Thus, sheer literary value or standards appropriate to other times or other countries are irrelevant when it

---

*Saitō Shōzō, KBHS, p. 50, suggests that although the content of *Princess Fumiko* was not objectionable, the title may have been considered disrespectful of an actual member of the nobility of that name. See also MBHS, p. 98.

comes to deciding whether or not a piece is injurious to public morals. Judge Imamura recognizes that there may be some subjectivity in determining what constitutes "generally held contemporary moral concepts," but this, he says, is unavoidable. All he can do is act according to his beliefs, and he advises writers to do the same. "Go ahead and write all you want," he says, but "expect to be banned." [17]

The phrase "contemporary community standards" entered the American judicial scene in the famous Roth case of 1957, although the courts have been wrestling with the concept since 1915, when Judge Learned Hand introduced similar terminology to help end the Comstock era. [18] Judge Imamura may perhaps be credited with having anticipated Judge Hand by seven years with his new formulation and its attendant subjectivity and confusion.

NATURALISTIC SUICIDE AND RAPE

Less than three weeks after the verdict was announced in the trial of "The City," and before the publicity had had time to die down, a scandal hit the headlines that was seen as an actual instance of moral turpitude among the educated younger generation induced by naturalism.

"CLIMAX OF NATURALISM," read the headline in the March 25 *Asahi*. "Failed love suicide of lady and gentleman. He: university degree holder, novelist. She: graduate of the women's college." He was Morita Sōhei, a bright but erratic protégé of Natsume Sōseki with literary aspirations but also with a wife and a four-year-old son. She was Hiratsuka Haruko (later Raichō), a graduate of Japan's only college for women [19] who had sworn to her mother that she would remain single and devote her life to literature. They had met at an academy where Sōhei taught English. They had fallen in love and had decided that death was the only way out of their predicament. A policeman had stopped the suspicious-looking couple as they made their way into the mountains of Shiobara, where they had intended to hurl themselves from a cliff. "Love suicides are not so unusual," concluded the paper, "but it is simply unprecedented for a gentleman and lady like this, who have received the ultimate in education, to act like such fools. This bizarre event represents the climax of naturalism and sexual gratification-ism (*seiyoku manzoku-shugi*)." [20]

The following day's paper carried an even longer report, including not only details on Sōhei's liaison with another woman but also a discussion of his literary interests. Sōhei was an outstanding student of Western literature, having studied under both Natsume Sōseki and Ueda Bin, it said. He especially admired D'Annunzio's *Triumph of Death*, "a novel with a strong modern scent." According to Futabatei Shimei, Sōhei was extremely fond of the climactic scene in which the hero leaps over the cliff edge with the heroine in his arms. A certain poet said of him, "Sōhei is fond of the Turgenev story 'A Desperate Character'—which is exactly what he is." His only pleasure was said to be sinking himself in philosophical speculation. A good bit of his conversation seems to have consisted of plots for novels that he had in mind, according to two literary figures interviewed for the report. Yosano Akiko told of a recent visit Sōhei had paid to her, in which he outlined the story of a man with an obsession that he was being followed by a woman he hated; the man tries to kill himself, fails, returns to his wife and child, and in the last scene grasps his wife's hand across the *kotatsu*—"a very naturalistic ending," Yosano Akiko remarked, perhaps impressed with the down-to-earth realism of the heating device.

The literary element was emphasized in the account of Hiratsuka Haruko's background as well. A former classmate at the women's college noted that she smoked and tried to give the impression of being a fast woman, but in fact she merely enjoyed toying with men. An unnamed poetess well acquainted with her said that "her ideas are thoroughly Western. She loves to draw men to her but spurn them when they come too close." She was "an avid reader of Russian literature, has a good collection of Turgenev and others which she is always reading."

In a brief statement, Sōseki generally defended Sōhei, saying that "the minds of the youth of the new age are very complicated." But overall, the report of the affair was critical, ending with remarks by the dean of the women's college that beautifully summarize the prevailing conservative attitude toward literature, individualism, and the younger generation:

> It is a matter of extreme self-centeredness—and in direct conflict with the principles of this college—when people act just as they please, claiming that love is "sacred" and entering into illicit relationships. They talk about "the individual," but we believe that the individual depends upon the existence of society and gains significance only after contributing to the path of righteousness. Thus, we have striven to annihilate such evil philosophies as "the aesthetic life" and "individualism" from the moment they began to spread. Had our educational policies taken their full effect, the present example of self-centered recklessness should never have happened.* I am filled with remorse to think that our efforts proved insufficient.
>
> On the other hand, it occurs to me that it was *after* she had graduated from

---

*Dean Asō uses the term *jiko-hon'i*, the self-centeredness that Sōseki would elevate to the highest ethical principle in his famous 1914 lecture. See Jay Rubin, "Sōseki on Individualism: 'Watakushi no Kojinshugi,'" MN 34, no. 1 (Spring 1979): 34.

here that Haruko fell into her present naturalistic tendencies. It was then that the popular literature she so relished began to work its evil and she was finally converted to the enveloping tide. I do wish that the newspapers and periodicals would join together to eradicate this malicious tendency. A hint of sympathy for actions like this, and the poison will be spread not only to the schools but to society at large.

Despite the considerable literary accomplishments of the new writers, the public image of naturalism was still so distorted as to encourage a statement like this from a college dean. But if the view of this suicide attempt was colored by the atmosphere surrounding the trial of "The City," another event which surfaced in the press at this time, and which became a far more durable symbol of naturalism's baneful influence on society, carried the distortion beyond all reasonable limits. This was the so-called Debakame Incident.

On the night of March 22, 1908, a gardener named Ikeda Kametarō, whose distinctive physiognomy had earned him the nickname "Debakame" (Bucktooth Kame), followed a young married woman home from the neighborhood public bath, where he had become aroused while spying on her through a knothole. Forcing the woman into a deserted area, he proceeded to rape her, gagging her screams with the towel she was carrying and, in the process, suffocating her to death.

Although he escaped that night, Ikeda apparently continued his habits of spying on the women's bath and openly masturbating in the men's tub (the latter an activity that had earned him the additional nickname "Senzuri-Kame"), and the police picked him up. He confessed, was tried and sentenced to life imprisonment; an appeal to the Great Court of Cassation was rejected in June the following year. The case caused a sensation in the press, and one prevalent view seems to have been that Ikeda's crime was an acting out of naturalist fiction. The word "Debakame-ism" (*Debakame-shugi*) was coined as a synonym for naturalism.[21]

The identification of Debakame and naturalism was more an accident of timing than common sense. Surely no one was suggesting that a semiliterate gardener was combing the literary and intellectual journals to find naturalist debauchery for himself. A major element in the public uproar over naturalism was the fact that a comparatively small percentage of the population was actually reading the new fiction. Devotees of naturalism were far outnumbered by readers of the *kōdan* then being serialized in the daily papers.[22] These were essentially transcriptions of a traditional form of narrative entertainment (*kōdan* or *kōshaku*) that concentrated on more-or-less "true" stories, the bulk of their material coming from well-known samurai adventures. It was far more likely that Ikeda Kametarō was reading *kōdan* than modern fiction—if he was reading anything at all—for *kōdan* were still being performed before enthusiastic audiences.*

On the day that *Kokumin Shimbun* reported the discovery of the murder, it also printed chapter 85 of *Nightstorm Okinu* (*Yoarashi Okinu*), a *kōdan* by one of the most popular performers of the day, Shinryūsai Teisui. This was Teisui's retelling of the tale of Okinu, the notorious poison woman whose story had been such a hit in 1878 (see above, pp. 37–38). By this point in the action, Okinu has been through an incredible series of adventures, many with erotic, scatological, and homicidal overtones. In chapter 13, for example, she is attempting to urinate over the side of a boat (which "must have been a matter of great satisfaction for the fish looking up from beneath," remarks Teisui) when suddenly she is pushed overboard by a servant hoping to thwart her intended marriage to his rich master's son.[23] She is found on the beach, naked in the moonlight, which is only the first of countless opportunities for Teisui's illustrator to show readers Okinu's fulsome breasts.

After the man who found her goes to prison for murdering her father, Okinu becomes the mistress of a daimyō (feudal lord) with the approval of his barren wife, and she bears him a son.[24] When the daimyō dies, she becomes a nun. By the time Ikeda Kametarō raped and murdered his victim on the night of March 22, 1908, Okinu has been through a sordid affair, the Meiji period has begun, and she is living with a usurer named Kobayashi Kinpei while buying the favors of Kabuki actors on the side, especially one Arashi Rihaku. Kinpei is suspicious, and in chapter 85 he demands to know the identity of the man whose letter has just fallen out of Okinu's sash. When she refuses to confess, he tears her clothes off, ties her to a pillar, and commences to beat her. The illustration shows him in the act of violently stripping off her kimono. The following day's illustration shows Okinu tied to the pillar, breasts protruding voluptuously through the ropes, blood dripping from her face. She convinces Kinpei that she has not been unfaithful to him. (Thereafter, she becomes pregnant by Rihaku, poisons Kinpei, is tried and executed for the murder two weeks after giving birth to Rihaku's child: thus is Virtue Encouraged and Vice Chastised.)

"*Kōdan* are what cause the Japanese people to win wars," Count Ōkuma Shigenobu is supposed to have said, probably with rousing tales of the Forty-Seven Loyal Retainers in mind.[25] But *Okinu* seems to have been one of Teisui's most popular pieces in performance, and there was plenty of sex and violence in the tales of such underworld heroes (*yakuza*) as Kunisada Chūji,[26] which constituted a major part of the *kōdan* repertory. Especially after the Ikuta Kizan trial, however, the new, Western-tainted naturalism had become ines-

---

*The *kōdanshi* does not "write" (*kaku*) his stories, even when they appear in print; he "reads" (*yomu*, i.e., "recites") them.

capably identified with sexual depravity, while the traditional *kōdan* never came under suspicion because their characters acted in accordance with (or in violation of) the familiar moral code; the code itself was never called into question. So completely were *kōdan* identified with the good old values of loyalty and patriotism that, in 1911, the Ministry of Education actually formulated a policy of promoting their production. And, as we shall see, one of the first *kōdan* performers they turned to was Shinryūsai Teisui himself.[27]

Such media events as the trial of "The City," the Morita Sōhei/Hiratsuka Haruko suicide attempt, and the Debakame Incident were raising a groundswell of public indignation against naturalism at a time when political developments were moving in a distinctly conservative direction.

7

Literature and Life / Art and the State

As public sentiment crystallized in opposition to the new literature, the government began to take action. The official position was stated by one Inoue Takaya, Ministerial Secretary in the Police Bureau, when he was interviewed in the major legal journal, *Hōritsu Shimbun*, on February 29, 1908, just two days after the trial of Ikuta Kizan. It was a matter of deep regret to the bureau, he said, that "this literature of the flesh or literature of the naturalist school or whatever it is called, which advocates the lewdest passions and describes all sorts of physical matters, is gaining such momentum." I don't know what these naturalists think they are doing, he continued, but the things they write are so obscene they can't be read aloud to the family. The young people in our society, said Inoue, are showing enough signs of decadence as it is, without actually having to be taught by writers how to degrade themselves. Their apologists argue that they are simply recording what actually goes on in society, but surely this is the dark side of things that they are blowing up out of all proportion. Further, he went on, there are many who misunderstand our prohibitions, who say that we tend to be particularly severe in suppressing portrayals of the upper classes or accuse us of singling out the naturalist school, but this is entirely false. We are concerned, Inoue declared, only with public morals. "I sincerely hope that people—and especially the writers—will see the truth in what I am saying and take a good, hard look at themselves."[1]

Looking at themselves was precisely what writers were doing, of course, but not in the way Inoue meant. Instead of accepting the values of their elders, they were looking inside themselves. These writers were not verbal performers for the aural entertainment of the family circle. They were the silently read conspirators of the young. They were subversive agents threatening communal solidarity not with obscenity but with something far more insidious: privacy.[2]

Serious works of literature were beginning to appear among the Edo erotica, sex manuals, and pornography on the Police Bureau lists. Throughout 1908 the question of "the regulation of literature" (*bungei torishimari*) occupied a prominent place in the journals. A recurring theme was the need for mutual understanding between writers and censors, which was to be achieved through publication of the government's still-secret standards on obscenity, or through shifting the censorship function from the Home Ministry to the Ministry of Education, or perhaps through the establishment of an academy after the French model.

The censors' standards were never published, but the call for communication did not go unheeded. In January 1909 the Minister of Education held a gathering for writers at which such problems were discussed. Not until May 1911, however, did the academy come into being, and after two years of government frustration, its life was finally snuffed out by a fiscal retrenchment. This would be the government's last attempt, until the militarist era, to influence writers by organizing them.

Response among writers to the question of their relationship to government varied widely, but as this crucial period developed, and as writers became more certain of their social role, open contempt increased for any official steps taken to control literature. In the end, neither side could claim a clear-cut victory, but literature emerged from the ordeal with its integrity uncompromised.

LITERATURE, LIFE, AND FUZZY THINKING: TENKEI, KATAI, AND TAKUBOKU

"At last," wrote the critic Maeda Akira in March 1908, "the interaction between literature and society has grown close in Japan! No longer is literature a plaything, an amusement for men of leisure. It is one of the great and serious undertakings in life"—and one of genuine concern to the government. Until the previous year, Maeda continued, the conflict between the new and the old literature was confined to writers only—a lively enough debate but not dangerous. The censors' recent strictness, however, had introduced a whole new coloration to the arguments. People had begun to assume that a banned work must be from the naturalist school; they had begun to take sides with the government and to attack naturalism. "Yes, I suppose if one is always satisfied with—always applauding—the government, then he need never worry about being punished himself, but that is a pretty despicable way to live. . . . The few mediocre works that are banned now will someday find a prominent place as martyrs in world literary history. . . . But naturalism has found its meaning in undermining the very foundations of all authority, all ideals, all fantasy, and beginning anew the study of life." *

Maeda's position of looking to the historical process for ultimate vindication would, in the end, prove most typical. By contrast, Hasegawa Tenkei, writing in *Taiyō* (June 1908), began calling for the establishment of a literary academy as a means of solving the conflict between the writers and the government. † Tenkei was the critic who had declared the advent of the "Age of Disillusionment" (see pp. 60–61), but his argument for an academy reveals how imperfectly this forceful spokesman for naturalism as the enemy of established values understood the implications of his own pronouncements.[3]

The case of Ikuta Kizan's "The City" is still in appeals, Tenkei notes, and already Fūyō's *Shattered Love* and translations of Zola's *Paris* and the complete works of Molière have fallen like dominoes before the censors.‡ This is an unfortunate situation, he knows, but he recognizes that some degree of censorship is necessary for the maintenance of public morals. Tenkei goes on to defend literary control by analogy to the family. Even the most liberal head of a household sets limits to keep his children from going astray, he observes, but rather than criticize such a father, we see that his act is an entirely natural part of his emotional concern (*ninjō*) for his children's welfare. "The censors, the moralists, and the educators all hand down their stern rules out of this parental feeling, which is why society ought to be most grateful to them and, at the same time, should hope for a rigorous exercise of their decision-making function."

Tenkei does have one misgiving, however, when it comes to the censors'

---

*"Bungaku zakkan," TY (March 1, 1908), pp. 142–44. For a shocked response to this sort of pronouncement, see Esui [pseudonym], "Bungei no anryū," *Teikoku Bungaku* (July 1908): 1048–50. "This is extreme individualism. As I see it, man is also a social being, and in sacrificing his desires for the common good, he does not annihilate himself. He merely sacrifices his small ego for the sake of his great ego. This is what distinguishes men from the animals. . . . The naturalists are plotting the destruction of morality."

†In fact, Tenkei had been asking for an academy as early as June 1906, but at that time the censorship question had been only a side issue. As he had seen it then, the main benefit an academy would bestow on literature would be to express the nation's appreciation to writers for "raising the nation's spiritual honor" in the eyes of the world. See TY (June 1, 1906), pp. 153–60.

‡The second volume of *Paris* was banned on May 4, 1908, even though the first volume carried an enthusiastic letter of praise to the translator written by Prime Minister Saionji Kinmochi. He had not read Zola for thirty years, he said. It was like meeting an old friend, and he eagerly awaited the appearance of the second volume. See KBHS, pp. 19, 53–54; and Naimushō Keihokyoku, ed., *Kinshi tankōbon mokuroku*, p. 89. The second volume of the three-volume Molière collection was banned on April 30, 1908. The translator attempted to publish the three volumes as one in 1916 but was stopped again. See KBHS, pp. 19, 52; and Naimushō Keihokyoku, ed., *Kinshi tankōbon mokuroku*, p. 110.

literary judgment: "They are human and can make mistakes." It is for this reason that he suggests the formation of a literary review board composed of widely respected scholars. The censors and writers view each other suspiciously, Tenkei believes, because they have no opportunity for an exchange of views. He notes that of the many ways to accomplish such an exchange, the best might be to hold a large, friendly gathering for censors, writers, and critics.[4]

Tenkei was still asking for an academy in November. It would be a way to "bring us together," he argues, to avoid the kind of "misunderstanding" seen in the Kizan case. He is pleased at the censors' increasing stringency, he says, for this will do away with the exploiters who have caused so much of the misunderstanding. We serious writers and critics, he states, want to have the charlatans weeded out. "Far from being decadent, practitioners of naturalism taken to the extreme would have to live like Zen monks because their true aim is to live the life of outside observers, attaching value to nothing."[5]

If Tenkei seems to be arguing that literature is a harmless pastime of no concern to the government, he is neither the spokesman for all of naturalism nor is he by any means alone in declaring naturalism to be strictly an artistic theory with no bearing on "real life." * His views on the need for accommodation between literature and government do, however, derive from an affirmation of the status quo startling in a man who had proclaimed naturalism to be the "Art for an Age of Disillusionment."

In a second article in the June 1908 *Taiyō*, Tenkei spells out the limits that nature places on art. Tenkei begins "Aspects of Realism" ("Genjitsushugi no shosō") with a declaration of the need for "fulfillment of the individual's existence," but he goes on to appeal to the "self-evident truth" that "the ego gradually expands its boundaries" until it encompasses the entire nation (no larger expansion than this being possible within the limits of "reality"). He thus affirms that the "fifty million brothers and sisters" of Japan are crowned by "a line of Emperors unbroken for ages eternal." All have been nurtured by the same air, the same land, and the same thoughts through twenty-six hundred years of history. Tenkei insists that the Japanese should receive a "Japanist" education based upon this reality rather than upon abstract concepts of man derived from Buddhism, Christianity, or socialism. An idealistic education, he asserts, is perfect for producing cowardly hypocrites who mouth

---

*See Hasegawa Tenkei, "Sho-ronkaku ni ichigon o teisu," TY (May 1, 1909), p. 154. The naturalist theory of Shimamura Hōgetsu also stressed uninvolved observation. See Hōgetsu, "Geijutsu to jitsujinsei ni yokotawaru issen" (September 1908), KBHT 3:233–45. For a classic statement of Japanese intellectual passivity, see Hōgetsu, "Ima no bundan to shin-shizenshugi" (June 1907), KBHT 3:52–55, in which he propounds a Zen-like attitude of unconditional surrender of the writer's ego to nature. Only a theoretician could have written this piece.

ideals while living by a wholly different set of necessities. The Ministry of
Education would be doing the nation a service if it would shut down all
religious schools.

Though Tenkei here equates Christianity with other objectionable doctrines, the foreign religion was something of a bête noire for him. He had
attacked Christianity in the May 1907 *Taiyō* and again in the August 1908
Taiyō for reasons that show him to be in full accord with the Meiji state and its
imperialistic mission. "We desire geographical development. We hope for the
development of the nation. But Christianity sets up supernatural ideals. How
can godly ideals so out of touch with reality fulfill these aspirations? . . . If
one is to be a true believer in their teachings, it follows that one must cherish
ideals that clash with the *kokutai.*" Appealing to the Confucian concept that "a
man cannot serve two masters," Tenkei asserts that the spread of Christianity
in Japan could only produce an increasingly large—and dangerous—number
of hypocrites who could be completely true neither to their religion nor to the
laws of Japan.[6]

Tenkei does have one objection to present-day nationalistic education:
namely, its tendency to fashion people according to ideals abstracted from
mankind in general, probably as a result of infatuation with Western educational techniques. The great defect in modern education is its attempt to turn
all children—those of grocers, farmers, aristocrats, and soldiers—into ideal
human beings by subjecting them to the same training. This only encourages
people to cherish ambitions unbefitting their station in life. The best education, says Tenkei, awakens each student to the reality of his particular position. Likewise, the best literature depicts the reality of life as it is: namely,
naturalistic literature, which inevitably expresses the national character because of its emphasis on the real.[7]

Hasegawa Tenkei was supposedly an intellectual in the vanguard of a Euro-
pean-inspired movement bent on destroying all traditional values, but here we
see him expressing thoughts that would not only have been congenial to the
Meiji oligarchs but even to the Tokugawa rulers who had sought to keep their
four-class society immobile and the stain of foreign influence shut out. Whatever such concepts as "individualism" or "ego" meant to Tenkei in his frequent
usage of them (in "Aspects of Realism," "ego" might just as well be defined as
kokutai), it is clear that the literature of the real (i.e., the given) had no more
political potential for him than it did for Oguri Fūyō. "The illusions of
religion have been destroyed, the sacredness of nature has been reduced to a
catalogue of cells, gasses and elements," he had proclaimed. But still, somehow, the *kokutai* survived intact, admitting room for individual conscience
neither in religion nor—if Tenkei could see the implications of his argument
—in literature.

Tenkei was only a critic, a theoretician, but he had a close counterpart among practicing authors in Tayama Katai, whom Yoshida Seiichi has characterized as the Zola—the foremost propagandist—of Japanese naturalism.[8] Expanding on a remark of Shimazaki Tōson, Katai insisted that naturalist writers were "war correspondents in the battlefield of life." Unlike "cowardly" romantics who lost themselves in fantasy, naturalists boldly entered the field of battle but restricted themselves to recording in detail the actions of the combatants. As were real war correspondents, they were bound to be considered a nuisance by the troops. Adopting the "attitude of an outside observer" (*bōkanteki taido*), the writer should limit his technique to "surface description" (*heimen byōsha*) without voicing overt criticism or interpretation, which could only distort reality by imposing upon it the writer's subjective values. For Katai, too, reality was a given. The writer had no business criticizing it or trying to change it. Exactly what his business *was* was not very clear—other than an artistic "discovery of life's truths." Katai explicitly denied the possibility that art might influence social change.[9]

There is some danger in taking theories of fiction too literally, however, even when they originate from the author. For example, Katai's best-known statement on the technique of "surface description," in his interview "The Experiment in *Life*" ("*Sei* ni okeru kokoroyomi," *Waseda Bungaku*, September 1908), is simply not an accurate account of the technique as he employed it in that novel. As even the brief quotations below clearly demonstrate, the interview is in error when it states that the author does not enter into the minds of his characters but describes them only as they would be seen by an objective observer. The narrator of *Life* is, in fact, omniscient. He provides not only a historical panorama of the plot of ground upon which the novel's action occurs, but he freely reports the thoughts of every character in the book, including some very minor ones. One scholar has suggested that Katai's interviewer, Sōma Gyofū, probably interpreted his remarks too freely, and that Katai meant nothing more doctrinaire by "surface description" than "eschewing fictionalization," as he later glossed the term.[10]

Sometimes in his fiction Katai behaves exactly as his theory might suggest—that is, as a technician with little to distinguish him from Oguri Fūyō, who could also sound very somber when talking about his art. The narrator of Katai's 1902 Zolaist story "The Death of Jūemon" ("Jūemon no saigo") likes to comment, with the aid of many exclamation points, on the unimaginable realness of reality and the animal forces in human nature. But the author's central interest is less with these pseudo-profundities than with an exploration of the various legitimate ways a dramatized narrator can come by his information.[11]

Katai is still experimenting with technique in "The Next Room" ("Rinshitsu," January 1907), trying to convince us with a lot of heavy truisms about death and human ugliness that he has something profound to say. The piece describes the experience of listening to a man die in the next room of an inn, confining the visual element of the story to a few peeks through a crack by the door. So busily is Katai playing with his narrative gimmick that he seems almost unaware that he has raised some important ethical questions. The narrator blames the innkeeper for abandoning the man to die alone, but he himself could simply have walked through the door had he wanted to become involved. He is disgusted to see the innkeeper snooping in the dead man's suitcase, but he does not attempt to stop him. In the end, he merely hurries away to catch a train.[12]

Had Katai stopped writing with "The Next Room," he would have gone the way of Oguri Fūyō or Kosugi Tengai as a now-unreadable contributor to the development of realism in Japan. He went on, however, to examine himself in the ethically ambiguous role of the observer, producing a series of works that are remarkable precisely for their lumpy mixture of piercing self-criticism and apparent critical blind spots. Katai's fiction is as contradictory in its way as is Tengai's criticism. They are true contemporaries, sharing this strange mixture of iconoclasm and conservatism. Katai, however, has the artist's ability to create characters embodying his view of the world. The work assuring him of a permanent place in literary history is *The Quilt*, an autobiographical short novel appearing in September 1907 and winning him the praise of *Waseda Bungaku* as the year's outstanding contributor to the new literature.

One of the first things the narrator of *The Quilt* tells us about his protagonist, Takenaka Tokio, is that "as a writer, he had the ability to study his own psychology objectively." But the remarkable thing about this novel is that Katai succeeds in convincing us that the statement is generally true about Tayama Katai precisely because it is a false assessment of Takenaka Tokio. Tokio emerges as a hypocrite with enormous powers of self-deception, an ineffectual bookworm living vicariously through Western literature, a self-styled member of the new generation whose true sympathies lie with traditional values but who appeals to the freer modern morality whenever it suits his convenience. Tokio's intellectualizing amounts to nothing but a smoke-screen behind which hides an ordinary man in his mid-thirties who has tired of his wife and is dying for some fresh, young sex.

Tokio is an unsuccessful writer of prettified love novels who supports his family by editing geography books. His wife of eight years is in her third pregnancy, and he walks about fantasizing affairs with young girls, wondering what he could manage if his wife were to die in childbirth. Suddenly letters begin arriving from one Yokoyama Yoshiko asking if she can become his literary disciple. He is intrigued by her cultured style, but he writes back discouraging her from a literary career: as a woman, it is her biological duty to bear children. Still, he checks the map to find the location of her village, and it takes only one more letter from her to make him relent. They begin to correspond, and in the corner of one letter he writes in tiny characters a request for a photograph then crosses it out.

Yoshiko's father brings her to Tokyo shortly after Tokio's third son is born. She comes from a rich Christian family, and she has all the virtues and faults of the modern educated woman: she is beautiful, idealistic, and vain—a product of the last few years during which female education has been on the upswing. Tokio now regrets that he was content to marry a woman who could boast of nothing but her matronly chignon, her ducklike walk, and her submissiveness and chastity. Nevertheless, when Yoshiko comes to live with them temporarily, he is thrilled by her many domestic skills. The wife's jealousy and the misgivings of Yoshiko's family convince him to find a room for her elsewhere.

During the next year and a half, Tokio "teaches" her "self-awareness" and defends her to his "old-fashioned" wife, who is scandalized at her consorting with male friends. When Yoshiko confesses to him that she has found "sacred" love with a young Kyoto Christian on her way back from a stay at home, however, Tokio is thunderstruck. As an apologist for the modern ways, Tokio feels he ought to help the young couple, but he berates himself for having let her slip from his own grasp, just as he has always missed his chances in life. "I am Turgenev's superfluous man!" he laments, drinking himself into oblivion.

For three days, Tokio struggles with the dilemma. Finally he decides to work for the happiness of the woman he loves. "It will be hard, but life is hard." To carry out his duty as Yoshiko's teacher, he will bring her back to his own house and install her in a second-floor room. "There is nothing so pitiful, so evanescent as man when he comes in touch with that irresistible force that lurks in the depths of nature," he thinks, in one of those moments when Tayama Katai loses his distance from Tokio.

Tokio's noble resolve must face some stern tests. When Tokio hears from Yoshiko the modern decisiveness with which she and her lover are planning their future together, Katai informs us that Tokio wants to approve of this change in mores but cannot suppress his tradition-bound misgivings. Soon he is reading her mail to find if their "sacred" love might have a physical element and preaching to her in pseudo-modern rhetoric that the preservation of her chastity is a woman's guarantee of her freedom.

As the lovers meet with increasing frequency and disturbingly modern openness, the distraught Tokio realizes that he can end their relationship by informing her parents. He does so in the guise of a plea on Yoshiko's behalf. His jealousy only increases when she determines to go ahead with her marriage plans despite parental opposition; he also resents her dereliction of her obligation to him as her mentor. (She is a *giri-shirazu*, he says, using the traditional phraseology.) When Tokio learns without a doubt that she has indeed given herself body and soul, he arranges to have her father take her home, regretting that he never took advantage of her deflowered state, but glad at least that he has managed to snatch her from his rival's hands.

As the time for her departure draws near, Tokio reflects that he would "certainly" have married Yoshiko had he been single. They could have had an ideal literary life together; "she would have comforted him in the unbearable pangs of creation." Perhaps fate would bring them together in the future? Perhaps her loss of purity would be the determining factor?

The bleakness of domestic existence returns to the Takenaka household; the same loneliness amid the noise of children that had been there three years ago before Yoshiko had entered his life. A few days after her departure a letter arrives, its unwonted formality seeming to suggest that she has been tamed. Tokio goes to her second-story room to search for traces of his lost love. He finds a soiled hair ribbon and sniffs it. He finds the quilt on which she slept, and he sinks his face into the soiled velvet collar of her sleeping robe, inhaling her odor to his heart's content. "Suddenly overcome with desire and sorrow and despair, Tokio spread the quilt and lay the robe atop it. He wept, burying his face in the cold, soiled collar of velvet." *

The Quilt came as a shock to the reading public for the unsparing honesty with which the author exposed the shameful, ugly elements of his own personality, and particularly for the confessed physicality of his sexual longing in the concluding scene. [13] Such confessional honesty was in part colored, however, by the conventions of morbid Zolaist interest in the ugly truth. Thus it seems far less courageous than Katai's intellectual honesty in suggesting an element of affectation and self-deception in the very foundation of his literary career—his knowledge of Western literature. Here, his self-analysis reaches a level of detachment that could not reasonably be expected of any late Meiji literary figure so committed to the West. There were limits beyond which he could not go, of course: he was deadly serious about "the unbearable pangs of creation." But he recognized the strong layer of traditional sentiment against which his modern ideas had to struggle and which he could not manipulate freely because it was more deeply rooted. And finally, he had the artistic discipline to objectify this insight in a literary work.

Katai revealed how strong indeed his traditional sentiments were in his next important piece, the novel *Life*, serialized in the *Yomiuri Shimbun* from April to July 1908. Perhaps the sordid afterglow of the Debakame Incident (see

*GNBZ 20:31–58. Both *The Quilt* and "A Morbid Weakness for Young Girls" have now been translated. See Kenneth G. Henshall, *The Quilt and Other Stories by Tayama Katai* (University of Tokyo Press, 1981).

above, p. 91) caused conservative critics to pounce on this novel as another dangerous example of naturalism, for the tremendously strong pull of family embodied in the self-portrait of Katai should have been obvious to any fair-minded reader.

The central action of *Life* takes place over four and a half months, during which time the matriarch of the Yoshida family is slowly dying of intestinal cancer and making everyone's life miserable. Having raised her four children single-handedly after the death of her husband in the Satsuma Rebellion, the mother has always been a difficult and domineering family head. But terminal illness is unleashing all of her frustrations and resentments, which pour out on the heads of her children and their spouses. The situation is so very particularized and the attitude of the children so understanding, however, that the novel is in no way a protest against the weight of the traditional family on modern individuals longing for liberation. Katai is not unaware of the issue, however: he has an onlooker remark, as the funeral passes by, that the children will have an easier time of it now that the old woman is dead. But in its context, the observation is filled with irony. It only serves to emphasize the unimaginably complicated mix of feelings among the individual family members, none of whom has looked forward to the mother's death or has even indirectly questioned the authority of the traditional system. There is no sense of a determination to reject the old patterns and claim a long-delayed independence; in fact, when the Katai figure, Sennosuke, is given his independence through the mother's death, he sobs like a helpless child.

On the night of the fortieth-day anniversary of the mother's death, Sennosuke returns from the observances. The Milky Way stretches across a beautifully clear sky, and he is overwhelmed by sentiment:

> Suddenly the tears began to pour out of him. A parent had given her all for her children, but what had the children ever done for the parent? Their mother had been a difficult person, it was true, but she had also been warm and loving. From the bottom of her heart, she had sorrowed for them, grieved for them, and raged for them. She had been difficult only because she had been truly kind. Yet what had her children done to repay her for this?
>
> A choking sense of the despicableness of mankind suddenly pressed in upon him. Soon, however, he saw it in another light.
>
> "This," he said to himself, "yes, this, after all, is man. This is nature. Let him pass who must pass. Let him perish who must perish."
>
> His tears overflowed endlessly. . . .
>
> "Is something wrong?" asked his wife, Oume.
>
> "My mother is dead. I'm all alone."
>
> The sight of her husband in tears moved Oume deeply. She could find no words of comfort.

"I'm all alone," Sennosuke repeated. "I have no more source of strength. Now the two of us must make our way through the world alone."

Oume, too, was in tears. For a while, neither of them spoke. At length, she said, "You are right. Mother was a wonderful source of strength. But there is no way to bring her back. We shall try our best, do whatever we must. . . ."

For the first time in their lives, Sennosuke and Oume felt the piercing sadness of having touched the shifting waves of this transient world. Now they were more than just husband and wife: a powerful closeness had grown between them.[14]

It is sometimes asserted that *Life* suggests a passing of the old family pattern to be replaced by a conjugal-centered family more congenial to the modern ego. But this book contains no such modern egos, and though the happy ending is worthy of any domestic drama, no guarantee exists that the young families established by the next generation will not develop along traditional lines. The fecund sister has gone back to the country to suffer at the hands of her drunken husband. The youngest brother has triumphed in winning the bride of his choice, but as a military man he is pleased with his career and evidences no wish to change. The eldest brother has been able to enjoy his new bride now that round-the-clock nursing of the sick mother no longer inhibits their love life, but he is a simple and traditional person. And in answer to the subtly suggested theme of conflict between marital sex and filial piety, the supposedly Westernized writer, Sennosuke, has shown himself to be anything but liberated:

A sensitive man, Sennosuke could not entirely rid himself of the feeling that there was something immoral, even sinful in his wife's having become pregnant. Long ago, a husband and wife could not share a bedroom for three years while mourning for a parent. . . . This ancient Chinese moral teaching mysteriously reasserted itself in Sennosuke's heart.[15]

It is also Sennosuke who is most upset at the selling of an heirloom painting that symbolizes the family's feudal roots, and he who bemoans the redistribution to the children of their umbilical cords following the mother's death.* Nor does he question the family pride that leads the eldest brother to insist on an expensive funeral.

What offended conservative readers of *Life* was the cold eye with which Katai had described the slow, sickening death of his mother.[16] There are fond

*Japanese mothers usually preserve the nub of a child's umbilical cord when it dries and falls off.

memories of her as a young woman, and expressions of pity for her suffering and her fear of death, but she is not worshipped. She is revealed in ugly moods and in her physical ugliness as she rots away, exuding horrid smells that draw flies. Katai later wrote that his decision to write the novel was reached only after much painful deliberation. We may fault him for having overcome his misgivings only to exploit his family in the name of art. His cold eye was not trained on them alone, however, but on himself as well, and his self-portrait had nearly as many strains and contradictions as the close-up portrait of *The Quilt*.

Tayama Katai did not have the intellectual capacity to unite his fragmented image of life into a coherent statement: indeed, when he presumed to offer his thoughts, as in the tearful scene above, he became simply embarrassing. But with his dispassionate stare, he implied that life was too complex for summary and truth too elusive ever to be capitalized. He demonstrated, as Hasegawa Tenkei's theory never could, that Japanese naturalism was in fact the art for an age of disillusionment.

Katai's neutral descriptive pen could appear, however, to be no more of a challenge to orthodoxy than Tenkei's theory—and Katai's own—would suggest. Certainly this was the view of Ishikawa Takuboku when he accused both men of practicing a "shameful kind of self-deception."[17] Tenkei, he said, was guilty of "the most characteristic Japanese form of cowardice" when he insisted that naturalism's battle against the old morality did not conflict with the national family because its technique was limited to the observation of given reality. If naturalism's objectivity was no threat to the state, Takuboku pointed out, then it was no threat to the old morality, either. Turning to Katai's fiction, Takuboku said that Katai's unvarying *professional* detachment was a form of *personal* cowardice. Surface description was a laudable means of ridding literature of elements that could not be verified in actual experience, but Katai had dismissed authorial criticism too rashly when he asserted that solutions to life's problems lay beyond observable reality.

As evidence of Katai's lack of critical spirit, Takuboku cited the juvenility of the self-portraits in Katai's stories and novels. This criticism only makes sense, however, if we assume that the Katai figures in the fiction are silly and hypocritical because Katai was unaware of how much he was revealing of himself. We would then have to assume that Katai quite mindlessly put all of his worst traits into the protagonist of "A Morbid Weakness for Young Girls" (see above, p. 62), then ran a train over him at the end for no other purpose than to end the story. We would have to ignore the obvious deepening of this self-portrait in *The Quilt* and assume that Katai was offended when critics praised him for boldly revealing what a hypocrite he could be. It is difficult to say how far he would have had to go to please Takuboku; possibly only speechifying—ideas on the crude level of propaganda—would have done it.

This is suggested both by Takuboku's later political writings at the time of the High Treason case (see below, chap. 11) and by the impatience of the recent convert revealed in his critique of Katai. Until "yesterday," he remarks twice in the short, fragmented essay, he himself was guilty of the kind of cowardly self-deception he is attacking in others. It is a widespread malaise, he implies, and it calls for immediate treatment. Such indirect methods as objective description of life's surface would never do.

Takuboku's confession does serve to remind us of how strongly rooted were the traditional assumptions and how effectively they impeded any widespread perception of censorship as an intrusion of public values into the private realm. For what sort of private realm exists when even a new wave of literature—meant to destroy all established values—is seen as part of the national mission? If Hasegawa Tenkei, an intellectual in the vanguard of naturalism, identified himself with the *kokutai*, the systematic propagation of which was just beginning to be reflected in such steps as textbook revision, little hope existed for widespread support of writers who asserted their separateness from that monolithic body.

But Tenkei's was only one view of the relationship of the individual to nation and society. Uchida Roan, in Tenkei's own magazine, *Taiyō*, brought a far more liberated intelligence to bear on the problem. Roan was the author who had so vehemently protested the suppression of his story "Broken Fence" in 1901. Interviewed in the June 1908 issue of *Taiyō*, Roan said that he could not agree with those who thought (as he once had) that the problem of excessive censorship could be solved by transferring jurisdiction from the Home Ministry to the Ministry of Education. The problem, he said, lay not with the censors but with something far more basic.

We really *do* have a problem when the collected works of Molière are banned, said Roan. It is pointless, however, to complain about police insensitivity to literature. "Police" sounds very terrible, of course, but they are nothing compared with the educators and scholars who encourage the censors when they express such delight at seeing recent fiction banned. As Roan perceived it, the real problem of censorship arose from the discrepancy between the moral concepts of these traditionalists and the new morality of the writers. Shifting the censorship function to the Ministry of Education would not change anything, he felt, because the writers would still be at the mercy of men like Inoue Tetsujirō, the University of Tokyo philosophy professor who condemned Christianity as heresy for its failure to teach loyalty and filial piety.* In fact, added Roan with a twinkle, we are probably better off with

---

*For the conflict between Inoue and the Christian evangelist Uchimura Kanzō, see Tatsuo Arima, *The Failure of Freedom*, pp. 34–36.

poorly educated police censors who cannot understand Shakespeare and Schopenhauer well enough to realize that they would want to suppress them.[18]

One month after Roan's marks appeared, a government came into power that was even more willing to mobilize its forces in the cause of the old morality. And these were the men who would eventually give Tenkei his academy.

8

The Government Moves Right

THE SECOND KATSURA CABINET

Looming over the disintegration of early Meiji cohesiveness was one of the giants of the Restoration, Yamagata Aritomo (1839–1922). A military man and perhaps the most rigidly conservative of the surviving autocrats who had guided Japan into the modern era, Yamagata had never approved of Prime Minister Saionji, whom he considered far too liberal. In particular, he disapproved of Saionji's blasé attitude toward socialism, which Yamagata feared as a dangerous foreign ideology.[1] He had made certain that Saionji's predecessor—and his own protégé—Katsura Tarō, had taken strong measures against the Socialists, and he had also succeeded in pressuring Saionji into taking a hard line. Saionji was never harsh enough to please him, however. Several developments, culminating in the Red Flag Incident of June 22, 1908 (when leftists waved banners inscribed "socialism" and "revolution" to greet a comrade emerging from prison), convinced Yamagata that the only way to expunge all dangerous thoughts would be to remove Saionji from office. He was able to effect Saionji's resignation, and on July 14, Katsura Tarō, General of the Army and one of Yamagata's "four horsemen," became Prime Minister for the second time.[2]

To a government obsessed with dangerous thoughts, all -isms were the same—socialism, naturalism, anarchism, individualism, egotism, free love.[3] To combat them (or "it"), a program of suppression and indoctrination would be necessary. The leaders believed that they could find and further inculcate the good old virtues of loyalty, filial piety, and patriotism in the young men of the countryside, many of whom would eventually go to the city. This had prompted the inauguration of the Local Improvement Movement (Chihō kairyō undō). Under Saionji, most of the practical steps taken in this direction—

administrative reorganization of villages, shrine mergers, centralization of grass-roots organizations—had been handled under the jurisdiction of the Home Ministry.[4] Katsura's approach included both a stepped-up police campaign against dangerous thoughts and a program of national re-education to be run by the Ministry of Education under the direction of Komatsubara Eitarō, a former chief of the Police Bureau under Yamagata and another of Yamagata's "four horsemen."

Komatsubara participated in the planning for a new imperial rescript, the *Boshin Shōsho*, which was drafted by the Home Minister, Hirata Tōsuke, under whom he had worked in the Local Improvement Movement.[5] This document was designed to inspire a "campaign of national mobilization" and to "stem the evil tide of extravagance and frivolity."[6] Speaking at the promulgation ceremony on October 13, 1908, the Vice-Minister of Education, Okada Ryōhei, said that the *Boshin Shōsho* had been prompted by a decline in the spirit of national unity caused by "many undesirable phenomena . . . such as naturalism and extreme individualism."[7]

As a counterpart to the Home Ministry's Local Improvement Movement, Komatsubara instituted programs of continuing education and so-called popular education (*tsūzoku kyōiku*). Further, under Komatsubara's personal direction a "top-flight committee was established . . . and instructed to 'rectify and review elementary school ethics, history and language texts.'"[8] This produced in 1910 a new formulation in ethics textbooks known as "national morals" (*kokumin dōtoku*), or, as later scholars tend to label it, the "family state" (*kazoku kokka*) ideology—the ultimate codification and spiritualization of the pro-imperial, anti-Tokugawa thought upon which the Restoration leaders had been bred. These ideas had been more or less taken for granted throughout the Meiji period (Hasegawa Tenkei was no product of the new textbooks!), but now they were consciously propagated as a national myth to combat the recent social unrest.*

From this time, Japanese children were taught Shintō myth as historical fact. The emperor was the "sacred and inviolable" descendant of the Sun Goddess through a family line "unbroken for ages eternal." "The nation was not *like* a family, it *was* a family, by virtue of the fact that the distant ancestors of ordinary Japanese households were offshoots of the main imperial family line." Filial piety for the individual family head was one and the same as loyalty to the warm, loving father of the national family, which in turn was synonymous with patriotism.[9] A parallel spiritualization of military codes and manuals took place between 1908 and 1914.[10]

---

*The myth was by no means fashioned out of whole cloth. Even during its most desperate days in the sixteenth century, the imperial house retained its mystique. Its shogunal commission was the ultimate prize for which the warlords fought. For sources of the mystique, see John Whitney Hall, "A Monarch for Modern Japan," pp. 11–64.

This warmly emotional nationalism became the orthodox myth taught, with increasing emphasis on national ethics, through 1945. Literature stood in direct opposition to the state's orthodoxy whenever it questioned the sanctity of the family, or implied a change in the family structure by portraying liberated women, or suggested that an individual might live for himself and not for his family as part of the family-state, or that the fulfillment of his own sexual drives was a legitimate end in itself, quite apart from the maintenance of the family line.

It was precisely all the family-centered values that naturalism questioned, and its emergence was taken by the government as another sign of familial and societal breakdown. A clash—and the expansion of censorship—was inevitable. In effect, just as Japanese fiction was reaching its maturity and formulating its disillusioned vision of modern man, the government was formulating its own program for the propagation of illusion. (Ironically, the Katsura regime would be hoist with its own petard, accused of producing textbooks that called into question the myth of an unbroken imperial line because of their vague account of the fourteenth-century split between the northern and southern courts. This debacle not only contributed to the fall of the government but left Komatsubara Eitarō as the only member of the Katsura cabinet without an aristocratic title.) [11]

THE QUESTION OF AN ACADEMY: KOMATSUBARA'S PARTY

The advent of the Katsura regime conveyed a strong sense that the government and conservative society were bearing down on literature with increasing severity. A need was felt for ameliorative action. Rumors began to circulate of government moves toward the establishment of an academy of the arts or literature, and several essays and interviews appeared, suggesting the functions that such a body might perform.

Newly returned from Paris, Nagai Kafū recounted his knowledge of the French Academy, but he made it very clear that he viewed the idea of any such establishment with suspicion. Even in France, he noted, the genuine creators of literature encountered more suppression and censure than protection from the academy. "If we Japanese naturalists [sic] are true to our principles, we should go unscathed by attacks and suppression meted out by society and government; indeed, I believe we will develop all the more fruitfully." An academy of dried-up old men, he added, would probably be of no help to literature and might impede the spread of ideas.*

*Nagai Kafū, "Akademī no naiyō," Shinchō (February 1909), in KZ 27:6–10. The identification of Kafū with naturalism, whether due to the interviewer or Kafū himself, indicates how all-inclusive the "school" was at this time.

Few other commentators shared Kafū's skepticism at this stage.[12] The January 1909 *Taiyō* featured a symposium, however, the title of which left no doubt that the growing interest in the idea of an academy was the result of censorship: "An Academy of the Arts and the Problem of the Regulation of Literature" ("Bungei torishimari mondai to geijutsuin"). It was a typical piece in that the majority of those interviewed looked to the establishment of an academy as a step toward understanding between writers and the government which would reduce the incidence of suppression, perhaps by acting as a review board in difficult cases.

Only one interviewee, the writer Kosugi Tengai, suggested that the "regulation" problem might actually be exacerbated if the government attempted to exploit such an academy for its own ends. The critic Miyake Setsurei went so far as to assert that regulation was a positive good because it forced writers to polish their skills in euphemism and thus contributed to the development of literary expression. As for an academy, he noted that the government was fond of setting up all sorts of committees and then ignoring their recommendations. The Katsura government especially, being of the Yamagata line, was not about to entrust censorship to such a body, something that might have been at least conceivable under Saionji.

All of the respondents assumed that censorship was unavoidable, primarily because the police had to adopt standards suited to the masses, who might actually be harmed by the views of the advanced few. According to Uchida Roan, however, the problem lay primarily in the writers' attitudes, not in the actions of the government. His spirited interview merits our attention.

As one lacking the talent to be a creative writer, said Roan, he respected those with the ability. He only wished they would respect themselves a little more. They fawned on the authorities the way they fawned on publishers, grateful for whatever crumbs they were thrown and frightened to ask for more. "I asked one publisher why he didn't pay more for manuscript, and he said it was because the writers are happy with what they get—they don't ask for higher fees." It was no wonder the politicians saw writers as sniveling, insignificant little men, he declared. Writers, he said, should realize that the government was finally powerless to hold back the surge of the intellectual tide.

Informed by the interviewer that plans for establishment of an academy were supposedly nearing completion, Roan was incredulous.

> I heard that Mori Ōgai made some sort of proposal to the government, but that's impossible! He's far too intelligent to do such a thing. It can't be true.* Just look

---

*But it was true. Ōgai records in his diary for November 5, 1908, that he sent a written opinion to Okada Ryōhei, Vice-Minister of Education, entitled "Government Measures to Be Taken With Regard to Novelists" ("Shōsetsuka ni taisuru seifu no shochi"). He followed on

at the Katsura government: they don't see any pressing need for or value in an academy. . . . Of course, I would be in favor of it, but no one really knows if it is going to be formed or not. In any case, the main thing, if it really comes up, is for the writers not to act like spineless parasites the way they usually do. They should say what they have to say, and if there's no agreement, then it's time for a fight! I want to see the writers write and not give a damn when the government starts banning their work.[13]

Roan would not have long to wait. *Taiyō*'s symposium appeared on New Year's Day 1909, and the first move toward some rapprochement with writers was taken by the government later that month. On the evening of January 19, Minister of Education Komatsubara Eitarō held a party for literary men at his official residence. Guests included Mori Ōgai, Natsume Sōseki, Ueda Bin (influential translator of European literature), naturalist critic Shimamura Hōgetsu, scholars Ueda Mannen and Haga Yaichi, and such traditional writers as Kōda Rohan, Iwaya Sazanami, and Tsukahara Jūshien. They were to meet with several officials of the Education and Home Ministries, including the Home Minister himself, Hirata Tōsuke.

Meetings between writers and the upper echelons of the government were not entirely unprecedented, but Prime Minister Saionji's "Gatherings in the Murmuring Rain" (*Useikai*, begun in 1907) had seemed more like private affairs reflecting his own interest in literature.* Komatsubara told his guests that he sought their opinions on what steps the government might take to encourage the "wholesome, high-toned development of literature."

As they sipped their drinks and Haga Yaichi explained to an appreciative Sōseki the difference between sherry and vermouth, the company discussed the "new literature" and its appeal for young people. The conversation focused on foreign literary academies and the possibility that the establishment of one such in Japan might benefit the development of literature. Sōseki said that he was not absolutely opposed to government "encouragement" of literature, although he feared it could have some undesirable effects. For one thing, any system of awarding prizes would probably be unfair since it would depend

---

November 9 with a hurried telegram when he found that the earlier piece had been leaked to the press. According to the report, Ōgai attributed Japan's decadence to the lack of artists among the leaders of society. He recommended the establishment of a foreign-style academy of some fifty members with a broad representation of poets and novelists, including Sōseki and Fūyō. See Mori Junzaburō, *Ōgai Mori Rintarō*, p. 179.

*Imai Yasuko argues convincingly that Saionji had some thoughts about developing a literary academy which were encouraged by several writers' naive enjoyment of this attention from the Prime Minister. All came to naught when his government fell. See Imai Yasuko, "Meiji-matsu bundan no ichi-chōkanzu," pp. 32–38.

Uchida Roan

總理大臣兼大藏大臣桂侯爵

Mori Ōgai (*Taiyō*, February 1909)

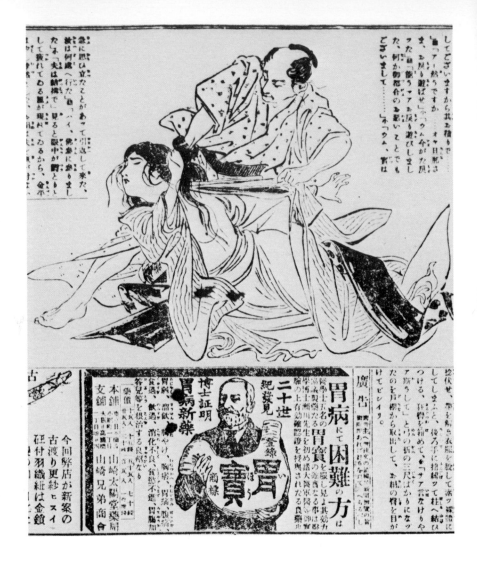

Nightstorm Okinu, Chapter 85 (*Kokumin Shimbun*, March 24, 1908)

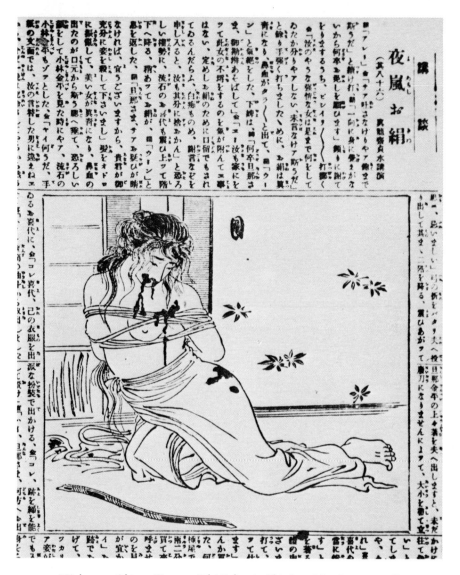

Nightstorm Okinu, Chapter 86 (*Kokumin Shimbun*, March 25, 1908)

Minister of Education Komatsubara Eitarō.
(*Taiyō*, August 1908)

Prime Minister and Minister of Finance Katsura Tarō
(*Taiyō*, August 1908)

Hiraide Shū, 1913

Natsume Sōseki, 1910

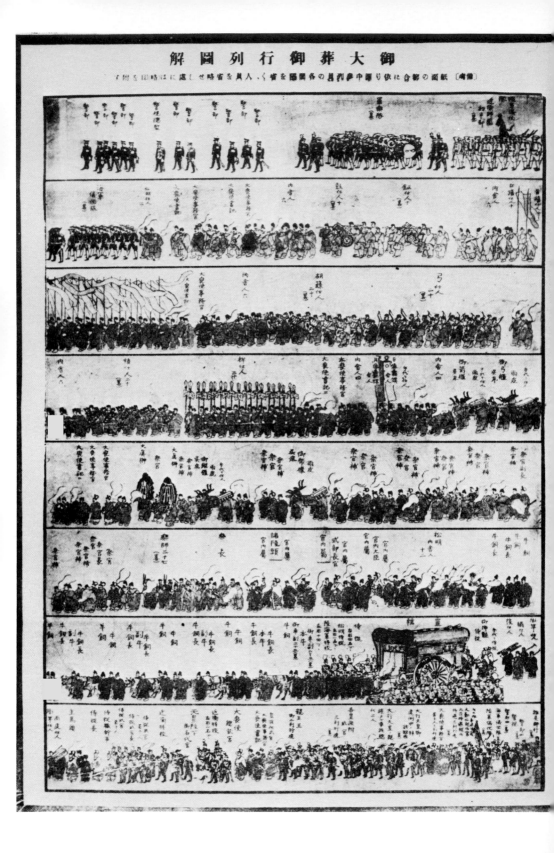

Above: General Nogi with the Peers' School Swim Club at Katase near Kamakura
(*Nihon oyobi Nihonjin*, October 1912)

Facing page: The funeral of the Meiji Emperor (artist's conception in *Asahi Shimbun*,
September 13, 1912)

General Count Nogi Maresuke

Tanizaki Jun'ichirō, 1913

upon the subjective views of a few contest judges. It was conceivable, too, that an officially sanctioned group would encourage works only of a type they approved, discouraging other types.

Hōgetsu remarked on the need for some means of recognizing the literary value of even those works considered harmful by the administrators, while Sazanami asked for the establishment of a system whereby bans could be lifted in deserving cases. The suggestion was made that an academy might actually purchase banned books for later resale when standards had changed.

After their catered Western dinner, Hirata Tōsuke spoke, in almost apologetic terms, about the "differences of opinion" that occasionally arose between writers and censors, saying that the policemen were the ones who decided what was banned: as Home Minister, he merely signed the documents. He was pleased to have this opportunity for frank discussion, he said, a view echoed by Ueda Bin, who added that he was glad of this chance to defend naturalism against the false charge that it was mere pornography.

All in all, the conversation seems to have been good-natured and rather desultory, ranging at one point to the subject of pederasty in Saga Province. Komatsubara later remarked that the gathering had been most informative for him, that he now hoped to be able to encourage literature for its own sake rather than as a means of preventing the decay of morals, and he hoped that concrete ideas would be forthcoming in future get-togethers. Vice-Minister of Education Okada Ryōhei, for example, had asked Mori Ōgai to look into the workings of the Schillerpreis as a possible model for a Japanese system. Everyone agreed that this was to be the beginning of a long and fruitful exchange.[14]

Over the next few months there were rumors that the government was investigating the private lives of certain writers as potential academy members, but the anticipated subsequent get-togethers never took place. One guess was that the sheer expense of such lavish banquets was prohibitive. A more likely obstacle was the kind of reaction aroused both by the first gathering and by the increasingly severe censorship being practiced by Hirata's Home Ministry, especially when (that July) it involved so important a potential member of the committee as Mori Ōgai.[15] There began to surface in this period an attitude of mistrust of the government and an independence of mind on the part of writers and critics that was almost more than the bureaucrats could comprehend.

Perhaps the most surprising reaction to the news of Komatsubara's dinner, considering the consistency with which he had advocated the establishment of an academy, was that of Hasegawa Tenkei. Literature was practically the only component of Japan's modern civilization that had developed so successfully without government support, he said, and it was simply creepy the way all of a sudden now this government, which had either ignored or suppressed literature, was beginning to act friendly. "We had better be careful, or we'll be finding ground glass in our rice and morphine in our sake. My only purpose in advocating an academy has been as a means of explaining to the authorities what literature is, not from any parasitic desire for government patronage. Any writer in such dire straits that he would stoop to accepting government support would be better advised to kill himself." [16]

A more balanced commentary, by one Shōkei (pseudonym), appeared in *Chūō Kōron*. Considering how strict this cabinet's censorship had been and how conservative—even reactionary—Komatsubara had been in such matters as the reform of the orthographic system, and the prohibition of drama in public schools, Shōkei found the Minister of Education to be surprisingly open and pleasant at the dinner. Of course, his remarks on literature showed him to be naive about modern fiction: it disappoints him when it is not full of heroic action. But perhaps, said Shōkei, we can hope that increased contact with writers may result in some lessening of the government's pressure. [17]

Some popular enthusiasm was evident in a silly contest concocted by *Taiyō* to have its readers pick the most promising people in various fields, from Prime Minister to Sumō Grand Champion. In one category, readers were to vote for the four most nearly ideal members of an arts academy (one each in the fields of belles lettres, criticism, fine arts, and music) if one were to be established. (As it turned out, Natsume Sōseki was the winning writer, but he refused the award.) [18]

More typical of what was to come, however, was the snide remark of a *Chūō Kōron* columnist to the effect that he could see Saionji mixing with writers, but he could not imagine men like Komatsubara and Hirata doing so. This growing contempt for the obtuseness of the Katsura government would doom the academy once the government became convinced of the need to establish it (in May 1911). By then the authorities had succeeded admirably in convincing the literate public that its only interest in free speech was to suppress it, and that its only interest in literature was to make it into an organ for preaching Confucian homilies.

9

Working Under the Mature System

THE DIET MAKES A PRESS LAW

If Komatsubara's dinner raised hopes for an easing of censorship, it did not do so for long. When the year had run its course, several commentators would note that 1909 had been the worst yet for the suppression of literature.[1] One set of figures showed a rise in morals bans from thirty in 1908 to forty-three in 1909.[2] More impressive than the figures, however, was the stature of the banned authors and works. Such major writers as Nagai Kafū, Mori Ōgai, and Tokuda Shūsei were banned, plus such other unimpeachably serious men as Gotō Chūgai and Uchida Roan. Translations of Tolstoy, Sienkiewicz, Andreev, and Gorki were forbidden (not to mention the "obvious" choice of Maupassant). 1909 was also distinguished as the year which saw the passage of the Diet's Press Law to replace the pre-parliamentary Press Regulations of 1887.

As originally presented to the Twenty-Fifth Diet, the Muramatsu Bill of 1908 would have left intact many important restrictions of the Press Regulations. But it would have done away with the court's ability to suspend publication of an offending periodical as well as prison terms with hard labor, and it would have allowed the reporting of preliminary judicial hearings. In this Diet session, however, Katsura had entered into an "understanding" with the anti-Yamagata Seiyūkai party, which had an unprecedented absolute majority. His cabinet was able to manipulate the parliamentary mechanisms as never before.[3] Thus, when the bill emerged from committee the next year, it had not only been gutted of its liberalizations but, in several important ways, had given the government an even freer hand.

According to Article 11, printed copies now had to be submitted to four censoring agencies instead of three, with the district procurator being added to the local procurator, the local police, and the Home Ministry.[4]

Article 12 stated that the indemnities newspapers and magazines were required to deposit were doubled to ¥2000 for Tokyo and Osaka and their environs, raised to ¥1000 for other cities over 70,000 population, and to ¥500 for the provinces. (A supplementary provision gave existing newspapers three years to make up the difference.)

In Article 23, the final authority for administrative bans was returned from the courts to the Home Minister, who could forbid the sale or distribution of any issue of a paper he deemed disruptive to peace and order or harmful to public morals. The Home Minister still could not prohibit the *publication* of a paper (that power he had lost in 1897), but he could (and, in the case of some leftist journals, actually did) ban every issue of a paper until either its registration became invalid (one hundred days without an issue could effect that in most cases [Article 7]) or it died for lack of income.[5] The prohibition of a paper's publication was left to the courts, which could take this action upon conviction for violation of news embargoes by the Ministers of the Army and Navy and the Minister of Foreign Affairs, or for violation of the prohibition against printing material "disruptive to peace and order or harmful to public morals" or which constituted "desecration of the dignity of the Imperial House." These broadened powers were spelled out in Articles 27, 40, 41, 42 and 43.

While there was some easing of the imposition of hard labor sentences, Article 9 stated that editorial responsibility was now shared equally by the editor-of-record and the actual editor. In Articles 19 and 36, prohibitions against the reporting of preliminary hearings were made even stricter, with a ¥500 fine involved.

The Diet's Press Law was in itself a reactionary document, containing all of the limitations on freedom of expression seen in the preconstitutional Press Regulations and reversing the Diet's earlier timorous step away from leaving unchecked power in the hands of the Home Minister.

Even with its "understanding," the Katsura government apparently had to do a good bit of cajoling to have the bill passed by the lower house, after which the House of Peers was pleased to add its approval. The Press Law went into effect on May 6, 1909.[6]

One English language paper, the *Japan Chronicle*, commenting on the new legislation, suggested that doing away with dummy editors would lessen the number of libelous articles (since it was here, rather than the political cases, that the practice was being abused). The paper also pointed out that interest was paid on the larger—but not excessive—bonds. It expressed shock, however, that both houses of the Diet had actually passed such a backward law, and it surmised that certain increased powers of the courts might lead to collusion between the administration and the judiciary.[7]

Within weeks of its implementation, the newspapers were complaining about the difficulties the Press Law was causing them.[8] By the end of the next

Diet session, on March 22, 1910, the increased censorship seems to have caused some regrets among a group of fifty-four members of the lower house. They felt—or claimed—that they had been deceived into passing the "revised Regulations," as one representative ironically referred to the new Press Law. The government had repeatedly assured them that although the new code might have some potential for limiting the people's rights, it would be implemented with the utmost discretion. Now, however, not even the most serious and patriotic publications were safe from the government.[9]

Whatever political games these men were playing, the fact was that the censors' pace had picked up considerably since the new Press Law had gone into effect, perhaps in part because it did make things more convenient for the police. Finally, however, these changes in legal text were less important than the changes in policy they represented. The Publication Law of 1893, which required submission of the finished book three days prior to publication, was left unaltered. But it, too, provoked controversy as enforcement became more stringent. The Katsura cabinet was ushering in a new era of repression.

Two Separate Worlds: Nagai Kafū

Earlier, we saw a 1908 advocate of manuscript censorship arguing that the banning of books was ineffective as anything but a financial burden to the publisher, because the Home Ministry did not usually take action until a book had been on sale for several days and the first edition had sold out (see above, chap. 2, p. 27). It came as a shock, then, to Nagai Kafū and the publisher of his *French Stories* (*Furansu monogatari*) when that large volume, containing over five hundred fifty pages of fiction, drama, impressionistic sketches, and essays, much of which had been published in periodicals, was banned on the very day it was submitted to the censors. This was probably on March 22, 1909, since the colophon of the few copies in "temporary binding" that survived shows a publication date of March 25.[10] In any event, the police confiscated the newly printed volumes so quickly that not a single copy could be distributed to the bookstores. "From *their* point of view, it was a great success," remarked Kafū dryly. The publishing company lost its entire investment and made the "outrageous" demand that Kafū repay his royalty on the first edition.[11]

Since most of the other pieces in the volume had been published in periodicals without incident, Kafū assumed that the story "Dissipation" ("Hōtō") and the play "Love in a Foreign Land" ("Ikyō no koi"), both previously unpublished and given special prominence as the first two works in the book, were at fault. Of course, the mere fact that the police had overlooked something in a magazine was no guarantee that it would measure up to their standards the second time around, as we have seen. An examination of some of the other stories and their subsequent publishing history suggests that these two pieces were not alone in catching the censor's eye.

The dissipation in the story of that title was doubtless considered objectionable because it involved no ordinary citizen but a government official, a young Japanese diplomat stationed in Paris. So disillusioned has he become with his country, his work, and even with the prostitutes whose aid he has sought in attempting to drown his sorrows, that he would like to commit suicide. "His is not the bravura manner, however, and we leave him hoping to be run down by a streetcar," notes Edward Seidensticker. "The story is a very wordy one, and it must have been still wordier when the industrious censor pushed his way through it." [12]

But Seidensticker was reading the story in the 1948 complete works version, by which time it had been restored to something approximating its original form. It had been excluded from both the 1915 revised (i.e., expurgated) version of French Stories and the 1919 complete works, but Kafū published it in a 1923 collection with the new title "Clouds" ("Kumo") and containing ten suppressed passages with fuseji* totaling 510 characters—or about a page's worth. The second edition of the complete works was published in 1926 at the height of the "Taishō democracy" years, when censorship policy was generally more liberal, and "Clouds" was included among the French Stories for the first time. Even more remarkable, seven of its suppressed passages were restored. That text has since remained standard, but the editors of the Iwanami complete works (1962–1965) have supplied the three missing passages in their notes. Of the three, only one is erotic, briefly describing the heat of a nearby fire against naked flesh. The other two passages question the value of serving the country and assert that the only reports of the Russo-Japanese War that ever made it through censorship were reports of victory. [13]

Seidensticker describes "Love in a Foreign Land" as "the sort of play one can scarcely imagine seeing performed. It has to do with a young Japanese who commits suicide with a young American lady, and another young Japanese who goes over the whole problem very articulately and finally returns to Japan, 'where human emotions are killed.'" [14] Kafū himself assumed that the following speech mocking the glories of Meiji civilization had something to do with the censors' decision:

> Ladies and gentlemen. I am grateful to be allowed the honor of introducing the up-to-date Japanese Empire to my dear American friends. . . . It is so peaceful a country that drunken gentlemen sleep happily in gutters. The state and the police and the people are as close as parents and children. Wherever the people gather, therefore, at political meetings, at performances of various sorts,

*See above, pp. 29–30, for an explanation of fuseji.

at athletic contests, there the police are in their grand uniforms, a source of boundless popular pride. . . . Wishing to make the earth in which their ancestors sleep as rich as possible, the Japanese decline to build sewers, but rather see to it that the last drop of sewage sinks into the earth and is not lost in the maws of fishes.[15]

Kafū also suggests that the police censor may have been disturbed by an exchange in which America is blamed for the vulgarization of Japan. Another unflattering view of Japan was contained in the story "Revulsion" ("Akkan"), which had been printed earlier in 1909 but which did not resurface until its postwar inclusion in the complete works—with a new title: "A Few Hours in Singapore" ("Shingapōru no sūjikan").*

At this rate, there seem to have been more diplomatic and political than moral elements involved in the banning of *French Stories*, despite the official rationale. "Love in a Foreign Land" and "Revulsion" were not even reprinted in the daring 1926 complete works, and in fact the play had to wait until the publication of the drama volume of the postwar complete works in 1953 before it could join a definitive edition of Kafū.[16] Readers in 1909 were not entirely deprived of these works, however: an article in the May *Waseda Bungaku* protesting the banning of *French Stories* gave detailed summaries of both.[17]

"Dissipation" and "Love in a Foreign Land" were probably not the only pieces that the censors objected to in March 1909. "Dance" ("Butō;" later "Yowa no butō" or "Midnight Dance") and "The Dancer" ("Maihime"; originally "Opera no maihime" or "Opera Dancer") had appeared together in a magazine in December 1908. They would not be included uncut in *French Stories* until the 1926 complete works, probably owing to the glimpses of bare thigh in "Dance" and the narrator's still more physical longing for a dancer on the Lyon opera stage: "This yearning can only be assuaged on that night when you allow my hands and lips to caress your tender flesh."[18] The vignette "Past Noon" ("Hirusugi") had not been published before and was never seen in print until 1948, in the postwar complete works. This short piece evokes the narrator's dreamlike mood when he awakens in the late afternoon to find the ravishing Paulette sleeping naked on his arm (presumably after a night of passionate lovemaking): "Your opulent breast rests against my cheek like a ripe fruit about to fall."[19] Japan needed forty years to prepare itself for such unbridled eroticism. (Or perhaps the censors had better literary judgment than they were given credit for. The volume, full of "young artists . . . bent on parodying themselves,"[20] might have been banned for offensive silliness.

*Discussed by Edward Seidensticker, *Kafū the Scribbler*, pp. 30–32. See also Seidensticker's quotation from "Port Said" ("Pōtosetto"; originally "Sabaku" or "The Desert") on page 30. This piece first appeared in June 1918 and was included in the 1919 complete works.

What else but good sense could explain the elimination of "Worshipping the Statue of Maupassant" {"Mōpasan no sekizō o hai-su"} from all but the postwar editions? Kafū's abject prostration of himself before the image of Maupassant is almost embarrassing.)[21]

Having spent his anger on the previous year's bannings of Molière and Zola, Kafū told a newspaper reporter, the suppression of his own work did not come as such a dreadful shock. He did not see how either "Dissipation" or "Love in a Foreign Land" could disrupt the public morality, but he concluded that "my thoughts on the matter are irrelevant." He was, he said, just a weak poet facing a strong government. No Japanese has ever fought for his rights in court as Flaubert, Baudelaire and others did to bring French art to its present state of freedom. I know, he continued, that the proper thing to do now is fight, but when I consider my chances of winning, I recall the general tone of freedom-loving French society, where art is highly prized: "If an author is going to struggle with the authorities for his rights, he must have sympathy derived from the general drift of society." Contemporary Japanese society has no great need for either freedom or art. The only ones who demand these are the few stepchildren of society who may have read Western books. The majority are pleased to have Japan's glory rest on military accomplishments.[22]

Kafū had two more occasions to express himself on censorship that year, and each time he stressed his identification with the stepchildren of society, the sensitive young artists in a hostile land. "As a writer, I have no particular thoughts regarding the suppression of a literary work in Japan," Kafū told an interviewer in the July 1909 *Chūō Kōron* after the June issue had been banned for Oguri Fūyō's story "Big Sister's Little Sister" ("Ane no imōto"). "The authorities don't read our stories and novels as literature or art: they treat them strictly as 'printed matter.'" He went on to say that writers neither knew nor needed to know the standards employed by the authorities. "We who publish fiction and the authorities who suppress it live in different worlds." Rather cynically, Kafū noted that they had banned Fūyō's story because "they wanted to, that is all. Of course, this sort of incident is deplorable for Japanese literature, but that is true only for those few of us who comprise the society of writers; for the state, which declines to recognize the existence of fiction and the other arts, it is simply a matter of course. . . . For them, fiction is nothing but a filthy abscess. . . . In order for the state to recognize the existence of art, the people must first come to respect art."[23] In another interview, Kafū added, "If we simply write what we believe and the authorities act on their perceptions, I see no objection to that. But as the age progresses, this problem will become increasingly difficult and will eventually have to be brought to some sort of conclusion."[24]

Kafū himself was not prepared to force the issue, and while he implied that writers ought to take the censors to court, he knew very well that there existed no judicial apparatus by which this could be done. In the end, faced with an impossible situation, Kafū could only conclude that writers and policemen lived in two separate worlds, that art was an irrelevancy, a means of escape. He concluded this and concluded this and concluded this over and over and over again in fiction, poetry, essays, and interviews until he had fashioned for himself and the public a unique persona embodying his bitter rejection of all that was respectable and thus acceptable to the state. There may well have been useless outsiders in Japan who dabbled in Edo art and erotica because they felt there was no place for them in the authoritarian state, but we do not know about them. They did not make a public career of it as Kafū did. "Look at me," his works say, "I am useless in your ugly, materialistic, hypocritical police state." Call it a pose; call it a rationalization for cowardice (although the fact is that most of his countrymen would have supported the censors all the way); the one thing that Kafū's stance did *not* represent was smug self-satisfaction. He tells us what he is escaping from and why. Nor is he afraid to admit that the escape is not completely satisfactory.

A story Kafū published in July 1909 is of interest both as an early example of the persona that Kafū spent his life creating and as a concrete demonstration of the kinds of steps taken by writers and editors to deal with the censors. While it does tend to be "wordy" and "diffuse," as Seidensticker says,[25] "Pleasure" ("Kanraku") is a simple narrative of three love affairs in the life of a writer in his forties as told to a younger associate. The theme is the collision between passion and reality, and in the course of spelling out the decline of passion in his life, the writer provides—at the cost of narrative cohesion, to be sure—something of a theory of art as practiced by Nagai Kafū.

It should be kept in mind that we have the story in four forms: (1) the magazine galley proofs with editorial markings; (2) the text as published in the magazine, which (to confuse matters) *was* banned, but not for "Pleasure";[26] (3) the text as it appeared in the book *Pleasure*, published on September 20, 1909, which was also quickly banned, apparently owing to the title piece and one or two other stories; and (4) the modern text.

As presented in "Pleasure," the writer (or "poet") lives for emotion, for recreating the profound, selfless ecstasy aroused by the sensual experience of life in all its varied forms:

> For me, there is nothing else but this passion, this desire to sing—without purpose or plan—of the whole of life and nature as my eyes have seen it and my heart has felt it. . . . To write good poetry, one must prize solitude. One must insulate oneself from family encumbrances, from the sanctions of society. . . . Now, I am utterly indifferent to what my family thinks of me. I am a poet; they are ordinary human beings. We belong to different lands, different races. Neither do I feel anger toward the state for its treatment of art. It was my choice and mine

alone to rebel against parents and teachers and become a poet, a man unneeded—
indeed, violently suppressed—by the state. . . . The state may try, with the
sickle of the law, to cut poets down to nothing, but they can never succeed: we are
like weeds that shoot up after the rain. . . . We are non-citizens, . . . and so I
have lived alone in rooms and chosen not to mix with people of good family. My
only park has been the streets of shame and degradation, my only gospel Baudelaire's *Flowers of Evil.* . . . Not even the birds could match my freedom, for I was
not merely indifferent to the welfare of my parents and to whether my brothers
were alive or dead: I truly paid no heed to my own tomorrow.[27]

The magazine editor took most of this in stride, but he apparently felt that
in the last sentence Kafū had gone too far, for the original manuscript read, "I
was not merely indifferent to whether my parents might die or *the country might
perish (kuni no sonbō)*." Kafū wrote a note in the margin of the galley proofs
saying he saw no objection to the italicized phrase, but that the editor could
suppress it with *fuseji* if he wished—which he did.[28] The modern text quoted
above follows the phraseology as Kafū rewrote it shortly afterward for the
book—which, of course, was banned anyway.*

In this story about the pleasures of love for a writer determined to live life
fully and sensually, several passages had to be composed with an eye to the
censor. Kafū claimed in one interview that he never wrote with such questions
in mind but left those decisions to the editor or publisher.[29] This was not
entirely true in practice, as the following passages demonstrate: "At dawn, the
weather suddenly turned cold, *and in our sleep we tightened our embrace, pressing
our bodies together ever more closely*, until at length we awoke from the sheer
discomfort." The italicized section was crossed out in the galley proof, becoming *fuseji* in the magazine. The book and the modern text read: "At dawn, the
weather suddenly turned cold, and feeling this we awoke."[30] Another passage
originally read as follows: "I would sit by a window or a pillar of the veranda,
*arms folded as I felt her leaning against me, the warmth of her skin seeping through the
soft silk of my sleeping robe*. And I would gaze at the shapes of the trees." The
proof page containing this and the sentence previously quoted has a marginal
note from the editor asking Kafū to revise the marked passages. Here again,
the magazine substituted *fuseji* for the italicized section, and Kafū later rewrote the sentence as follows: "Folding my arms across the soft silk of my
sleeping robe, I would sit by a pillar of the veranda or a window, and gaze at the
shapes of the trees." This revision appeared in the banned book and appears in
the modern text of the complete works.[31]

---

*In Sōseki's *Sanshirō* (1908), a major character says flatly, "Japan is going to perish." The
censors let it go, both in the newspaper and in the book. See SZ 4:22; for a translation, see Jay
Rubin, *Sanshiro* (Seattle: University of Washington Press, 1977), p. 15.

Having been angered by the publisher's demand for repayment of his first edition royalty on *French Stories*, Kafū was doubly gratified—and obligated—when the publisher of *Pleasure* (a different company) made no mention of his returning their advance of one hundred yen. He had submitted his manuscript in good faith, assuming that the previous untroubled publication of all nine stories meant no risk was involved. He immediately submitted a safer manuscript when the book was suppressed, and in late October of 1909 (just one month after the publication date of *Pleasure*) A *Kafū Anthology* (*Kafū shū*) was published with six of the nine stories and one additional piece. Missing were "Pleasure," plus a moving prose-poem on another Kafū-style social misfit entitled "Behind the Prison" ("Kangokusho no ura") and a story with a checkered past entitled "A Toast" ("Shukuhai").[32]

Like Masamune Hakuchō's 1908 story "Where?" (see above, pp. 65, 81), "Behind the Prison" might be seen as another predecessor to Sōseki's *And Then*, the ultimate portrait of a young Meiji intellectual too aware of his society's hypocrisy to become its willing participant. *And Then* would begin serialization in June 1909. Sōseki's protagonist, like the narrator of "Behind the Prison" (March 1909), would also be a thirty-year-old supported by a wealthy, sternly moralistic father and unable even to conceive of a suitable profession. In both works the change of the seasons plays a major role, but the seasons are primarily a backdrop to Sōseki's Westernized love melodrama. In Kafū's more traditional, contemplative short story the delicate, sensual perception of seasonal change becomes the central concern. Kafū has neither the space nor the intellectual apparatus for the extended development of ideas seen in the Sōseki novel, but "Behind the Prison" is not lacking in sharp social commentary. Here is one passage that may have excluded the story from the safer anthology:

> I thought of becoming an artist. But no, Japan is Japan, not the West. Japanese society does not need artists; indeed, it finds them a nuisance. The state has established education-by-intimidation and forces us to learn grotesque languages made up of sounds that no member of the Yamato Race ever pronounced—T, V, D, F. And if you can't say them, you have no right to exist in Meiji society. They have done this in the hopes that someday we will be able to invent some new-style torpedo or gun, certainly not to have us read the poems of Verlaine or Mallarmé—and still less to have us sing the "Marseillaise" or the "Internationale," with their messages of revolution and pacifism.[33]

Such observations were not arbitrarily inserted into the protagonist's mouth but were to be understood as the rationale both for his subdued lifestyle and for the somber tone of the whole. Uchida Roan was only reaffirming his antipathy toward escapist literature when he enthusiastically endorsed "Behind the Prison," hailing Kafū as Japan's "first authentic artist in the European sense": not an irrelevant entertainer, but "a man who draws the pure air of creativity from the foul stench of real life."[34]

The other story excluded from *A Kafū Anthology*, "A Toast," tells us less about the author than about the uses of *fuseji*. If moralistic critics needed any proof that the young could be corrupted by what they read, "A Toast" was it. The protagonist of this ugly little piece learns most of what he needs to know about sex from Edo erotica, modern novels, medical textbooks, and newspapers—plus variety theater performances and advice from his barber. Then he goes on to the whorehouses and searches for other ways to fulfill his "low, shameful, selfish desire" to fool around with women while he is still a student and unprepared to commit himself to anything permanent. His most despicable act is to help his similarly cultivated friend, Iwasa, hide out from the waitress whom Iwasa has made pregnant. Ten years go by, and Iwasa, now a respectable bank employee with a family of his own, hears that the waitress had a miscarriage and has become a prosperous madame. He cries out in joy to his friend, "We must have a toast! . . . My old sins are obliterated! . . . If only I had known, my conscience wouldn't have bothered me all these years!"[35] It is unclear at the end whether we are meant to join in the two men's laughter or condemn them for their hypocrisy.

With its ambiguous moral stance, "A Toast" leaves a bad aftertaste, and it received mixed reviews when it appeared in the May 1909 *Chūō Kōron*.[36] Several reviewers mentioned the unusually large number of suppressed passages. Apparently there were suggestions that many of these *fuseji* had been inserted in obviously innocuous places merely for the sake of arousing the reader's curiosity, and that because "A Toast" had been such a big hit for *Chūō Kōron*, the magazine was planning to print an even bolder piece in June with even more *fuseji*. "We were shocked at such slanderous notions," said the editors, "but even more shocking are the rumors that the police believed such articles and waited, ready to pounce on the next issue the very day it appeared." The editors related this in a special appendix to the July issue devoted to the banning of the previous month's issue for Fūyō's "Big Sister's Little Sister." "We are worshippers of literature and we are law-abiding citizens," they continued. "Thus we took the step of inserting a few *fuseji* in 'A Toast,' a fine piece of fiction, in order to make it harmonize with the law of the land. We agonized over each phrase, discussing it among ourselves for half a day."[37]

But "A Toast" had more than just "a few" *fuseji*, and some of them may well have been inserted gratuitously. *Chūō Kōron* is justly admired as a last bastion of liberal thought in the 1940s, but at this stage in its career—and especially in comparison with *Taiyō*—it was not an entirely serious magazine. Much of the hoopla it raised over literary censorship, beginning with the Fūyō appendix, seems to have been more in the interest of commercial gain than intellectual freedom.

A few examples of *fuseji* in the *Chūō Kōron* version of "A Toast" will serve to suggest the editors' approach. The narrator's nocturnal restlessness frequently brings him to bookstores, where, after some hesitation, he becomes "bolder and increasingly shameless, ardently poring over OOOOOOO books of fiction, art, or OOOOOOOOOOO medicine and such, not only for the momentary relief they provided, but in a calculated attempt to gain knowledge for future experimentation." In the modern complete works, the first omission has been filled in with "all sorts of," and the second—into which it would be grammatically impossible to fit anything much worse than nouns such as "anatomy" or "physiology"—has simply been eliminated.[38] In the modern text, the description of the narrator's first encounter with a prostitute moves directly from his awkward attempts at sophistication beforehand to his leaving the pleasure quarters the next morning, describing nothing in between. The magazine version is equally reticent, but it underscores the silence with a full column of dots. A little later in the text, the word "experienced" has been turned into *fuseji*.[39]

The censors could not have been ignorant of all the controversy surrounding "A Toast" and almost certainly banned *Pleasure* in part to make up for having missed the story the first time around. Apparently they took a bit more time to ban *Pleasure* than they had with *French Stories*, however.[40] Enough copies were distributed for the book to be not only widely reviewed but eventually praised by *Waseda Bungaku* as the outstanding work of fiction for 1909.

Since *Waseda Bungaku* was supposed to be a naturalist journal, and since Kafū was supposed to be a decadent antinaturalist, this event gave rise to one of the most heated (if typically pointless) literary debates of the late Meiji years. The naturalists were accused of not knowing their own minds, and apologists for the magazine tried to prove that Kafū's writing was perfectly acceptable as naturalism (after all, he had started out as a Zolaist, hadn't he?). In other words, this theoretical war, which raged on for months during 1910, had as its object a book that could not legally be sold but which everyone seemed to have read. The fact that it had been banned was never made an issue, even by the *Waseda Bungaku* editors who honored Kafū.[41] As with *French Stories*, the individual works eventually found their way into print, but the collection *Pleasure* was not reassembled in its original form until 1964, when the Iwanami publishers brought out volume 4 of the current complete works.[42]

PROTESTS AND COUNTERCHARGES

We have seen how closely Nagai Kafū's fortunes at the Police Bureau were intertwined with those of Oguri Fūyō. Several commentators suggested that in banning the June 1909 *Chūō Kōron* for Fūyō's "Big Sister's Little Sister," the censors were attempting to make up for having allowed "A Toast" to slip by. Whatever the actual causes may have been, the most noteworthy aspect of this case was the magazine's reaction, which was the first instance of something resembling organized opposition to literary censorship. For not only did the main body of the July issue carry strong criticism of the censors' action, but the editors attached a thirty-page appendix filled with their own indignation (some of which was cited above in the discussion of *fuseji* in "A Toast") and with statements from thirty different writers and critics representing a broad sweep of the literary world.

Unfortunately for *Chūō Kōron* and those who cooperated, the story in question no longer seems to have been worth the effort, as it might have been for Kafū's *Pleasure*, for example. Kafū was a maturing artist, while Fūyō was on his way out, and his drab little tale seems to reflect this. Wearily, it tells the story of the wife of a customs bureau employee who sacrifices her chastity to augment the family budget. She is led to take this step by her elder sister, a policeman's widow who prospers now as the madame of a brothel.[43]

Masquerading as a naturalist view of life's hard realities, the story is actually a rather sleazy presentation of the far-from-objective thesis that a whore lurks just beneath the skin of every respectable woman. The censors probably would have taken this in stride, however, had the heroine and her sister not been the wives of underpaid government officials. They were perhaps reacting as they had to Kafū's story of the dissipated diplomat. One critic was pointing in the right direction when he said it was the prime minister's fault, not Fūyō's, if people were living in Japan as shown in the story. And while another agreed that it was the portrait of petty officialdom to which the censors objected, most took the morals ban literally and either grumbled about the lack of published standards or asserted that the story was *not* obscene—in contrast to the low-minded censors themselves.

Despite the large number of contributors, the appendix was not very impressive. After all, it was a magazine's publishing venture, not something organized by writers banding together for social action based on a common conviction. Those who bothered to express an opinion on censorship in general said they agreed that obscenity ought to be suppressed by the government. A few practical suggestions did emerge—the institution of a means of appeal, a new system of temporary bans while the censors sought out expert literary opinion, a laissez-faire policy for writers of established reputation—but these came up at random as part of the scattershot approach. One *Chūō Kōron* columnist noted that Thomas Hardy, George Meredith, and other British authors had banded together in a protest to the London *Times* when Maeterlinck's *Monna Vanna* was banned from the stage,* but that such joint action could not be hoped for in Japan as yet, although he did not say why. The appendix to his own magazine seemed to bear him out.

We have already cited Nagai Kafū's contribution to the protest (see above, p. 120), but few of the others stand out. Perhaps most noteworthy are the lively remarks of Aoyagi Yūbi, himself a frequently banned author. Women may be stupid, he grants, but not stupid enough to turn to whoring just because Fūyō has shown them how it can help make ends meet. Aoyagi was being only partly facetious, and the fact that several issues of *Chūō Kōron* devoted a good deal of space to his farcical theories of sexual stereotypes[44] speaks well neither for the intellectual standards of the magazine at that time nor for its rather spasmodic activities on behalf of free speech. After its July effort for Fūyō, the August issue carried an article that unfavorably compared Japan's recent "dark" fiction with the novels of Dumas and the Chinese picaresque novel *The Water Margin* (*Shui-hu chuan*), concluding, "No wonder the authorities ban writing like this. If there were a god of literature, he wouldn't wait for the authorities to act!"[45]

A few months later, the magazine was again righteously defending a piece of third-rate fiction. The February 1910 issue of *Chūō Kōron* was banned for a story by the young naturalist writer Mizuno Yōshū. "The Inn" ("Ryosha") is a slice-of-melodrama about a man who again seduces an old love, now a wife and mother, causing both of them great pain when the time comes to part. Rather like a throwback to Zolaist-era Fūyō, with a dash of psychology and some heavy philosophizing about the meaninglessness of life thrown in for good measure, the wonder of this story is that *Chūō Kōron* wanted to print it at all, let alone fight for it.

But fight is what they did, and the next issue carried a large advertisement

---

*This incident may have made a greater impression in Japan than in England. I happened across references to it not only here, CK (July 1909): 183, but in CK (April 1910): 90, and NoN (November 1910): 95. The "protest" was a 22-line letter to the *Times* editor (June 20, 1902) which concluded, "We, the undersigned, are of the opinion that some protest should be made against a decision of the censorship by which the representation, in French, of a play by a distinguished French writer, of the highest moral reputation, has been forbidden in England." The array of signatories was more impressive than the letter itself, for included were not only Hardy and Meredith but Swinburne, Symons, Yeats, and eight others. An amused editorial on the same page noted how easy it was for patrons of a banned play to "form a 'society' for the nonce, subscribe the price of their seats in advance, hire a suburban hall, and the thing is done," which is exactly what happened with *Monna Vanna* and among other more recent works, *The Rose Tattoo* and *A View From the Bridge*. The English stage is still governed by the 1843 Theatres Act. See Morris L. Ernst and Alan V. Schwartz, *Censorship*, pp. 142–43.

announcing a lecture meeting to be held at noon on March 13, 1910, under the auspices of the magazine. Scheduled to speak on the problem of "the protection of literature" were several writers and critics, including the author himself. The April 1910 issue carried stenographers' transcripts of the speeches and noted that a crowd of more than twelve hundred had attended. The editors said they hoped that this feature would open the eyes of the authorities to how unfairly they had been suppressing literature and would demonstrate the seriousness of literature to those who still thought it frivolous.

The authorities were not likely to learn anything new from this tedious group of transcripts, however. The best that Mizuno Yōshū could do was ask the censors to be a little more open-minded and not approach everything they read as though dealing with criminals. The critic Kaneko Chikusui, speaking on the "collision of literature and morality," offered the usual dangerous argument that literary people want to have the truly bad stuff banned for them by the state.* And so forth.

Whether or not there was a commercial taint to these activities of *Chūō Kōron*, it is clear that the magazine had a long way to go before it would ultimately become the champion of liberal values in the militarist era. Perhaps it was as the sounding board for Yoshino Sakuzō, whose warnings against military encroachment upon the political sphere appeared from 1916 to 1930, that *Chūō Kōron* first earned the enmity of the government.[46] In later chapters we shall see the magazine as both hysterically antileftist (chap. 10) and as one of the last holdouts against the extinction of human rights in Japan (chap. 16).

Chūō Kōron was not alone in printing feature articles on censorship. The August 1909 *Taiyō* interviewed six writers under the title "How I Felt When the Sale of My Work Was Prohibited." Uchida Roan recounted his experience with "Broken Fence" in 1901, commenting that the authorities invoked bans so commonly nowadays that the practice was becoming meaningless. "If something of mine were banned now, when they are doing such stupid things as banning Molière, I would feel none of the shame I did then, and I suspect that everyone else feels as I do." (Three months later, Roan's translation of a novel by Henryk Sienkiewicz would be banned, provoking an outburst from Hasegawa Tenkei. Yes, he said, it contained a little kissing and hugging, but nothing provocative. At this rate, the words "husband and wife" would soon be outlawed. The authorities are always enjoining the people from doing

---

*For another example of this argument, see Hasegawa Tenkei, "Hatsubai kinshi mondai," TY (July 1, 1909), pp. 159–60. The effect of all this may have been merely to magnify Yōshū in the sights of the censors, for they shot him down again in June and August of 1909 and in the following April. When his works did appear, they were rarely free of *fuseji*. The censors did not do him in, however. His popularity faded quickly on its own.

anything that would be embarrassing if the foreigners got wind of it, but how embarrassing it would be for us if they were to hear we have been banning Sienkiewicz, Molière and Zola!)[47]

Kosugi Tengai, whose popular novel *Demon Winds of Love* (*Makaze koikaze*) had been taken out of circulation at the Imperial Library and forbidden stage performance by the police, said in the August 1909 *Taiyō*, "I don't expect the censors to have the literary insight of a writer—or even a critic, but they should at least have the level of appreciation of an ordinary reader and not approach these things as though being forced to watch people defecate." Tengai also voiced the all-too-often-encountered argument that he would like to see some real obscenity eradicated by the police. In the same issue of *Taiyō*, Tokuda Shūsei, whose miserable little story "The Go-Between" ("Baikaisha") had caused the banning of the April 1909 *Tōa Bungei*, said, "I don't know what their standards are—probably because they don't, either."*

Responding to the frequent charges of arbitrariness and unfairness, the Chief of the Police Bureau, Arimatsu Hideyoshi, explained in a newspaper interview that their Book Section had only four readers and it was impossible for them to get to everything. The bureau's standards were not stricter than before, he insisted, there were just many more works that deserved suppression. And it was not true that they were tougher with books and magazines than newspaper novels: these were simply harder to keep track of, coming out as they did in little snippets. The charges of an antinaturalist bias were not true: they not only had no idea what "schools" writers belonged to, they intentionally avoided remembering individual names so as to avoid prejudging any one work.[48]

The reporter who took this interview obviously knew where to go for it. This could not be said for the author of a curious piece on censorship appearing in the November *Nihon oyobi Nihonjin* which chiefly illustrated a general ignorance of the administration of censorship. Concerned that the recent number of banned works was astoundingly high, the reporter first visited the Tokyo Metropolitan Police Department, where an official in the censorship office told him that the department had no policies of its own but simply followed the orders of the Home Minister. Although the department was doing a certain amount of censorship, the one or two men assigned to the task could only read a fraction of what was published. In fact, very few books came to the department at all: here, they were more concerned with newspapers. It was the Home Ministry that received copies of all the books—and news-

---

*TY (August 1, 1909), pp. 135–44. Odagiri, *Hakkin sakuhin shū* (1948), pp. 423–24, suspects that "The Go-Between," a piece "utterly devoid of literary value," was written for Shūsei by a disciple. Whether he wrote it or not, Shūsei did appear in court when, in a rare case, he was prosecuted for having written the story. (See above, chap. 6, footnote p. 84).

papers, and magazines—published in Japan. "Properly speaking, the Metropolitan Police Department does not engage in the censorship of books." A second official told the reporter that all the newspapers were wrong in saying that the department was responsible for banning things: it simply carried out the instructions of the Home Ministry's Police Bureau, where the reporter should go for more informed opinions.

It was only then that the reporter went to interview Arimatsu Hideyoshi, who confirmed for him everything that he had been told by the Metropolitan Police, adding: "It's not *our* fault. Just look at what they are publishing these days!" Here, too, Arimatsu defended the bureau against charges of inconsistency by explaining that they only had three or four men who could not give everything equal attention. Besides, the process was a slow and careful one:

> The censor first shows a dubious work to the Ministerial Secretary, who shows it to me, and I am supposed to take it to the Minister himself. Of course, *he* is busy, too, like the rest of us, and he is *very* concerned about literature. "Let's think about it a while," he'll say, which goes to show you that we are not as precipitous in our actions as has often been charged. It is just that there are so many unavoidable cases. . . . And finally, the Police Bureau does not control literature as such. We are merely in the business of controlling publications from the point of view of public morality. If you see it this way, there should be no resentment or criticism. I wish the writers would have a little appreciation for the difficult job we are doing and not add to our burdens. . . . Do they have to write this kind of stuff? Isn't there anyone who wants to develop wholesome literature?[49]

MORI ŌGAI'S *VITA SEXUALIS*

In July 1909, the month that *Chūō Kōron* carried its appendix protesting the suppression of the Fūyō story, the much less widely read literary journal *Subaru* caused a good deal of comment when it printed a short novel tracing the sexual development of a high-ranking bureaucrat, the Surgeon General of the Army. Everyone wondered whether it should—or would—be banned, and the Ministries of the Army, Education, and Home Affairs all greeted the event with consternation.[50] The Surgeon General himself was not outraged, however, for it was he who had written the novel and littered it with enough parallels to his own life so that the autobiographical intent was unmistakable.

Mori Ōgai's readers should not have been surprised to find him writing in this personal vein, for he had begun to pick up the pieces of his nearly abandoned literary career in March 1909 with a story of domestic crisis, "Half a Day" ("Hannichi"), a work so uncomfortably close to home that Ōgai's wife forbade its subsequent publication.[51] And if anyone could remember back to

1890, he had caused quite a stir with his first story, "The Dancer" ("Mai-hime"), when he was fresh home from Germany and an affair like the one in the story.

Ōgai had faded quickly as a writer of fiction, however, producing only three stories, all of which derived from his German experience. After the last of the trilogy appeared in January 1891, Ōgai had confined his literary activities to criticism and translation. When the new writers began to emerge after the Russo-Japanese War, he had had the unsettling experience of reading about himself in the past tense, listed among the now useless "old men" along with Ozaki Kōyō, Kōda Rohan, and Tsubouchi Shōyō, whose "gold-plated" writing consisted of nothing but stylistic polish and clever plots.[52]

As Ōgai tells the story in *Vita Sexualis*, the writing of Natsume Sōseki first made his arm "itch" with the desire to show that he, too, could write intelligently. This would have been in 1905, when Sōseki published *I Am a Cat*, but before Ōgai could respond, other writers had produced parodies with such titles as *I, Too, Am a Cat* or *I Am a Dog*, which had given him second thoughts.

> Meanwhile Naturalism had begun. When he read works of this genre Kanai [i.e., Ōgai] felt no particular desire to emulate them, but for all that he found them very entertaining. He was amused but at the same time a strange thought occurred to him.
>
> Whenever he read a Naturalist novel it seemed that whatever the characters in the story were doing it invariably involved the representation of sexual desire, and criticism seemed to accept this as a true reflection of life. While he doubted whether life really was like that, he did sometimes wonder whether he perhaps deviated from the normal human psychological state in that he felt indifferent towards sexual desire; in particular he worried that he might have been born with that abnormal characteristic called frigidity.[53]

Ōgai's protagonist goes on to explore the major turning points in his sexual development with almost clinical detachment (not to say tedium), beginning at the age of six, continuing through twenty-one, and concluding that, yes, he supposed the sexual drive was indeed a very strong one but that, with a little effort, it could and should be controlled. In his own case, he decides that "he had known himself too thoroughly, even as a boy. His intellect had withered his passion while it was still germinating."[54] This may be all to the good, he feels, but he is still hesitant to allow his son to read the manuscript, less from a fear of corrupting him than from a concern that it might make the boy as indifferent to sex as he. At the end, Kanai decides not to publish the manuscript—a decision Ōgai negated by publishing it as *Vita Sexualis*, only to have it banned, after some hesitation, by the authorities.

What Ōgai has done in this short novel, then, is "scientifically" to have studied sex as the naturalists claimed to do. But he has come to very different conclusions. The sexual urge is not an irresistible force but an occasional annoyance. In the process of presenting his frigid protagonist, however, he has been less than fair to naturalism—particularly since the above-quoted characterization of naturalism is specifically limited to the period *before* the Debakame Incident, during which time, as we saw earlier, sexual themes were relatively rare. In this ensuing year and a half, a good deal more explicitly erotic literature had appeared, most notably from the pen of the antinaturalist Nagai Kafū, whom Mori Ōgai would recommend for a professorship at Keiō University in January. Ōgai's own "Half a Day" had suggested that the conflict between a mother-in-law and daughter-in-law had a strong element of sexual rivalry: at one point, the young wife even calls the protagonist's mother "sexcrazy."[55] His "Hypnotism" ("Masui"), which preceded *Vita Sexualis* in *Subaru* by one month, raised eyebrows by portraying a doctor who uses hypnotism to seduce his female patients. There seems to have been a "model" problem with this story, too, as was often the case with naturalist fiction, but in this instance the writer was reprimanded by Prime Minister Katsura himself.[56] The closer we look, the more absurd appears the distinction between naturalism and its opponents.

It is well known that Mori Ōgai was the first to introduce the name of Zola to Japan (in 1889, the year after he returned from Germany) and that his primary purpose in writing at the time was to condemn French naturalism as pornography. According to Richard Bowring, however, Kobori Keiichirō has convincingly demonstrated that at this early stage Ōgai was relying entirely on the arguments of Rudolf von Gottschall, which had been in vogue during his stay in Germany (1884–1888).[57] In 1893, he wrote that "the so-called Realists are getting more and more obscene and bestial. . . . What is realism? One could define it as that which is based on psychological study and which uses shock tactics such as brutality or obscenity."[58]

Thus, when Japanese writers after 1906 began giving their work the naturalist label that Ōgai had rejected twenty years before, he was better prepared than anyone in Japan to assume that this was a literary throwback bound to be "obsessed with sexual instincts,"[59] and to join in the uproar against "Debakame-ism." The view of naturalism in *Vita Sexualis* is little more than an expression of Ōgai's long-standing prejudice against European naturalism.

This was just the beginning of one of the most thoughtful and creative periods in Ōgai's life, however. *Vita Sexualis* appeared a mere four months after "Half a Day," which was the very first story Ōgai had written in modern colloquial Japanese, and which inaugurated an unprecedented spate of original and translated fiction. After the shock of having his own work banned, and after seeing the Home Ministry's campaign against the twin evils of socialism and individualism, Ōgai abandoned the view seen in *Vita Sexualis*. "It is quite natural that literature should penetrate the impulsive side of life," he wrote in November 1910, "and when it does so, the impulse of sexual desire must be revealed." [60]

Ōgai went on to do a good bit of such "revealing" both in his translations and his original writing.* Far more abhorrent to him than the naturalists' interest in sex—an interest that Ōgai shared and was stimulated to pursue because of the obvious seriousness of the new writers—was the Home Ministry's attempts to suppress the "dangerous" writings of the younger novelists. By banning *Vita Sexualis*, a work that in fact reflected some of the popular and official misconceptions about naturalism, the government succeeded only in encouraging Ōgai in his sympathies for the young iconoclasts. "If we cannot make a thing public because it is considered dangerous," he said in October 1909, "we will be unable to translate any works that express modern ideas, and that includes Tolstoy, Ibsen, Maeterlinck and Hofmannsthal. You would have to reject the whole of modern literature and enforce a kind of literary seclusion policy." [61] (For an examination of Ōgai's literary opposition to censorship, see below, chap. 10.)

Ōgai's unique position made the banning of *Vita Sexualis* a sensitive problem for the bureaucracy. *Subaru* appeared on July 1, and rumors flew all month while the authorities hesitated to take action. For one thing, Ōgai was being considered by the Ministry of Education for receipt of the Doctor of Letters degree—awkward to award a newly labeled pornographer. The degree was bestowed on the twenty-fourth of the month, and on the twenty-eighth, well after most issues had been sold, *Subaru* was banned. Although no official mention was made of the specific work that had been found offensive, Ōgai "heard" that *Vita Sexualis* was at fault. He mentioned this "circumspectly" to Army Minister Terauchi, but on the sixth of August, the head of the Police Bureau came in person to the Army Ministry on the matter. As a result, Ōgai was reprimanded by Ishimoto Shinroku, the Vice-Minister of the Army. [62]

Nihon oyobi Nihonjin somehow got wind of this, adding to its account of the interview that Ishimoto had asked Ōgai to end his literary activities. Ōgai reportedly listened, expressionless, but he was no longer the man who had allowed his superiors to "exile" him to Kyushu ten years earlier. He was determined to continue his writing. [63] This is exactly what he did, of course, but Ishimoto wanted a clean division between Ōgai's military and literary careers. That November, he ordered Ōgai not to sign his legal name—Mori Rintarō—to unofficial articles in newspapers, so as to avoid giving the impression that he was speaking or writing from his official capacity. [64]

*For a good look at these writings, see Richard John Bowring, *Mori Ōgai and the Modernization of Japanese Culture*, pp. 171–81, 228, 264, 266.

Owing to bureaucratic confusion and delay over how to deal with *Vita Sexualis*, a rumor began to circulate that Ōgai could publish things that for anyone else would have been banned immediately.[65] One reporter specifically asked Police Bureau Chief Arimatsu about the matter. "That's ridiculous!" Arimatsu fumed, insisting that some irregularity in the submission of the magazine to the censors had taken a week to correct and had resulted in a delayed reading.[66] This hardly explains the twenty-seven-day hiatus, but it does bring the dates of the Home Ministry's decision on the ban and the Education Ministry's decision on the doctoral award into a position where one would have been more likely to influence the other. (The doctoral committee had asked Ōgai for an up-to-date curriculum vitae on July 6.)[67]

Since the ban had been instituted so late, *Vita Sexualis* was another of those works widely reviewed and discussed despite its having been suppressed. The January *Chūō Kōron* termed it one of the more noteworthy novels of the year, without even bothering to mention that it had been banned. According to one fugitive report, some used book stores were selling copies of the banned *Subaru* for four times the original newsstand price.[68] (If true, they were taking quite a chance, since Article 175 of the Penal Code stipulated a maximum fine of five hundred yen.)[69]

One critic who came to the defense of *Vita Sexualis* during the suspenseful month of July was Ōmachi Keigetsu, the man who had so scathingly denounced Yosano Akiko for the "traitorous" epistolary poem to her brother fighting at Port Arthur (see chap. 5). According to his antagonist Hiraide Shū, Keigetsu was even more violently opposed to portrayals of the dark, ugly side of life than were the officials of the Home and Education Ministries. But for *Vita Sexualis* Keigetsu had only the highest praise. "Not only is it harmless to public morals," he said, "but every boy and young man in the country should be encouraged to read it. . . . I respectfully urge them to grasp the extraordinary character of the man as they read Ōgai's sexual history; it fairly dances on the page."[70]

Uchida Roan wrote a three-part article for the *Asahi* literary column in which he deplored the authorities' decision to ban Ōgai's "bold, scientific" study of sex. Like Keigetsu, he saw its value as an educational document.* Had such an important book by such an important man been suppressed in Europe, Roan said, it would have become a major social issue. But because almost no one read *Subaru*, banning it had simply transferred it from one form of obscurity to another. In the West, he noted, the mystery surrounding

---

*A rather less penetrating assessment of the book doubtless prompted the University of Washington Library's decision to confine its single copy of the English translation of *Vita Sexualis* to the Health Sciences branch where, like other books on sex (and drugs), it is kept under lock and key. Thanks to Linda Rubenstein for this bit of information.

procreation since primitive times was giving way to research—Krafft-Ebing, Ellis—but in Japan the traditional antiscientific morality and the traditional hypocrisy still prevailed. Ōgai's book was a serious study, said Roan, and should not have been banned until the *real* vita sexualis being flaunted by politicians and gentlemen in the houses of assignation was banned.[71]

Just a few days after the magazine was released, Ōgai heard that a publisher was interested in producing *Vita Sexualis* as a book. Nothing ever came of the plan, of course, and in 1924, two years after Ōgai's death, one student of censorship was still wondering whether the novel would be included in the first complete works, then beginning to appear.[72] Because the ban had only named *Subaru*, there was no legal impediment to printing *Vita Sexualis*, and indeed this time the censors did not prevent its inclusion, apparently uncut. There were several prewar editions of the full text.

EXTRALEGAL ARRANGEMENTS:
MORITA SŌHEI AND TANIZAKI JUN'ICHIRŌ

As our final illustration of conditions for writers and publishers working under the mature censorship system, we shall examine two cases handled through extralegal channels. The first demonstrates the increasingly public, widespread nature of such practices. The second expands on this and, using the example of one of Japan's best-known novelists, illustrates some of the difficulties of starting a career in the Katsura era.

A major event—or nonevent—in the publishing world during the latter half of 1909 was the delayed appearance of volume one of the novel *Sooty Smoke* (*Baien*), Morita Sōhei's fictionalized account of his affair with Hiratsuka Raichō. This was the liaison that had caused such an uproar as the "Climax of Naturalism" when the couple was prevented from committing their planned love suicide in March 1908. (See above, pp. 89–91. The affair itself is anachronistically known as the Sooty Smoke Incident.) The sensation had made of Morita Sōhei a virtual social outcast, but Natsume Sōseki had arranged for him to serialize his novelization in the *Asahi Shimbun* from January to May of 1909. "All the girls are reading it," said one female educator, who insisted she had no choice but to read it herself to find out what interested her students. The *Asahi* was forbidden on the campus of Raichō's alma mater.[73] Some idea of the eagerness with which each day's installment was awaited can be gained from Sōseki's own *Asahi* novel of that year, *And Then*, although Sōseki's protagonist is clearly contemptuous both of the work's imported modernity and the "fleshy smell" that was attracting so many readers.[74]

The censors, too, were attracted, and apparently they cautioned the *Asahi* several times without actually resorting to a ban. When it came time to publish the book, however, they were not so lenient. As early as July they were rumored to be forbidding its publication or at least threatening a ban unless Sōhei did some revising.[75] Meanwhile, both Natsume Sōseki and Mori Ōgai were writing prefaces for the forthcoming book. Sōseki printed his as the inaugural article of his *Asahi* literary column on November 25, 1909, calling it "Preface to Volume One of *Sooty Smoke.*" (Ōgai's appeared in the December *Subaru.*)*

Sōseki's preface revealed that there was not supposed to *be* a volume one of *Sooty Smoke*, that in fact Sōhei had hoped to publish the entire novel as soon as its serialization ended in May. But the new regime's strict censorship had rendered all but the early chapters—about one-fifth of the book—unprintable. The publisher had gone so far as to have the type set, but he had checked with the Chief of the Police Bureau, who had warned him that its sale would definitely be prohibited, and so the project had been abandoned. Then someone had suggested that at least the inoffensive part might be brought out as a book, which they could call "volume one." It would portray the hero Yōkichi on a long-delayed visit to his rural birthplace, where his insufferably ordinary wife and their new baby were staying. It would bring him back to Tokyo, but it would not introduce the modern, liberated (cigarette-smoking!) heroine or show the torrid love affair that had excited so much comment.

No one could possibly object to this part of the book, says Sōseki. "And as far as I am concerned, this section is actually better than the rest. . . . The latter half of *Sooty Smoke* is full of ostentatious nonsense."[76] An illustration of Sōseki's ungracious observation can be found in the dialogue in chapter 19 from which the title derives: "I love to watch black, sooty smoke rising like this," says the heroine, Tomoko. Yōkichi responds, "Is that because it seems to express symbolically [*shinborikaru-ni*] the tumult in your heart?"[77]

Volume one finally appeared in February 1910. The publisher resorted to yet another extralegal technique, substituting *fuseji* for many of the novel's inflammatory passages, in producing the three subsequent volumes between then and November 1913. It is not always clear, however, why the publishers chose the lines they did for suppression. A 1930 edition preserves the narrator's commentary, "She knew that she was inflaming his masculine desire." On the same page we find a row of Xs instead of the italicized line in the following: "The waiter went out again. Yōkichi took advantage of the opportunity to slide over and touch her fingertips. Immediately Tomoko relaxed the stiff posture she had been maintaining and, *grasping Yōkichi by the wrist, she suddenly pulled him toward her.* His chair fell with a clatter, and at last their four lips met.

---

*A one-act, two-scene dialogue, Ōgai's "Shadow and Form" ("Kage to katachi") viewed Sōhei's hero and heroine as reincarnations of the principal characters of D'Annunzio's *Triumph of Death*, but it said nothing about censorship. *Subaru* (December 1909): 99–107.

They held their breath as long as they could endure it."[78] Apparently it was more shocking that the woman had taken the initiative than that they had actually kissed—and so messily, too.

Sooty Smoke was not the only work to go public with its extralegal negotiations. In Sōseki's preface and in other sources, however, we see that the channels for such communication were far from regularized. One gossip column item claimed that a certain author had been confident his book would not be banned, because he had asked an official he knew at the Ministry of Education to request a friend of his with the police to have a censor look at the risky passages. Only then did he dare to publish it.[79] Satō Kōroku told an interviewer that his publisher had sent the contents of an anthology of his to the censors, one story at a time (presumably as the type was being set), and was forbidden to publish only "Revenge," the sleazy little story mentioned earlier (see above, p. 64).[80] By the 1920s, however, extralegal arrangements would have become so formalized that the issuing of cautionary notices and expurgation orders would be included in Police Bureau statistics.

The most startling instance that I have seen of public acknowledgment of cooperation between the producers and censors of literature occurred in 1917. This involved a story by Tanizaki Jun'ichirō (1886–1965), a writer well known in the West for such erotic masterpieces as *The Key* (*Kagi*, 1956) and *Diary of a Mad Old Man* (*Fūten rōjin nikki*, 1961–1962).* A discussion of this incident will take us well beyond the period in question, but it will provide us with an excellent opportunity to trace the early years of a career that began at this time, one that was frequently beset by censorship problems (and so will be of recurring interest to us), but a career that succeeded nonetheless in exploring those dark areas of the human psyche for which there could be no room in the *kokutai*.

Tanizaki, age twenty-four, and a few literary friends at Tokyo Imperial University had barely managed to publish the founding issue of their journal *Shinshichō* on September 6, 1910, and to begin selling its five hundred copies when the Home Ministry banned its sale. The ban was not for erotic content, however, and certainly not for Tanizaki's contribution, a rather pointless one-act play, "The Birth" ("Tanjō"), which recreated the superstitious atmosphere surrounding the birth of an important eleventh-century figure.† The police

---

*Translated by Howard S. Hibbett as *The Key* (New York: Alfred A. Knopf, 1961) and as *Diary of a Mad Old Man* (New York: Alfred A. Knopf, 1965).

†One might see here Tanizaki's "history-shaped-by-the-flesh" theme, but aside from the wild atmosphere of chanting priests and possessed mediums, the point of the piece is a bit of historical pedantry. This is the birth of the future Emperor Goīchijō (r. 1016–1036) to the Empress Akiko in 1008 and so the beginning of Fujiwara no Michinaga's unshakable hold on the throne—which is no doubt what the infant "whispers" to Michinaga at the end.

suddenly confiscated the unsold copies one night because someone had been tardy in submitting the required sample copies to the Home Ministry. Upon payment of a small fine, the ban was lifted a few months later and the confiscated copies were returned. The whole business was thought by some to have been a cynical attempt by the police to nip a new journal in the bud.[81]

Although this particular ban on a technicality came as a surprise, Tanizaki and the others had been aware of the need to take the censors into account when launching their new magazine. This is why "The Birth" became Tanizaki's first published work rather than his famous story "Tattoo" ("Shisei"), which he had written earlier. The members of the coterie had met to discuss the contents of the first issue and had decided that the story should be rewritten to reduce the likelihood of a ban. Never a speedy writer, Tanizaki could not manage the task by press time and had substituted "The Birth."

Despite the delay, Tanizaki always considered "Tattoo" his maiden work. It surely does comprise the archetypal statement of his sado-masochistic, fetishistic view of the sexes. A sadistic tattooer, who has long wished to engrave his art upon the skin of a beautiful woman, finds the perfect living canvas through a fleeting glimpse of her foot. She is an innocent young girl, but he quickly awakens her to the vampire lurking within and tattoos a large spider on her back, himself like a male spider sacrificing his life's blood. Not Tanizaki's most subtle piece, it is nevertheless a perfectly crafted little tale which looms much larger in the memory than the six or eight pages required to print it.* So perfectly is the late Edo setting matched to the story's lush beauty, and so precisely does the outlawed craft of tattooing symbolize the artist as a rebel in Tokugawa society, that one can hardly imagine the story as anything but an Edo piece. Yet this may be a case in which the threat of censorship helped improve a work of art, for according to Tanizaki, the little gem of a tale we have now had been much longer and had had a contemporary setting until he rewrote it for the third issue of *Shinshichō* that November.[82]

Not only did the story itself appear in that issue but also a piece called, in English, "Real Conversation," purporting to record an actual editorial meeting in which the revision of "Tattoo" was discussed. "Look at this manuscript," says Kimura Sōta, "All these good lines crossed out—and with such obvious reluctance! Like cold-blooded murder." Watsuji Tetsurō opens the manuscript and replies, "I see what you mean. 'Skin' has been changed from the sensuous '*hada*' to the clinical '*hifu*.'" "That's nothing," counters Kimura. "It must have killed him to take out a line like this: 'Her sleeping flesh lovingly swallowed each sharp-pointed shaft.' And then the bath scene!"[83]

Continuing financial difficulties coupled with another ban in March the

---

*Translated by Howard S. Hibbett as "The Tattooer," in *Seven Japanese Tales* (New York: Alfred A. Knopf, 1963).

following year put an end to *Shinshichō* after only seven issues, but Tanizaki went on publishing in other small journals, such as *Subaru* and Keiō University's *Mita Bungaku*. His first work to cause a ban was a story called "Blizzards" ("Hyōfū"), which Nagai Kafū, the editor of *Mita Bungaku*, chose to include in the October 1911 issue. Perhaps Kafū himself liberally scattered the story with *fuseji* to ward off the censors (although he claimed it arrived too late for him even to read it before sending it off to the printers), but the effort proved wasted and *Mita Bungaku* suffered its second ban in four issues.*

Tanizaki's tenth published work, "Blizzards" ranks with "Tattoo," the shockingly scatological and sado-masochistic "Children" ("Shōnen," June 1911), and the slightly less perverse study of male masochism "The Jester" ("Hōkan," September 1911).[84] With enormous vitality and irony, Tanizaki tells the story of Naokichi, an artist who has preserved his chastity to the age of twenty-four, but who loses all control when he becomes infatuated with a courtesan whose "nostrils, viewed from beneath, had something eerie about them."[85] For these nostrils, Naokichi nearly destroys himself with sexual overindulgence. To regain his health, he embarks on a six-month's walking trip, vowing to keep himself pure for his love. (She, of course, is free to go on selling her body.) With the return of his vigor, however, comes an epic battle to uphold his vow. He manages to ward off all temptation and to come through the terrible blizzards of the north, only to return to Tokyo in even greater physical debilitation than when he left. In this outrageous comedy's final black curtain, the emaciated Naokichi dies of apoplexy when sexually aroused.

Despite the ban and the *fuseji* (which Tanizaki never did fill in), the results of publishing "Blizzards" were fortunate indeed for him. The story caught the eye of Takita Choin, the influential editor of *Chūō Kōron*, who sought out the young writer in his tenement lodgings and commissioned him to write his first story for a commercial publication.[86] Thereafter, the major portion of Tanizaki's works appeared in *Chūō Kōron* company publications. His career was off and running.

As much as *Chūō Kōron* supported Tanizaki, however, there seems to have been at least one moment of hesitation.[87] This came in 1916 after Tanizaki's works suffered four bans in close succession, two of them in two separate magazines in the same month (September 1916)—surely a record of some sort—which made Tanizaki appear to be a favorite target of the Police Bureau.[88] *Chūō Kōron* had been banned in March 1916 because of him, and they were apparently hesitant to go through that again merely on the strength of his name. The work in question, "Sorrow of the Heretic" ("Itansha no kana-

---

*As a result, the Keiō administration ordered him to submit the edited proofs to them for examination before printing. He did this gladly, leaving questions of reputation up to them, so that editorial decisions could be entirely literary. See "Fumihogo," KZ 14:347–51.

shimi"), had little that could be used against it besides the Tanizaki name—
certainly nothing overtly erotic, as in the stories that got him in trouble. It is
toward the extralegal negotiations regarding the publication of this story in
July 1917 that the foregoing discussion has been circuitously heading.

Readers familiar with Tanizaki in English translation will not be surprised
to learn that his intense sensuality was often more than the censors could
abide. It is perhaps less well known that this most imaginative creator of
highly wrought fiction did occasionally write in an autobiographical mode
closer to the Japanese mainstream. "Sorrow of the Heretic" is one such piece,
and it is devoid of the obsessive Tanizaki sexuality. Thus there is some irony in
the fact that this story should have been handled so prudently, as Tanizaki
himself set forth in an introduction first printed with the story in *Chūō Kōron*.
The following is a paraphrase:

> This story was supposed to have appeared nearly a year ago, in the September
> [1916] issue. I completed it in August, the type was set, but then some of the
> editors began to feel that it might cause the magazine to be banned and decided
> to postpone its release. According to the editors, there is a moralistic tone to this
> work that is rare in my fiction, but the clashes between father and son are
> presented too nakedly; they hurl crude phrases at each other that the censors
> would be certain to take out of context, and the story would be banned as
> potentially corruptive of lowbrow readers. It also happened that a new Chief of
> the Police Bureau had come into office just then, and we thought it best to get
> a line on his new policies if we could and revise the necessary passages according
> to those.*
>
> I have almost never written stories based on real-life models, first because it
> might be embarrassing to them, and secondly because I myself find the idea of
> self-exposure unbearable. This story, however, is different. It is the most faithful
> representation I could make of my family—the four of us—at that time. It is my
> only confessional work. I had long postponed writing it, fearing that it would
> only add to the burdens of my parents' already difficult life. But when their
> business began to succeed the year before last and my wife presented them with
> their first grandchild (somehow, it seemed, making up for my years of filial
> impiety), I finally felt secure enough to undertake the work. The publication of

*Nagata Hidejirō (1876–1943) had been governor of Mie Prefecture until coming to this
post in the autumn of 1916. See his *Nagata Hidejirō senshū* (Chōbunkaku, 1942), p. 101. He
would later serve as mayor of Tokyo and in two cabinet positions. A classmate of the haiku poet
Takahama Kyoshi, he published his own haiku under the pen name "Seiran." He also authored
an unqualified hymn of praise for the sacred, loving imperial house, *Hei-i naru kōshitsuron*
(Keibunkan, 1921), plus a testament to the joy of imperialistic expansion, *Kokumin no sho*
(Jinbun shoin, 1939).

the story was postponed in September, however, and then suddenly in May of this year my mother died.

I publish this story in her memory. It is based on the most unfilial period of my life, about seven or eight years ago (i.e., 1909–10), as my writing career was just getting started. This is now the only thing left on earth of my mother and sister. I do not present them as superior human beings, however. They were not superior. But even so, they no doubt wanted to live. Death is nothingness. Life is at least something. I want this story to help them live on as something. Perhaps then I can take heart that my having become an artist was not entirely pointless.

In closing, I would like to express my profoundest gratitude to Chief Nagata Hidejirō of the Police Bureau for having made time in his busy schedule to read the manuscript prior to publication and, in addition, for having kindly written a detailed commentary.[89]

One searches in vain here for a hint of facetiousness. Tanizaki was in dead earnest about this story, and the emotional tone of the introduction was an extension of the story itself. It alerted even the very first readers of the piece to the fact that this was autobiography; they were free to enter into the typical understanding with the writer of an I-novel and evaluate it for its author's sincerity rather than his technique. And indeed, as we read "Sorrow of the Heretic," it is fascinating to watch even so shrewd—and self-consciously satanic—a writer as Tanizaki losing his composure as he indulges in an outpouring of his sins.[90]

"Sorrow of the Heretic" escaped banning, but as we shall see in subsequent chapters, this was far from the end of Tanizaki's troubles with the censors. Tanizaki was never noncontroversial, either before or after the Pacific War. *The Key* was denounced as pornography in the National Diet in 1956.[91] For a writer of Tanizaki's creative drive, however, the censorship system was little more than an occasional annoyance, one with which he was willing to make small compromises if it meant he could continue exploring and communicating from his idiosyncratic world.

Tanizaki has taken us well beyond the 1909–1910 period that we have been discussing, but his appearance on the literary scene, the reemergence of Ōgai, and the popularity of Nagai Kafū at this time should all be noted as part of the blossoming vitality of Japanese fiction in the wake of naturalism. Thanks to both the writers and the critics, the breakthrough to modern fiction had been accomplished. That the debate between naturalism and antinaturalism was anachronistic and irrelevant was attested to by the silly uproar occasioned by *Waseda Bungaku*'s praise of Kafū (see p. 125). One of the leading naturalist theoreticians, Hasegawa Tenkei, seeing that there was nothing more for him to accomplish, left for England and sent travel impressions back to *Taiyō* instead of the stimulating naturalist propaganda that he had been producing each month. His replacement, Kaneko Chikusui, preferred abstract, philosophical questions. Kaneko concentrated on European literature, changing the entire literary thrust of *Taiyō* after July 1910.

Far more important than definitions of naturalism and opposing -isms was the distinction between those who had made the breakthrough and those who saw modern literature's free exploration of individual life as a threat to traditional values. "If put to good use," said one official in 1910, "literature can be of enormous benefit to the nation, but there are many who, instead, abuse it, and seek to inflict harm on the nation. I would like to ask writers to remember always that literature, too, is an activity carried out within the national family."[92]

These were the words of a man who had not the slightest inkling of what writers had accomplished in Japan during the preceding five years. And if there were still writers at the mid-point of 1910 whom the censors had not succeeded in alienating from the national family, the startling events of the next several months would complete the process.

Part Three

HIGH TREASON AND AFTER

10

Mori Ōgai and Hiraide Shū:
Inside the High Treason Case

THE POLITICAL AND INTELLECTUAL CLIMATE

Yamagata's antileftist pressure did not abate after he helped to replace Saionji with Katsura (see above, p. 108), and he saw to it that the police kept hounding the Socialists. They were especially worried about Kōtoku Shūsui, long Japan's most visible Socialist and pacifist as publisher of *Heimin Shimbun*, but a recent convert to the "direct action" of anarcho-syndicalism.

Kōtoku was rumored to be contemplating anti-imperial violence, and in fact he had been approached in February 1909 by one of his readers, a mechanic named Miyashita Takichi, who had asked him to participate in a plot to assassinate the emperor, but he had hesitated to become involved until the police pressure convinced him that it was something he must do. His enthusiasm cooled after a few short weeks, however, when government hounding caused his mistress, Kanno Sugako, to suffer a nervous breakdown. Kōtoku's attitude remained ambivalent, but Kanno was determined to go through with it, and she renewed her ties with Miyashita and the two other plotters in May 1910. She won the privilege of throwing the first bomb, but the police moved in before any action could be taken. Unaware of these developments, Kōtoku was unexpectedly swept off to jail on June 1, and a nationwide roundup of all types of leftists followed.[1]

The press carried little more than rumor and conjecture on the meaning of the arrests until November 9, 1910, when the Great Court of Cassation's Procurator General released its written findings, for not only was there an immediate embargo on hard news of the incident, but the Press Law as a matter of course forbade any reporting of preliminary hearings. Whatever had happened, the press suggested, it was terribly frightening and it involved bombs. By September, the *Asahi* had picked up a wire report from New York that suggested a plot directed against the emperor. Finally, in November, 1910, the court documents listed not four or five but twenty-six defendants and traced their supposed grand conspiracy back to Kōtoku's involvement with American and expatriate Japanese radicals in San Francisco beginning in November 1905.[2]

The initial reaction was one of outrage against the conspirators and gratitude toward the government for having detected and foiled the assassination. But meanwhile there had been building a critical attitude toward the government's heavy-handed policing. By the time Kōtoku and eleven others were executed (January 24 and 25, 1911), the government's failure to redress social ills was being blamed for the rise of socialism and the increasing radicalization of leftists. In response to this criticism the government began to make some feeble moves in the direction of providing social welfare.[3]

On the issue of free speech, also, the government was subject to much criticism during the confused months between the leftist roundup and the release of the Procurator General's report. The number of bannings that occurred was simply unprecedented. The censors set themselves the task of rooting out all the leftist writings they could find, not just those appearing currently but books published as early as 1902. During September they banned some ninety volumes, including all of Kōtoku's books, and all the novels of the Socialist Kinoshita Naoe. The Ministry of Education cooperated by ordering libraries to lock up their Socialist holdings. Bookstore and library shelves were swept clean of Socialist titles. This situation would prevail for the next decade, the period known as the "winter years" of socialism.[4]

Even before the September purge had been completed, the young critic Uozumi Setsuro (1883–1910) printed a blistering attack in the *Asahi Shimbun* (September 16, 1910) that not only accused the censors of blind recklessness but called upon Japan's "Well-Behaved Freethinkers" ("Onken naru jiyū-shisōka," as he called his piece) to recognize the danger they were in. Uozumi argued that many recent bannings (for example, that of the literary journal *Hototogisu*'s September 1910 issue) demonstrated the authorities' determination to limit not only particular ideologies and obvious obscenity but anything and everything that could be called free thought. "Up to now, writers and those who are pleased to call themselves freethinkers have looked on indifferently at the suppression of socialism and anarchism, as though it were a fire on the opposite shore. Some have tried to show that their own position shares nothing with such dangerous extremism. They have been unaware—or pretended to be unaware—that *as* free thinkers, their position in the history of civilization puts them into the same category as those others." Now that the censors were proceeding logically to suppress all free thought, he said, the time was coming when freethinkers would have to take a stand.[5]

Uozumi was not alone in his willingness to speak out against the authorities. Had typhoid fever not killed him that December, when he was twenty-seven, he would have been pleased not only by the increasing bitterness and irony with which the victims of censorship fought back but by their awareness that the government's pairing of socialism and naturalism was not just a historical coincidence.

One particularly strong piece appeared in *Taiyō* two weeks after Uozumi's essay, when that magazine's political commentator, Asada Kōson (or Hikoichi), accused the government of carrying out an "intellectual coup d'etat." In outline, Asada's argument ran as follows:

> There is genuine fear running through the publishing world. Our officials are living in the past, they distrust the people, misunderstand the role of the individual in society, and immediately resort to force to maintain the status quo. They may win the battle for now, but any such victory over ideas must be temporary, superficial, and pointless. Look at what a century of struggle has netted the Russians: they have the world's most radical, desperate revolutionaries, so what can the Katsura regime hope to accomplish? They cherish the grand ambition of remaking and controlling the entire intellectual climate, but this is a vain illusion—especially for politicians incapable of understanding the ideas of the age. Society is pluralistic, alive, and austerely selective: inferior and dangerous ideas will be weeded out naturally. Aside from Debakame-style disruption of public morals and Kōtoku-style disruption of the public peace, the rest can be safely left alone.

Asada then offered the Katsura regime his modest proposal: If the government actually believed it could refashion and control the age's intellectual climate, why should it stop at negative measures like banning? It should get into the publishing and printing business, should issue some sort of "Regulations for the Purchase of Publishable Manuscripts," and should buy only manuscripts written in the approved vocabulary from approved authors only. Asada suggested other measures, including: buying up the rights to all previously published material and disposing of what was undesirable; searching every home in the country; taxing the importation of foreign publications; reading all mail that appeared to contain published material; prohibiting foreign study; and enlarging the official gazette as the only permitted newspaper. Since government publications would be as tasteless as the tobacco sold by the government monopoly, an "Enforced Reading Law" would almost certainly be necessary to ensure sale of the product. Unless the government were willing to go that far, Asada concluded, what they were now doing was meaningless.[6]

Taiyō printed several other views of the situation during October and November, before the Procurator General's document appeared. These ranged

from hysterical expressions of fear of all "dangerous thoughts" to more reasoned considerations of the meaning of socialism. By far, the dominant theme
was the need for educating the public. Socialism and anarchism were *not* the
same, they pointed out, and certainly these were something quite different
from naturalism. Even *Taiyō*'s sophisticated readers could not be assumed to
be clear on these issues.

Doctor of Laws Shiosawa Masasada carefully noted the different types of
socialism that had sprung up in Europe. He criticized the folly of excluding
any intellectual discipline of social analysis as "dangerous": the complexities of
society required constant, open-minded study and could not be interpreted by
one exclusive ideology. If freedom of thought were sacrificed for the annihila-
tion of socialism, he asserted, the impossibility of rational long-range planning would do great harm to the nation.

By contrast, a former head of the Police Bureau said that the censors had no
special standards other than to stop "them" from destroying morality and the
nation. The Vice-Minister of Home Affairs, Ichiki Kitokurō, expressed shock
at the authors' "irresponsibility" and sadness at the stern measures that had to
be taken, "but the fact is that the amount of harmful writing is on the
increase." He insisted that censorship was not a fruitless exercise, offering the
remarkable view that it made some sense to ban once-serialized novels when
they were published in book form, because a book's continuity could be far
more stimulating to the reader than short installments.

An anonymous former official expressed impatience at the censors' ignorance
of the distinctions among the different -isms. They seemed to be bringing
back the old Reign of Terror that had prevailed under the libel regulations of
1875 and to be treating people like idiots. Not only was it a shame, he said, to
snatch away freedom of healthy inquiry but it was downright stupid of the
police to revive interest in now-forgotten books by banning them.

Even Inoue Tetsujirō, while waxing eloquent on the mystical oneness of the
Japanese nation, called for a more reasoned approach. It was regrettable that
some of Japan's Socialists had changed into anarchists, he said. Socialism did
have some admirable goals, but Kōtoku and his gang wanted to destroy the
irreplaceable ancient customs that bound the nation together, and the government had to stop them. Unfortunately, he continued, the authorities were not
going about this task intelligently, the way they were banning any book with
"society" in the title. "In order to progress, we must study social problems. It
is also important," he added, "to distinguish between socialism and naturalism." Inoue had no objection to *literary* naturalism, but he criticized the
"instinctual wing" of naturalism, which seduced youth into seeking unlimited
sexual gratification.[7]

Even after the Procurator General's version of the case had been released in
November, *Taiyō* maintained its generally objective tone. Asada Kōson wrote

in the December retrospective issue that the worst impression left by the year 1910 was the government's treatment of the intellectual world. The authorities had done well to suppress anarchists who advocated direct action, he said, but they had confused socialism with anarchism and attempted to deprive the people of their freedom of thought.

In his summary of the year's literary events, Shimamura Hōgetsu said he was pleased at the great variety that had come to replace the exclusive naturalist dominance of previous years (1910 was indeed remarkable for the richness and variety of its fiction, most of which did not negate naturalism but built upon the modern foundation it had erected), but he noted that a major problem had been the official policy of suppression, which had employed the "crafty" approach of trying to force socialism and naturalism into the same category in order to foist the public's opposition to socialism off onto naturalism. The ultimate practical effect of this policy was minimal, but it "ought to be recorded as one example of the present administration's misgovernment."

The anonymous writer of another *Taiyō* summary of the literary events of 1910 voiced his belief that the only reason Katsura had been brought in to replace Saionji was to institute stricter controls over socialism and naturalism. Unfortunately, he said, the censors could not distinguish between naturalism and the obscenity of writers like Satō Kōroku and Ikuta Kizan, whom he blamed for giving naturalism a bad name. It would not have any notable effect on literature, he averred, if meaningless fleshy stuff like theirs would be difficult to publish for a while.[8]

The ideological confusion was not without its amusing aspects. During the September 1910 purge of Socialist books, one overzealous censor banned a book by the French entomologist Jean Henri Fabre when the translator gave it the title *Konchū Shakai* (Insect Society).[9] By March, the idea seems to have gotten across that "social" did not always mean "Socialist," but the word was still sensational enough to be exploited by clever entrepreneurs. One advertisement in the *Asahi* asked, "WHAT is a SOCIAL EXPERIMENT?" and answered in minuscule type that a social experiment could be conducted by the widest possible use of this particular company's medicine in an attempt to cure the entire population of pimples.[10] The *Asahi* had contributed to the uproar in September with an article entitled "Dangerous Western Books" ("Kiken naru yōsho"), which drew a storm of criticism by arguing for a ban on the import of all modern European literature as morally corrupting. And because his novel *Sneers* (*Reishō*) had presented such a devastating view of Japan's cultural provincialism, even so epicurean a writer as Nagai Kafū was suspected of being a Socialist.[11]

There was little commentary on the problem of radicals in *Nihon oyobi Nihonjin* until the trial had run its course. The literary column carried an assessment of the year's censorship that was similar to the others we saw above, and an editorial counseled readers to bear up under the increased pressure. Freedom is a matter of endurance, it said. Any literary progress that could be stopped by banning was not true progress and was therefore no great loss. Occasional remarks in the magazine's literary gossip column reflected the growing concern over censorship and publishers' attempts to forestall bannings by substituting *fuseji* for controversial words. Some writers were finding this dull, noted one column, and so they were using foreign words instead of the usual marks, the "leader" in this being none other than the Surgeon General of the Army himself, Mori Ōgai. (Ōgai's writings are, in fact, liberally sprinkled with foreign words, but these are hardly limited to "racy passages," as suggested here!) Another column carried an anecdote concerning a certain translator of Russian literature who was visited by a stream of young readers asking him to fill in the circles. He obliged them with a list of suppressed words. [12]

Considering its earlier activities on behalf of free speech (and perhaps increased sales), *Chūō Kōron* remained strangely quiet on the censorship issue, having almost nothing to say on the leftists aside from speculating that whatever they had done, it must have been pretty bad, and chiding the Home Minister for ignoring everyday crime as he sent the nationally run Tokyo metropolitan police out chasing after Socialists and anarchists. [13] When the Procurator General's report came out, however, the editors must have regretted even this hint of criticism, for the magazine exploded with a raging editorial, "Oh, The Traitors!" ("Aa, ranshin zokushi"). *

The editorialist noted that the twenty-six defendants would be tried under Article 73 of the Criminal Code, which called for the death sentence. He declared that "we should go ahead and execute them without regard to the protests of foreign Socialists," for the emperor would have been the latest in a long line of anarchist victims, including Czar Alexander in 1881, President Carnot of France (1894), the Austro-Hungarian Empress Elizabeth (1898), Italy's King Humbert (1900), President McKinley of the United States (1901), and King Carlos of Portugal (1908).

> Our *kokutai* stands peerless in the world. The dignity of the Imperial House is
> absolute and incomparable. We cannot permit the slightest insult to any of its
> members, let alone the inflicting of injury upon them. Our national sentiments

---

*This traditional term for traitor had been used by Ōmachi Keigetsu in denouncing Yosano Akiko for her poetic plea to her brother not to die in the Russo-Japanese War (see above, p. 57). This was especially strong language in Japan, where "from ancient times to the present there has never in fact been a rebellious subject. Nor will there be one in the future" (Fukuzawa Yukichi, 1888). See Albert M. Craig, "Fukuzawa Yukichi: The Philosophical Foundations of Meiji Nationalism," In Robert E. Ward, ed., *Political Development in Modern Japan* (Princeton: Princeton University Press, 1968), pp. 132–33.

and the thoughts of our people arise from nature. The laws that we have fashioned based upon these are like the sun and moon, shining with a radiance that our fine judicial officers cannot obscure.

In addition to the text of the Procurator General's report, printed "in full for future generations," the magazine carried an article by Takebe Tongo, one of the "seven doctors" who had called for the opening of hostilities with Russia in 1904. This essay beautifully represented the fear of foreign influences and the confused view of socialism and naturalism as equally dangerous forces acting upon the nation.[14]

A later report in *Chūō Kōron* noted that the trial of the anarchists had been ordered closed at the first session on December 10 owing to its potential for disrupting peace and order. Security was exceptionally tight. The Great Court was said to have received tens of thousands of letters demanding the death penalty for the traitors in a frightening display of national wrath. American Socialists were protesting, but Japan's "sacred" courts would never pervert the law merely to accommodate them.*

Thus, the atmosphere surrounding the trial was chaotic, and the government's instinctive decision to hold the proceedings *in camera* was representative of the confusion pervading all levels of society and government. When it was suggested to him later by liberal Diet members that the government's lack of social policies had been a factor in breeding discontent, Home Minister Hirata Tōsuke said, "This is all new to me. Perhaps I have confused the terms 'socialism' and 'social policy.' I regret this and hope to maintain the distinction. Are the policies I mentioned earlier—rehabilitation of criminals, founding industrial unions—*social* policies? I simply avoided using the term for fear of being misunderstood."†

ŌGAI AS EDUCATOR

Among Japan's writers, Mori Ōgai was the only one to produce a series of intentionally didactic stories and articles that grasped the intellectual chaos concerning socialism. He attempted to spell out the differences among such controversial concepts as socialism, anarchism, naturalism, and individualism, and he asserted the need for intellectual freedom.

---

*CK (January 1911): 194. Whatever the official rationale for a closed trial, it is well known that Yamagata was opposed to any public airing of views that might compromise the emperor's divinity. See F. G. Notehelfer, *Kōtoku Shūsui, Portrait of a Japanese Radical*, p. 187.

†Furoku, "Taigyaku jiken (2)," TY (May 15, 1911), p. 49. MITC, pp. 24–25, shows the authorities beginning to become more sophisticated in the summer of 1911.

In one short essay from this time, Ōgai warns that the various "ism" labels attached to literature are, at best, rough approximations that should not be taken too seriously. Those who label naturalism evil or threatening, he says, are doing it out of ignorance or some ulterior motive:

> The most ridiculous thing one hears is that naturalism stands for free love, which is actually something that the Socialists preach [the press made much of the relationship of Kōtoku and Kanno] and which has nothing to do with the recent tendency for art to be true to nature. More talked about than naturalism, lately, is individualism. In that art is concerned with the inner life, it is, properly speaking, individualistic. Unlike anarchism and egotism, to which the term is often incorrectly applied, individualism presents no threat to family, society, or nation. To persecute art in order to obliterate anarchism and socialism, all under the vague heading of individualism, can only do harm to the nation. No country can expect to flourish that prevents free academic inquiry and the free development of art.[15]

The September 1910 issue of *Mita Bungaku* carried "Fasces" ("Fuasu-chiesu"), Ōgai's answer to Judge Imamura of the 1908 Ikuta Kizan trial. Imamura's widely publicized affirmation of "generally held contemporary community standards" had been the only thing approximating an official response to the call for publication of the censors' guidelines. In the first part of this dramatic dialogue, Ōgai presents a gaunt, high-strung reporter in his thirties interviewing a ruddy, corpulent judge in his forties who confidently espouses such views as Judge Imamura gave to the various reporters who interviewed him for the literary and intellectual journals.

The judge expounds on the importance of his three touchstones, emphasizing that foreign standards are irrelevant to the Japanese case, and that writers who happen to be ahead of their times will often have to be punished like ordinary pornographers since they, too, are out of line with *contemporary* values. The reporter concludes, logically, that at least all contemporary books will receive equal treatment. "Quite the contrary," responds the judge, as confidently as ever. Since censorship is practiced by the Police Bureau, the Metropolitan Police, and the Procurator, he notes, each office will bring different preconceptions to the task. Indeed, the same person will react differently on different days. It is no business of the court if the censors happen to miss now and then. Inconsistenty of enforcement is no defense. The judge underscores the absurdity of all this by cautioning the reporter not to take these remarks as his personal standards: they are based on "our society in general." The reporter seems satisfied and goes off to write up the interview. (Ōgai surely had in mind Judge Imamura's most recent interview in *Taiyō*.)[16]

In the second part of the dialogue, Ōgai introduces a pale, shaggy-haired writer. He has read the reporter's interview, and has come to see the judge to test his own ideas on him, since, as he says, the judge has given the clearest statement yet of the official view of censorship. He speaks in the obsequious tones appropriate to the traditional image of the writer as a cheap entertainer, but his ideas are precise and challenging. He wants to know how the judge can determine something as vague as the "generally held idea" of what is morally acceptable. The judge says it is very simple: the standards come to him after a little dispassionate thought on the matter. The writer does not press this point or any other, and when the two are about to part, a demon appears in a coolie hat and ankle-length coat. The demon gives them both a sound tongue-lashing—the writer for cringing before the judge and not asserting his right-ful authority as an authentic literary visionary; the judge for his arbitrary and dogmatic exploitation of authority and his failure to give due respect to art and learning.[17]

Ōgai published another piece on censorship in *Mita Bungaku* two months later (November 1910). This story, "The Tower of Silence" ("Chinmoku no tō"), took an even more critical view of the government for its suppression of "dangerous Western books" that introduced socialism and naturalism, echo-ing the phrase that had become so controversial after the *Asahi* article in September. "To translate was to retail the dangerous goods themselves, and to write original work was to copy the Westerners and thus produce dangerous goods, imitation imports! Ideas that were destructive of peace and social order, ideas that corrupted public morals were transmitted through dangerous West-ern books!"[18]

In this allegory, set in India, the Parsi rulers are carrying out mass execu-tions of their young men who read such books, and each day wagons carry piles of bodies to the Tower of Silence. The narrator points out that the coupling of naturalism and socialism is a strange one and that the sexuality in the native naturalism is but a pale shadow of the Western model, a slightly less restrained presentation of what has always been very restrained. It is being so ruthlessly suppressed, he notes, because by coincidence, a violent revolutionary move-ment has begun. Hysterical fear of revolution has fanned the flames of anti-naturalism—a view with which Uozumi Setsuro would certainly have taken exception.

> From the Parsi point of view any art in the world today which is of the slightest value and not absolutely trite is considered a danger. This is only to be expected.
>
> Values recognized by art entail the destruction of convention. Any work which loiters within the bounds of convention is bound to be mediocre. All art when seen through the eyes of convention appears dangerous.

Art penetrates through surface considerations to the impulses which lurk
beneath. . . . It is quite natural that literature should penetrate the impulsive
side of life, and when it does so, the impulse of sexual desire must be revealed.[19]

Ōgai published another didactic piece, "The Lunchroom" ("Shokudō"), in
the December 1910 *Mita Bungaku*. In this story, set in a government ministry
lunchroom just after the release of the Procurator General's report on the
anarchist plot, a bureaucrat (and spare-time scholar) named Kimura responds
to the queries of an innocent, young colleague concerning radical thought.
The office spy, Inuzuka, tries to trap Kimura into making some committed
remark that would be worth reporting to their superiors. The fictional setting
enables Ōgai to give the impression that Kimura would be making more
liberal statements if it were not for the presence of Inuzuka (literally, "dog
mound"; a "dog" is a spy in Japanese). "It is not entirely pointless" to suppress
books that foment violence, says Kimura, "but all I am saying is that I believe
in the importance of freedom of expression and think it is a shame that the
banning of books is being carried out on too broad a scale. Of course I, too,
realize that there are instances when it becomes an unavoidable tactic."[20]

Aside from presenting a pocket history of anarchism, Ōgai seems to be using
the story to offer indirect advice to the government authorities. They are the
ones who can prevent an increase in the number of radicals, not by suppression
but by reducing the number of disadvantaged people in society. Further, he
says, since the conspirators apparently want to die as martyrs, the best thing
the government could do would be to keep them alive. There is a hint here,
too, that this was about as direct as Ōgai could be with his official colleagues:
Kimura always speaks more politely to Inuzuka than to the others, which gives
Inuzuka the impression that he is being kept at a respectful distance.

Ōgai's "educational" activities were not limited to his creative writing but
extended—indirectly, again—into the proceedings of the High Treason trial
itself. As a long-time mentor of the Myōjō school of modern poets and the
major contributor to the magazine *Subaru*, which several former Myōjō poets
had begun publishing in January 1909 after the demise of *Myōjō*, Ōgai was
well acquainted with the lawyer-poet Hiraide Shū, in whose home the editorial office of *Subaru* was located. We have discussed Hiraide in his role as
counsel for the defense in the Ikuta Kizan trial, but he also became involved in
the High Treason case when the former editor-publisher of *Myōjō*, Yosano
Hiroshi, asked him to argue in behalf of two lesser defendants in the case with
whom Yosano was indirectly connected.

The request apparently came in August. Between that time and the day he
spoke in court, December 28, 1910, Hiraide had a great deal of cramming to
do. At Yosano's suggestion, he turned to Ōgai to be filled in on the back-

ground of socialism and anarchism. He and Yosano visited Ōgai's home several evenings during October, and Ōgai willingly spoke to them on the history of European leftist movements, drawing from his up-to-date library and current newspapers.[21]

It was precisely Ōgai's contribution to the defense, namely, Hiraide's scholarly presentation of the history of anarchism, that impressed the senior members of the defense team. Ōgai also thought highly enough of Hiraide to exploit his privileged connection with the Ministry of Education by passing a written opinion of Hiraide's on to an important ministry official (see below, chap. 12, p. 210). Students of Ōgai have always marveled at how he could mix on an equal footing with the highest echelons of Japanese officialdom— visiting the imperial palace and the prime minister's residence on New Year's day, writing poetry and drinking with Yamagata (which he did on the very night he completed "Fasces")—and still could maintain genuinely close ties with literary men, himself writing stories critical of government suppression of art and learning.* Whether he attempted to influence his official colleagues to see things as his literary associates did will probably always remain a matter of speculation (not to say wishful thinking), but his relationship with Hiraide and his other activities suggest that he was indeed active behind the scenes. Both for what it reveals of this side of Ōgai and as a little-known view of the issues and personalities involved in the High Treason incident, the career of Hiraide Shū is worth exploring in some detail.

HIRAIDE AS DEFENSE COUNSEL

Hiraide was Shū's second adoptive name. He was born Kodama Shū[22] in 1878, the tenth and last child, eighth son of a Niigata farmer. A bright student, he was to have been educated by a merchant family that adopted him at the age of fifteen, but when the agreement was not carried through, he returned to the Kodamas and soon became an elementary school teacher. He was interested in literature and, taking the pen name Roka, he began contributing poetry and criticism to local newspapers and magazines in 1898. By 1900 he was sending his work to Yosano Hiroshi and publishing in *Myōjō* under the latter's tu-

---

*The frequency of Ōgai's meetings with men in the highest echelons of government is especially remarkable at this time in his literary career. See Ōgai's diary entries for January 1, 1909, and August 21, 1910, in OZ 20:393, 535. Moriyama Shigeo, *Taigyaku jiken*, p. 83, has noted that Ōgai dined with Home Minister Hirata, Education Minister Komatsubara, and Professor Hozumi Yatsuka (the major force behind spiritualization of ethics textbooks) at Yamagata Aritomo's Chinzansō estate on the evening of October 29, 1910, just three days before "The Tower of Silence" appeared in *Mita Bungaku* and, simultaneously, the Procurator General submitted his finding of "all defendants guilty" to the Great Court of Cassation.

telage. To further his education, he agreed to become the adopted husband of Rai, the younger sister of a lawyer named Hiraide Zenkichi. In 1901 he took Rai to Tokyo and entered her brother's alma mater, Meiji Hōritsu Gakkō. Graduating at the top of his class in 1903, he briefly went to work for the Justice Ministry but left the following year to open a private practice.

In Tokyo, Hiraide's involvement with *Myōjō* became deeper than ever. He was strongly supportive of Yosano when an anonymous pamphlet appeared in 1901, slandering Yosano and sending the circulation of *Myōjō* down.[23] As we described earlier, he accompanied Yosano and another colleague to deliver an in-person rebuttal to the critic Ōmachi Keigetsu, who had denounced Yosano Akiko's famous antiwar poem as treasonous (see above, p. 58).

Relations between the Hiraides and the Yosanos grew increasingly close and remained so even after a literary dispute led to the demise of *Myōjō* in November 1908. Following this Hiraide, Ishikawa Takuboku, and other Myōjō poets began publishing *Subaru* from the Hiraide house, where Hiraide also conducted his legal activities. One reason this responsibility fell to Hiraide was that, thanks to his law practice, he was probably the only poet in Japan who could afford to own a house large enough to accommodate a publishing enterprise; he also contributed to the magazine's operating capital. *Subaru* became for him not only his central literary activity but also an advertising medium in which he offered his services "in all matters pertaining to civil and criminal suits and patent law," the address and telephone number in the advertisement being identical to those of *Subaru*. Understandably, as reported by Hiraide's son Akira, the house was always in an uproar.[24]

It was natural, then, for Yosano to turn to Hiraide when followers of a friend who had become deeply implicated in the High Treason case found themselves in need of a defense attorney as they, too, were sucked into the spreading swamp. As Hiraide began to work on the case and to suspect that the government was inventing the greater part of the conspiracy, the *Subaru* office became a source of underground information. Hiraide was allowed to take sections of the procurator's records home to prepare the defense, but because he was required to return them immediately, he and his brother would spend whole nights making pencil-on-rice-paper copies of the materials.

Ishikawa Takuboku, whose ideas were becoming increasingly radicalized during this period, saw the seventeen-volume Great Court records in Hiraide's house and managed to read two of them himself. Determined to "leave a record of the truth for future generations," Takuboku borrowed several documents from Hiraide and spent many hours copying them late into the night. He died in April 1912 after compiling a detailed record of the case based primarily on newspaper reports and a few of Hiraide's materials. These came to light only after the end of the Pacific War.[25]

As was the more famous Takuboku, Hiraide was a young victim of illness.

But after his death in March 1914, his wife preserved the penciled materials, the transcript of Hiraide's court presentation with his reactions to the verdict, and the letters of appreciation that Hiraide had received from Kōtoku, Kanno, and other imprisoned defendants, wrapping them all in a white cloth *furoshiki* (wrapper). The family always referred to this bundle as "the valuables" (*kichōhin*) and kept it stored far back in a closet, taking particular care of it whenever they moved. Rai would tell the children, "The day will come when these will be published," but as they waited, the white *furoshiki* turned slowly gray.

Young Akira, who has provided this account, went off to the front during the Pacific War. The Hiraide house was destroyed in the Tokyo air raids, but "the valuables" were saved and were eventually published in full—fifty years after the death of Hiraide Shū and seventeen years after Rai's own death.[26] The copies of the procurator's records that Hiraide and his brother had made came to form the cornerstone of some of the most important postwar revelations concerning the long-misunderstood High Treason case.[27] (The story ends disappointingly. Hiraide's elder son, Hiizu, became a prominent legal scholar who wrote a book strongly supportive of wartime censorship and himself served as a thought procurator.)[28]

Hiraide's clients in the High Treason case were Takagi Kenmei (46) and Sakikubo Seiichi (27), members of the five-man so-called Kishū Gang of leftists from the old Kishū region (the coast of the Kii Peninsula in modern Wakayama Prefecture). The leader of the group was Yosano Hiroshi's friend Ōishi Seinosuke, an American-educated physician who had become interested in socialism in 1897 and had cultivated the friendship of such well-known leftists as Kōtoku Shūsui, Katayama Sen, and Sakai Toshihiko. His frequent contributions to Kōtoku's *Heimin Shimbun* and other periodicals had attracted a large local following, and he became the cultural/intellectual nucleus of the region around his hometown of Shingū. He was also admired and respected in the area for his selfless devotion to medicine and his willingness to treat the local Eta pariahs. Takagi, a priest indignant at the plight of his Eta parishoners, and Sakikubo, a local journalist, had the misfortune to be present at a meeting in January 1909 when Ōishi recounted a recent conversation with Kōtoku in Tokyo. Ill (Ōishi had just diagnosed him for intestinal tuberculosis) and increasingly desperate from police hounding, Kōtoku had reportedly mused, "If only we had forty or fifty good men who were willing to die! We could plunder the rich, burn down government offices, and, if we had any strength left, mount an attack on the palace."[29]

Hiraide argued in court that the government's entire case against the Kishū Gang rested on their presence at this secondhand report of Kōtoku's "sheer fantasizing." In the year and a half between this meeting and the discovery of Miyashita Takichi's bomb plot (which had been broached to Kōtoku only after

Ōishi had left Tokyo), twenty of the twenty-six defendants *knew* nothing and *did* nothing, Hiraide insisted. The most tangible act committed by the Kishū Gang was their expression of approval for Ōishi's story, which was not a violation of the law—and certainly not of Article 73 of the Criminal Code, which prescribes the death penalty for "Every person who has committed or has attempted to commit, a dangerous (or injurious) act against (the person of) the Emperor" or other members of the imperial family.[30]

Hiraide argued that the government's case, as presented by procurator Hiranuma Kiichirō, had failed to prove that his clients (and, by extension, the eighteen others whom he considered innocent) had attempted to commit—or had even *intended* to commit (as the Japanese text could be interpreted) such crimes. What Hiranuma had done was to posit a worldwide, monolithic anarchist conspiracy in blind disregard of the actual history of anarchism as it had developed under the guidance of various personalities in different countries, and to impose this violent, horrifying monster on Japan's anarchists. (In the detailed analysis here, and in the observation that the Kaiser himself could be seen regularly on the streets of Berlin, safe from anarchists, we surely discover Ōgai's influence.) In effect, Hiranuma's argument was that Japan's anarchists and Socialists had been corrupted by dangerous foreign ideas that had aroused in them the intent to assassinate the emperor.*

Hiraide's reply to Hiranuma's argument may be summarized as follows:

> *All* new ideas are dangerous when judged by the status quo. Foreign ideas for which there is no internal need will have no effect, and if there is such a need, the suppression of ideas will have no effect. In spite of the fact that it is our national policy (*kokuze*) to import foreign ideas, we have men like Inoue Tetsujirō arguing that Christianity conflicts with the *kokutai*. Meanwhile, Procurator Itakura has pointed to two of the defendants' refusal to join the Methodist church as evidence of the danger of anarchism, whereas if this had happened fifteen years ago, their *not* having converted to the "dangerous" religion would have counted in their favor. No ideas are inherently dangerous. The present case merely demonstrates that excessive control leads to resistance, not that the idea of anarchism is dangerous in itself.
>
> In particular, when we examine how anarchism has supposedly manifested itself in Takagi and Sakikubo, we find that both profess only to being Socialists,

---

*Richard H. Mitchell has shown what a bête noire these "dangerous foreign ideas" were for Hiranuma and how, as the key figure in the Justice Ministry and organizer of right-wing study groups (one of which included, among others, Tōjō Hideki), Hiranuma went on to set the tone for prewar thought control. On Kōtoku, Hiranuma wrote that a "flawed" education in Japan's past had been responsible for the plot: if his education had ended with Chinese studies and had not gone on to include English and French, the affair never would have materialized. See MITC, pp. 36–38, 43–44.

and that they have only the vaguest idea of what even "socialism" means. Takagi, especially, has confused utopian socialism with his Buddhist millenarianism, positing a future heaven-on-earth of perfect equality. This is what he means when he says he recognizes only the existence of Amida Buddha and not that of the Imperial House or the government. Both Takagi and Sakikubo simply had vague wishes for a better life that led them to share their dissatisfactions with Ōishi—and even Ōishi is far from being a committed revolutionary. These men may be disappointed with social inequities, but they are true Japanese subjects who share in the spirit of reverence for Japan's unique Imperial House, and would never knowingly commit the heinous crime with which they have been charged.

All but one or two of the defendants revere the Imperial House, they know full well the meaning of *kokutai*, and in this courtroom they have unanimously decried the unjustness of the records of the preliminary hearings. They have sought to cleanse themselves of the foul brand of treason against the Emperor.

As a loyal Japanese, I detest crimes against the Imperial House as much as anyone, and I would insist upon the supreme penalty for anyone who had knowingly perpetrated such a crime. But look at how these defendants sit here humbly, awestruck whenever mention is made of the Imperial House. Even if we accept the trumped-up contention that they participated in a plot in January 1909, the phrase "attempted to commit" in Article 73 is designed only to punish those discovered to be actually involved in a conspiracy; the spirit of the law is not to punish men who have plotted and repented. Neither Takagi nor Sakikubo had any intention of committing such a crime, and they should not be judged according to Article 73. These are not simply my words as counsel for the defense. This is, in fact, the public cry raised by the loyal subjects of the Empire of Japan.[31]

Hiraide was shocked when, three weeks after he had spoken in court, all twenty-six defendants were found guilty and twenty-four of them, including the Kishū Gang, were sentenced to death.* That day (January 18) he appended a short postscript to his formal defense memorandum, in which he recorded his conviction that the procurator's records were far removed from the truth of the situation. The bomb plot, he wrote, was clearly the work of Miyashita Takichi, Kanno Sugako, and Niimura Tadao, but even the motives of Furukawa Rikisaku, the one other defendant involved in the plot, were extremely vague. Kōtoku Shūsui bore some responsibility, he continued, as disseminator of his ideology, and the evidence against Ōishi Seinosuke could

---

*The other two were found guilty only of breaking laws regulating the possession of explosive materials. They were released after serving several years in prison. See *Taigyaku jiken arubamu*, pp. 102–03.

not be explained away, but the case against the other twenty hinged on one absurd statement that Kōtoku made a year and a half before the arrests started.*

In order to penetrate to the truth, however, and to render a proper verdict, Hiraide added, "one would first of all have to have a clear mind and possess the new knowledge required for interpreting the age; one would have to be a person who was honest enough neither to toady to superiors nor pander to the masses, and compassionate enough truly to prize human liberty and equality." Hiraide had envied the judges in this case for the rare opportunity given them to demonstrate the fairness and authority of the Japanese court system, but they had let the chance slip through their fingers. Now, would they actually execute all twenty-four convicts, like fish on a cutting board? "What good did it do for me to go to court sixteen times? What good did it do for me to speak two hours for the defense? All my tears and efforts and anger were a waste. But this verdict will do nothing to shake my convictions. The truth I have seen is still the truth. It will never change. For now, at least, I must be satisfied with that and hold my peace."[32]

The day after Hiraide wrote this, an imperial order of clemency commuted the sentences of twelve of the condemned twenty-four—including Takagi and Sakikubo—to life imprisonment. Kōtoku, Ōishi, the four conspirators, and six others were executed just a few days later.†

Hiraide was by no means satisfied to hold his peace. Again he turned to Mori Ōgai, not only as an advisor when he began to write fiction but possibly also as a conduit for disseminating his views of the trial within the government. To his combined defense memorandum and postscript he affixed the title, "Written Opinion on the High Treason Incident" ("Taigyaku jiken ikensho"). This may have been the "written opinion of Hiraide Shū's" that Ōgai mentioned in his diary that June as having passed on to an official at the Ministry of Education named Fukuhara Ryōjirō. Of course, Ōgai's term, "written opinion," may have referred to some other document, and there is always the question of what Ōgai hoped to accomplish through Fukuhara. As we shall see, however, at least one magazine at the time suggested that Fukuhara's views were becoming noticeably more liberal.

---

*Before the verdict was announced, Hiraide told Ishikawa Takuboku that if he were judge, he would sentence the four plotters to death, imprison Kōtoku and Ōishi for life, imprison one other defendant for five years for *lèse majesté*, and pronounce the rest innocent. See Takuboku's diary entry for January 3, 1911, in TZ 16:129.

†Takagi eventually killed himself after three and one-half years in prison. Four others died behind bars. Sakikubo was paroled in 1929 and his civil rights were restored in 1948, seven years before his death. There were three other such survivors and three more parolees who were not fortunate enough to outlast the Japanese Empire. See *Taigyaku jiken arubamu*, pp. 78–101.

Before we discuss Hiraide's fictional treatment of the High Treason incident, it would be helpful to summarize some of his own inner struggle. In
much of what he wrote, we see a desperate desire to believe that the system
works. His courtroom remarks on the imperial house, for example, should not
be taken as mere rhetoric. He agreed with the view often expressed at those
times that anyone who could bring himself to harm the emperor was literally
not a Japanese.* Nonetheless, he had a far more rational view of the legal
system to which he had devoted his life than did the *Chūō Kōron* editor who
imagined the "radiant" laws of the land as having been based upon Japan's
unique "national sentiments" that "arise from nature." For him, the proper
functioning of the Meiji legal structure would prove that Japan was a modern,
civilized nation that had succeeded in assimilating Western law.

Sometimes Hiraide's faith in the system could go beyond the bounds of
common sense. In an essay written while waiting for the verdict of the High
Treason trial, he argued that it was the fault of the Diet, not the administrative
authorities, that the people had lost their freedoms of speech and assembly.
Japan's politics were the politics of the people, not of the government, he said.
The people's Diet approved the laws and charged the government to carry
them out. If the Diet had not been so wrapped up in debates on taxes and
military expansion, said Hiraide, they would not have allowed the administration to place "limits" on the "law" that went beyond the spirit of the constitution, and the excessive pressure that caused the anarchists' plot would never
have come into being.[33]

He is right, of course, in that that is how the system was supposed to work,
but the "people" who had constituted the 1908 electorate amounted to a mere
3% of the population, i.e., 1,590,000 voters who were wealthy enough to pay
"the minumum ten-yen direct tax that entitled male citizens to vote."[34]

Hiraide went through this tortured process of reasoning, finally, to restore
for himself his original faith in the constitution's "absolute" guarantee of
freedom of expression, which, he said was only to be limited by the law in truly
unavoidable situations. Such freedom was necessary, in his view, to assure the
proper functioning of the national character, which, in its most patriotic
aspect, had always consisted in the ability to assimilate foreign influences
selectively, rejecting elements inconsistent with the national customs. This
process of natural selection worked best in a free situation. (The question of
inalienable individual rights did not come up.)[35]

---

*When the distinguished French jurist Gustave Boissonade helped the early Meiji govern-
ment draft the criminal code in force from 1882 to 1908, he recommended encoding crimes
against the imperial house under a specific title. His advice was ignored as unnecessary. It was
assumed that, as a foreigner, he could not grasp the perfect unity of the Japanese people which
would render such crimes unthinkable. See Furoku, "Taigyaku jiken (2)," TY (May 15, 1911),
p. 47.

Hiraide's faith in the system must have been sorely tested by another court case from this time in which he unsuccessfully defended a young man accused of *lèse majesté* and infractions of the Press Law. The man was known to have some connection with Kōtoku, and was under investigation for having published an article entitled "Undercurrent of Revolution" ("Kakumei no anryū"). His room was searched by the police, who discovered a diary containing remarks disrespectful to the emperor. For this, he was tried and convicted under Article 74 of the Criminal Code, which forbade "disrespectful acts" against the imperial house. Hiraide appealed the case through the Great Court, but the appeal was rejected on March 3, 1911. As a result of this case, a landmark in prewar law, Article 74 carried the following annotation: "*Lèse Majesté* is consummated when a disrespectful declaration of intention is made. It does not matter whether others have obtained knowledge of such declaration or not." [36]

HIRAIDE AS AUTHOR

Mori Ōgai helped Hiraide revise his first two stories when he decided to try his hand at fiction that spring. But it was not until September of the following year that Hiraide published a story drawing from his experience in the High Treason case, and yet another year would go by before he published "The Rebels" ("Gyakuto"), the one piece of fiction in which he captured the atmosphere of the trial and expressed his bitter view of Japanese justice. (Most of his other stories, including several conventional pieces on the troubled love affairs of geisha, have been justifiably forgotten.) [37]

Of Hiraide's three stories derived from the Kōtoku case, the first, "The Way of the Brutes" ("Chikushōdō") is the least successful. It is a brief "self-portrait" narrated by a once-prominent attorney whose conscience has been bothering him in the two years since he refused to join the Kōtoku defense team. He lives a brutally sensual, materialistic existence, knowing that he declined to participate in the defense attempt to demonstrate to the world the fairness of the Japanese court system. He had had two despicable reasons: several letters threatening death to the other defense attorneys had frightened him; and he knew that, taking the job as public defender, he would have made no money on the case. Hiraide Akira has written that the protagonist was modeled on a lawyer who actually did refuse to take the case. It was also a fact that some of the defense lawyers had received threatening letters and that resentment against them for having become involved at all was not limited to the uneducated. [38]

"The Plan" ("Keikaku"), which appeared the following month (October 1912), is a commendable effort to analyze the relationship between Kōtoku

Shūsui and Kanno Sugako (here called Akiyama Kōichi and Mano Suzuko) as an explanation for Kōtoku's ambivalent connection to the bomb plot. We see them at a hotspring spa like the one at which Kōtoku and Kanno spent their last days together before she left him and the arrests began. Having struck a deal with the government to take the police off their backs, he has regained some peace in the countryside, but she finds herself turning into his domestic servant and secretly longs to reassert her identity by rejoining "the plan" before they both die of tuberculosis. She would like to have Kōichi come with her so they can die together, but she knows there is no hope of getting him to participate in the violence. Kōichi thinks to himself, "I had no intention of promoting this kind of violent XXX-ism ["anarchism," with *mu-sei-fu* suppressed by Hiraide or the editor]," and regrets that he had encouraged Mano and the others by momentarily letting government pressure get the better of him. But when Mano announces that she will be leaving him, he knows what she has in mind and asks to be let in on the plan. Shocked at this turn of events, she decides she must save him so that he can pursue his scholarship. She lies to him, saying that she will leave both him and the plan. As they part, he is hoping for a word from her that will encourage him to plead with her to stay, but she has made her decision.[39]

This is an effective—and probably very accurate—presentation of Kōtoku as a vague, vacillating idealist, and of Kanno as a different sort of romantic— restless and destructive. It suggests (but only suggests) ironies and unfairnesses that were never taken into consideration by the court, but it is far from being a whitewash: Kōtoku is seen as a sad, desperate man who might have joined the plot if given one last chance.

A year after "The Way of the Brutes" and "The Plan" appeared in *Subaru*, the September 1913 issue of *Taiyō* suffered the first banning in that often controversial magazine's nineteen-year history when it carried Hiraide's powerful impression of the High Treason trial, "The Rebels."[40] The story merits discussion in detail, not only because it is a fine piece of documentary fiction but because it was the only such piece written by anyone at that time.

Hiraide claimed to have compromised a good deal in revising the story to avoid its being "misunderstood" by the authorities, but it is difficult to imagine why he and the editors ever thought that the censors would read much past the title and opening paragraph. The action of the story is set in the courtroom on January 18, 1911. The guilty verdict against "Akiyama Kōichi" and the others has just been pronounced. The narrator observes that the chief justice's written explanation of the verdict was of necessity a "long, long" document, because it tried to bring together so many disparate acts by so many people and view them all as one grand conspiracy. The judge's authoritative, objective tone in reading his explanation is unchanged from the opening of the proceedings, when it had convinced some of the defendants that they were

going to receive a genuine trial. The narrator recalls the rumor-filled atmosphere during the news blackout following the arrests, and the remorseless
stand-up grilling of all the suspects. Then he zeroes in on one young defendant
whose eccentric behavior in court had suggested that he was something of a
simpleton.

Modeled after Miura Yasutarō, a tin worker who was twenty-three when
arrested, Mimura Yasusaburō is depicted as a pitiful character. His revolutionary bluster had been a charade that had given way to sheer cringing terror when
he had realized with what a horrendous crime he was being charged. A
flashback shows him confused and alone in his cell one night, when suddenly
he is overcome by a desperate need for companionship and begins pounding on
the door. The guards come running and unlock the cell, and he joyfully rushes
out to embrace them—only to be beaten to the floor. He is thrown back
inside, bruised and handcuffed, but at least he has overcome the horror of the
night. Later, in court, he describes a thwarted attempt to hang himself in his
cell, speaking with such childish enthusiasm that the courtroom fills with
smiles.*

The narrative returns to the expectant atmosphere of the courtroom just
before the reading of the verdict. The spectators' seats are filled, mostly by
students, but a few laborers are present as well. Security is heavy, guards
alternating seats with defendants. The chief justice begins to read his opinion,
and the "young defense attorney," who has been mentioned earlier as observing much of the action, immediately senses: "He's going to execute them all!"
Finally, all but three are sentenced to death (no doubt a conscious departure
from the actual case), and the judges file out quickly.

The young lawyer ponders the reason for their rapid departure. "More than
thirty years had gone by since Japan's court system had been constructed after
the model of the civilized nations," and this legal system requires its judges to
dispense the law with complete impartiality. In capital cases, they must
"endure the unendurable" by imposing the death penalty, but once this duty is
carried out, they become ordinary men again and cannot bear to confront those
whom they have just condemned. The young lawyer tries thus to view their
rapid withdrawal in the best light, but this is just the beginning of his
struggle. He has too many doubts about the fairness of the trial, the lumping
together of the central conspirators and those only peripherally involved, to be
as certain as the disinterested spectators, who file out quietly, that the "civilized" court system has done its job. The trial had simply been a rehash of the
preliminary hearings, in which the procurators had wrung out confessions and

---

*Miura Yasutarō is thought to have gone mad and killed himself in prison in 1916. There is
no known grave. *Taigyaku jiken arubamu*, p. 93; Itoya Toshio, *Taigyaku jiken*, p. 274.

had constructed their reports so as to eliminate details inconsistent with their interpretation.

He walks over to comfort his two clients, who had been "far from the center of the crime" and deserved no more than a five-year sentence. Standing there, he nods silently to Mano Suzuko, with whom he has never spoken. She was one of the two defendants who had taken the opportunity granted by the legal procedure to make a final statement. "My only regret is that our plan failed," she had said. "I believe that the meaning of my sacrifice will be clear to later generations." The young lawyer had found her absurd, her talk of sacrifice ludicrous. The government's exaggerated reaction to the case, their outlandish security measures, only made this woman and her accomplices all the more certain of their glory. But Suzuko had had still more to say. She had gone on to argue, forcefully and emotionally, that she was fully prepared to die as one of the four conspirators, but that she could not resign herself to death knowing how many others had been wrongfully implicated in the plot.* Her words had moved the young lawyer profoundly, but they had done no good.

As she is leaving the courtroom, Suzuko calls a last farewell to the others, which arouses a mood of resistance. "Hurrah for XX-ism!" shouts Mimura, and the others echo the cry, not because they believe in anarchism,[41] thinks the lawyer, but to express their contempt for the verdict. He himself is torn between a desire to see the convicts' lives spared and a need to believe in the authority of the verdict, confessing to himself at the end that this is a belief to which he cannot subscribe.[42]

Hiraide felt like a fool, he wrote in the next month's *Taiyō*, at having made a considerable number of compromises that went against his artistic conscience so as to avoid being misunderstood by the authorities, only to have them treat *Taiyō*'s elite intellectual readership like a pack of lust-crazed revolutionaries. Since it was impossible to provoke any intelligible response from the censors, he said, he hoped that the magazine's readers would appreciate the great care he had lavished on his manuscript out of concern for "the present ludicrous regime," and he probably went on to quote passages from the just-banned story, but the *Taiyō* editors substituted a note indicating that they had decided to suppress this section of the essay.

In criticizing the authorities, Hiraide made it clear that he was not arguing from a position of belief in the supremacy of art, but that politicians were

---

*This is consistent with the view of herself that Kanno wrote in a passionate memoir composed in the week between her sentencing and her execution, "Lingering on the Way to Death" ("Shide no michikusa"), one of the many documents relating to the case that came to light only after the Pacific War. See Moriyama Shigeo, *Taigyaku jiken*, pp. 7–11. Kanno's last farewell, attributed to "Suzuko," is also recorded in Moriyama.

certainly guilty of a tendency to believe in the supremacy of politics. His argument ran as follows:

> One hears politicians grumbling that Japan has never contributed anything to world civilization, but let them think about what that means. If Japan is going to contribute anything, it will be in the fields of art and learning. Even politicians can be proud of *The Tale of Genji*, but Japan is not going to give the world a better political system than constitutional government, nor can strength in battle be counted as a contribution to civilization. The day is long past when the only function of government was to guarantee the nation's existence. Now it must also support the nation's development, which is to say the development of its individuals. This is the normal function of government, while police measures are merely emergency actions, but Japan's politicians do not seem to realize that the casual use of these emergency measures is a great moral defeat for them.[43]

About the time he wrote this, Hiraide was diagnosed for spinal caries. When he went to Kamakura for treatment in December 1913, *Subaru* ceased publication, and by March 1914, Hiraide was dead. A nonreligious memorial service was held at his request and attended by some five hundred people, before whom spoke such literary figures as Yosano Hiroshi, Sōma Gyofū, Abe Jirō, and Mori Ōgai, plus the senior defense counsel in the Kōtoku trial, Hanai Takuzō.*

Hiraide was certainly not a great writer and was probably not a great attorney, but in "The Rebels" he left a vivid narrative that effectively exploited his unique experience. There emerges from his writing, too, the image of an extremely decent man who had the intellectual capacity and the compassion and courage to sort out the political and human complications of a crime that he abhorred. In a letter she wrote just after his death, Yosano Akiko abjectly "confessed" that she had been "too cowardly" to respond to the request for a copy of her poems from "the woman who committed High Treason." She probably did not know, as we have learned from a letter preserved in the white *furoshiki*, that Hiraide had sent a copy of Yosano Akiko's book into prison and had made Kanno Sugako very happy.[44]

---

*Furukawa Kiyohiko, "Hiraide Shū, hito to sakuhin," THS, p. 436. A member of the Diet, Hanai confronted the Home Minister when he appeared before the appropriations committee on January 26, 1911, insisting that the government was morally at fault for having persecuted the socialists ever since the Red Flag Incident. Katsura, Hirata, and Komatsubara came under strong criticism from other Diet members at this time, however, for not taking strong enough measures against anarchism. Furoku, "Taikyaku jiken (1)(2)," TY (May 15, 1911), pp. 44–49.

FEAR AND IGNORANCE

As we go on to examine other literary reactions to the High Treason case, we should take note of Yosano Akiko's fear of becoming involved. Her husband was a friend of one of the convicts, she was close to both Hiraide Shū and Mori Ōgai, and she was a strong-willed, intelligent woman—all conditions that should have permitted a more rational assessment of the risk involved. But she was afraid, and probably not just of the police. The official view of the anarchists as horribly dangerous, violent beasts was the widely held view. One newspaper captioned a smiling photograph of Kōtoku "The Face of the Devil" on the day the verdict came through.[45] Although *Taiyō*'s editorial policy never took the foaming-at-the-mouth approach of *Chūō Kōron*, the magazine did carry a number of alarmist diatribes to match its more levelheaded pieces. And few readers could have been comforted by one large photograph in the December 1910 issue of *Taiyō* which showed the Los Angeles *Times* building 75 percent destroyed, black soot stains rising from the few remaining window frames, after it had been bombed by a local labor union (i.e., anarchists), resulting in one death and scores injured.

Speaking for a less well-educated segment of the populace, the mistress of a Shimbashi geisha house said of Kōtoku in a *Taiyō* interview, "I'm afraid even to mention his name. I think it is the fault of present-day society that a man like that has appeared. As I said before, you can't be careless for a minute. I just think these are frightening times."

Asada Kōson, who had mordantly urged the government to start writing and printing all books if they *really* wanted to destroy independent thought, and who had sharply criticized the administration for causing a greater sense of terror than the criminals merited by making a great show of their security measures and holding the trial in secret, still was pleased to say that the country could breathe a sigh of relief now that most of the anarchists were to be executed. They got what they deserved, he said, and what the people have been expecting.[46]

Asada's was a typical approach to criticizing the government's handling of the case and its all-too-willing suppression of free speech. Even those who blamed the Katsura cabinet's lack of social conscience for the rise of desperate anarchists never doubted that all of them *were* desperate and dangerous. There were very few people in the country—whether geisha or political commentators or novelists—who could share Hiraide's balanced view of the case. He himself did not attempt to publish "The Rebels" until September 1913— nearly three years after the executions, when Katsura was out of office and the Home Minister whose policemen banned *Taiyō* was none other than Saionji's associate, Hara Kei, the consummate anti-Yamagata politician.

There was simply not a widespread belief that the government had perpetrated a frame-up, and apolitical writers who were not convinced that an injustice had been carried out could hardly be expected to start writing critical pieces. Not even Socialists or anarchists were doing that. It is true that the "winter years" were just starting. The bookstores would not start selling Socialist titles freely again for nearly a decade, after which time quite a lot of material by and about Kōtoku was published.[47] The details of the frame-up, however, would not be reconstructed until after the Pacific War. Bourgeois writers did not hesitate to speak out against censorship and attempts at indoctrination, as we shall see. But for the present, the few literary reflections of the High Treason case tended to see it not as a crisis of conscience but a source of fear, and these views were as slow to appear as Hiraide's stories.

11

Other Writers React

THE PROBLEM OF ESCAPISM

"The Japanese naturalists let the tyranny of the government go unchallenged during the Kōtoku incident," wrote Tatsuo Arima in 1969. Earlier, Marius Jansen had asserted that "The facts of the Kōtoku incident . . . were widely available despite the official censorship," but the writers' only response was "withdrawal, retreat, or indifference." And recently Janet Walker has written that the apolitical thrust of naturalism was confirmed when the execution of the conspirators "made it clear that political freedom of the individual was not a goal to be achieved in late Meiji."[1]

I have long doubted that the High Treason case made anything "clear" to anyone, and Japanese commentators are far from unanimous on the literary response to this event. No one has been so sanguine as to attempt to document a concerted struggle for justice. There was no such thing. The most positive move in this direction has been made by postwar Marxist scholars who have contributed a short list of works that somehow "reflect" the case or the atmosphere surrounding it. The list quantitatively demonstrates that universal silence was not the rule, but until very recently (in the work of Moriyama Shigeo) there has been little commentary to suggest the variety or degree of response.[2]

In this chapter we shall examine some of the more frequently cited contemporary "reflections" on the High Treason case to determine whether the few writers who expressed themselves on the subject knew something that their silent colleagues did not know—or pretended not to know. The situation was far from simple. There was no black-and-white "crisis of conscience" in which a handful of courageous writers spoke out against injustice while the rest (and particularly, the naturalists) saw what was happening but chose to turn their backs. Such a view springs from an essentially antiliterary bias, which would have writers cease writing to become political activists. Nor do the few "courageous" figures look so heroic when we see what they were saying—and when. One thing we do find, however, is the continued vitality of naturalist and postnaturalist writing through the darkest days of the Katsura regime.

TOKUTOMI ROKA: "ON REBELLION"

The one writer who took some action that he hoped would change the course of events in the High Treason case was Tokutomi Roka (Kenjirō), a man who came out of the same Christian-inspired, socially concerned Min'yūsha background as Uchida Roan.*

As the younger brother of Min'yūsha's founder, Tokutomi Sohō (Iichirō), Roka seems to have had difficulty achieving emotional independence, even after his tearful domestic novel, *The Cuckoo* (*Hototogisu*, 1898–1900)† won him financial independence. After breaking with Min'yūsha in 1902 when the editors of the company's newspaper removed some antigovernment phrases from an article he had contributed, he caused a small sensation the following year by prefacing his next novel with a declaration of independence from Sohō. A "spiritual revolution" he experienced on Mount Fuji in 1905 was followed by an ostensible reconciliation, but Sohō was too grimly establishmentarian and Roka too unstable for any permanent relationship to develop. A tour of the Holy Land and a visit to Tolstoy in Yasnaya Polyana convinced Roka that he had been wrong to support the war against Russia and influenced him to take up a bucolic lifestyle in Kasuya on the outskirts of Tokyo.

It was here, on January 19, 1911, that Roka first read of the death sentences that had been meted out to the twenty-four convicts on the day before. To his wife he could speak of nothing else, and when news arrived on the twenty-first that only twelve of the condemned had been granted life sentences by the emperor, he wrote to Sohō, asking him to appeal to Katsura for clemency, Sohō being a close associate (and later the official biographer) of the prime minister. Roka apparently included with his letter an appeal addressed directly to Katsura, and a copy is known to have survived at least until 1929, when it was slated for inclusion in Roka's complete works. Instead, there was a note from the editor saying that the authorities had forced its suppression, and present-day scholars are still hoping to learn what happened to it.[3]

In any event, when his letter prompted no reply, Roka sent an appeal via

*Min'yūsha was the publisher of *Kokumin no Tomo* and *Kokumin Shimbun*. See above, p. 45.
†Translated by Sakae Shioya and E. F. Edgett as *Nami-ko* (Tokyo: Yurakusha, 1904), and by Isaac Goldberg as *The Heart of Nami-san* (Boston: Stratford, 1918).

Ikebe Sanzan, editor-in-chief of the *Asahi Shimbun*, in the form of an open letter to the emperor, asking that the remaining twelve be granted commutations. "They, too, are Your Majesty's children," he wrote. They were not mere criminals, he continued, but had always worked for the sake of others. Their "imprudence" in this instance was owing in part to the overzealousness of officials which had driven them to desperation. "It would be a shame for those same officials, who had not allowed them to know the full measure of their Imperial Father's benevolence, to kill them for plotting to kill their Father."[4]

Roka had the letter rushed to the nearest post office before noon on January 25, only to learn when the papers reached Kasuya at three o'clock that the first eleven had been executed the day before, and Kanno Sugako that morning. As Kenneth Strong has recounted the incident, Roka (Kenjirō) and his wife

> wept at the news, and talked of fetching the bodies and burying them in their own land, till they found that in this at least they had been anticipated by friends of the dead. But for them the incident was still not yet over. On the 22nd, two students from the First National Higher School . . . came to Kasuya to invite Kenjirō to speak at the big annual meeting of the School's Oratorical Society [on February 1]. When he agreed, they asked him to suggest a subject. One of them . . . recalls his amazement when Kenjirō, with the firetongs from the porcelain brazier around which they were sitting, traced in the charcoal-ash the characters MUHON-RON, "On Rebellion." Such a title being too dangerous to publish in advance, the subject was given out as "Not Yet Decided" till the morning of the meeting, when the posting on a notice-board of the explosive words quickly filled the hall to overflowing, with students who were unable to push their way in packing the opened windows from the outside.[5]

Roka spoke extemporaneously, but he had written out two slightly different versions in preparation for the talk, and these manuscripts plus some fragments have been collated and edited to produce the most nearly authoritative version of the talk that we have today.[6]

Roka began with an account of the oppressiveness of life in the Tokugawa period, when anyone who wanted to do something new was considered a rebel. The world now, he said, is like Japan was sixty years ago: divided by borders that can only be crossed at certain checkpoints. But the great world current still flooding into Japan is an ideal of the oneness of man. Many will be sacrificed for the realization of this ideal. For Japan and Russia to join hands, the blood of tens of thousands was shed. And "here, at the outset of the forty-fourth year of Meiji, we have already killed twelve rebels." (The last three words were expunged from the text available before the Pacific War: *"Koko ni XXX no XXX o X-su koto to natta."* Xs below will indicate a few other such instances.) In paraphrase, Roka's speech continued as follows:

My young friends, my standpoint is rather different from that of XX [Kōtoku] and the others. I am a coward and hate to shed blood. I do not know whether they seriously intended to commit the crime of XX [High Treason]. I do not know whether, as XXXXX [Ōishi Seinosuke] said, this is all a case of truth being fabricated from a lie. I do not know if, having their tongues tied and pens broken, they were desperately determined to commit forced suicide with XXXX [His Majesty the Emperor]. If there was a plot, I am glad it failed, but I did not want to see them executed. They were not ordinary X [traitors] but XX [*shishi*, heroic patriots] who, with dreams of a new world of liberty and equality, meant to sacrifice themselves for the sake of all mankind. The XX [government] is responsible for having changed them from harmless Socialists into XXXXXX [anarchists].

The blood of the Restoration Loyalists still flows in our veins. ⋯⋯⋯⋯⋯⋯⋯⋯⋯⋯⋯⋯. [I love His Majesty the Emperor / *Boku wa Tennō Heika ga daisuki de aru.*] He is the model of Japanese manhood. It was not he but his advisors (*hohitsu*) who lacked the compassion to spare the twelve. If only some of the great early Meiji advisors were still alive! If only the Crown Prince XXXXXXXXXXXXX [were the actual son of the Empress], a woman of formidable intelligence! [Presumably, Roka means by this that the Emperor did not always have her there to advise him because the mother of the Crown Prince was a concubine.] Because there is no one who will dare to confront and advise the Emperor out of loyalty, we have killed twelve anarchists only to sow the seeds for countless more. The true loyalists are not the cabinet ministers but the twelve who were killed, for the warning they have given the Imperial House.

This was a perfect opportunity to raise Japan in the eyes of the world, to show them that we have a benevolent Emperor who does not execute unruly subjects but gives them an opportunity for self-evaluation. The ministers are not wise and kind but cold and calculating: XXXXXXXXXXXXXX [if there had been twenty-five under sentence of death, would they have spared twelve and one-half]? They engaged in an ugly show of force, hiding behind the Emperor as a shield. But they are not the only ones to blame. Was there no one in the Diet who could overcome the awe inspired by the words "High Treason"? Was there not a single religious leader to step forth and beg for the rebels' lives? All fifty million of us bear the responsibility, but primarily to blame is the government. Perhaps they thought they were serving the nation, but seen through the eyes of Heaven, this was sheer XX [premeditated murder] carried out in secret. They wanted to frighten the people with the death penalty, then curry a little favor with clemency for twelve, and then they went ahead and XX [assassinated] the rest!

But still, we must be fair and try to see things from the government's point of view. Position restricts one, and the years bring old age. The authorities are balding men who can think of nothing but unity and order. They have forgotten their own spirited youth.

My young friends, you must not fear rebellion. You must not fear to become rebels yourselves. "Fear not them which kill the body, but are not able to kill the soul." [Matt. 10:28] A dead soul is one which has ceased to grow, and to grow one must continually rebel. Kōtoku and the others rebelled politically and went to their deaths. But they are already resurrected. Their graves are empty. They died as traitors on the gallows, and while we may not approve of what they did, who can doubt their pure, patriotic motives? Saigō Takamori was also a traitor, but today no one is admired more as a hero of his country. Through an error in judgment, Kōtoku and the others became traitorous subjects, but a hundred years from now everyone will lament the frustration of their high purpose.[7]

Strong describes the aftermath of the speech as follows:

The end of the speech was met with total silence, and then with prolonged and enthusiastic applause. There were repercussions, however, which Kenjirō had not foreseen. When the content of the speech became known, Nitobe Inazō, the School's Principal, who had given formal permission to the students to invite Kenjirō, but without knowing the subject of his lecture, at once offered his resignation to the Ministry of Education. There was a flurry of comings and goings, on and off the campus: students "apologized" to Nitobe and to the Minister, assuring them both that nobody had been "influenced" by Kenjirō's dangerous ideas. Kenjirō wrote to the Minister of Education and to the Prime Minister, urging them not to accept Nitobe's resignation. In the end, Nitobe was only censured. No action was taken against Kenjirō himself, perhaps because of his brother's connections: though for a while he was violently attacked, in the press and at public meetings, for "lack of patriotism," and a Christian College where he had been asked to speak suddenly cancelled the invitation. Kenjirō was unrepentant. He had recently built a small library on to his cottage, and now named it the "Shūsui Room," after the leader of the executed radicals.[8]

As Strong points out in a footnote, Roka received lavish praise for his courage throughout the affair when the facts became known after the Pacific War, and even in paraphrase the passion and daring of the speech are evident. There are, however, certain features of the talk that should be noted. First of all, Roka, like most Japanese, was ignorant of the details of the government's fabricated case. He accepted the official conclusion that the convicted twenty-four had been plotting to assassinate the emperor. He criticized the government, therefore, primarily for the use of heavy-handed tactics that could only inspire increased numbers of equally dangerous conspirators.

Second, the declarations of his "love" for the emperor contain not the least bit of false rhetoric. Roka was making the classic distinction between the emperor and his malicious advisors that nearly all critics of the government would make—and had made throughout the better part of Japan's history. To cite another instance, this was essentially the argument of Miyake Setsurei, who was one of several speakers to address an overflow audience of more than one thousand attending a "High Treason Case Lecture Meeting" held on February 6, 1911, at the conservative Kokugakuin University. Kōtoku had proved himself a filial son and a loyal disciple, noted Setsurei, but wicked ministers (*kansha*) at the emperor's side (*kunsoku*) had hidden from him the divine glow of the imperial benevolence (*kun'on*), and the trial had given him no opportunity to defend himself. (So enraged was a Diet member named Arakawa Gorō, an invited guest, that he demanded an opportunity to reply to Setsurei. When the chairman of the proceedings attempted to restrain him, Arakawa threw the man bodily into the audience. The crowd—mostly students—was on its feet and shouting. After Arakawa had managed to deliver an emotional blast at Setsurei's "shallow" criticism of the government, the students sent the smiling Setsurei off with cheers.)[9]

Roka's criticism of these wicked ministers contained yet another traditional element. He resented the treatment of high-minded idealists as common criminals. Their ideas—and his—may have been modern and cosmopolitan, but their spirits were as pure as those of the greatest "noble failures" in Japanese history, including Saigō, the apotheosized leader of the 1877 Satsuma Rebellion.*

As a third and final point, let us not gloss over the fact that, despite Roka's genuine passion for justice, he often argued like a man seriously out of touch with reality. If we take him at his word, he equated the soldiers who died in the Russo-Japanese War (so that the two countries could "join hands," no less) with "other" rebels working toward the ideal of a unified world, such as Kōtoku. His reference to the empress might be taken as a daring stroke, but what could it possibly accomplish? Courage from a man who wore dark glasses "to protect others, so he said, from the abnormal brightness of his eyes"[10] can hardly be accepted at face value. If Roka was left alone by the Katsura government, it was probably less out of respect for his brother's connections than awareness that his somewhat fuddled attack was not a very great threat.†

Moriyama Shigeo is willing to grant that "On Rebellion" might possibly qualify as the one Japanese parallel to Zola's "J'accuse," but only upon stipulating that the High Treason case had none of the far-reaching consequences

---

*See Ivan Morris, *The Nobility of Failure* (New York: Holt, Rinehart and Winston, 1975), pp. 217–75. Roka was right: Kōtoku was a *shishi*, not a modern revolutionary, as F. G. Notehelfer has demonstrated in *Kōtoku Shūsui, Portrait of a Japanese Radical*.

†Nakano Yoshio suggests that the sudden flare-up of the textbook problem (see above, p. 110) may have distracted the government's attention from this relatively isolated incident. See Nakano Yoshio, *Roka Tokutomi Kenjirō*, 3 vols. (Chikuma shobō, 1974) 3:42–44.

of the Dreyfus affair,[11] which had brought France to the brink of civil war and would permanently alter that country's political and religious life. Japan was not split down the middle by a clear-cut issue of injustice, nor did Roka, with his belief in the emperor, represent an especially penetrating view of the issues that were involved. For a more lucid perception of the times, we will have to turn to the makers of the new literature, whose gazes were more reliably trained upon the real world. First, however, we must deal with one of their most effective critics.

Ishikawa Takuboku: The Impotence of Naturalism

Of all the writers whom we are considering in connection with the High Treason case, only two have emerged since the dismantling of Meiji state censorship in 1945 with a tinge of heroism attached to their names. The first is Tokutomi Roka, who spoke out boldly in spite of his ignorance. The other is Ishikawa Takuboku, who gained an unusually detailed knowledge of the case through his friend Hiraide Shū and resolved to leave a true record for future generations (see above, p. 156), while maintaining a discreet silence for the present.

Earlier, we saw Takuboku as an effective critic of naturalist theory, writing in 1909 to decry the "characteristic Japanese form of cowardice" he saw in Hasegawa Tenkei's attempts to reconcile the new literature and the *kokutai* (see above, p. 105). As the High Treason case unfolded, Takuboku's disgust for the Katsura regime and his growing awareness of socialism joined with his disappointment in naturalism to emerge as the period's most influential critique of escapism in modern Japanese literature. This was the essay entitled "The Impasse of Our Age" ("Jidai heisoku no genjō"). Here we shall examine the rapid development of Takuboku's antinaturalist thought during the High Treason case, considering its implications both for his own poetry and for literature in general.

It is well known that "The Impasse of Our Age" was, in part, a critique of the Katsura regime's repressiveness, but the timing of its appearance is not often discussed. The opening sentence tells us that Takuboku wrote the piece in response to an essay by Uozumi Setsuro which had appeared in the *Asahi* literary column on August 22 and 23, 1910, and that he intended his critique to run in the same column "a few days" later. The fact that he *did* not publish the essay is sometimes taken to mean that he *could* not because of the threat of censorship, but there is no evidence to support this. Takuboku's essay does not seem much more outspoken in its critique of "authority" than Uozumi's, and in fact Uozumi would go on to publish his scathing denunciation of censorship and of "Well-Behaved Freethinkers" in the *Asahi* on September 16, 1910 (see

above, p. 146), while "The Impasse of Our Age" would appear without difficulty in May 1913, posthumously. When he wrote the piece, Takuboku's
connections with the *Asahi* were good and were improving all the time (he was
editing Futabatei Shimei's complete works for the *Asahi*, and in September
1910 he became head of the paper's new tanka column), which would suggest
that Takuboku himself was the one who decided not to go ahead with
publication.

The essay that sparked Takuboku's was itself a response to an earlier piece. In
"Naturalism as an Ideology of Self-Assertion" ("Jiko-shuchō no shisō toshite
no shizenshugi"), Uozumi had voiced his agreement with another writer's idea
that naturalism was one manifestation of a tendency toward assertion of the self
which had become evident in the preceding decade, and that conservative old
men would be better advised to lead the young in good directions than attempt
to suppress them. Flabby as this may sound, Uozumi did not hesitate to name
the "hated enemies" of the young as the state, society, and—in Japan—the
family, which had conspired with the state over the centuries to obstruct
individual development; and he found ludicrous such attempts to reconcile
naturalism and nationalism as the "deficient naturalism" of Hasegawa Tenkei,
Tayama Katai, and Iwano Hōmei.[12]

In resorting to such phrases, Uozumi obviously had a terminology problem.
It was on his vague definition of "naturalism" that Takuboku leapt, crushing
Uozumi's slim little effort under a major analysis of the relationship of young
intellectuals and the state. In the end, however, Takuboku was in far greater
agreement with Uozumi than his highly charged rhetoric would imply.
Uozumi had simply failed to take into account the fact that "naturalism" could
no longer encompass all the new writing, and rather than conclude that the
label was inappropriate, he had tried to redefine the label. Takuboku only
added to the confusion when, instead of noting this defect, he accused Uozumi
of falsely asserting that the "scientific, fatalistic tendency" of "pure naturalism" had been joined with the new generation's self-assertive tendency in a
conscious conspiracy against their common enemy, the state—an extreme
(and finally meaningless) overstatement of Uozumi's point.

For Takuboku, the state was indeed the enemy. "The air enveloping us
young men is stagnant. The power of the state reaches everywhere. . . . We
must stand together and declare war on the impasse of our age." But naturalism had chosen to ignore the existence of the enemy. "'The nation must be
strong. We have no reason to oppose this. But we refuse to take part in it!' Is
this not the totality of the patriotism that can be expected from the reasonably
well-educated young, nearly all of whom are like strangers to the state?"
Takuboku went on to say that naturalism had performed a useful function at
the beginning when it had turned youth from baseless idealism and religious
daydreaming to the discovery and affirmation of mundane reality, but the time

was now past when the simple recognition of reality contained the stimulus of criticism. Naturalism had now declined to the level of a mere record or tale. What was needed, declared Takuboku, was a bold, free, and rigorous critical analysis of *today* in order to determine the shape of *tomorrow*, for one thing was certain: "It is utterly impossible for us to build our own new world with our own strength if we leave all 'establishment' as it is and try to work within it." [13]

This raises the question of just how far Takuboku was willing to go. As he wrote in August, the facts of the High Treason case were just beginning to trickle out, Hiraide was just getting to work on the defense, and Takuboku would not have his privileged look at the court records until January. Imai Yasuko has noted Takuboku's lack of sympathy in this essay for what he calls the anarchists' "blind resistance" to authority, but she argues that even at this stage Takuboku was willing to question the legitimacy of the imperial institution, the ultimate taboo that so few dared challenge.

Imai points specifically to the essay of Tenkei's cited earlier (see above, pp. 97–98, 105) as representative of the kind of "naturalism" that Takuboku was criticizing. Tenkei had argued that since naturalism was predicated upon reality, it conformed perfectly to the reality of Japan as reigned over by an unbroken line of emperors. It is this kind of reasoning, Imai argues, that Takuboku means by the phrase "that special Japanese logic" which has delayed a free investigation into the power of the state. [14]

I suspect that Takuboku felt he had gone too far in "The Impasse of Our Age" with his euphemistic references to the "weakest planks" comprising the box in which "the most radical among us" found themselves compressed to the point of having to "lash out blindly." [15] If, in his mind, these were all-too-clear references to the emperor system, then his decision (assuming it was his) to file this essay among his materials compiled for future generations becomes more understandable. Imai is probably correct in her interpretation, but her efforts vividly demonstrate what a close, thoughtful reading is required to abstract the anti-imperial element. The editor of a posthumous collection did not seem to think the piece too strong for inclusion, and it does not show up on lists of banned materials.

If Takuboku was hinting at the need for a political upheaval, and if he found naturalism (or rather, certain obsolete naturalist theory) insufficient for this task, what role did he assign to literature? In other words, where did he fit in as a poet? Although "The Impasse of Our Age" is a widely quoted essay, Takuboku's reputation rests primarily on his poetry—particularly his tanka, which "today enjoy greater popularity than any written in the thousand year history of the form," according to Donald Keene. [16]

Takuboku exploited the tanka's seemingly fossilized thirty-one-syllable framework to make deeply felt personal statements that rank him among the major modern Japanese writers. Probably no other writer has attained such

critical stature on so small a body of works, and in fact this reputation might
not be diminished if all we had today were the one tanka collection he published in his lifetime, *A Handful of Sand* (*Ichiaku no suna*). Published in
December 1910, while Takuboku was still learning about socialism and the
High Treason case, some half dozen of its 551 poems (420 of which were
written in 1910) manage to reflect his growing political awareness. Four of
them suggest an apprehension (expressed more directly elsewhere)[17] that he
was moving in the same dangerous direction as those who were being imprisoned. For example:

> My friend,
> The one they used to call a genius,
> Is in prison now.
> The autumn wind is blowing.[18]

> two friends
> just like me:
> one dead
> one, out of jail,
> now sick[19]

There are these two on censorship:

> The state
> Has banned this book with the worn, red cover.
> Have to search for it these days
> In the bottom of a suitcase.[20]

> They wouldn't let him sell his book,
> And now I'm meeting with him
> On the street like this:
> Autumn morning.[21]

And this little beauty on the present regime:

> Woke with a shock!
> Dreaming Prime Minister Katsura
> Had me by the arm.
> Autumn: two a.m.[22]

The night he wrote most of these (September 9, 1910), Takuboku also wrote
a group of eight tanka more or less connected with the Kōtoku case which were

published under the collective title "A September Night's Discontent" ("Kugatsu no yoru no fuhei") but not anthologized with the others—for perfectly sound literary reasons. The following two are noteworthy:

> More careful now
> About "revolution"—
> A word I always
> Used to like—
> I've entered autumn.[23]

> Come to think of it,
> Something about him suggests
> That he, too,
> Was an accomplice
> Of Shūsui's.[24]

After the trial and executions, when he had completed his compilation of secret materials, Takuboku wrote a series of longer, modern-style poems that appeared in July 1911 under the title "After Endless Discussions" ("Hateshi-naki giron no ato"), a phrase that he had drawn from an English translation of Kropotkin's *Memoirs of a Revolutionist*. As Imai Yasuko has noted, the poems themselves are little more than romanticized scenes suggested to him by his reading of Kropotkin.[25] They depict an imaginary cell of Japanese revolution-aries—some cowardly theoreticians, at least one mechanic ready to take action (reminiscent of Miyashita Takichi)—meeting secretly in a dark attic and engaging in heated debate by candlelight.* The narrator, an idealized young intellectual, tells us in the most strongly worded piece, "A Spoonful of Cocoa" ("Kokoa no hitosaji") that he understands the sadness of the terrorist, who "would like to speak through action / Those words that have been wrested from him," and who is willing to "hurl his flesh against the enemy." In a five-hour debate that almost comes to blows, a "young economist" shouts at the narrator that his ideas on the management of power in the "new society" are "inflammatory."[26]

The narrator of "After Endless Discussions" is, of course, Takuboku's own best image of himself, and it was precisely "to inflame the ideas of the young" that Takuboku conceived a plan consonant with his future-oriented activities at the time.[27] By no means a believer in violence, he decided to publish a magazine. He wrote to Hiraide Shū on January 22, 1911:

---

*The title piece has been translated as "After a Fruitless Argument" in Geoffrey Bownas and Anthony Thwaite, *The Penguin Book of Japanese Verse* (Harmondsworth: Penguin Books, 1964), pp. 182–83.

For a long while I have been daydreaming about publishing a magazine that
would advocate unicameralism, universal suffrage, and international peace. . . .
Even if I had the money to put out such a magazine, its sale would almost always
be forbidden by our present "military government," as you call it. Thus I have
conceived a plan for . . . something that would be *called*—but which in fact
would not be—a literary magazine. . . . Its purpose would be to cultivate perhaps
a hundred or two hundred young people who would be prepared to accept
progressive ideas at such time as we—or others—were able to advocate them.
Through a most gradual approach, and keeping within the bounds set both by
our literary character and by the government (so as to avoid banning), I would
demand that our readers clarify their awareness of the circumstances of contemporary youth and the inner dynamism of the people's life.[28]

Full of plans for this new venture that was somehow to transcend literature,
Takuboku neglected his health, despite a doctor's warning that his chronic
pleurisy could kill him within a year. He and his partner, the poet Toki
Zenmaro, managed to borrow the money they needed for the first issue, but it
was lost when the printer went bankrupt that April (1911). Takuboku was
working on his second collection of tanka when he died a year later at the age of
twenty-six.[29] Toki managed to carry their plans forward in September 1913 by
founding the magazine *Seikatsu to Geijutsu* (Life and Art), in which published
such prominent leftists as Sakai Toshihiko, Ōsugi Sakae, and Arahata Kanson,
but its minuscule circulation—ranging from 1,000 to 1,500—reflected the
vastly reduced activities of Japan's leftists during the "winter years."*

"Takuboku died so young that it is foolish to tax him for a lack of maturity,"
Donald Keene has written. "Nevertheless, it is hard to escape the feeling that
he remained to the end a brilliant, headstrong child, capable of strong passions
but not always of understanding them."[30] In "After Endless Discussions," we
recognize that romantic strain shared by so many who have looked to socialism
for solutions to political and social injustice.† Another tendency in Takuboku

---

*GNBD, p. 603; NPBT 1:406. Ōsugi and Arahata were able to publish *Kindai Shisō*
between October 1912 and September 1914 without posting a bond or registering as a periodical by limiting the forty-page monthly to literary and intellectual theory, and by avoiding
current events, as implied in Article 2 of the Publication Law. (See above, chap. 2, p. 23.) This
would mean that they were required to submit their nonmagazine to the censors three days prior
to publication as though it were a book. Fed up with such "intellectual masturbation," they
abandoned the magazine and reissued Kōtoku's old *Heimin Shimbun*. They started up the
magazine again, however, when continual bans destroyed the paper. This time, with slightly
bolder contents, *Kindai Shisō* lasted only from October 1915 to January 1916. See GNBD,
pp. 339–40.
†The paucity of political poems in the second tanka collection, *Kanashiki gangu*, suggests

often seen in leftward-oriented thinkers was his move toward viewing literature as a device to be used for political ends. His new journal "would be
called—but . . . in fact *would not be*—a literary magazine," as he wrote to
Hiraide. Carried to extremes, this is the road to socialist realism. It is also the
kind of argument that plays into the hands of some of the more intolerant
Western students of Japanese history, who are so eager to prove the political
impotence of Japanese writers and intellectuals. To them it matters little that
naturalism succeeded in establishing the novel in Japan as "the literary form
which most directly reveals to us the complexity, the difficulty, and the
interest of life in society, and best instructs us in our human variety and
contradiction," to borrow Lionel Trilling's defense of the novel from *The
Liberal Imagination*.[31]

The only answers that could satisfy critics of a writer who had "failed" to
take political action would be either the writer's engagement in political
activity quite separate from his profession or the commitment of his writing to
the expression of his political views. Such critics either have no use for literature, or else they want to see propaganda; they devalue "all the gratuitous
manifestations of feeling, of thought, and of art, of all such energies of the
human spirit as are marked by spontaneity, complexity, and variety."[32] Literary freedom is abhorrent to doctrinaire critics of both the left and the right: the
charge of narrowness leveled against writing that "failed" to deal with social
problems would eventually give way to the charge of narrowness for "failing"
to cooperate with the war effort. Hasegawa Tenkei may not have understood all
the implications of his heralding the advent of the Age of Disillusionment, but
many of the practicing writers went on to study their lives and themselves
relatively free from traditional preconceptions. By communicating their original thoughts and feelings to their countrymen, they were engaged in a political act "which affirmed the value of individual existence in all its variousness,
complexity, and difficulty."[33]

Takuboku himself had, in effect, taken this position when he saw the need
for what he called "poems to eat," by which he meant "poems that are down to
earth, poems with feelings unremoved from real life. Not delicacies, not a
feast, but poems that taste like our daily meals; poems, then, that are *necessities*
to us."[34] When he wrote this, late in 1909, Takuboku was repudiating all of
his earlier works with their "hackneyed sentiments" and self-conscious posing.
During the next two years, in the midst of which came the High Treason case,

---

that those in the first represented the mood of the time (autumn 1910—hence the many autumn
poems, though see Moriyama Shigeo, *Taigyaku jiken*, p. 41) rather than a developing ideology.
See, for example, NKBT 23:188.3, 192.3, 199.6, 199.7, and 201.9. The poem "Ie"
("Home"), which follows the "socialist" poems in *Yobiko to kuchibue*, seems a shocking admission that what Takuboku *really* wanted was a comfortable home, his pipe, and his slippers.

he wrote the few hundred tanka for which he is best remembered, many of
which have been beautifully translated by Carl Sesar:

> wrote GREAT
> in the sand
> a hundred times
> forgot about dying
> and went on home [35]

> kidding around
> carried my mother
> piggy-back
> I stopped dead, and cried
> she's so light . . . [36]

> give me
> the creeps
> some memories
> like putting on
> dirty socks [37]

> pathetic, my father—
> tired again
> of reading the paper
> he plays with ants
> in the garden [38]

> late at night
> no hat, a man
> enters the station
> stands, sits down
> finally leaves [39]

> late at night
> from a room somewhere [in the hospital]
> a commotion
> guess somebody died—
> I hold my breath [40]

I do not like to think Takuboku would have repudiated memorable poems like
these for the same shallow political reasons that prompted him to repudiate

naturalism. But this much is certain: if naturalism is irrelevant, so are "poems to eat." Neither provides a program, a doctrine, a way past the "impasse of the age."

Trilling reminds us that the rational organization of modern society exists to guarantee the integrity of each person's inner life—his "pursuit of happiness" as defined for him by his particular intellectual and emotional—irrational—needs. Inherent in the organizational impulse, however, is the tendency to snip off loose ends and get rid of unpredictable and complicating emotional factors, that is, a tendency to forget the liberal purpose for which the organization was created. It is here that literature comes into play, by keeping alive a sense of the messy variety of human happiness and suffering, for "literature is the human activity that takes the fullest and most precise account of variousness, possibility, complexity, and difficulty."[41]

Without such a *sense* of human variety, the purposes of liberal organization can give way to mere organization, Trilling warns us. It seems to me just as certain that without this sense, there is no hope of establishing a liberal organization where none exists. Thus it is precisely the writer who has the ability to convey a sense of inner vitality and curiosity through powerful imagery who contributes to the liberalization of society. If Natsume Sōseki has emerged as Japan's greatest modern novelist, it is not because of the speeches his characters deliver, and certainly not because of any doctrines or slogans they spout, but because of the indelible imagery with which he conveys his view of the world—in other words, what he shares with a sensualist like Tanizaki Jun'ichirō (the second most likely candidate for "greatest") rather than with a liberal theoretician like Yoshino Sakuzō. Of these two Takuboku poems, I would say that the vivid individuality of the second was potentially more dangerous to the Meiji state than the first, with its one controversial abstraction:

> More careful now
> About "revolution"—
> A word I always
> Used to like—
> I've entered autumn.

> give me
> the creeps
> some memories
> like putting on
> dirty socks

Naturalism's single greatest contribution to the development of modern Japanese literature—and society—lay in its messiness. The very fact that it never was—and never has been—successfully defined; that no two of its writers (when they could be identified) ever fit neatly into any of its theories; that it represented no ideology; that "it" was actually many writers who took a variety of positions with regard to change and the status quo; all this is ample demonstration that "naturalism" was merely a convenient and misleading label for the beginning of the representation of "variousness, possibility, complexity, and difficulty" in Japanese literature. *Waseda Bungaku* illustrated this in February 1910 when it named the "decadent" Nagai Kafū as the previous year's outstanding writer. Admirers of pat labels were outraged and accused the supposedly naturalist journal of not knowing its own mind (see above, p. 125). But the journal was not out looking for the right doctrine expressed in the proper jargon: it showed an open-minded response to what it considered a unique version of "the new literature" which was "firmly anchored in reality" while "decrying all restraints on life."[42]

The same flexibility could not be attributed to the story we will turn to next, a crude example of leftist impatience with the literary representation of individual life.

ARAHATA KANSON: ESCAPISTS RIGHT AND LEFT

Hiraide Shū's "The Rebels" was the only more-or-less contemporary literary work that focused directly on the events of the High Treason trial itself. By the time the proletarian literature movement took off in the 1920s, there seems to have been virtually no interest in the case. Moriyama Shigeo has found that neither of the major proletarian journals printed any literary work based on the Kōtoku incident, the one possible exception being a single act of a four-act play that might have had some indirect connection. And the only worthwhile prewar fictionalization of the Kōtoku-Kanno relationship, he says, was Hiraide's "The Plan" (see above, pp. 162–63).[43] One contemporary work by a leftist commented on the case: a story called "Escapists" ("Tōhisha"), which appeared in Toki Zenmaro's *Seikatsu to Geijutsu* in October 1913, the month after "The Rebels" was banned. This was written by Arahata Kanson, a well-known Socialist who devoted some of his earlier publishing efforts to fiction.[44] It is of interest both as a view of the "winter years" atmosphere and as a critique of escapism in mainstream literature.

The story is short and portrays a meeting of some twenty "comrades" in the house of "S" (Sakai Toshihiko), after which A(rahata) and Ō(sugi Sakae) are shown walking home together. The focus remains throughout on the strong temptation felt by all to leave "the movement" because of police pressure.

In the ceremonial alcove of Sakai's house hangs the last poem that K(ōtoku) wrote in prison, pictures of comrades executed in the High Treason case, and pictures of famous foreign Socialists and anarchists. Sakai opens the meeting by criticizing mainstream literary people for not understanding the causes of crime and the suffering of the poor but accepting them as fate; and for misunderstanding the capitalist origins of war and supporting the army's "righteous" causes. To them, he says, everything is insoluble; they shut their eyes to these ugly, unpleasant phenomena and lose themselves in drink and lust, becoming uninvolved observers of life, taking the attitude of escapists. "But these problems are *not* insoluble! If only they knew that the process of social evolution is making a new society, they would have to join our movement!"

Of course, what the new writers found insoluble were not the particular social problems but the broader human condition. Masamune Hakuchō would later write: "The more outstanding a work of literature is in its pursuit of life, the more apt it is to show life as unresolved." Which in turn recalls this analysis of Hemingway and Faulkner by Lionel Trilling: "They seldom make the attempt at formulated solution, they rest content with the 'negative capability.' And this negative capability, this willingness to remain in uncertainties, mysteries, and doubts, is not, as one tendency of modern feeling would suppose, an abdication of intellectual activity. Quite the contrary, it is precisely an aspect of their intelligence, of their seeing the full force and complexity of their subject matter."[45]

The next to speak is M(orita Yūshū), who has not been to one of these meetings since the High Treason case, which, he confesses, frightened him off and made him, too, an escapist. Nor does he intend to return here after this one visit. He is a father now and locked in the "shackles" of family-supporting and child-rearing. Despite his having left the movement, police still tail him and plainclothesmen question his family, who then vent their distress on him. His child, too, he fears, will have to suffer for what he did.

The narrator then tells us that under the increasing persecution of socialism, various comrades have been jailed, their rights of speech, assembly, and publication curtailed, and their jobs, homes, and friends lost. Some have died in prison (where their jailers refused to speak to them); some have gone mad and killed themselves; another has publicly renounced the movement and is now actually engaged in propagandizing to convince laborers to be satisfied with their lot.[46] Of those who escaped arrest in the High Treason case, many have scattered throughout the country, losing themselves in religion, drink, and sex, although some of these are merely biding their time, keeping true to the cause (if that is what this heavily expurgated passage means).

Having presented to the comrades a disturbing reflection of their own doubts, Morita leaves the meeting. Long, abstract discussions ensue, during which Arahata realizes that not only those who leave the movement but also those who remain to do nothing but discuss are escapists—a conclusion not unlike Takuboku's in "After Endless Discussions."

Spies watch the comrades leave after the meeting breaks up. Arahata and Ōsugi walk together, engaged in an intense (and partially suppressed) discussion of the escapist problem, their faces glowing with youthful vitality, their eyes burning with a piercing gleam of intelligence and passion. Continuing on alone, Arahata decides that it is all to the good if the middle-class intellectual young are frightened off, for then a true proletarian movement will begin and "the time will come when, instead of being led by the middle class and spoken for by the youthful intelligentsia, OOOOOOOO, OOOOO." Arahata walks home beneath the dome of the stars, a nearby hill echoing with the sound of his voice as he sings aloud the Marseillaise—in English.[47]

Perhaps the best thing that can be said for this story is that poor Morita is not summarily dismissed as a turncoat. He (or rather, his position, since there are no characters in the story, only ideological positions) and the other comrades are presented as having to face a real dilemma—not as to what constitutes the truth but how one is to relate to it. Sakai says at one point, "Leaving the movement doesn't make anybody a hero, and neither does ten years of unswerving loyalty. We are all weak, ordinary men controlled by circumstances. Those for whom it is convenient to quit will do so, and those who persist will OOOOOOOOOOOOO."[48]

What we do *not* have here is an analysis of the High Treason trial or of the personalities or issues involved. It is viewed simply as some terrible storm that burst over the radical movement, leaving in its aftermath a troupe of lurking detectives. This much can be found in the works of "escapist" mainstream writers, and at least two such stories, we shall see, are by bona fide naturalists.

HAKUCHŌ, MOKUTARŌ, AND KATAI: THE BOURGEOIS VIEW

When Hasegawa Tenkei labeled Masamune Hakuchō a "nihilistic" writer, the police are thought to have overreacted to the term and assigned men to tail him as an accomplice of Kōtoku.* He described his dealings with the police in the

---

*GNBZ 97:401. This is the usual explanation, but Moriyama Shigeo, *Taigyaku jiken*, pp. 172–73, notes that Hakuchō may have been under suspicion because his name had been found on a Heiminsha mailing list, perhaps for receipt of a Kropotkin translation by Kōtoku. The trip to Kōtoku's birthplace, Shikoku, may also have looked suspicious, he says (Moriyama, ibid., p. 174). According to Uchida Roan in "Shōsetsu kyakuhon o tsūjite mitaru gendai shakai," TY (February 15, 1911), p. 108, the provincial birthplace of the naturalist Tokuda (Chikamatsu) Shūkō was searched, even though he himself no longer ventured out of Tokyo. The police were also said to be rifling Tayama Katai's wastebasket in search of incriminating evidence. See OHSS, p. 425.

story "A Dangerous Character" ("Kiken jinbutsu"). Unlike "The Rebels" and "Escapists," this story did not appear nearly three years after the executions but just two weeks after they had taken place, in the February 1911 *Chūō Kōron*.

Instead of ideological speeches, what we find in "A Dangerous Character" is contempt for the stupidity and wastefulness of a government that is unable to distinguish between violent radicals and introspective writers. Having succeeded in selling a manuscript, the protagonist, a restless young writer, uses the money to travel aimlessly from his provincial home, deciding after he leaves to visit his mother's birthplace on the island of Shikoku. He has never been there before, and he vaguely hopes to find there something that will help him understand his inner turmoil.

He has a five-hour layover to kill in Okayama, and while he is visiting a friend in that city, there is a knock on the door. The rather creepy fellow who had earlier directed him to the house comes in, hesitantly introducing himself as Detective Kurozuka of the Okayama Police Department. Kurozuka has been assigned to "accompany" him while he is away from home. This explains to him why he has had the feeling that he was being followed, but a sense of annoyance quickly replaces the satisfaction of having solved the problem. It is, however, only a sense of annoyance. We see here none of the terror usually associated with lurking detectives—but then, the policemen themselves are disarmingly open about their work. "Well, I'm catching the six o'clock train for Uno," says the writer, "so you can wait for me either here or at the station." He leaves Kurozuka to warm himself by a charcoal brazier near the front door.

The writer tells his amused friend that neither he nor anyone else is capable of writing "dangerous" stuff these days, and he goes on to recount the spy activities of the policeman in his village, who had actually complained to the writer when his superiors had docked him 25 percent for not doing a thorough enough investigation of the writer's daily routine. The policeman is supposed to do this even if it means slacking off on gamblers and burglars. The writer observes that "it's practically impossible to watch someone who stays shut up indoors all day. You can't report something that hasn't happened." No wonder taxes keep going up if the government is spending money on such foolishness, he adds.

The writer leaves his friend's house with the detective, who shows him a shortcut to the station and remarks, "I feel bad about having to bother you writers, but it's my job." They do not sit together on the train, but some time later the detective comes over to tell him that the next stop is Uno, where they will be separating, although "I won't talk to you when we get off."

The writer transfers to a ferry that takes him across to Shikoku, and he is followed to the inn where he sleeps that night, but he seems to have lost this second (or third) detective at the station the next morning. Instead of rejoicing over this, however, he actually goes looking for the detective at the station master's office! When there is no sign of the man on the train, the writer becomes concerned. He realizes that they have assumed he will be going to the end of the line, since there are no famous scenic spots along the way, and it only then dawns on him that by disembarking at his mother's old village he will be free. This puts him in a good mood, which, however, does not survive the distaste he feels for the local geisha he hires.

On the train the next day, he notices some worried-looking policemen rushing around at stations along the way and overhears something about a "notebook." That night at the inn, he realizes he has lost the notebook in which he has been recording his memories and little snatches of everyday life for the past three years, things that he would prefer to keep secret, although he imagines how disappointed the police will be at their innocuousness. He spends a lonely night recalling the contents of the notebook, which brings the story to a close.[49]

Even some of the policemen in this tedious little sketch seem to suspect that policy is being set by fools. Through them, and through the ironic detachment of the protagonist, Hakuchō conveys a sense that what is real is to be apprehended by the open eyes, ears, and mind of the individual rather than by an unquestioning acceptance of the official line. Kanson, in "Escapists," believes not so much in reality as Truth.

The terror that was absent from "A Dangerous Character" became the central motif of a one-act play published in *Subaru* the following month (March 1911): "Izumiya Dyers" ("Izumiya somemonomise") by Kinoshita Mokutarō. This piece is invariably cited as a reflection of the High Treason case,[50] but it is an incredibly puerile work, especially in comparison with the products of Mokutarō's *Subaru* associates, Hiraide Shū, Ishikawa Takuboku, and Mori Ōgai. It consists of a lot of frenzied comings and goings, whispered suspicions, horrified gasps, and high-minded speeches by handsome young men whose black capes are picturesquely flecked with the snow of the New Year's night. But perhaps we should not expect too much: Mokutarō was one of several Ōgai disciples who were pouring their energies into what were, after all, some of the first stirrings of Japan's modern drama.

Mokutarō himself insisted that his primary interest lay in the burning eyes and the atmosphere projected by his intense young characters as they come dashing into the dyer's old shop.[51] But these are not unrelated to the play's central theme—the almost unimaginably broad philosophical gap separating the head of a traditional craftsman's household and his idealistic son, who has found the meaning of life among the working masses. Although he had been too late to join "it" in Tokyo, the son declares that those who were arrested are "great men," for more important than traditional ties of obligation are "the commands of one's own heart" that they followed, only to be branded criminals. Then, out of the audience's hearing, the son whispers to the father what he has *really* been doing in Tokyo, and the old man is horrified: Bow down to the ground! Beg the forgiveness of *okami*** and our ancestors! he commands, but the son goes off into the night.[52]

The time of the play is purposely skewed, and the whole is set against a mine uprising reminiscent of the Ashio copper mine disturbance of 1907 in order to prevent a factual identification with the Kōtoku arrests. But clearly this is what "it" is supposed to suggest. Mokutarō gives no evidence of having benefitted from Hiraide's analysis of the case,[53] and his romantic identification with the plotters suggests near-perfect ignorance of the participants' political philosophies.

The terror among the uninformed seen in "Izumiya Dyers" also underlies a story by Tayama Katai, "Perpetual Calendar" ("Tokoyogoyomi"), which appeared in March 1914. Although Katai was a major spokesman for the writer as uninvolved observer (see above, p. 99), this story is a far more effective representation of the "winter years" oppression than is "Escapists." Both works are based on factual characters, but we come away from "Perpetual Calendar" with a more tangible impression of the suffering experienced by the protagonist, Yūkichi, who was modeled after the poet Narumi Yōkichi, a former disciple of Katai's whose life was ruined by false accusations that he was a Socialist.

The events of the story unfold against the background of spreading terror. According to one news report, in August following the High Treason arrests, the Minister of Education had secretly notified school principals throughout the country that the mere mention of socialism was grounds for expulsion of any student or firing of any teacher.[54] Yūkichi has never been a Socialist, but he has been friendly with one of the executed twelve during a brief stay in Tokyo, and some of his poems have suggested a socialistic inclination. This has been enough for the police and the county school overseers where he has taught. He is dismissed without a trial or hearing—or even the filing of formal charges. When he loses his job, his pregnant wife says that she will leave him immediately if he is "one of them." "I'm frightened! I don't want to die!" If he is really not a Socialist, he ought to have a good alibi, she says, since the *okami* do not do such incomprehensible things.

He is able to convince her to stay, but his superiors are intractable. The family makes it through that first winter on its savings. Detectives show up and chat, and Yūkichi tries to explain his poems and show them his dead friend's letters, but it is no use; he will never be allowed back into the teaching

---

*"Honorable superiors," a term embracing the entire ruling structure. The father could be saying "Throw yourself on the mercy of the police," or, more abstractly, "Beg His Majesty's forgiveness."

profession. He is reduced to trekking through the mountains of Hokkaidō, selling patent medicines and putting all his spare cash into the failing homestead farm where he and his family now live. As if this were not bad enough, he hears that the police have begun hounding Socialists even in this remote area. To escape from them and his miserable existence, he decides to sell his land and go to Tokyo, where he can lose himself in the crowd and invest the money in the production of a perpetual calendar that he once invented. As the story ends, he has failed on both accounts: the calendars do not sell, and the detectives seem to find him wherever he goes.[55]

"Perpetual Calendar" is not typical of Katai, whose focus at this time was almost exclusively limited to his private life.[56] But while it may be atypical, it is not incongruous. For an "engaged" writer like Kanson, a similar departure from his preconceived notion of fiction would have been not merely incongruous but unthinkable.

KAFŪ THE CRITIC

There is one other work that deserves mention here as a contemporary reaction to repressive government policies, if not precisely to the High Treason case, namely Nagai Kafū's Death of a Scribbler (Gesakusha no shi), which was begun late in 1912 and serialized in Mita Bungaku through April 1913, then extensively revised and republished the following year as Willows Shedding Their Leaves at an Evening Window (Chiru yanagi mado no yūbae).[57]

Edward Seidensticker has noted that Death of a Scribbler was part of "an excursion, the only extended one of [Kafū's] career, into historical fiction,"[58] and he tends to minimize its contemporary relevance. But Kafū makes it clear that he intends this story of events set in 1842 to be read as a critique of his own day. At several points, characters mention the traditional technique of disguising a commentary on current events as historical fiction or drama—even painting, as if to remind the reader that that is exactly what Kafū is doing. And Kafū's protagonist, the Edo novelist Ryūtei Tanehiko (1783–1842), is in trouble with the authorities for having rewritten the eleventh-century classic, The Tale of Genji, as an indirect exposé of the contemporary ruler's decadence.[59]

The absurd aspect of the Tokugawa authorities' sudden interest in Tanehiko's The False Murasaki and the Rustic Genji (Nise-Murasaki inaka-Genji) was that it was "a work that had begun to appear twelve years earlier, a book which was moreover not in objectionable taste."[60] The change had occurred not in Tanehiko's writing, nor in any of the other artistic and social practices that the government was now finding objectionable (objectionable primarily because conspicuous consumption only demonstrated that the money was no longer in samurai hands): Kafū's point is that the sumptuary edicts of the

Tenpō Reforms, which were robbing daily life of all color and enjoyment, were simply arbitrary changes inaugurated by an oppressive government.

Kafū portrays the authorities as devoid of sympathy for the suffering of the ordinary townspeople, caused in the hopes of restoring a puritanical atmosphere more appropriate to periods of war or natural disaster than to the peaceful Tokugawa period. The legendary phoenix has at last appeared to signal peace and prosperity, says one of Tanehiko's young disciples, and all the authorities want to do is wring its neck. The most a writer can do at times like this, he says, is subtly ridicule the authorities in comic poetry. But while waiting for restrictions to ease, an aging writer like Tanehiko might go blind, and—what is worse—the new crisis has aroused in him an anguish that cannot be joked away.

Tanehiko does not tell his disciples this, but he has just learned more than he bargained for from an inquiry to a friendly official concerning the likelihood of his being punished. Until recently, the official has been a comrade in dissipation, but he has suddenly become grave and duty-minded on learning that foreign "black ships" have been making alarming appearances at several ports. Tanehiko is shocked to see the change in his friend, and even more shocked to find that his own childhood samurai training still has a grip on his heart. For Tanehiko *is* a samurai. When the official asks Tanehiko to exploit his intimate knowledge of popular sentiment to help the ruling class explain the intent of the sumptuary regulations to the masses, he begins to regret that his frivolous life has rendered him useless in this threatening situation. Still, having long ago decided to throw in his lot with the people, unfettered as they are by official duties, he resents the government's sudden intrusions into their lives.

Everywhere he walks through Edo, Tanehiko sees the new regulations bearing down on the lives of the people, but he can do nothing to help. Years of cowardly artistic compromise have convinced him that protest would be useless. He turns from the present, where there is "only terror," and gives himself over to "profitless memories of the past."[61] As if to emphasize the self-accusation of cowardice, Kafū has Tanehiko die of a stroke brought on by the arrival of a summons. (The exact circumstances of Tanehiko's death are not known.)[62]

Death of a Scribbler was written by a man who had been doing a lot of thinking about his function as a writer living under an oppressive regime. More particularly, this was a writer from a respectable family who had consciously turned his back on establishmentarian hypocrisy to embrace a romantic conception of the demimonde as the only locus of true feeling. Kafū's conversion from "samurai" to "townsman" was far from complete, however: there was still the nagging awareness that he ought to be "useful" in a manner that could be recognized by respectable society. This tension can probably be cited as the vital force behind all of Kafū's writing.

It is important to emphasize that Kafū's works do exhibit this tension. They are not the writings of an author who has settled comfortably in a groove. Kafū himself is wrong about his own works in the famous paragraph he penned in the 1919 essay "Fireworks" ("Hanabi") which seems so neatly to summarize the effect of the High Treason case on his attitude toward his profession:

> In [1910], when I was teaching in Keiō University, I often chanced on my way to class to see five or six police wagons go past Yotsuya [carrying Kōtoku and the other defendants] to the Hibiya courthouse. Of all the public incidents I had witnessed or heard of, none had filled me with such loathing. I could not, as a man of letters, remain silent in this matter of principle. Had not the novelist Zola, pleading the truth in the Dreyfus Case, had to flee his country? But I, along with the other writers of my land, said nothing. The pangs of conscience that resulted were scarcely endurable. I felt intensely ashamed of myself as a writer. I concluded that I could do no better than drag myself down to the level of the Tokugawa writer of frivolous and amatory fiction. Arming myself with the tobacco pouch that was the mark of the old-style dandy, I set out to collect Ukiyoe prints, and I began to learn the samisen. It was a matter of no interest to such inferior persons as the writer of light Edo fiction or the maker of color prints that Perry's Black Ships had arrived at Uraga, or that Ii Kamon no Kami, Great Minister of the Shogunate, was assassinated at the castle gate. They thought it better to know their place and remain silent. Quite as if nothing had happened, they went on writing their indecent books and making their indecent prints.[63]

But Kafū was no more successful at shutting out the real world than his Tanehiko had been, as demonstrated not only by his fiction (witness the omnipresent policemen in "A Strange Tale from East of the River" ["Bokutō kidan," 1936–1937])* but by the essay "Fireworks" itself. It poses as an elegant little divertissement, but it is in fact a unified essay with a clearly stated theme.

It opens when the "pop" of distant fireworks reminds Kafū that most of Tokyo is off celebrating Armistice Day, while he is engaged in the elegant pastime of reading old letters and discarded manuscript sheets that he is using to patch a crumbling section of wall. He is moved to realize how withdrawn he has become from what interests most other people, and he goes on to make some astute observations. Celebrations such as today's are a modern phenomenon imported from the West and are quite distinct from traditional Shintō festivals. They are marked by pompous headlines, displays of the national flag, and huge crowds that invariably trample to death some child or old woman. And "beneath the surface of these modern festivals there usually lurks some

---

*Translated by Edward Seidensticker in *Kafū the Scribbler*, pp. 278–328.

ulterior political motive." Kafū describes his minimal relationship to several other examples of orchestrated nationalism and to various major public events, including the Kōtoku incident, remarking that official holidays bear a marked similarity to riots. One of the great successes of bureaucratically inspired nationalism, he says, was to bring out to the Taishō emperor's enthronement ceremony a large contingent of painted prostitutes—who were, unfortunately, set upon by the savage crowd and, in several instances, raped in broad daylight.[64]

Seidensticker is surely correct when he says that Kafū "had never shown much sign of being a Zola," and "the common notion that the Kōtoku case was somehow crucial to Kafū's writings . . . has about it an ex-post-facto look."* Granted, Kafū was no Zola—and no Sōseki, for that matter—but he was a modern writer, too conscious of his inner life and its relation to society ever to become a mere Edo scribbler (if, in fact, Edo writers were "mere" scribblers). It was this that Uchida Roan had in mind when he called Kafū Japan's first genuine artist in the European sense (see above, pp. 123–24).

ROAN'S CONCLUSION ON ART IN SOCIETY

In bringing to a close this assessment of the relationship of the new literature to the High Treason case, we can do no better than to cite an essay by Uchida Roan, spokesman for the social and political conscience of the Meiji literary world. By this time (February 1911), Roan obviously felt that it was no longer necessary for him to chide writers for acting like spineless parasites (see above, pp. 49–50, 111–12). It is not they who live in Shangri-La, he says, but those politicians, businessmen, educators, and moralists who do not read the new literature and are therefore unqualified to discuss modern ideas. In the works of the new generation, says Roan, we find authentic images of contemporary Japanese society and contemporary ideas filtered through the individuality of each writer. To be sure, he notes, their ideas clash with the traditional morality based on loyalty and filial piety, but those concepts only served to enslave people to their superiors. Trying to teach such ideas now, Roan feels, when there *are* no superiors (with the all-too-obvious exception of His Divine Majesty), is like trying to drag Japan back into the feudal age despite the fact that the country is destined for democracy.

The Home Ministry and the Ministry of Education see resistance to the old morality in the writings of the young, Roan continues, and they decry such

---

*Edward Seidensticker, *Kafū the Scribbler*, pp. 46–47. Seidensticker is by no means the only skeptic when it comes to the literal truth of this passage. See Moriyama Shigeo, *Taigyaku jiken*, pp. 114–15.

"dangerous thoughts," but ideas are free and the government will not be able to control them until it perfects some castration-like technique for remaking brains. In closing, Roan advises old men who would like to escape from Shangri-La and regain their youth to read the works of the naturalists and other writers of the younger generation that can be found in such presumably antinaturalist literary journals as *Shirakaba*, *Mita Bungaku*, and *Subaru*.[65]

Here we see one of the most ethically demanding critics of the Meiji period cutting through the empty rhetoric of "naturalist" and "antinaturalist" to recognize the enormous democratic potential of Japan's new literature.*

---

*Oka Yoshitake, "Nichiro sensō-go ni okeru atarashii sedai no seichō," Part II, p. 104, cites a 1914 analysis of the growth of democratic thought which specifically credits the young naturalists with planting the individualistic seeds of democracy.

12

A Crashing Stalemate:
The Committee on Literature

Sōseki and the Writers' Contempt for Official Recognition

Although few of the authors discussed in the foregoing chapter were committed to any clear-cut political stand, they did choose to write fiction (or, as did Roka, to make a speech) that commented more or less overtly on the contemporary political scene. In this chapter we shall see how some of those writers, plus several more of even less definable political persuasion, chose other means to react to—and against—official policy following the High Treason case.

Less than one month after the execution of the twelve "anarchists," Natsume Sōseki treated the Katsura government to a shock that it was not prepared to handle. By this time, the outcries against censorship fell only on deaf ears, but suddenly the apolitical act of an individual writer left the bureaucrats in bewilderment. Without public reference to censorship or to the Kōtoku incident, and probably without any political intent in his own mind, Sōseki refused the Ministry of Education's conferral upon him of the Doctor of Letters degree. He did this solely in defense of his personal integrity, but he made of it a public act, demonstrating by his simple indifference to official "honor" that it was possible for a socially responsible individual to live according to his own values.

In contrast with most educated men of his generation, Sōseki had never been interested in politics, even in his youth.[1] To find any mention of Kōtoku in his writings, we must go back to *And Then* of 1909, which contains a catalog of recent foolishness that includes the government's comical fear of Kōtoku, to spy on whom the Shinjuku police alone were spending over one hundred yen per month.[2] Most of Sōseki's attention during the seven months in which the drama of the High Treason case was being played out was devoted not to politics but to his stomach ulcers. They had hemorrhaged, nearly killing him, on August 24, 1910, while he was recuperating at the Shuzenji hot springs after a prolonged treatment in a Tokyo clinic. But Sōseki was well enough by October 1910 to return to the hospital in Tokyo and begin writing again. Despite his contacts with Ishikawa Takuboku at the time, and his later attending a memorial service for Hiraide Shū,[3] Sōseki recorded no reaction to the High Treason case. His reaction to the award of the degree, however, was swift, decisive, and very public.

The Ministry of Education sent notice of the award on February 20, 1911. Sōseki first heard about it when his wife brought the notice to the hospital on the afternoon of February 21. (Meanwhile she had telephoned the ministry to say he would not be able to attend the ceremony that day.) Sōseki wrote to the official in charge, a bureau chief named Fukuhara Ryōjirō, and gave a copy of the letter to the Asahi Shimbun. It was printed on the twenty-fourth along with an interview in which Sōseki recited the details of the incident. In the letter, Sōseki respectfully declined the award because "I have made my way thus far through life as plain, ordinary Natsume, and I would like to go on living that way in the future."* He pointed out in the interview that his letter had crossed with the delivery of the diploma from the ministry, and he had returned it immediately. "And just look at this notice!" he complained to the Asahi reporter. It had no salutation; it was merely a curt order to appear. It had arrived at ten o'clock at night, instructing him to send a proxy if he were unable to attend the award ceremony at ten the next morning.[4] This arrogance was something he would not stand for.

Sōseki wrote an article on the incident and he gave another interview, which appeared in the Asahi on March 6–8, 1911. What he most resented, he said in the interview, was the ministry's having failed to ask him whether he even wanted their degree. He felt sorry, he said, about causing the authorities any difficulty, but he hoped they would stop treating people like toys and would take individual scholars' feelings into account in the future—when the gradual development of individual awareness would no doubt lead to more refusals. If the law provided both for awarding of the degree and for stripping of it when the recipient proved morally unworthy, he said, then it ought to provide for refusal so that one need not be saddled with this potential source of dishonor. For who was to say that the individual's view of moral worth would always correspond to the ministry's?[5]

On April 11, 1911, Sōseki was visited by two holders of the degree, the scholars Ueda Mannen and Haga Yaichi, and by Bureau Chief Fukuhara himself, but no understanding was reached. Fukuhara wrote the following day

---

*SZ 15:33. The English section of Taiyō carried a brief report on the controversy, noting that Sōseki wished to be known as "Mr. Prain" (sic). See The Taiyo (April 1, 1911), p. 4.

to say that the imperial decree awarding him the Doctorate of Letters could not be undone, to which Sōseki replied that he was most annoyed with the ministry for ignoring his wishes despite the fact that the law was vague enough to allow them to interpret it in his favor. In any event, he said, he was returning the diploma again, and he did not consider himself a Doctor of Letters, whatever the ministry's view of the situation. (The ministry's view was that Sōseki was a Doctor of Letters; his name continued to appear on the official roster. Meanwhile, Sōseki took care to see that the "mistaken" title not be attached to his name.)* He also noted that the doctoral system had many more evils than virtues, a remark that he expanded upon in an article for the *Asahi*, in which he quoted this second letter to Fukuhara. He said in effect that the greatest danger of this system of honorary awards from the Ministry of Education lay in its creation of an officially approved elite that would seem to possess academic authority, while perfectly capable scholars who did not happen to hold the degree might be thought less worthy. He was opposed to it on principle, just as he was opposed to the French Academy.†

Sōseki received many letters of praise and sympathy for the position he had taken, including one from the author of the monumental *History of Japan*, James Murdoch, with whom Sōseki had studied English and history twenty years earlier. The letter congratulated him on his "moral backbone." And when Sōseki briefly referred to his refusal of the degree in a lecture that August, he had to ask the audience not to applaud.[6]

One can only imagine what sort of impression all this made on Mori Ōgai. As a Doctor of Letters himself, he had been a member of the committee that awarded the degree to Sōseki.[7] And his own public reaction to receipt of the degree two years earlier could not have been in starker contrast. "I feel more embarrassed than happy" about the award, he had told an *Asahi* reporter. "There are many others far more worthy of this honor than I am," he had said, protesting in all modesty that he did not even deserve the Doctorate of Medicine that he had been awarded in 1891.[8]

Ōgai had a weakness for public recognition. In contrast to Sōseki's rejection of the *Taiyō* popularity prize, Ōgai not only accepted *Bunshō Sekai*'s designa-

---

*SZ 15:53; Fujiwara Kiyozō, *Meiji Taishō Shōwa kyōiku shisō gakusetsu jinbutsu shi*, 2:666. When he was preparing to deliver his famous lecture on individualism at the Peers' School in 1914, Sōseki specifically requested that announcements of his talk not add the "mistaken" title to his name. See SZ 15:409. See also Jay Rubin, "Sōseki on Individualism," p. 26 n22.

†"Hakase mondai no nariyuki," SZ 11:271–73. Komiya Toyotaka has noted that Sōseki had, in 1909, defended his personal integrity against so unofficial an encroachment as the *Taiyō* popularity contest (see above, p. 114), the prize from which he returned because it indirectly threatened to compromise "each man's freedom to evaluate himself." See Natsume Sōseki, "*Taiyō* zasshi boshū meika tōhyō ni tsuite," SZ 11:209, quoted in Komiya Toyotaka, *Natsume Sōseki*, 3 vols. (Iwanami shoten, 1953), 3:110–11.

tion as the most popular translator but he willingly posed for a photograph to be used in making the plaster bust of himself that was given to him by the magazine as his prize.[9] And where Sōseki chose to live his life as "plain, ordinary Natsume," Ōgai waited until he was on his deathbed to renounce worldly honor. In his last testament of July 6, 1922, Ōgai directed that he be buried without the elaborate ceremony due him for his many high military and civilian posts: "I wish to die as Mori Rintarō, man of Iwami."*

Had Ōgai been smugly satisfied with his honors, however, there would have been nothing to distinguish him from the bemedaled bureaucrats whose portraits appeared in the magazines' rotogravure sections, oozing with pride at being close to the head of the national family; and there would have been no monumental thirty-eight-volume complete works of Ōgai moaning on every other page with the inner struggle he experienced between an unconquerable need to do his duty and a nagging wish to have done with all the meaningless claptrap.

Sōseki's rejection of the doctorate must have been a slap in the face to Ōgai. But I feel certain that not only did he understand Sōseki but secretly envied him, wishing that he himself had been immune enough to the pull of conventional values to have considered doing the same thing. This would be consonant with Ōgai's self-parody (as Mōri Ōson) in the novel *Youth* (*Seinen*), which he completed in August 1911 and which shows him inordinately impressed with Sōseki's having left his teaching post to become a professional novelist while Ōgai himself continued to work for the bureaucracy.[10] Sōseki's act represented an attitude shared by many writers of the new literature which less reflective bureaucrats simply could not fathom.

Thus, when the Ministry of Education finally instituted its academy (or, as the body was officially called, the Committee on Literature, or Bungei Iinkai) as part of the post-Kōtoku attempt to recapture the national essence, it met with continued frustration. There were those, such as Sōseki, who rejected it out of hand, and a few who were pleased with the government recognition. And then there were those, such as Ōgai and the critic Shimamura Hōgetsu, who chose to participate in the hopes of swaying the government in favor of the new literature. Too much had happened since that cordial dinner at Komatsubara's in January 1909 for an academy to be accepted calmly and to function as smoothly as it might have then.

---

*OZ 19:304. When Yamagata Aritomo's loyalty to the throne was impugned in a controversy over the choice of a Crown Princess, he asked to be stripped of all his worldly honors, writing in a letter of February 21, 1921: "The major principle of my life has been to serve the Emperor first, last and always. If I am fortunate enough to have my wish granted, I am determined to die for my Emperor and my country as plain Yamagata Kyōsuke" (quoted in Roger F. Hackett, *Yamagata Aritomo in the Rise of Modern Japan*, pp. 339–40).

THE GOVERNMENT'S GIFT HORSE

Coming before the Appropriations Committee of the Lower House in January 1911, the month of the executions, Minister of Education Komatsubara noted that he had taken steps "since the outbreak of the recent incident" to assure that the schools would properly inculcate the spirit of the 1890 Imperial Rescript on Education, which had established the principle of education for service to the state. "However," he argued, "there is a need to perfect social education outside the schools, and to accomplish this I believe that we must establish facilities for continuing education and the reform of literature."[11]

Elsewhere, Komatsubara spoke of the need to encourage literature that was "wholesome and of benefit to public morality. . . . The young men today must be saved from their tendency toward depravity and decadence and from the dangerous thoughts that threaten to infect them. This is truly one of the most urgent tasks now facing the country."[12]

To produce concrete suggestions for a program in popular education, Komatsubara appointed a Committee for the Investigation of Popular Education (Tsūzoku Kyōiku Chōsa Iinkai), created by Imperial Decree (no. 165) and officially announced on May 17, 1911. The committee eventually recommended the production of desirable books, slides and films, the establishment of libraries to house such materials, and the presentation of lectures, shows, and storytelling by professionals (*kōdanshi*) who could be trained to deliver uplifting tales of loyal warriors, filial children, and faithful wives.[13] Foremost among the *kōdanshi* they recruited "in order to foster our unique Bushidō" was none other than Shinryūsai Teisui, author of *Nightstorm Okinu* (see above, pp. 92–93).*

On the same day that the Ministry of Education announced the Committee for the Investigation of Popular Education, it also announced the formation by Imperial Decree (no. 164) of the Committee on Literature.[14] The chairman of both was to be Vice-Minister of Education Okada Ryōhei, and the Executive Secretary of the Committee on Literature would be Chief of the Ministry's Bureau of Specialized Education (Senmon gakumukyoku) Fukuhara Ryōjirō, the very official who had refused the return of Sōseki's degree.

The appointees to the Committee on Literature read almost like a list of the guests at Komatsubara's dinner. Heading the roster was Senior Grade Fourth Court Rank, Second Order of Merit Third Class, Doctor of Medical Science, and Doctor of Letters Mori Rintarō, followed by fifteen others with decreasingly impressive titles. These included such ministry favorites as Ueda Mannen and Haga Yaichi, the scholars who had tried, with Fukuhara, to persuade Sōseki to accept the degree. There were such literary traditionalists as

---

*"Bungei zatsuji," NoN (June 15, 1911), p. 65. The quotation on Bushidō (the Way of the

the novelist/classicist Kōda Rohan, Ōmachi Keigetsu (the angry critic of Yosano Akiko), Tsukahara Jūshien, Sasa Seisetsu, and Aeba Kōson. More closely related to recent literature was Ueda Bin, the influential translator of symbolist poetry, who had joined with his friend Ōgai in recommending Nagai Kafū for the teaching post at Keiō, and who was also the godfather of Hiraide Shū's eldest daughter.[15] There was, however, only one member directly connected with naturalism: the theorist Shimamura Hōgetsu, an occasional critic of censorship.[16] Other notable appointees were Tokutomi Sohō, brother of Tokutomi Roka and publisher of *Kokumin Shimbun*; Iwaya Sazanami, a writer known mainly for his children's stories; and Anesaki Chōfū (Masaharu), the eminent scholar of religion.[17]

Since the committee's charter specified only that it was to "investigate matters pertaining to literature," Secretary Fukuhara took it upon himself to explain to the newspapers and magazines what the ministry had in mind. The committee would be deciding its specific policies when it met, he said, but tentatively the government was proposing three functions: to award prizes to current works; to call for the submission of new historical dramas; and to commission translations of "great" foreign literature containing "great ideas." "The Ministry of Education has always had a positive attitude toward literature and wishes to encourage it in the hopes of promoting wholesome great literature and great ideas."[18] The ministry may bring suggestions or requests to the committee, but it has no intention of limiting its freedom in any way, he concluded.

According to another semiofficial view carried in the *Asahi*, Japan's military might was equal to that of any nation, but the country had almost nothing in the way of art or literature to boast of to the world. The establishment of the committee was a first step in attempting to remedy this embarrassing situation.

No sooner had the formation of the committee been announced than opinions began appearing in the newspapers, few of which could have been comforting to Fukuhara and his superiors. Under the headline "USELESS COMMITTEE," Miyake Setsurei stated his views to an *Asahi* reporter with characteristic bluntness. He had had nothing to do with this committee from the start, he said, and had they asked him to participate he would have refused. The Ministry of Education liked to appoint all sorts of investigative bodies and committees, none of which accomplished anything. He had heard that several writers, including Natsume Sōseki, Tsubouchi Shōyō, and Ikebe Sanzan, had

---

Warrior) comes from an interview with Executive Secretary Tadokoro of the Committee for the Investigation of Popular Education. See "Tsūzoku kyōiku no shudan," AS (May 19, 1911), p. 5.

turned them down, and most of the sixteen who had accepted should have done so as well. Without Sōseki and the others, said Setsurei, the committee would not be worth much. Its only benefit might be to encourage writers opposed to it to outdo its members. No one with any pride or ability would submit his works to it. "After all, literature can only be produced through the perseverance of hard-studying, creative men who don't give a damn about some fart-like 'committee.' . . . In any case, it's a useless, harmless thing and in two or three years we won't even know it still exists."

Shimamura Hōgetsu declared that he had not known of his appointment, but that he thought the establishment of the Committee on Literature was a good idea. The only attention paid to literature by the state thus far had been negative, through the action of the police. Now literature would be treated as something belonging to the nation. He looked forward to "interesting" cases of conflict between the committee and the censors. "If the government's left hand disapproves of what its right hand is doing, this will be a clear case of internal inconsistency. We must cleverly cut our way through this contradiction and not lose our foothold. . . . We must put all our energies into casting off the shackles imposed on us by the administrators." [19]

Tsubouchi Shōyō told the *Asahi* that he had indeed turned down the appointment, but simply because he was too busy. The committee's ¥10,000 budget was too small to go very far, he noted, so people should not expect it to accomplish much.

Others noted the small budget—one writer with considerable satisfaction, since that would prevent the committee from doing much damage. Some pointed out that it was most unusual for a committee of outside experts like this to have a chairman appointed from within the bureaucracy, which only added fuel to the many rumors suggesting that the government was aiming more at the control than the encouragement of literature. [20]

Most of these remarks appeared in the form of newspaper interviews. Only one writer, Sōseki, had been disturbed enough by rumors of the impending announcement of the committee to begin putting his ideas on paper in anticipation, and when the news came out on May 18, 1911, he was ready with a three-part article for the *Asahi*. Sōseki was too much of an outsider to join with Ōgai and Hōgetsu in attempting to influence the bureaucracy from within, but in the socially useful role that he saw for himself *as* an outsider he decided it was time for him to take a stand. He called his article "What Will the Members of the Literary Academy Be Doing?" and wrote it in the form of an open letter to the members of the soon-to-be-announced "academy." (His ignorance of both the committee's official designation and the names of the members would seem to indicate that he had completed the article before the government's announcement on May 17.)

Addressing "you gentlemen" who are about to be appointed, Sōseki opens his remarks on behalf of his fellow writers (the *bundan*) by making an important distinction:

> The government (*seifu*), in a sense, represents the nation (*kokka*)—or at least it has the power to conduct itself in all affairs with the appearance of representing the nation. Undeniably, then, the government's new literary academy will be a national institution and you who constitute its membership must suddenly leave the category of "ordinary writer" to become national men of letters. Not that you will be doing so because of the value of your own unique creations or criticisms or insights: when you are instantaneously transformed from fish into dragons it will be thanks to the backing of a government that is far greater than you in terms of practical power. I would imagine that, for you who call yourselves literary men and writers, this will be an excruciating experience.
>
> If you say that you are prepared to endure this pain for the sake of the nation, then I have only the greatest respect for you. But I believe that it is incumbent upon you to tell us precisely where you stand. How far are you prepared to go for the sake of the nation?
>
> It is a most reasonable attitude for the government, as the managing directors of civilization, to seek to patronize and encourage literature as one small part of the nation's business. But it would be as mistaken of them to think that these objectives can be realized merely by instituting a literary academy as it would be for a grower of fruit trees to give all his attention to caring for the branches of his trees while neglecting the soil in which they grow. It goes without saying that the development of literature presupposes the existence of a society capable of appreciating literature. It is equally obvious that the first objective of a government that supposedly wants to patronize and encourage literature must be the cultivation of a society with this ability, which is something that can come to the surface of the general public only as a result of care for the roots—that is, the education of the nation's people. Once the roots are firm, any other paraphernalia are simply window dressing (if we do not count the positive harm they can do).

Among the types of positive harm that Sōseki goes on to enumerate is the false impression of authoritative certainty that necessarily subjective critical judgments will give to aspiring writers when those judgments are backed by governmental authority, which is something fundamentally irrelevant to literature. Worse still,

> it is not difficult to imagine that the government, having established the members of the academy as if they were the final judges of literature, will, by means of this institution, and employing the most distasteful methods, encourage only those works amenable to their administrative purposes and suppress all

others under the ostensibly laudable—but vague—banner of encouraging the development of wholesome literature. Surely there will be many cases where the "wholesome literature" of an unbiased critic does not coincide with what the government calls wholesome, and then he will find the establishment of a literary academy most distressing.

Sōseki then sees a precedent in the Ministry of Education's annual art exhibits (Monbushō bijutsu tenrankai, or Bunten), a program inaugurated in 1907 and administered by the Committee for the Judging of Art (Bijutsu shinsa iinkai). He admits that Japanese painting has improved over the years, but is reluctant to credit this solely to the policies of the Ministry of Education. "For if, in fact, Japan's artists have improved as a result of that sort of artificial stimulus, then even as their skill has been raised by the Ministry of Education, their heads have been lowered by it. As a group, their lack of self-respect is almost pitiful."*

Up to now, Sōseki avers, the government has not only failed to patronize literature, it has meddled with it. In spite of that, the artistic accomplishment of the fiction appearing in the monthly magazines rivals anything being produced in England—indeed, far excels it. There is no sense, he says, in transferring to an artificial hothouse atmosphere something that has done so admirably in the wild.

> The government's vanity causes it to think that what present-day writers need for their work is the opinions and criticisms and evaluations of you academy members who represent the nation. . . . That is not what they need. Money is what they need. A reasonably comfortable life is what they need. It is disgraceful how they suffer for lack of money. Today's so-called literary slump is not a slump on the production end but on the purchasing end. The writers themselves would tell you that it is a slump in the rice bin.†

If an academy could cure that—and he does not see how it could—then Sōseki might relent and give his approval as a way through the writers' current

*Perhaps Sōseki knew that Saionji's Minister of Education, Makino Shinken, had instituted the program at the suggestion of a Kyōto educator who wanted to encourage the "orthodox development of art expressing the national essence." Fujiwara Kiyozō, *Meiji Taishō Shōwa*, 2:822. Mori Ōgai became head of division two of this committee on August 17, 1911.

†With the lessened frenzy over naturalism in 1910 came a somewhat less receptive market. The literary gossip column in *Nihon oyobi Nihonjin* alluded to this several times, noting that naturalism was down, *kōdan* up. See "Bungei zatsuji," NoN (September 1, 1910), p. 29; ibid. (September 15, 1910), p. 84; ibid. (October 15, 1910), p. 73. The moralistic Inoue Tetsujirō expressed his satisfaction, "for the sake of public morals," that naturalism was not selling well, in "Gendai shisō no keikō ni tsuite," TY (November 1910), p. 67.

financial difficulties. He goes on to present his proposal for a relatively harmless method of distributing the money allotted by the government for the patronage and encouragement of literature. The government could make up for the magazines' low fees by dividing this money evenly among the writers of all stories for the month that had "surpassed a certain standard."

> Of course, each writer's share would not amount to much, but if he could get a thirty-to-fifty-Yen prize for a short story, that would help out a little with the practical problem of making ends meet—and the glory be damned. . . .
>
> As stated above, then, I am fundamentally opposed to the establishment of a literary academy, but if we were fortunate enough to have the members set up an equitable method for distributing the money earmarked for patronage, then I would have no choice but to express my approval of that one activity. Nor, of course, would I see a need to censure all of the academy's other programs. In general, however, such programs would have to be devised by some sort of writers' group or union independent of the government and, under the auspices of that organization, understandings reached with the government administrators. Regrettably, however, Japan's writers are a pack of egotists—helpless, isolated men who have neither the time nor the money nor the inclination to devise methods for the preservation of their species.[21]

It would be difficult to imagine a more straightforward, concrete, and unambiguous statement. The government's only legitimate role in literature is teaching the people how to read; any meddling beyond that will lead to suppression and enervation; writers do not need the "authoritative" opinions of critics artificially created by the government; they need money. Sōseki is almost crude. And if he is willing to waffle a bit when it comes to accepting government money, we should be less eager to chide him for lack of ideological purity than to recognize his awareness of the ambiguities inherent in any relationship between art or scholarship and modern constitutional government—that gray area in which today thrive federal contracts with universities and government grants to individual artists and scholars.* In this working

---

*There is nothing ambiguous in the relationship of totalitarian governments with art and scholarship, but "the double problem in a democracy is to improve the conditions of work of the creative artist and the creative thinker [i.e., to protect them against the vulgarizing pressures of the mass marketplace], and to preserve their freedom [i.e., to protect them against being exploited by government for propaganda purposes]" (Richard McKeon, Robert K. Merton, and Walter Gellhorn, *The Freedom to Read*, p. 17). Sōseki did not finally believe in the practicability of arrangements between artists and governments. If the artist cannot derive an income directly from the public, he said in a lecture, "then all he can do is starve to death." ("Dōraku to shokugyō," [August 1911], SZ 11:317) The best insurance against artistic prostitution he saw in the growth of individualism and pluralism with their attendant tolerance for a wide range of

writer's assessment of the needs of his profession, we see Sōseki defending the identity that he had chosen for himself when he left the government's university in 1907 to join the staff of the *Asahi Shimbun*. This identity allowed him to be at once an outsider to established authority and a citizen of his nation with a social role: he had a job to perform that made his living for him and was no better or worse than any other job.

This sense of his professional identity enabled Sōseki to be a perfectly appropriate spokesman for the new writers, naturalist or otherwise. The attitude toward authority inherent in the new writers' social role began to dog the workings of the Committee on Literature from the very start.

THE RISE AND FALL OF THE COMMITTEE

The committee's first activity was a semiofficial one, another banquet at Komatsubara's residence, this time for the newly appointed members.[22] (Missing was Tokutomi Sohō, who was traveling in Japan's newly annexed possession, Korea, at the time, and who, as it turned out, never attended a single meeting.) The highlight of this gathering on the evening of May 22, 1911, was not, as before, the frank exchange of views that had proved to be such a pleasant surprise for participants and observers alike. This time it was a rousing address by Komatsubara that left the group in stunned silence, for it seemed to indicate that the intervening two years had taught him nothing.

Komatsubara spoke of his keen regret that no grandly heroic works of literature had yet appeared that fully expressed the glory of the Meiji era and the welling vitality of the Japanese people. Instead, pornography was everywhere, taking its toll on the moral fiber of the nation. This committee would have before it the urgent task of encouraging the development of wholesome, uplifting literature, he said, and he went on to outline the ministry's suggestions for the steps that might be taken, central to which was a prize competition for plays and novels.

So strikingly awkward were the moments following Komatsubara's address that a waggish writer calling himself Rokkaku turned them into a short play, "The Committee on Literature: A Tragedy in One Act," for the June 1911 *Shinchō*. The piece is a very funny view of the members' inability to respond to Komatsubara with anything but incoherent mumbling, in spite of the coax-

---

self-expression, for "Art begins with self-expression and ends with self-expression." See "Bunten to geijutsu" (October 1912), SZ 11:389–420 (esp. 389, 395, 399–401). In an interesting contrast to Sōseki's disbelief in the state's ability to accommodate artistic freedom, George Steiner has recently demonstrated the dangers inherent in the absolutist position that high art should be protected by the state from mass defilement. See his "Reflections (Anthony Blunt)," *New Yorker* (December 8, 1980), pp. 158–95.

ings of the bureau chief, who is described as inordinately diffident in his
approach, owing to the recent bitter experience of having had a doctorate
thrown back in his face.

As the newspapers reported the incident, the first to break the silence was
Ōgai. He, Rohan, and some others pointed out that certain magazines had run
contests of the sort Komatsubara was suggesting. These contests had produced
nothing of value; it would probably do more harm than good to attempt to lure
out wholesome literature with prizes. This did not dampen Komatsubara's
enthusiasm, however. "Those contests failed *because* they were run by magazine
and newspaper companies," he insisted. "But when we call for masterpieces in
the name of the Committee on Literature, distinguished novels and plays are
bound to come forth." Obviously, Komatsubara was as much a believer in the
Confucian method of government as eighteenth-century rulers had been: when
the commoners threatened to get out of hand, Matsudaira Sadanobu had
resorted to suppression, indoctrination, and the awarding of "prizes for chastity, piety, and similar virtues."[23] The party ended with these differences of
opinion unresolved, noted the *Asahi*'s report, concluding that the Ministry of
Education "seemed to be attempting to manipulate literature as an organ
of government."

Lest there be any lingering doubt on this point, an *Asahi* reporter visited
Komatsubara a few days later and asked him directly whether his real aim in
establishing the committee was to promote the development of literature or
merely to promote the unity and wholesomeness of the thoughts of the people—and of the youth in particular—in response to the fear aroused by the
High Treason case. In what the reporter considered a "shrewd" reply, Komatsubara said that his immediate aim was to promote the development of literature, but that he also hoped for those other results as a by-product. Less than
shrewd himself, the reporter said he had considered asking Komatsubara to
define "wholesome," but he did not want to back an old man into a corner just
to hear the Confucian saw about the need for moral values in literature.

It did not take long for the magazines to give full expression to this kind of
skepticism. The June 1911 issues carried a wide variety of negative views,
ranging from Rokkaku's farce to unemotional statements that the committee
was part of a bureaucratic bid for the control of ideas (Masamune Hakuchō,
Kaneko Chikusui, Tokuda Shūsei), to cries of alarm, to bitter irony and
explosions of outrage.[24] Just about the only benefit widely anticipated from the
committee was its support of translations, but even here optimism was not
unanimous. Tokuda Shūsei agreed that translating was likely to be the committee's most useful function but that limits would be placed on the moral
sensitivity of the works chosen.[25]

Baba Kochō was even less encouraging. "This is almost ludicrous," he
fumed, pointing out what should have been an obvious contradiction. "To me,

it is simply beyond comprehension that the present government, which considers all foreign thought dangerous, would actually have people translating these dangerous foreign books. . . . They do all they can to spread loyalty and filial piety, so why on earth should they put out translations of the kind of books that are bound to destroy these very concepts? Do governments *do* such paradoxical things? . . . In his address to the members, the Minister said that one purpose of the Committee is to produce literature that is grandly heroic and wholesome. But the kind of literature that truly fulfills these qualifications, that truly benefits the nation and all mankind," Kochō concluded, with a note of the cosmopolitanism that would flourish in coming years, "is literature that will totally destroy the old morality that the government is doing its best to preserve." [26]

This disgust for the old on the part of spokesmen for the new was evident in the many objections raised to the personnel of the committee. Almost none of the members have shown any understanding of the new thought, said Tokuda Shūsei and several others. The committee included a writer in the purest Edo-period style, a travel essayist, some classical scholars, two newsmen, not a few failed critics, and "several old has-beens who should have handed the store over to their sons long ago," wrote a *Chūō Kōron* columnist. [27] One cynic offered a "mathematical" formula that referred to Iwaya Sazanami's reputation as a writer of children's stories: "Moralism + Fairy Tales = Committee on Literature." [28] Mori Ōgai, Shimamura Hōgetsu, and Ueda Bin were recognized by Tayama Katai as the only capable members, while Baba Kochō and Satō Kōroku saw them as mere token representatives of the new thought on a body dominated by people congenial to the government.

The last scene of Rokkaku's "Tragedy in One Act" was especially interesting. It showed Ōgai and Hōgetsu together in Komatsubara's hallway, escaping from the tobacco smoke and the speechifying. As it turned out, this antinaturalist writer and foremost naturalist critic would become the leaders of the committee's recalcitrant faction. Obvious choices like Tōson and Katai were excluded from the committee because they were naturalists, said Kōroku, and Sōseki's rejection of the degree had of course eliminated him. [29] Mizuno Yōshū wrote that the committee would be a veritable Tower of Babel: "One will say 'naturalism,' and the others will hear 'lust.'" Mizuno and Gotō Chūgai objected that any literature selected by such a heterogeneous group would have to be the lowest common denominator. [30] Shūsei took the reasonable position that such a varied group could not possibly reflect one fixed official policy, but he questioned whether this mixed bag of writers, scholars, and antiquarians could do a proper job of literary appreciation. [31]

A few writers felt that some cautionary words were called for. "The wolves are preparing to eat the lambs," warned Togawa Shūkotsu. "The Tokugawa neo-Confucian reformers are at it again," said Kamitsukasa Shōken; "they are trying to annihilate literature; the committee will be nothing but a branch police station for thought control—although perhaps we should count it as 'progress' when literature is mentioned in the official gazette in anything other than a banning notification." Satō Kōroku advised writers to be very careful of the kind of "encouragement" that this oppressive government claimed to be offering, while Mizuno Yōshū saw that now mere indifference was no longer possible: the time was coming when writers would have to fight this "false authority" which was bound to confuse the great mass of people, who have "immature perceptions and inadequate understanding."[32]

Almost no one shared Miyake Setsurei's view that the committee was harmless and powerless and would simply fade away, although the pride and independence of professional writers he spoke of would finally be the single greatest factor in the fulfillment of his prophesy. Aside from a few feeble statements by Shimazaki Tōson, Tayama Katai, and Morita Sōhei calling for substantial government patronage for art, the reactions from the literary community showed writers to be anything but the spineless parasites that Uchida Roan had spoken of long before.[33]

It was precisely the fawning of parasitic second-raters that Satō Kōroku, Gotō Chūgai, and Masamune Hakuchō thought the committee would encourage, particularly if prizes were offered in a competitive format. No serious, self-respecting writer would actually submit a work to such a committee, they said, echoing Setsurei.[34] The benighted masses will attach some weight to the committee, said Shūsei, and this may well serve the function of alerting more people to the importance of literature; but authentic literary artists will simply go on writing what they believe in, without a second thought for the committee.[35] "We writers want to carry on without the solicitude of the government," he said. Any "investigation into matters pertaining to literature" that this committee is supposed to do can be carried out far more effectively by the reading public, whose judgments have always been fair.[36]

Time and again, as writers reflected on the relationship of literature and government, they came to the conclusion reached by Sōseki and Tenkei: modern Japanese literature had advanced, *in spite of* the government, to where it could be favorably compared with that of any other in the world. Now there was serious talk of translating Japanese fiction into Western languages, a position that would actually be endorsed (although it was never acted upon) by the Committee on Literature at one of its earliest meetings.[37] One of the strongest statements on the accomplishments of Japanese literature was made by Togawa Shūkotsu, a prolific translator of English literature:

> There is not much that is Japanese that is worth boasting of abroad—perhaps
> tea, silk, and the army. Ah, the army! It eats up hundreds of millions of Yen, for
> which we are all making an enormous sacrifice, so that *it* might possibly be worth

a second glance. The only other thing rather worth looking at is our recent literature, which has developed entirely on its own, often persecuted but never protected, to the point where much of what is produced today could be sent to foreign countries without the least embarrassment. We can't export airplanes and wireless radios back to the West . . . but you could take a Sōseki novel to London or Paris and it would be perfectly respectable. In fact, any of the fiction in our monthly magazines looks good in comparison with what is appearing in the Western journals. So now the government dares to tell us they want to "protect" and "encourage" our literature after it has grown to maturity on its own despite *their* persecution! What gall! What blind stupidity!

Writing is strictly an individual activity, Shūkotsu added, saying it was cowardly to establish literary standards through government authority. On this point, he said, he agreed completely with Sōseki.[38]

Mizuno Yōshū was another writer who took the time to set his thoughts to paper rather than wait for the interviewers. He, too, spoke out strongly against the possible debilitating effect of government interference with literature, ascribing the attempt to an insufficient recognition of the existence of the individual in Japan. It was Mizuno who had expressed relief that the small budget would prevent the committee from growing into a monster. Protection—patronage—works only when there is respect for the freedom of art, he said, never when the patron wants to inaugurate the creation of a particular kind of art, especially if its purpose is to destroy something less congenial to the patron. "The development of the freedom of art means the development of freedom, and this is what Japan is so sorely in need of today. It is the very best means for advancing our people to a better position than the one they now occupy."[39]

If Ministry of Education officials believed that none of this uproar would taint the atmosphere of the committee itself, their illusion did not survive for long.[40] Perhaps the calmest meeting was the first one, held June 3, 1911, in which the bylaws were drafted, but even some of those unremarkable provisions would later prove disruptive. The committee decided that: a simple majority would rule in all cases except the awarding of prizes or other recognition, which would require a three-fourths majority; the proceedings were to be kept secret; individual members would suggest works for consideration by the whole; authors could submit their own works for consideration; members and their works were not eligible; and so forth. Although they did not include it among the bylaws, the committee agreed that individuals chosen for public recognition would first be contacted privately to be certain that they would accept.[41] Clearly, Sōseki's influence was at work here! The question was also raised at this meeting of what would be done if the committee were to choose a work that the Home Ministry had banned, but this was left as unfinished business for the next meeting, two days later. In between, Mori Ōgai and Ueda Bin would have lunch with Hiraide Shū.[42]

When the committee reconvened on June 5, 1911, Shimamura Hōgetsu opened discussion on two issues that were to prove crucial. First, he asked that the committee provide financial aid for the surviving family members of men who had made great contributions to the development of modern Japanese literature. This was an ongoing concern of Hōgetsu's which he expressed at every suitable opportunity, although at this meeting the bureaucrats could only reply that they would have to look into the legality of such "indirect encouragement" of literature. Second, Hōgetsu asked that the Ministry of Education begin negotiations with the Home Ministry to establish a system whereby the latter would consult with the Committee on Literature whenever they were about to invoke a ban.

This sparked a vigorous debate between Secretary Fukuhara and Chairman Okada on one side and Hōgetsu, Ōgai, Ueda Bin, and Anesaki Chōfū on the other. Hōgetsu insisted on knowing what the Ministry of Education was prepared to do about the banning of works widely recognized to be good literature; works of Nagai Kafū and translations of Molière and Maupassant had been suppressed by the Home Ministry, and such cases were bound to occur frequently in the future. Was the committee to assume that the banning of a piece automatically excluded it from consideration? For that would mean the committee was supposed to be blindly obedient to the Home Ministry. Ōgai criticized the Home Ministry, pointing out that in Germany bans were occasionally lifted, but that such a thing had never happened in Japan.

The ministry people were extremely annoyed by this onslaught. Okada tried to avoid the issue by insisting that the sort of conflicts they mentioned were very unlikely to occur, and that such "extreme" instances could be handled on an ad hoc basis. In the end, Fukuhara whispered something to the four contentious members which brought smiles to their faces and convinced them to relent, leaving the issue unresolved. (Perhaps it was at this moment that Mori Ōgai handed Hiraide Shū's written opinion to Fukuhara.)*

If the Ministry people were upset with some of the members, the members in turn were provoked by discussion of the idea that Komatsubara had raïsed of a literary competition. The bylaws had been left vague enough to allow for

---

*OZ 20:592. See pp. 155, 160 above. Although Hiraide's combined defense memorandum and postscript was the only document he left entitled "written opinion" (*ikensho*), Ōgai's diary could conceivably have been referring to something else. Hiraide did leave one unpublished manuscript from 1910 entitled "On the Sale Prohibited System" ("Hatsubai kinshi ron"). He made a case for *Vita Sexualis*—although mainly by citing a published essay by Ōmachi Keigetsu. See THS, pp. 174–75.

such a system, but at the June 3 meeting the committee had decided against calling for the submission of works. Instead, they decided that they would discuss works published since the beginning of the previous fiscal year (i.e., after April 1910). These would be brought up by the members at each meeting, and publicity would be limited to one annual announcement of the results, with prizes of money, trophies, and certificates of recognition going to the winners. Apparently dissatisfied with such a subdued approach, the ministry officers kept pressing for the more conspicuous and colorful plan of a widely publicized contest, insisting that offering a cash prize was the surest way to bring forth outstanding fiction and drama.* It would also fit the committee's assigned task of the encouragement of literature in a more direct manner than Hōgetsu's proposed method. They could not find a single ally among the membership, however, and once again Ōgai, Hōgetsu, and Chōfū led the opposition. Writers do not write for money alone, they said, and besides, such a contest can never be run fairly. This discussion also ended with no more definite results than the annoyance of Okada and Fukuhara. A newspaper report some days later said they were still hoping to have their plan adopted, but in fact the issue never came up again.

Little or none of the preceding account should have been available to us, of course, but the Committee on Literature was a wonderfully leaky committee. "I'm so angry I can't stand it, to think there is such an ungentlemanly individual among us!" complained Ōmachi Keigetsu. "Judging from the accuracy of the leaks, it could only have been someone who has access to both the Committee and the Ministry of Education," which would seem to suggest it was Ueda Mannen or Haga Yaichi, but it could have been anyone and probably was everyone (although Keigetsu insisted that he had never broken his vow of secrecy).[43]

Certainly, news of the subcommittee on translations leaked out quickly. The members—Ōgai, Hōgetsu, Bin, and Chōfū—met on June 8, and Ōgai visited Fukuhara the next day to tell him the results. The June 10, 1911, *Asahi* carried a sarcastic anonymous interview that purported to conjecture on the kinds of innocuous translations the committee as a whole would sponsor. "You

---

*A recent parallel, in which promoters of official orthodoxy have been replaced by the potentially even more threatening promoters of conglomerate profits, was seen in the summer of 1979 following "the decision of the Association of American Publishers, in July, to replace their annual National Book Awards, in which meritorious books in seven categories were honored on the basis of recommendations made by a board of writers and book critics, with a new program, to be called the American Book Awards, in which books in seventeen categories, including Westerns, mysteries, [etc.] would be chosen for awards through a process of balloting [which would obviously be] 'nothing more than a popularity contest, another ratification of the best-seller lists'" (Thomas Whiteside, "Onward and Upward With the Arts / The Blockbuster Complex II," *The New Yorker* [October 6, 1980], pp. 118–20).

can be sure they won't do anything Russian. They'll pick classics—Dante, Cervantes, Goethe—probably *Faust*, though I'd like to see something of a little more interest to modern youth. . . . Maybe Chōfū will drag out some Sanskrit thing and frighten everybody to death." *

At the July 3 regular meeting, the full committee confirmed the subcommittee's choices: Ōgai would do *Faust*; Bin, *The Divine Comedy*; Hōgetsu, *Don Quixote*; and Chōfū, *The Ramayana*.[44] (As it turned out, *Faust* would be the only translation actually seen through to completion.)†

Otherwise, the meeting was rather uneventful. Haga Yaichi was named to head a committee for the compilation of folk tales, an apparently harmless enough task, except that such a volume had been banned in 1909 even though the publishers had suppressed the earthier passages, thus destroying much of the book's documentary value.[45] Ōgai, Ueda Mannen, and Kōda Rohan were assigned the task of designing a gold commemorative medal. Hōgetsu got his reply concerning the feasibility of support for the families of deceased writers: the terms under which the ministry had obtained the allocation from the Diet did not permit of such "indirect encouragement" of literature. This may well have been decided in retaliation for the committee's having rejected the ministry's favored "direct" method. Hōgetsu, at least, was not convinced that the law had to be interpreted so narrowly. He was also disappointed to learn at this meeting that there would be no funds for sending young writers abroad as he had suggested.[46]

The voting for outstanding works went on in a routine manner at this and at the next meeting, on September 16, 1911.‡ The only noteworthy event in September (aside from Chōfū's lament that *The Ramayana* was a *very big* book, and he wished he could postpone translating it) was the announcement by Fukuhara Ryōjirō that he had been promoted to Vice-Minister of Education

---

*This interview contains a tongue-in-cheek defense of Okada and Fukuhara against the charge that they were acting solely in behalf of traditional values and *shakabikushugi*, a wonderful neologism, which he defines "*Shaka*ishugi no shaka o kiku to *biku*ri-to suru" (to become frightened upon hearing just the first two syllables of the word "socialism"). AS (June 10, 1911), p. 5.

†Ōgai finished the uncut translation of Parts I and II on January 5, 1912. This was an impressive feat in itself, but breathtaking to note this was in addition to producing some of his most interesting original fiction and putting in his full time at the Army Ministry. The proofreading was not completed until February 1913, a month before the publication and gala performance of scenes from Part I. See AS (March 23, 1913), p. 5; AS (March 25, 1913), p. 1; AS (March 27, 1913), p. 6; OZ 21:4, 85.

‡There was, however, some uncertainty as to how they ought to handle a work submitted by an author. In the first—and probably the only—such instance, Yosano Hiroshi submitted his poetry collection *Oak Leaves* (*Kashi no ha*). They decided to handle it in the same manner as the other works.

following the inauguration of the second Saionji cabinet on August 30, 1911, which meant that he was now chairman of the committee. A new man was introduced as executive secretary. Komatsubara had been replaced as minister by Haseba Junkō, who sat in on this meeting for an hour.[47]

Although the end of the Katsura regime did usher in an era of less severe censorship, the change in personnel does not seem to have had any effect on the functioning of the committee. For the moment, however, Fukuhara's new responsibilities must have kept him unusually busy. He asked the committee to postpone the October meeting, and in fact they did not convene again until December 2.

At this final meeting of 1911, the sixty works chosen in the preliminary voting were divided into four categories—fiction, poetry, drama, and miscellaneous—and assigned to subcommittees in preparation for the final balloting. It was decided to award the winner in each category a gold medal and an equal share of the ¥3000 prize money. Owing to the postponement of a meeting, the final balloting did not take place until March 3, 1912, by which time the mounting suspense had aroused speculation in the press, especially concerning the fiction category, with the usual accurate leaks but no definitive word.[48]

Kōda Rohan, chairman of the poetry subcommittee, recommended Yosano Akiko's tanka collection, *Spring Thaw* (*Shundeishū*, January 1911), while Ōgai's fiction subcommittee recommended Natsume Sōseki's *The Gate* (*Mon*, January 1911), Shimazaki Tōson's *The Family* (*Ie*, November 1911), Masamune Hakuchō's "Faint Light" ("Bikō," October 1910), Nagai Kafū's "The River Sumida" ("Sumidagawa," originally published in December 1909 but anthologized in March 1911), and Tanizaki Jun'ichirō's "Tattoo" ("Shisei," November 1910).

This was a powerful demonstration of the fiction subcommittee's critical acumen: each piece has lasted through the years as a major work of a major author. It is not difficult to imagine, however, that even the "liberal" Saionji cabinet's Ministry of Education would be reluctant to bestow official recognition on any of these works.

Yosano Akiko had long since established herself as "that woman responsible for the spreading taste for obscene fantasy" with her poems of tangled hair and throbbing breasts,[49] a reputation that even the bland melancholy of *Spring Thaw* could not have dispelled.

Sōseki's *The Gate** is in no way erotic, but it does depict the sufferings of a husband and wife who have come together through an adulterous affair and

*Translated by Francis Mathy as *Mon* (London: Peter Owen; Tokyo: Tuttle, 1972).

who live as virtual social outcasts. And of course little need be said of the ministry's fondness for their recalcitrant doctor.

In *The Family** Tōson depicts the sufferings of individuals oppressed by the weight of the traditional family system, characterizing his two family heads as swindlers and carriers of venereal disease, and suggesting various illicit liaisons and uncontrolled primal urges.

Hakuchō's "Faint Light" remains decorously silent where bedroom scenes can be assumed, but it presents a vivid, complex portrait of a kept woman whose tenuous family ties have failed to protect her from a degraded life. Seduced at sixteen, she has left her illegitimate daughter in the country and now drifts from man to man toward a life of prostitution.

Kafū's well-known "The River Sumida" † suggests the temptations of respectability for those who live in the world of the entertainer and the geisha, but in the end it reaffirms Kafū's preference for what he sees as the freedom and honesty of the stagnant Edo twilight, as compared with the constricting hypocrisy of bureaucratic success.

The first of Tanizaki's five bans for obscenity had occurred not under the Katsura regime but under Saionji in October 1911 when Kafū's *Mita Bungaku* was banned for "Blizzards," the wildly exaggerated account described earlier (see above, p. 139) of a young artist's fatal attachment to a prostitute with fascinating nostrils. "Tattoo" (see above, pp. 138–39) is Tanizaki's famous Edo-period tale of a young girl's awakening to the demonic power latent in her flesh.

Unfortunately, not a single work had been chosen that expressed the glory of the Meiji era and the welling vitality of the Japanese people—perhaps because not many were written that year. Just how sensitive Haseba Junkō's Ministry of Education was to the corruptive potential of these pieces is not clear. According to the March 5, 1912, *Kokumin Shimbun*, Fukuhara addressed the committee at the March 3 meeting when the final selection was about to be made, assuring them that it was absolutely untrue that the ministry was in agony over the preliminary choices. "We will respect your decision," he told them, and neither he nor any other official voiced opinions on the works. If we are to believe an article in *Nihon oyobi Nihonjin*, Fukuhara had actually been influenced by his contact with the "new literature types" on the committee. His original belief in "literature for education" had changed to "the harmonization of literature and education" and then to "literature comes first."[50] As an 1892 graduate of the University of Tokyo Law Faculty, Fukuhara was roughly contemporary with Hōgetsu and perhaps not entirely immune to his influence and to that of the others—and perhaps even of Hiraide Shū.

---

*Translated by Cecilia Segawa Seigle as *The Family* (Tokyo: University of Tokyo Press, 1976).
†Translated in Edward Seidensticker, *Kafū the Scribbler*, pp. 181–218.

The *Asahi*'s report of the balloting, however, gave a very different picture under headlines proclaiming "Ministry Officials' Foul Play" and "Committee Members' Rage." As part of their scheme to make certain that the morally questionable works would be eliminated (leaving what? we might ask), the officials are said to have arranged with Ueda Mannen and Haga Yaichi to take charge of the probureaucratic faction. But they were as surprised as anyone when, after an entire day of repeated balloting, the committee could not decide on a single work to award a prize. The drama and miscellaneous categories were no problem, but opinion was hopelessly divided when it came to poetry and fiction, the most obstinate in their choices being Anesaki Chōfū, Kōda Rohan, and Shimamura Hōgetsu.

Concerning *The Gate*, the probureaucratic faction argued that if Sōseki had gone so far as to reject the doctorate he would not accept the prize. The antibureaucrats argued that whether he accepted was up to him; it was not the function of the committee to read the recipient's mind but to recommend the best work. Sōseki's best work was *I Am a Cat*, not *The Gate*, rejoined the probureaucrats, and it would be a shame to honor him for an inferior novel.

The morning was taken up with this sort of arguing, and the actual balloting started after lunch. Perhaps because moral values comprised a major area of disagreement (according to *Kokumin Shimbun*), no single work could command the ten votes necessary for a three-fourths majority of the thirteen attending members. Nine was the closest they came (on *The Family* and *Spring Thaw*), but when they tried to break the deadlock, the probureaucrats read the other members' expressions and cleverly shifted their votes. Switching from paper ballots to a show of hands apparently made no difference.

The only work to receive the full ten or more votes in its field was Tsubouchi Shōyō's translation of *Romeo and Juliet*, but the members were reluctant to announce that they could agree on only one work. At that point, someone suggested that Shōyō's Literary Society (Bungei Kyōkai) had made such major, lasting contributions to the development of the drama in Japan that they would do well to honor him for his distinguished service to literature. This met with unanimous approval, for in addition to his work in drama, Shōyō was widely recognized as the father of modern realistic theory in Japan and a major experimenter himself in realistic fiction.* They decided to present him with a medal and the entire ¥3000 in prize money.

Thanks to Sōseki, perhaps, the matter did not end there. That very night, Hōgetsu, a colleague of Shōyō's and himself a key figure in the Literary Society, was sent to ask Shōyō whether he would be willing to accept the award. Shōyō was reluctant to do so at first, saying that he was far from being the only

*See Marleigh Grayer Ryan, *The Development of Realism in the Fiction of Tsuboichi Shōyō* (Seattle: University of Washington Press, 1975).

individual to have rendered service to literature and could not accept the prize
in those terms. Hōgetsu asked if he would be amenable to accepting it as the
head of the Literary Society. Yes, that would be all right, said Shōyō. Hōgetsu
brought the news, the certificate of award was rewritten, and the prizes
presented. Instead of keeping the money, however, Shōyō donated half of it to
the Literary Society and—in a move that must have delighted (if not surprised) Hōgetsu—gave the rest to the families of Futabatei Shimei, Kunikida
Doppo, and Yamada Bimyō, all of whom had indeed rendered "distinguished
service to literature" during their lifetimes.[51]

Reaction to this debacle was widespread and varied. Sōseki told the *Yomiuri
Shimbun* that he was enormously relieved. A rumor that his novel had won the
competition had made him apprehensive that his troubles with the Ministry of
Education were going to start all over again. Having refused to take back his
doctorate, the ministry would have had to inscribe that title on this new
certificate of award, which would then have made it impossible for him to
accept. He would also have had to refuse the award because he was opposed to
the Committee on Literature in principle. Of course, if his novel *had* been
chosen, he would have felt grateful, but the fact that no winner could be
determined only went to prove his earlier contention that the general level of
Japanese fiction was high, without any especially outstanding works: they
were all masterpieces and deserved perhaps ¥50 each.[52]

Tōson, whose novel had come within one vote of capturing the prize, and
who had once written of his "beautiful sense of yearning" for the Medicis'
genuine appreciation and patronage of art, was indignant. "I would like to see
literature treated with sincerity and understanding," he pleaded.[53]

To conclude its report on the thwarted competition, the *Asahi* maintained
that the ministry's "conspiracy" had left the antibureaucrat faction seething;
they were already hatching plans to hold their own meetings in order to
present a united front at next year's competition. If such a counterplot did
indeed get off the ground, it could not have stayed there for long, because over
the next few months the committee would shrivel up like a pricked balloon.
Taiyō commented that the whole thing had been a mistake from the start, that
soon the committee would just sink into the earth and no one would notice or
care.[54] *Nihon oyobi Nihonjin* took a more upbeat approach: after this spectacle,
the committee's allocation might be cut from the budget, which would signify
the writers' first successful blow against "the enemy."[55]

Soon the *Asahi* was criticizing the procrastination of those members who
had not, as Ōgai had, completed their assigned translations or editions but had
kept their fifty-yen monthly fee.[56] The May meeting promised to be a scene of
confrontation, noted a later article. Several members wanted to change the
committee's method of support for literature since the attempt to choose
outstanding works had proved abortive, but now the ministry was apparently

opposed to any change. Ōgai frankly told the *Asahi* he thought the present approach should be abandoned.[57] A few days later (May 5, 1912) the *Asahi* recommended that the committee be abolished along with several other nonessential Ministry of Education programs as part of a retrenchment package: it had been nothing but a failed attempt to manipulate the members under the guise of the encouragement of literature, and its budget could be put to better use elsewhere.[58]

The committee's May 1912 meeting was postponed, primarily because the ministry had gotten wind of the brewing confrontation, said the *Asahi* at the end of the month, and this was just one illustration of its chaotic state. The utter indifference of the Home Ministry toward the committee and toward the Ministry of Education was a source of frustration for the members. This had been underscored in May 1912 when the police had failed to consult the committee concerning their interference with the stage performance of Sudermann's *Heimat* (1892; known as *Magda* in English, *Kokyō* or *Maguda* in Japanese), which had been translated by Shimamura Hōgetsu and staged by Hōgetsu's and Shōyō's Literary Society, the group so recently honored by the committee. (The police had threatened to forbid its performance until the company revised the final scene to make it appear less like a victory of the "new" ideas over the "old." They wanted the heroine to blame herself for her father's apoplectic death, rather than say ambiguously, "I wish I had not come home." Hōgetsu had tried to explain that the clash of ideas was merely presented as a problem, without a clear-cut victor, but to no effect. He was willing to capitulate, he said, which apparently led to a successful run of several weeks.)* As if it had not been demonstrated conclusively already, this proved beyond a doubt that the committee was not going to have any effect at all on the censorship situation. Interviewed anonymously, one member said it would be a shame to dissolve the committee, but there was little hope of its accomplishing anything in its present form.[59]

In this atmosphere of hopelessness, the committee all but ceased to function. It finally inaugurated its second year of activity with a meeting in June 1912, at which the decision was made to produce a definitive edition of the great eighth-century poetry anthology, the *Man'yōshū*, which never got produced.

There probably would have been no summer meetings in any case, but

---

*Hōgetsu was well aware that the play had been criticized in Europe for pitting its complex heroine, a liberated "new woman" whose hard-won independence is still threatened by the old ways, against her one-dimensional father, a stubborn military man utterly lacking in appreciation for art (and especially the opera-singer's art to which his daughter has devoted her life). But Hōgetsu asserted that in fact the situation applied more perfectly to present-day Japan than to its European homeland. See "Bungei Kyōkai no *Kokyō*," in *Hōgetsu zenshū* 2:406, plus other articles on the performance, ibid., pp. 401–20.

suddenly, on July 21, 1912, the news broke that the emperor was gravely ill. From that day through the announcement of his death on July 30, the change of the reign name from Meiji to Taishō on August 1, and the spectacle of the funeral on September 13, the attention of the nation was riveted on one thing only. Before that excitement could even begin to die down, the news flashed throughout the country and the world that General Nogi Maresuke, military hero, world traveler, and national model of vigor and righteousness, had died with his wife in an archaic act of ritual suicide, following the emperor in death.

The upheavals associated with this, with the fall of the Saionji regime in December 1912 and the collapse of the third Katsura cabinet in February 1913 amid a constitutional crisis, must have obliterated whatever thought might have survived on either side for a rapprochement between government and literature. Ōgai's *Faust* appeared with the committee's imprint in March 1913, and in May Ōgai held a dinner to thank Fukuhara Ryōjirō and other Ministry officials for their support of his translation.[60] By then, however, *Faust* was being called "the only accomplishment left to us by the Committee on Literature."[61] And when, on June 13, 1913, Prime Minister Yamamoto carried out the fiscal retrenchment and bureaucratic reorganization that had been the primary political frustration of both his predecessors, the demise of the Committee on Literature was barely noticed amid the commotion. The *Asahi* observed drily that the other projected translations would not be produced and that, "in contrast to the Committee for the Investigation of Popular Education," which had lost only half its budget and would continue functioning in a different bureau of the ministry, the Committee on Literature would cease functioning entirely. The magazines said nothing at all.[62] Of far more general interest were the detailed reports on a love affair between Shimamura Hōgetsu and the Literary Society's leading actress, Matsui Sumako, which was producing a split between Hōgetsu and Tsubouchi Shōyō and breaking up the society.

By then the Yamamoto cabinet had been in power only four months, and complaints had begun to surface again of increased censorship activity, much of it now directed against the women's movement, which was exciting as much outrage among educators as had naturalism.* One commentator in an educa-

---

*Both *Taiyō* in June, 1913, and *Chūō Kōron* in July 1913, printed lavish special issues devoted to "the new woman." *Chūō Kōron*'s led to the founding of the women's magazine *Fujin Kōron*; it was edited by Shimanaka Yūsaku, who headed the company during the Pacific War. Hiratsuka Raichō, whose attempted "naturalist" suicide with Morita Sōhei had shocked the nation in 1908, was the most prominent "new woman." On the trend toward the banning of women's writings, see "Fujin zasshi hatsubai kinshi mondai," in *Ōsaka Asahi Shimbun* (April 23, 1913), reprinted in Nakajima Kenzō, ed., *Shimbun shūroku Taishō shi*, 15 vols. (Taishō shuppan kabushikigaisha, 1978) 1:267–68. Thanks to Sister Margit Nagy for finding this article and

tional journal noted that foreign observers had been citing "democratic tendencies" in recent Japanese politics. "This totally erroneous view is due to the fact that they do not know our unique *kokutai* and they observe us with the Western mentality. . . . Our Imperial Way consists in the perfect spiritual oneness of the Emperor and his people."[63]

The brief respite from censorship that literature had enjoyed under the second Saionji cabinet was at an end, the situation having reverted essentially to where it had been before the call for "understanding" between literature and government. Owing both to the contempt of writers who shared Sōseki's outsider's view, and to the stand of men like Ōgai and Hōgetsu who hoped to exploit their insider's privilege in defense of literature, this initial attempt by the government to organize writers ended in failure. The writers had been unable to influence the police, and the bureaucrats had elicited no compromise from the writers. The stalemate would persist until the rise of fanatical militarism in the 1930s changed the rules of the game.

THE END OF MEIJI

The death of the Meiji emperor on July 30, 1912, was an event that carried profound emotional impact for most Japanese, as readers of Natsume Sōseki's *Kokoro* are well aware. The novel's young narrator tells us that word of the emperor's illness, "which was spread throughout the nation by the newspapers, reached us like a gust of wind. . . . Every day, [my father] would wait for the newspaper to arrive. . . . When the newspaper announcing the Emperor's death arrived, my father said: 'Oh! Oh!' And then 'Oh, His Majesty is gone at last. I too. . . .'"[64]

The news touches not only this simple country gentleman but the darkly introspective protagonist, Sensei, as well. "Then at the height of the summer Emperor Meiji passed away. I felt as though the spirit of the Meiji era had begun with the Emperor and had ended with him. I was overcome with the feeling that I and the others who had been brought up in that era were now left behind to live as anachronisms. . . . On the night of the Imperial Funeral I sat in my study and listened to the booming of the cannon. To me, it sounded like the last lament for the passing of an age."[65]

To be sure, one of the most vibrant and creative periods of Japanese history had drawn to a close. Far from marking the end of the Meiji state, however, the death of the monarch was made into an event that symbolized the completion

---

the article on page 200 of the same volume dealing with the second banning of Hiratsuka Raichō's magazine *Seitō*. See also "Bungei zatsuji," NoN (June 15, 1913), p. 100.

of its structure and crystallized all the love and devotion for the throne that the Meiji leaders had nurtured in the populace throughout the nearly forty-five years of the reign of this "impressive and possibly influential figure." *

As the quotation, taken from a standard historical text, suggests, mystery was a large element of the emperor's appeal. Even now, historians are uncertain precisely what role his ideas played in the shaping of his period. As Asada Kōson wrote during the High Treason case in a backhanded slap at the Meiji leaders' manipulation of the imperial symbol:

> Our nation's strength lies in unity, and His Majesty the Emperor is the center of gravity. . . . He is the inexhaustible wellspring of the people's vitality, the paragon of our morality, the everlasting light that shines upon the road ahead. . . . For all the traditional awe and respect paid the Imperial House, however, too little is known of the particular, everyday *facts* of His Majesty the Present Emperor. . . . He is too hidden amidst the nine-fold clouds. . . . His ministers should not shroud him in secrecy; his joys and sorrows should be ours. . . . We do not need abstract lessons in loyalty and patriotism and the deeds of long-dead heroes: all we need is information on the daily life of His Majesty.[66]

That the Meiji leaders' manipulating had been enormously successful became clear with the outpouring of anxiety that greeted news of the emperor's grave illness. From July 21, 1912, the daily papers carried huge headlines above lengthy laments and detailed accounts of his condition. The *Asahi* featured a cumulative chart of medical data, adding a column or two each day to indicate changes in the emperor's temperature, pulse, and respiration, plus physical minutiae of a sort rarely seen even in these eager days of United States politicians' total public disclosure. The emperor may have been a god, but he was a Japanese "living god" [67] with a perishable body, and thus it was perfectly natural for the papers to report, in the most reverential language, that—for example—the doctors had taken a pint of urine from him with a catheter at 7:30 P.M. on July 20. Thanks to these reports, we know not only the volume of his urine but the weight of his feces, the frequency of his flatulence, and the color and texture of his tongue (it was a mossy brownish-black on July 22). Finally, on July 30, the tips of his extremities turned dark purple, and the following day's papers reported that he had "augustly succumbed."

"*Kakemakumo kashikoki* / Awesome beyond speech, O dread theme for my profane tongue!" began the *Asahi*'s report, harking back to the resonant language of the seventh-century Man'yō poets who tremblingly bemoaned the deaths of their god-emperors.[68] The government proceeded to orchestrate a

---

*John K. Fairbank, Edwin O. Reischauer, and Albert M. Craig, *East Asia*, p. 227.

funeral worthy of this sentiment, its preparation taking until the middle of September. Much of this time was devoted to opening an entire virgin mountain south of Kyoto to be the emperor's final resting place, and indeed this sepulchre at Momoyama is one of the most impressively grandiose monuments in Japan, done in a severe Shintō style that recalls the simplicity of the ancient emperors' burial mounds but which far outdoes them in sheer scale.

The funeral procession left the grounds of the imperial palace in Tokyo when a cannon sounded at 8:00 P.M. on September 13.[69] It was, as the headlines proclaimed over and over, an "Unprecedented Giant Funeral" (*kūzen no daisōgi*). Never in Japan's history had the death of an emperor been such an all-consuming national event, bringing troops and mourners from every part of the country and concerning all levels of the populace. The procession itself comprised at least 25,000 people, including both army and navy honor guards numbering over 10,000 troops. It extended two and one-half miles from end to end and took over two hours to pass any one point. Nine hundred specially installed arc lights illuminated the route. After the initial cannon blast within the palace grounds, two other cannon in the city kept up a volley of fire at one-minute intervals, each releasing 101 shots, while a fleet of warships on Tokyo Bay fired 300 blasts. To pay for this spectacle, an emergency session of the Imperial Diet had made an appropriation of ¥1,545,389, the rough equivalent of $5,500,000 (1980).[70]

The crowds that lined the three-mile route from the palace gate to the temporary altar in Aoyama had begun to gather at daybreak and filled every inch of available space by four o'clock that afternoon. A human wall of soldiers stood on either side of the route, 23,937 of whom had been sent to represent every regiment in the country. Just under 5,000 policemen were assigned to crowd-control duty, and plans had been laid carefully enough so that major accidents were avoided. The few shoving incidents were never enough to break the police cordon, and the mourners were generally well behaved. Among them were some 60,000 school children whose attendance had been arranged for by the Ministry of Education, four large grassy areas having been set aside for them, with school physicians providing first-aid care and with toilets assigned in nearby ministry buildings. The children were reminded to be especially quiet when the imperial casket (carried in an ox cart of the kind used by ancient nobility) and the foreign royalty passed, at which times they were to show their utmost respect by bowing the upper parts of their bodies forward to an angle of thirty degrees, as provided for in Education Ministry Directive (no. 18) of 1907.

Respect for the foreigners was expected not only of the children. Practically every breathless newspaper report on the monumental preparations being made included a reminder that Japan's "fifty million siblings" would be performing this national ritual before the eyes of the world and must behave accordingly, eschewing gaudy clothing and avoiding any offense whatever to the foreign representatives. Advice on "how to behave" was given through the papers by any number of officials.

Foremost among the foreign dignitaries was His Royal Highness Prince Arthur of Connaught, representing the British Crown, who had arrived aboard the battleship "Defense" on September 11, 1912, accompanied by three flagships. He had been greeted on board by General Count Nogi Maresuke and other officials who were assigned to accompany him in the cortege, and the new emperor had quickly dispatched Grand Chamberlain Prince Katsura Tarō to present him with the Grand Order of the Chrysanthemum.

The papers reported none of this great spectacle with detachment. Conscious of the deprivation that they had experienced as deeply as their readers, the reporters larded their prose with resonant archaisms. Along the route was not simply a crowd, but the very same "green grass of humanity" that had sprung up mysteriously in the cosmology of the eighth-century "bible," the *Kojiki*; and their tears did not simply fall but they "condensed as clouds and poured down as rain."[71] The subjects of this uniquely beloved emperor thronged out to see him take the road to death, even lining the railroad tracks for the casket's all-night trip to Kyoto (departing Tokyo at 1:00 A.M., arriving in Momoyama at 6:00 P.M. the next day).

Amid the news of this gigantic undertaking, the *Asahi* carried several columns of a shocking story that, in the following days, quickly overwhelmed coverage of the funeral itself. This was the suicide of Japan's consummate military man, General Nogi Maresuke, and his wife. The government could not have asked for a more perfect climax to the Meiji pageant. The timing and style were impeccable.*

Having lost his regiment's flag to the enemy during a battle in the Satsuma Rebellion (1877), Nogi had requested punishment for this act of near sacrilege. Instead he was pardoned and had gone on to become an internationally recognized military leader, the hero of the Russo-Japanese War (in which he lost two sons), President of the Peers' School, and one of the men most respected in Japan for his embodiment of the stoic samurai virtues. Now that he could no longer serve his "lord," however, he had determined to seize this as the opportunity for his long-delayed punishment and follow the emperor in death. Dressed in his uniform of mourning, he and his wife had sat for a photograph at breakfast before calling upon Prince Arthur of Connaught, presumably to convey his regrets at being unable to attend him that evening. Countess Nogi, also dressed in mourning, accompanied him to the palace.

---

*For a study of Nogi and his death, see Robert Jay Lifton, Shūichi Katō, and Michael R. Reich, *Six Lives / Six Deaths* (New Haven: Yale University Press, 1979), pp. 29–66. The following account is based on this and on reports in AS (September 12, 14, 1912).

Then, sending their servants out to watch the cortege, they locked themselves in an upstairs room of their home, composed their death poems, and at the sound of the cannon that signaled the start of the procession, they committed suicide in the time-honored samurai fashion, he disemboweling himself and she stabbing herself in the heart. A small Shintō shrine was erected in their memory at the foot of the mountain tomb of the emperor, where it seems to kneel in perpetual service.

As a recent study has demonstrated, "The Meiji regime as well as subsequent Japanese governments transformed Nogi Maresuke into a formidable instrument of militaristic and nationalistic propaganda."[72] In any case, Nogi's death was an event of great historical significance and was immediately recognized as such in the press. An editorial in the September 14, 1912 *Asahi* saw the challenge it presented the Japanese. "This will not go down as an individual's isolated act, nor will it end as a momentary shock. This presents a major problem with regard to Japanese mores and morals."

For a time, continued the editorial, the flood of new Western civilization destroyed this country's traditional morals and beliefs. But the people rediscovered the value of their own country through the Sino- and Russo-Japanese Wars, giving rise to a reaction against the destruction of the old civilization and a revival of Bushidō, the Way of the Warrior. Now, continued the article, some people insist that Bushidō is the very foundation of Japanese morality. It may well be a perfect military code, but it cannot be forced upon society as a whole.

General Nogi's *junshi* (self-sacrifice) to the spirit of the late emperor cannot but move us all, the editorial went on to say, but from a modern point of view, his act was strictly a matter of personal choice. We regret that he forgot he still had an individual self (*jiko*) to devote to the nation. "While we express great *emotional* respect for his act as a fitting climax to Japan's ancient Bushidō, *intellect* tells us to choose differently. We can only hope that it will not have an adverse long-range effect on Japan's morality. We are filled with admiration for the General's intent, but his act should not become a model for emulation."[73]

It was precisely to express this struggle between old heart and new mind in *Kokoro* that Natsume Sōseki seized upon the *junshi* of Nogi as the inexplicable impetus for his coldly rational protagonist's long-delayed suicide.* And the most compelling feature of Mori Ōgai's historical novellas on *seppuku* (disem-

---

*I cannot help thinking that a group photograph in AS (September 15, 1912), p. 6, and in NoN (October 1, 1912), appendix, of Nogi immersed in the naked flesh of the Peers' School Swim Club provided Sōseki with the inspiration for the opening beach scene of *Kokoro*. The towel, the man and the youth, the masses of unclothed humanity, and even the lone, unidentified foreigner in Japanese beachwear could all have been suggested by this picture. (The foreigner is visible at the far right of the NoN print). A less impressionistic indication of an intended parallel between the modern thinker Sensei and the anachronistic soldier Nogi is the

bowelment), written at this time, is their mingled sense of awe for samurai heroism and disgust for the destruction of individual life.* Indeed, we might say that the *Asahi* editorialist, writing within hours of Nogi's death, captured the struggle that most Japanese would experience—and writers among them—as they became increasingly sophisticated members of the world community while their government invested increasingly larger sums of money and manpower in programs designed to preserve the aura of a united family. Even as Japan was swept by the world trend toward cosmopolitanism that followed World War I, the emotional pull of the imperial myth remained strong, and official policy moved to keep it that way.

---

names of their wives: Shizuko (Nogi) and Shizu (Sensei). And if we take the concluding lines of the novel seriously, it is certain that Shizu, too, followed her husband in death.

*It is well known that Ōgai sent the completed manuscript of the first of these stories to *Chūō Kōron* on the day of Nogi's funeral, September 18, 1912. For background and translations, see David Dilworth and J. Thomas Rimer, eds., *The Incident at Sakai and Other Stories* (Honolulu: University Press of Hawaii, 1977).

Part Four

TOWARD NATIONAL MOBILIZATION

13

Overview:
Thought Control and Censorship After Meiji

Through the Taishō (1912–1926) and Shōwa (1926–) periods, serious writers continued to uphold the tradition of political and artistic independence that had been established in late Meiji. Meanwhile, official thinking also remained consistent: ranged against everything that was wholesomely Japanese were the alien forces of sedition and decadence, their deadly germs always threatening to infect the sacred *kokutai*. As a result, the relationship between writers and the state continued essentially unchanged.

The conservative position was remarkable not only for its continuity but for the evangelistic zeal with which it sought to bring wayward souls back from the regions of the damned. The missionary analogy is no exaggeration. If anything, it does not go far enough. To appreciate the complex of pressures to which the unorthodox were subjected, one must imagine a fundamentalist ladies' temperance union determined to effect a spiritual cure of every drinker in the country. They would be supported at first by private philanthropic organizations but eventually by generous appropriations from the national budget and the services of the police, the courts, the educational system, the media, religious institutions, social workers, and the friends and families of the alcoholic. Their work would be accomplished primarily at a number of regional detoxification centers, staffed in many instances by converted alcoholics and civilian volunteers. In the early stages, their propaganda efforts against demon rum would have been too successful, as a result of which even fully reformed alcoholics would be shunned by the public and unable to find work. The union ladies would quickly realize the need for educating the public concerning the special needs of converts, and soon public distrust would decline, "with some businessmen making special efforts to hire offenders." People would see that the alcoholic should not be treated as a criminal but as a patient, a fellow human being in need of love and understanding. He would be encouraged to "read good books and listen to good lectures," but by far it would be the outpouring of love all around him that would move him to renounce his selfish ways and rejoin the fold, the recidivism rate running at an amazingly low 1 to 3 percent.

What I am referring to here is the system of thought control that developed after the High Treason case, the mechanism known as the "peace preservation system" and described in stunning detail by Richard H. Mitchell, from whose book, *Thought Control in Prewar Japan*, the above quotations are taken.[1] The system's continuity of values is to be explained in part by its personnel: the chief procurator in the Kōtoku trial, Hiranuma Kiichirō, went on to become the single most influential shaper of policy in the Justice Ministry, where thought control policy was formulated, and his fear of "alien ideology" never changed (see above, chap. 10, footnote p. 158).

At the core of the system was Hiranuma's Peace Preservation Law (Chian iji hō), which was first promulgated in 1925 as an antileftist measure, but which was then revised and expanded in 1928 and 1941 until "few acts [were left] outside the scope of the law. Even a drunk who relieved himself in a dark corner of a neighborhood shrine might be charged with a violation."[2] As the law's scope expanded, so did the use of violence to enforce it. It is well known that the police tortured to death the foremost proletarian author, Kobayashi Takiji, in 1933 during one of their mass arrests of suspected radicals. During the war, procurators and police exploited the Peace Preservation Law to justify the arrest and torture of some prominent liberal journalists (see below, chap. 16).

Undeniably, then, "arrest, torture (or fear of it), interrogation, trial, imprisonment, and fear of death certainly played" an important role in keeping the orthodoxy as unsullied as possible,[3] but the Japanese system of thought control was historically unique in its assumption that everyone—enforcer and offender alike—was part of one big, happy family that could be brought into harmony again with love and patience. "Procurator Hirata Susumu summed up this view: No 'thought criminal was hopeless. . . . Since they were all Japanese, sooner or later they would all come around to realizing that their ideas were wrong.' . . . [D]aily indoctrination would reform even hardened thought criminals, whose Japaneseness was bound to surface sooner or later."[4]

Rather than using the Peace Preservation Law to try offenders in court and punish them with imprisonment, the Justice Ministry devised an ingenious administrative approach that kept suspects in a kind of legal limbo while they were being "treated" at regional "Protection and Supervision Centers," twenty-two of which were created by the legislature in 1936 to take up the role earlier played by philanthropic societies. "After enactment of this crucial legislation, Protection Division Chief Moriyama Takeichirō announced that the 'father-and-mother-type policy to control thought crimes has been established.'"[5] This parental policy stressed renunciation and conversion (*tenkō*) over incarceration and punishment. Mitchell's description of later developments shows us that the family-style cure for thought crimes was aimed at much more than the Red Menace:

> Protracted warfare in China and the diplomatic crisis with the United States during 1941 ushered in new standards for conversion. It was held that the thought offender must awaken to the fact of being Japanese, put his Japanese ideas into daily practice, fully accept and understand the concept of *kokutai*, and discard the unassimilable portions of Western culture (e.g., individualism, liberalism, Marxism, and other "inferior" ideas). . . . . Eventually, they would find their way out of the swamp of "modern individualism and materialism" which had prevented them from realizing their true Japaneseness.*

As the system expanded, the number of Japanese who had to be reminded of their Japaneseness became simply astounding—certainly many more than would have called themselves Communists, even supposing the illegal fifty-member party founded in 1922 had caught on like wildfire. Between 1928, when the notorious mass arrest of suspected radicals on March 15 inaugurated the systematic use of the Peace Preservation Law, and the full wartime mobilization of 1941, there were 65,921 arrests, only 14,426 of which led to judicial (5,559) or administrative (8,867) action. By 1938, only two years after their official founding as government agencies, "Protection and Supervision Centers had handled about 13,000 people. . . . the number of repeaters was a low one percent."[6]

The system could not have confined itself to tight, little Communist cells to produce these numbers; in fact, "the hard-core incorrigibles" numbered only about two hundred over the years.[7] This was a sprawling octopus that reached into every corner and tried to reach into every mind in the nation, a modern institutionalization of that "conspiracy" between state and family decried by Uozumi Setsuro at the beginning of the Kōtoku case (see p. 176). As one advisor to the government concluded in 1928, "the nation's strongest weapon in the thought war was 'love,'"[8] and the government took his advice, ingeniously exploiting the nation's great pool of regressive emotion to lure back the mavericks. There are signs that the "conspiracy" is still active today,† and

---

*MITC, pp. 137–38. One leftist writer who "awoke" put it this way: "Marxism can certainly never become a permanent support for the Japanese soul. . . . Even a convert (*tenkōsha*) who is unable to die for Marxism can gladly die for a great principle (*taigi*), because he too is a Japanese." See Donald Keene, "Japanese Literature and Politics in the 1930s" *Journal of Japanese Studies* 2, no. 2 (Spring 1976): 241.

†The protagonist of Abe Kōbō's 1967 play *Tomodachi* (translated by Donald Keene as *Friends*, in Howard Hibbett, ed., *Contemporary Japanese Literature* [New York: Alfred A. Knopf, 1977], pp. 53–109) is imprisoned and finally killed by a family spreading the gospel of neighborly

while it is surely true that all cultures offer oases in which the mature individual's taxing independence can give way to moments of childlike belonging, it took the prewar Japanese government to hold out the promise of Peter Pan with such methodical thoroughness and to beat into submission those few who continued openly to resist.[9]

Seen thus in summary, thought control may seem to have taken hold on the day of Kōtoku Shūsui's execution in 1911. The process was more gradual, of course, until after the Manchurian Incident of 1931.

As the transition was being made from Meiji to Taishō in 1912, the political parties were beginning to take power from the other ruling elites. In 1917, school textbooks were revised to include some of the internationalism associated with World War I, and the end of the war in 1918 brought to Japan the same mood favoring pacifism, constitutionalism, and international cooperation that was sweeping the rest of the world. The Rice Riots of that year also demonstrated the potential for widespread defiance of police attempts to hold the national family intact.[10] Japan's first May Day celebration was held in 1920 as the rise of the labor movement signaled that the post-Kōtoku "winter years" were coming to an end and Socialist titles began appearing in the book stores again. 1921 saw the founding of the first proletarian literary journal, *Tane Maku Hito*. Universal manhood suffrage expanded the electorate from 3,000,000 to 13,000,000 in 1925.[11]

Even as this period of "Taishō democracy" was flourishing, however, major strides were being taken toward the reestablishment of national harmony. The trial and imprisonment of Morito Tatsuo in 1920 for publishing an objective study of Kropotkin demonstrated the limits of Japanese academic freedom.* "Since the universities were viewed as the seedbeds of radicalism, the Hara cabinet (1918–1921) used an imperial ordinance to order them to pay more attention to 'the training of character and the cultivation of national thought'"[12]—and Hara was considered the foremost champion of democracy. The reaction to an attempted assassination of the Prince Regent, ostensibly in "revenge" for Kōtoku, in 1923, coupled with other leftist "shocks" and a

---

love. Perhaps even more startling is a thirty-minute film on Japan being distributed abroad since 1972 by the United States-Japan Trade Council, an agency of the Japanese government. Called "Growing Up Japanese," it is a lively, wonderfully colorful panorama of life in Japan that overflows with infectious energy and good will. "The Japanese," we are told behind a montage of hand-holding, snuggling, breast-feeding, and general "skinship," "are a very *touching* people." Obvious propaganda designed to counteract the "economic animal" image of the Japanese, the film captures a great variety of individuals in moments of spontaneous laughter and joyous participation in groups at work and play, never suggesting that there might be Japanese who simply loathe company picnics. Its title notwithstanding, the film is about *not* growing up.

*One might point out that the limits of British academic freedom were demonstrated in 1918 when Trinity College dismissed Bertrand Russell for opposing the war.

feeling that the great Kantō earthquake of that year was a form of punishment for excessive individualism, helped erode opposition to government control of radical movements. By 1925, when representative democracy was supposedly at its height (possibly *because* it was at its height: there was some sense of a trade-off), the Hiranuma faction was able to pass the Peace Preservation Law through the Diet "with overwhelming support," establishing the mysterious *kokutai* in law for the first time and repudiating the widely held rational view of the emperor as an organ of the state.[13]

The Taishō emperor died in December 1926, and Shōwa, the age of the present emperor, began. By this time the economy, never strong in Taishō, was in a state of collapse. There was widespread suffering, and to many it seemed that democracy and internationalism were already failing. The corrupt political parties were blamed, and young military patriots began searching for a "spiritual" solution to Japan's problems, which would lead to a wave of right-wing terrorism.[14]

The regime that came to power at this time of crisis under Tanaka Giichi (1927–1929), with its strong Hiranuma connections, was reminiscent of the second Katsura cabinet in its determination to root out subversion. This was the government that organized the nationwide arrest of 1600 suspected radicals on March 15, 1928, and set the mechanism of the peace preservation system into motion. Tanaka obtained a special ¥2,000,000 allocation from the Diet for expansion of the Special Higher Police, and the Police Bureau censorship budget more than doubled between 1927 and 1929 (the staff expanding from twenty-four to fifty-eight).[15] And as with Katsura, the censorship figures began to climb, initiating a trend that would continue—and dramatically intensify—through the war period.

Censorship played an important role in the thought control system, both through the Police Bureau mechanism we have seen at work thus far and under a number of new, mutually competitive agencies, including the Home Ministry's Special Higher Police Section (or Thought Police), the cabinet's increasingly powerful intelligence operations, and the military services' information sections.[16] Throughout the Taishō period the censors relaxed somewhat, and informal consultations between publishers and censors played a major role. The end of that period in 1926, however, saw a boom in commercial publishing which far outstripped the Police Bureau's capacity for individual consultation. In June 1927 the bureau announced an end to informal consultations, and immediately a movement for the revision of the censorship system came into being. This was quickly snuffed out by the Tanaka government, which took the unprecedented step of forbidding criticism of the system.

But this was only the beginning. Many things published in 1930 would never have seen the light of day in 1935. In 1930 a good deal of Marxist theory was still appearing in print, and an occasional arrest was considered, if anything, good advertising. The publishing business was booming.[17] The crucial turning point was the Manchurian Incident of 1931, after which the exigencies of war became the rationale for a tightened grip on the minds of the people. The crackdown on communism expanded to the suppression of left-leaning cultural and literary groups that had heretofore been considered legal. Then, beginning with the Takigawa Incident of 1933, there occurred a series of bans and court cases that demonstrated how far the government was going to go beyond the mere suppression of leftist writings.

Takigawa Yukitoki, professor of criminal law at Kyoto University, was the first of several "old liberals" whose works were suddenly labeled "un-Japanese" and no longer publishable. The most famous victim of this new movement was Minobe Tatsukichi, professor of law at the University of Tokyo, whose "organ theory" of the role of the emperor had been accepted as mainstream constitutional thinking and had even been incorporated into official documents. A crusade was launched against him in 1935 by Mitsui Kōshi, an old nemesis of Natsume Sōseki, and by others calling for "clarification of the national polity [kokutai meichō]." *

During these years in which the old liberals came under fire, the Home Ministry attempted to branch out from its traditional negative censorship role and move into the area of the protection and encouragement of literature, where Komatsubara Eitarō's Ministry of Education had fared so poorly, but again the writers proved difficult to handle. Their nearly complete subversion of this new Literary Chat Society was another bracing show of independence— but it was to be the last.

The Police Bureau was still the headquarters for censorship during this period, but after the China Incident of 1937, military intelligence bureaus began to vie with it, and with one another, and with several semiofficial right-wing organizations, for control of the written word. From this time, editors and publishers found themselves rushing from one obligatory "friendly get-together" to another. There they would be praised for cooperating with the war effort, criticized and threatened if they did not, and issued embargoes and other oral directives too sensitive to commit to writing. It was at these friendly get-togethers, too, that they finally ceded to the military whatever editorial autonomy they still retained.

Just as censoring agencies proliferated, the laws affecting written expression

---

*SSDS, pp. 13–14. Apparently there was some confusion as to what kind of "organ" Minobe had in mind. For Mitsui Kōshi and Natsume Sōseki, see Jay Rubin, "Sōseki on Individualism," pp. 47–48. SKG 3 (1935): 103–08 contains a fascinating Police Bureau account of the Kokutai Meichō movement's hysterical pressure on the government.

also increased in number.* The single greatest limitation on the wartime publishing industry, however, came not in the form of agencies and laws but in shortages of paper. Substantial cuts in paper consumption were being ordered as early as August 1938, and the situation was serious enough to require a rationing program beginning in July 1941. The most "deserving" periodicals received preferential treatment when paper was allotted, and nearly complete prior censorship was achieved regarding books when publishers were finally required to submit a detailed description of any manuscript before they could receive a paper allocation. This phase of control was administered not by the police or the military but by the publishing industry itself in a remarkable reversion to the days of the Tokugawa shoguns.

It should be obvious from even this brief overview that at least another volume as long as the present one would be needed to do a reasonably complete study of the 1913–1945 period. (The Occupation period presents yet a different set of problems, with writers confronting alien censors who were determined to expunge a perceived militaristic strain inherent in Japan's "feudal" society, even while the victors' guilt over their own unprecedented military atrocities—the atomic bombings, the still more lethal fire bombings of the cities—prompted them to suppress their victims' cries of pain and outrage. American puritanism helped launch the seven-year court battle over the 1950 translation of *Lady Chatterley's Lover* which has rendered a complete translation still illegal in Japan despite the book's 1959 vindication in the United States. Ironically, the Chatterley case set the precedent for the most celebrated obscenity trial in recent years involving a work that had nothing to do with the flood of pornography that followed the Allied nullification of the prewar publishing codes: Nagai Kafū's quaintly erotic early Taishō story, "What I Found Under the Papering in the Little Room" ["Yojōhan fusuma no shitabari"], reprinted in a humor magazine in 1972.)[18]

The following chapters are intended neither as a substitute for an exhaustive treatment nor even as episodes broadly representative of the period. They should, however, demonstrate both the direct contribution of late-Meiji offi-

---

*In addition to the Press and Publication Laws and the Peace Preservation Law, publishers had to worry about the Control of Subversive Documents Law (Fuon bunsho torishimari hō, 1936); the Military Secrets Law (Gunki hogo hō, 1899, broadened and strengthened in 1937); the War Materials Secrets Law (Gun'yō shigen himitsu hogo hō, 1939); the National General Mobilization Law (Kokka sōdōin hō, 1938); the National Defense and Public Peace Law (Kokubō hoan hō, 1941); the Emergency Law (and Enforcement Regulations) Controlling Speech, Publication, Assembly, Association, Etc. (Genron shuppan shūkai kessha tō rinji torishimari hō plus its shikō kisoku, 1941); the Press Industry Ordinance (Shinbun jigyō rei, 1943); the Publication Industry Ordinance (Shuppan jigyō rei, 1943); and others. SSDS, p. 132.

cial values to the massive indoctrination program supporting total national mobilization, and the equally direct resistance of writers whose commitment to intellectual independence was born in that same period of late Meiji. The discussion will be limited to the following topics: (1) the experience of Tanizaki Jun'ichirō as an apolitical Taishō period writer whose work was a frequent target of both book and theater censors; (2) problems surrounding the Shōwa publishing boom and the Home Ministry's attempted replay of the Committee on Literature; and (3) censorship and mobilization of writers under the military and the thought police, including a last look at Tanizaki, both as a libertarian and as a lukewarm supporter of the war.

14

Tanizaki in Taishō

We have seen in chapter 9 how the censors' omnipresence disturbed but did not disrupt the early career of Tanizaki Jun'ichirō. As his unique fictional and dramatic explorations of human sexuality and violence reached new levels of creative resourcefulness through the Taishō years, the police found it necessary to step in from time to time. But Tanizaki's rich literary legacy remains vivid evidence of how little the censorship system could do to a determined writer, particularly one whose works had the power to enter into what Sōseki called "the greater consciousness of society."

The censors made more trouble for Tanizaki as a dramatist than as a novelist. (Again, just as fiction went relatively unscathed until it became a mature medium of criticism during the naturalist years, so the flowering of the modern Japanese theater during Taishō led to the increasing importance of theater censorship.) We have noted the ban of Tanizaki's story "Blizzards" in 1911, but the number of outright bans suffered by his fiction thereafter came to no more than three. Of these, "Oiran" (a term designating the highest rank of courtesan in the licensed quarter) was the most unfortunate instance, for when its first installment caused the banning of the magazine *Arusu* in May 1915, Tanizaki chose not to continue a work that would surely have been delightful. Like "Blizzards," it would have propelled its virginal hero into an explosion of sensual discovery, but the fragment ends just as the sixteen-year-old apprentice is being sent on an errand to the pleasure quarters. There the mysterious Oiran lives whom he has heard the men discussing. His vague curiosity about her is the one weak spot in his armor of total sensual indifference. He works longer hours than anyone else in the shop, studies late into the night, cannot see why the grown-ups prefer one restaurant to another as long as they can fill their stomachs, and despises people for the time and energy they waste on personal hygiene; he would probably have ranked high among Tanizaki's many comical prudes.[1]

Tanizaki had two uninteresting stories banned in September 1916: "My Late Friend" ("Bōyū") in *Shinshōsetsu*, and "A Handsome Man" ("Binan") in *Shinchō*.[2] Because this unusual twin banning occurred just a year after the loss of "Oiran" and only two months after a play of Tanizaki's had caused the banning of *Chūō Kōron*, Tanizaki was beginning to look like a marked man. This no doubt contributed to the startling negotiations concerning "Sorrow of the Heretic" that we discussed in chapter 9.

Before we turn to the difficulties Tanizaki faced as a playwright, two more works of fiction should be mentioned, *A Fool's Love* (*Chijin no ai*, 1924–1925) and "The Story of Tomoda and Matsunaga" ("Tomoda to Matsunaga no hana-shi," 1926).[3] *A Fool's Love* is Tanizaki's full-length novelization, in contemporary setting, of the male-female relationship he first created in the 1910 story "Tattoo." Here again a man sensitive to the latent sensuality of a young girl grooms her to be his ideal woman, and when she has come to realize the power of her flesh, he becomes her unquestioning slave. "Tattoo" ends with the girl's realization that she has drawn the life-blood from her erstwhile master, but Naomi, the heroine of *A Fool's Love*, goes on to exploit her Western-tinged sexuality in affairs with a wide variety of men—even foreigners. This is the ultimate blow to Jōji, who had originally been attracted by her resemblance to Mary Pickford and the Western sound of the name "Naomi," which was such an excellent match to his own "George." He cannot bear to extricate himself from the relationship, however, and the story ends eight years after it began, with Jōji still married and more hopelessly enslaved than ever to Naomi.

Jōji tells us that he has presented the record of their relationship with the conviction that it will become a valuable reference for the reader: "Especially in this modern day, as Japan becomes increasingly cosmopolitan, as natives mingle more freely with foreigners, as a variety of philosophies and ideas come pouring into the country, and not only men but women, too, become fashionably Westernized, marriages like ours (something almost without precedent) should be springing up everywhere."[4]

A Fool's Love was written after Tanizaki had moved to the Osaka area following the near-destruction of Tokyo in the great earthquake of 1923. As such, it was a major document in his reconsideration of the Western influence in Japanese culture, particularly as it was manifested in the affectations of life in the Tokyo-Yokohama area. From the point of view of censors interested in cultural purity, the novel had much that should have been congenial. But while the West may be seen as the source of decadence in the novel, that decadence is presented with undeniable erotic allure. Young readers, especially, responded to Naomi as the embodiment of the *modan gāru* who was out to destroy feudal inhibitions, especially those concerned with sex. The term "Naomi-ism" became popular for a while.

This widespread interest was not lost on the police, who sent frequent warnings to the *Osaka Asahi Shimbun*, the newspaper that had begun to serialize the novel on March 20, 1924. Eventually, the *Asahi* caved in to the pressure and ended serialization with installment number 87 on June 14, 1924. The book was too important to Tanizaki, however, too much a part of this crucial transitional period in his life, merely to abandon. As he wrote to his readers, "This novel is my favorite of recent years and I have been writing it with mounting excitement. I intend, therefore, as soon as possible, to find another newspaper or magazine in which to continue serialization. I say this both by way of apology and as a promise."[5]

True to his word, Tanizaki resumed publication in November 1924 in the Osaka-based magazine *Josei*, which carried it through to completion in July 1925, apparently without incident.

Tanizaki serialized "The Story of Tomoda and Matsunaga" in the women's magazine *Shufu no Tomo* from January to May 1926. Its eighty-plus pages tell a fascinating variant version of the psychological struggle between East and West seen in *A Fool's Love*, *Some Prefer Nettles*,* and many other Tanizaki pieces. But it is noteworthy also as an example both of how absurdly arbitrary the use of *fuseji* could be and of how free writers still were at this stage to denigrate the sacrosanct foundations of Japanese society.

Matsunaga Gisuke is the head of a wealthy rural family, a devoted and dutiful—indeed, embarrassingly sentimental—husband and father. Mysteriously, however, he disappears from his home for four-year periods whenever he has been living at home for four years. While he is away, he assumes several names—including Jacques Moran in Paris, Tomoda Ginzō in Shanghai, Yokohama, and Kobe—and he lives an utterly dissolute life, drinking, whoring, even engaging in white slavery. He knows the finest in Western cultural and sensual fulfillments, dances a mean tango, and cannot even be recognized as a Japanese, so profoundly does his physical appearance become altered by a near doubling of body weight! Predictably enough, when Tomoda has had his fill of Western decadence, he shrivels to his former self and returns to the comforting familiarity of the Japanese countryside. The process does not end there, however, for it is something he cannot control: after four years on the farm, Matsunaga's body and soul begin to crave Western stimuli, and he must once again plunge into the dissolute life of Tomoda. His one hope for release from the cycle lies in the decrepitude of old age, that stage of life best suited to the restrained culture of Japan.

Forced by his widowed mother to marry and assume the family headship upon graduating from college, Matsunaga had longed for the pleasures of the city. "Then, when my mother finally died, it was like having an ugly growth

---

Tade kuu mushi (1928–1929), translated by Edward Seidensticker as *Some Prefer Nettles* (New York: Alfred A. Knopf, 1955).

removed. . . . Now there was no one to fear. . . . I loathe Japanese drink and Japanese women. I am a fanatical worshipper of the West. Today I realize that this is at least partly a reaction to having been raised in an old rural family and oppressed by its traditions." Matsunaga (speaking as the dissolute Tomoda) goes on to turn Tanizaki's famous aesthetic of shadows * on its head, negating the very core of Japan's cult of restraint and suggestion:

> Just as the interior of my country home was dark and gloomy, all oriental taste is dark and gloomy. "Refinement" and "elegance" are the very opposite of everything open and spontaneous. They are not suited to a young, healthy man who still possesses a full measure of vitality. No, these come from doddering old fogies who can only enjoy themselves by arbitrarily assigning value to things that have no innate value; they are nothing more than perverse slogans of withdrawal, servility and self-deception.[6]

He continues in this vein, lambasting all that is passive and negative in Japanese culture, insisting that the Japanese preference for half-revealed beauty is owing to their own physical ugliness and their lack of the physical stamina required by the dynamic expressiveness of Western culture.

Even in the context of the entire story, this passage is only partly ironical, for though overindulgence leads to Tomoda's physical debilitation and his longing for the mystery and reserve of Japan—the sweetly yellowish skin of its women, the familiar aroma of the morning bean soup—these in time come to disgust him and he is on the road again—at least until some time in the future when he is too old to respond to the West's sharp stimulus. Each excursion he makes is less distant from Japan's cultural cradle, Yamato: when age finally cripples him, perhaps he will settle there once and for all.

Censors can hardly be expected to take things in context, however, especially such a forceful condemnation as partially quoted above. They did not seem to mind this story, though. It was not banned, and the handful of *fuseji* did nothing whatever to obscure Tanizaki's point. Nor, when he supplied the missing phrases in postwar publication, did Tanizaki do anything more than illustrate how nervous and inconsistent editors could be in trying to anticipate police objections. Even expurgated, the story had "burning lips" and "clinging arms," but "snuggling up to comfort me" and "sharing sweet whispers with Susan" were not allowed. Perhaps because it suggested a longer time for dalliance, "He had her on his lap" was expunged, while "He pulled her onto his lap and embraced her" got through.[7]

Tanizaki's novel 卍 (*Manji*, serialized 1928–1930) might also be men-

---

* "In'ei raisan," translated by T. J. Harper and E. G. Seidensticker as *In Praise of Shadows* (New Haven: Leete's Island Books, 1977).

tioned here as an example of *fuseji* nonsense. A chronicle of disastrous hetero-
and bi-sexual relationships as convoluted as its title, it was liberally sprinkled
with *fuseji* in prewar publications. In 1947, however, Tanizaki found himelf
apologizing to readers of *Tokyo Shimbun* who had been taken in by a recent
publisher's advertisement claiming that the book was now complete and
without *fuseji*, as though he had filled in the missing words. In fact, all he had
done was direct the publisher to eliminate the *fuseji*, having decided that the
omitted passages were not worth restoring.[8]

Readers of Tanizaki in English will have been alerted by the foregoing
discussion to the fact that the few translations we have of his fiction are but a
small fraction of the colorful whole. Tanizaki's work as a playwright, however,
is all but unknown here. This is unfortunate; it might be said that the appeal of
his fiction owes much to its theatricality, while his dramatic works are always
written with an eye to keeping the stage alive. Especially when he adopts brash
Kabuki conventions, so in keeping with his love for hyperbole, there is no hint
of bookish stasis to his theater. This, combined with the shocking material he
often chose for the stage, brought him more often to the attention of the
theatrical censors than the overseers of the printed media.

Local police departments played a more prominent role in controlling the
entertainment media than they did with printed publications. As a practicing
playwright, Tanizaki had difficulties with the local police where his plays were
produced—that is, the Tokyo Metropolitan Police Department, which had its
own set of rules and guidelines for the theater, beginning with a licensing
procedure.

Producers were required to submit their scripts to the department for prior
censorship and were subject to arrest and fine if they staged any piece without
approval. Unlike publishers, however, producers did have access to a list of
standards they were expected to follow. The very first item on the list was an
astounding archaism that put the Tokyo police squarely in the camp of the
eighteenth-century Tokugawa government: no script could be produced
which was deemed to run counter to the principle of Encouraging Virtue and
Chastising Vice (see above, p. 19). There were also prohibitions against anything considered disgusting, obscene, or cruel; anything that might incite or
aid in the commission of a crime; anything considered an unseemly parody of
current events or which smacked of political discourse; anything that might
interfere with good diplomatic relations; anything deemed to present a bad
educational influence; and anything not covered by the above that could
disrupt the public peace or injure public morals. Even when permission had
been granted, any policeman had the authority to walk into a theater and close
down the show on the spot.[9]

Tanizaki began having trouble on many of these counts as early as 1913. In
May of that year, *Chūō Kōron* published his three-act play, *The Age to Learn of*

Love (*Koi o shiru koro*). It was not suppressed by the Home Ministry, but neither would the Tokyo police allow it to appear on the stage.

Shintarō, the central character of the play, is a highstrung, spoiled boy of twelve given to kicking the servants, throwing tantrums, and generally making himself hated by everyone including the audience (or reader). When the sixteen-year-old Okin enters the household as a maid, however, Shintarō suddenly becomes docile, smitten by her innocent beauty. She is far from innocent, however, and it does not take Shintarō long to realize that even though Okin is supposed to be his half-sister, born to the madame of a house of assignation, in fact she and her mother have merely hoodwinked his father into believing this. She is conspiring with a clerk, her lover, to take over the family and its lucrative cotton wholesaling business. He overhears Okin and her lover plotting to kill him—the family heir—as the one obstruction to their plans. Rather than expose the pair, he shocks Okin by telling her that he would gladly die for her, a remark she ascribes to coincidence. That night he lets her guide him out to a dark storage shed and is killed according to plan.[10]

Far from Encouraging Virtue and Chastising Vice, *The Age to Learn of Love* concludes with the apparent total victory of Okin, whose evil is so extreme as to verge on self-parody. (Most of Tanizaki's early "satanical" writings are pretty silly, after all.) Of course, she does not know that Shintarō sacrificed himself out of love for her and that the moral victory is actually his, which is the crux of the play. The censors were also apparently unaware of this. In addition they were opposed to having Okin appear on stage in the first act fresh from the bath and wearing only a single underkimono, much to the excitement of her lover and no doubt any audiences that would be harmed by seeing the play.

Before examining Tanizaki's reaction to this ban, which he wrote eight years later, we will look at a more successful and important piece that was suppressed in 1916. Tanizaki has explored the theme of deception in many different fictional forms, perhaps none more subtle and insinuating than *The Key*, "The Bridge of Dreams," and "A Portrait of Shunkin."* In each of these works, layer after layer of apparent truth is revealed, only to be negated by conflicting evidence, until the reader finds himself anxiously groping for some foothold that will not give way. *The Key* is especially unnerving in this respect, throwing the reader from one mendacious diary to another as it paints an ugly portrait of six loathsome individuals who use and finally destroy each other.

As unpleasant as the characters are in *The Key*, however, they hardly begin to measure up to the evil demons in Tanizaki's exuberantly bloody 1916 play, *The*

---

*"The Bridge of Dreams" and "A Portrait of Shunkin" ("Yume no ukihashi" [1960] and "Shunkin shō" [1933]) have been translated by Howard Hibbett in *Seven Japanese Tales* (New York: Alfred A. Knopf, 1963).

Age of Terror (*Kyōfu jidai*). Here, in an Edo-period setting, Tanizaki exploits hyperbolic Kabuki theatrical conventions to express his modern view of the physical and psychological fragility of man in a deceptive world. Of the play's ten main characters, nine lie dead either on or off stage at the end, while the tenth, a cowardly clown, lies in a faint amid six of the most gorily dispatched corpses. This is a suitably absurd ending to a black comedy of errors in which the plotters' evil is matched in full by their ineptitude.

The evil begins with the lord of the House of Harufuji, whose delight in the killing and torturing of his subjects has spawned a plot to overthrow him. The rebels, however, are by no means champions of righteousness. First among them is Ogin-no-kata, a former geisha who, eight years before, bore Harufuji the male heir his wife had been unable to produce, and who has since been his favorite concubine. The actual father of the child, however, was Harufuji's head retainer, Jinpu, Ogin's present ostensible coconspirator and lover. In order to obtain poison to dispense with Harufuji's now-pregnant wife, however, Ogin tells the clan doctor that the child was his (as it well could have been). Once she has the poison, she uses some of it on the doctor and watches in exultant fascination as he writhes in agony, bleeding from every orifice.

Ogin's unscrupulous maid, Umeno, hacks down one young girl who is planning to expose the plot, then threatens the girl's father until he agrees to poison Harufuji's wife, which he does. Umeno, at the end, is cruelly slashed by her lover Ionosuke, who is actually Ogin's lover. Ionosuke does this at the command of Harufuji, who has gone berserk with blood-lust at the sight of Ionosuke's killing of two righteous samurai spies who have been trying to convince Harufuji to mend his tyrannical ways—and execute the evil Ogin—before he forces his subjects to rebel. When Jinpu shouts that he has overheard Ionosuke and Ogin exulting at the elimination of Umeno (whom Ionosuke had pretended to love in order to deceive Jinpu), Ionosuke kills him, too, then kills Harufuji, who has just learned of the plot, following which Ionosuke and Ogin stab each other. (Don't try to keep this sorted out; the point is that Tanizaki has fashioned a typically labyrinthine Kabuki plot.)

The whole is written with such extreme bravura that a realistic presentation would probably verge on the comical. At one point in the action, Ogin sashays on stage with an exaggerated confidence in her sexual allure that could only be played by a Kabuki female impersonator—or by the late Mae West (the only female female impersonator, as she has been called).[11] The element that Tanizaki magnified most audaciously, however, was the blood. He filled his stage directions with so many gouts, geysers, and pools of shining gore that it is difficult to imagine how any stage production could handle them all. The effect on a reader's stomach can be distinctly unsettling. The censors seem to have shared this reaction, as a result of which the March 1916 issue of *Chūō Kōron* was banned.

Tanizaki published a revised version of the piece four years later. "Actually, the stage directions were the best part of this play," he wrote. "They depicted a fantasy of blood, but they have been all but eliminated since the ban of *Chūō Kōron*. The present revision is as flat as stale beer." [12]

In fact, little besides the detailed descriptions of torture and the mutilation of corpses was eliminated. The dialogue was practically untouched. Information on the various illicit liaisons, and revelations concerning the true identity of the "seed" borne by Ogin survived intact. Aside from the gore and such erotic gestures as a woman's resting a hand on a man's knee, the one interesting cut involved feudal values that the Meiji state was hoping to keep alive. When the two spies are remonstrating with Harufuji in the hopes of preserving his domain, they are described in the original script as "absurdly staunch in their loyalty," but in the later version the "absurdly" is gone. [13]

Certainly the intent of the play is clear even in the revised version, but Tanizaki was understandably frustrated as a writer that the immediate sense of horror and disgust which he hoped to convey to readers who might not see a stage production were largely diluted. Tanizaki wanted his readers to feel in their own flesh the ridiculous ease with which a living human being could be reduced to a heap of garbage. He wanted them to recognize the cruel instincts lying just beneath the surface of their own psyches which could be responsible for such destruction if released. For a writer like Tanizaki who believed in the truth of the senses, it was not enough to have the maid say "What fragile creatures humans are." [14] He wanted his audience to sense for themselves the fine line dividing civilization from barbarism.

Having had its March issue banned, *Chūō Kōron* featured a symposium on censorship in the May 1916 issue. Tanizaki contributed a rather feeble little piece calling for consultation about questionable manuscripts so that publishers could have the advantage of prior censorship enjoyed by theatrical producers. He also expressed his discomfort at being the author of the one piece in a magazine responsible for the suppression of all the others. [15]

Four months later, "My Late Friend" and "A Handsome Man" were banned and "Sorrow of the Heretic" was shelved. Finally, in 1921 Tanizaki wrote a story called "The Censor" ("Ken'etsukan"), based ostensibly on the prohibition of *The Age to Learn of Love* eight years earlier, but probably a distillation of his thoughts and feelings on censorship to date. Perhaps he did not wish to endanger other people's writings by printing the story in a magazine, taking instead the unusual step of publishing it for the first time in an anthology of his own recent works. Presented in the form of a dialogue between the censor, T, and the playwright, K, it contains some forceful criticism.

T and K have a long, often-heated discussion that touches upon a wide range of issues centering on two basic principles: (1) that censors have no business posing as literary critics; and (2) that, given the unavoidability of censorship, a writer like Tanizaki may reluctantly compromise on literary effect but he cannot compromise on the central meaning of his art.

The first principle is reminiscent of a famous—but ultimately dangerous—censorship case decided in the United States in 1933: Judge John M. Woolsey's enlightened decision to allow the importation of *Ulysses*. Since the text of the decision has been circulated as a preface to the novel, the judge has been widely admired for his literary perspicacity. But this has only served to obscure the point that not even literarily sophisticated judges should be telling people what books they are allowed to read, for "if we put criticism in their hands, or in the hands of a jury, we are risking unjust results." [16]

Tanizaki's censor, T, is a university graduate who claims to be a regular reader of K's and one of the "intelligent few" (he uses the English) with a profound understanding of art. He is worried, however, that most of the members of even the relatively elite audience who will see K's play *First Love* (*Hatsukoi*) will misunderstand the *artistic* intent of the after-bath scene in which the heroine is pinched by her lover through her single, thin under-kimono: instead of the proper aesthetic response, their base emotions will be aroused.

"Let me ask you something," says K. "You keep talking about other people's base emotions, but what about your own? Could it be that you assume everyone else is going to feel them because that's what *you* feel when you read my script?"

"Ha ha ha, now you're getting rough. I may not look the part, but I pride myself on having *some* appreciation for art. No, of course I do not feel anything of the sort. . . ."

"But this scene is *meant* to depict the strong passions of a man and a woman, and as such it is *supposed* to arouse base emotions even in those who understand art. If a person didn't feel them, it wouldn't be because he didn't appreciate art but because he wasn't human. Either that, or because the writer's technique was wanting."

Step by step, and always with the upper hand (the form is inherently biased, of course), K forces T to discard his literary pretensions and speak strictly as a policeman. "Perhaps there is no artistic objection to the arousing of base emotions, but as a public official I cannot simply let it go."

"Fine. So you want two layers covering the underclothes and no pinching, right?"

"Right."

K is willing to soften the impact of particular scenes in this way, but T soon makes it clear that he wants more than that. Killing a twelve-year-old boy is too cruel, he says, and he suggests kidnapping instead. K tries to explain that the boy *has* to be killed: it is the crux of the play. Besides, aren't there many cruel murders in the traditional theater? Yes, T admits, but there the requirements of Encouraging Virtue and Chastising Vice are met. K declares that no one, not even the censor himself, falls for that nonsense anymore. T halfway agrees but notes that a kidnapping would at least leave open the possibility that the boy later escaped and obtained justice; this would not obscure the boy's "first love" for the maid, which is the point, after all?

K explains at great length that that is *not* the point of the play: he wants to portray an all-consuming, transcendent love that suggests to the audience a spiritual world divorced from the flesh. If the censor cannot see how much more valuable that would be to an audience than childish moralisms, then he should stop trying to bargain the play away bit by bit like some street vendor and just ban the thing. K says he can stand the financial blow but not the loss of his artistic integrity.

Having given up any hope of approval for his play, K goes on to challenge T to live up to his own integrity, not as an official but as an individual human being. Instead of inflicting harm on society and impeding progress by trying to enforce outmoded moralistic rules that neither he nor anyone else believes in, salving his conscience all the while by claiming to be merely doing his duty, T should work to change the rules. But T insists that he is powerless to do so: he is under the thumb of the Chief of Police, the Home Minister, the Prime Minister, and "certain areas above even the Prime Minister." The best he can do is bend the rules slightly now and then. For writers, his advice is to go on writing what they believe in and not object to government policy. "And *you* will not object, I am sure," counters K, "if from now on we treat you as a despicable bootlicker. . . . If you are powerless to change the rules, you should resign."

Long after K has left his office, the censor sits with arms folded, sighing, deep in thought.[17]

Tanizaki had a good deal of trouble getting his work on the stage for a year or so after this. Both *The Eternal Idol* (*Eien no gūzō*, published March 1922) and *Because I Love Her* (*Ai sureba koso*, published December 1921 and January 1922) were refused production licenses, and *Okuni and Gohei* (*Okuni to Gohei*, published June 1922) could be staged only with extensive cuts. Tanizaki went public with these again in the form of interviews for drama magazines. The one concerning *The Eternal Idol* sounded almost like a replay of the story "The Censor," concluding that what the police were doing was not only bad for art but was an unhealthy way to run a country.[18] In another interview, he called for a complete change of air in the Police Department in order to rid the censors of their weird preconceptions. "I know it is a difficult order. Only broad-based public opinion is going to change things."[19]

Tanizaki continued vigorously writing for the stage, however, and most of his plays were produced. Although his reputation as a dramatist never quite matched his fame as a novelist, he was a major contributor to the Taishō flowering of the modern Japanese theater.[20] The Shōwa period, which began in December 1926, meant for Tanizaki extended excursions into the Japanese past, both through his original fiction and his modern translation of the classic *Tale of Genji*. In this work he would encounter obstacles set up for him by new, and more menacing, censors: the military.

15

The Shōwa Publishing Boom and the Literary Chat Society

After the naturalist scandals of 1908, writers' carryings-on (if not their writings) became newsworthy items. It was not until the exponential growth of the Shōwa period publishing industry, however, that successful writers became the wealthy public figures we know them as today. Here we shall examine the Shōwa publishing boom as an element of the mass diffusion of modern culture, and see how official (and semiofficial) attempts to restrain that growth led to another clash with writers.

The upsurge in periodical publications started with the expansion and modernization of newspapers following World War I, with prewar circulations of 400,000–500,000 shooting up to well over 1,000,000 in the 1920s. The mass-audience publisher Kōdansha instituted a number of entertainment magazines, creating a "magazine empire." One of their most successful publications was *King* (*Kingu*), which began appearing in January 1925 and saw its circulation leap from 740,000 for the inaugural issue to a high of 1,400,000 in 1928. *King* soon had many competitors, and some writers of "pure literature" such as Kikuchi Kan and Kume Masao turned to writing for this mass audience, beginning a new wave of popular fiction, detective stories, samurai adventure novels, and so forth.[1]

The publishing boom was given its biggest thrust by the Kaizōsha Publishing Company in November 1926, the month before the Taishō emperor's death. In a huge gamble intended to rescue the company from its "post-earthquake depression," Kaizōsha announced the publication of a sixty-three volume series entitled *Collected Works of Modern Japanese Literature* (*Gendai Nihon bungaku zenshū*), a chronologically arranged compendium of important works from Meiji and Taishō. Available only to series subscribers, a new volume would appear each month at the set price of one yen. The price quickly gave rise to the term *enbon* (one-yen books), which referred to this and similar sets that appeared when other publishers witnessed Kaizōsha's great success.

What made the *enbon* so attractive was their combination of low price and replete contents. Printed in triple columns in small type, they squeezed four books into the space of one and cost only half the price of a typical volume. There was also the well-timed emotional appeal: the earthquake of 1923 had given many the sense that a new epoch had begun, and the set was sold as a summation of Japan's accomplishments in modern literature. Both this and the bargain were hard to resist, and before long Kaizōsha had 230,000 subscribers, a figure that later rose to an estimated half million.[2] Long used to living in near poverty, Masamune Hakuchō took his Kaizōsha royalties and his wife on a yearlong world tour, and there were complaints from some publishers that the sudden wealth was making the established writers lazy.[3] Even this unexpected success was surpassed by Shinchōsha's *Collected Works of World Literature* (*Sekai bungaku zenshū*), which was announced in January 1927 and had 580,000 subscribers within three months—convincing evidence of an interest in foreign literature perhaps even more widespread than in the domestic product.

In any event, the "*enbon* wars" were launched, with over two hundred different series being produced in the next six years. After having remained fairly constant since late Meiji, the number of nonperiodical publications submitted to the Police Bureau underwent a 267 percent increase between 1924 and 1934. The number of periodicals registered with the bureau rose by 173 percent in the same period, showing in all a 560 percent increase over late Meiji. And this boom was happening during the worst years of the Depression.[4]

Although minuscule by comparison to the mass-market figures, a notable growth in leftist publications comprised a substantial element of the publishing boom. The proletarian journals *Senki* and *Bungei Sensen* had a combined circulation of close to 50,000 in 1929–1930.[5] Among several "dangerous" *enbon* series that appeared in the early 1930s were those such as *The Collected Works of Marx and Engels* (*Marukusu Engerusu zenshū*).[6] Nor was leftist fiction restricted to the leftist magazines. When he returned from his world tour in November 1929, Masamune Hakuchō was dismayed to find that all the editors who used to badger him for stories were going now to the proletarian stars Kobayashi Takiji and Tokunaga Sunao.[7] One historian of the proletarian movement has calculated that in the general magazines *Kaizō* and *Chūō Kōron*, proletarian works accounted for 29 percent of the fiction in 1929–1930 (through March), 44 percent in 1930–1931.[8]

Thus, both for its scale and contents, the publishing boom came as a shock to the censors. On June 28, 1927, the Home Ministry decided that, owing to the unprecedented overload, the Police Bureau's Censorship Division would be ending the consultation system immediately. The staff simply no longer had the time to meet with individual editors as they had done to advise on the publishability of manuscripts.[9]

Two weeks later, on July 12, a group calling itself the Censorship System Reform League (Ken'etsu Seido Kaisei Kisei Dōmei), apparently spearheaded by left-wing dramatists but claiming broad support among middle-class artists, filmmakers, theater people, publishers, and writers, met in Tokyo's Tsukiji Little Theater (the headquarters for leftist theater in Japan) to formulate a policy, deciding upon the "mass struggle" approach. After some fruitless conversations with the chief of the Police Bureau and several meetings held over the next few months, during which time the suppression of leftist art became increasingly violent, the league designated the week of January 18–24, 1928, Anti-Censorship Week, printed a pamphlet demanding reform (not abolition) of the system, and managed to gain at least some attention from the press.[10] Almost nothing is known about the league, however, for it seems not to have survived past the Tanaka cabinet's notorious roundup of leftists on March 15, 1928.[11] It certainly had no successors, and its only known impact was to have induced the Home Minister to begin suppressing criticism of the censorship system for the first time.[12] Some of the demands spelled out in its pamphlet are of interest, however, because they illustrate the trend brewing in the government toward suppression of modern culture in mass media.

Much of the pamphlet was devoted merely to reprinting the censorship laws to inform a broader segment of the public as to the specifics of the system. The league's demands included revision of the laws, reinstatement of the consultation system, institution of a route of appeal, establishment of nationally uniform standards of script censorship, establishment of prior censorship of film scenarios when requested by the studio, the return of certain confiscated items, financial restitution by the government in such patently unfair instances as opening-night prohibitions of plays, and the restriction of suppression only to situations actually covered by law. There *were* no laws concerning art exhibits, the pamphlet noted, and yet the police managed to have works (e.g., Rodin's "The Kiss") withdrawn all the time. A 1925 Home Ministry Ordinance not only required producers to submit films for censorship but actually charged them a "censorship fee." The fee could be waived, but this was done in practice only for films approved by the Ministry of Education or military propaganda films.[13]

Japan was experiencing its own version of the Roaring Twenties, and the censors did not like it. The mood of urban Japan in the late 1920s and early 1930s was characterized by the slogans *"ero-guro-nansensu"* (eroticism, grotesquerie, and nonsense) and "the three S's—sports, screen, and sex." Radio broadcasts began in 1925, and soon there were hit songs and soap operas, and the nation was divided into rival camps of fans listening to the baseball games of Waseda and Keiō Universities. Automobiles known as *entaku* (one-yen taxis: Fords and Chevrolets assembled in Japan and charging minimum one-yen fares) emerged with the *enbon* as symbols of the mass infiltration of modern culture. Talking pictures appeared in 1929. That year the "Casino Follies" review opened in Tokyo's Asakusa entertainment district, much of its eventual popularity owing to a novel serialized in the *Asahi* by the young "neoperceptionist" writer Kawabata Yasunari. Various parts of Tokyo saw the opening of dance halls such as the "Florida," where short-haired, short-skirted *moga* (modern girls) danced the night away with their long-haired *mobo* (modern boys), all of whom seemed to be wearing bell-bottomed trousers. Neon signs brightened the streets, and foreign temptresses like Clara Bow, Gloria Swanson, Marlene Dietrich, and Greta Garbo were appearing in the movie theaters. One of the strangest crazes to affect all parts of society—not only *mobo* and *moga* but students, children, office workers, and even the elderly—was the popularity of the yo-yo—"an undeniable manifestation of *fin-de-siècle*-type nihilism," concludes one modern historian.[14]

None of this was pleasing to the men who hoped to recapture Japan's uncorrupted native spirit, and when hostilities commenced with the Manchurian Incident of 1931, the national emergency rationale was invoked with increasing frequency to purge the unhealthy tendencies. Now the Peace Preservation Law was used not only against illegal political groups but cultural organizations such as leftist writers' societies that were suddenly perceived as Communist fronts. The arrest of writers such as Nakano Shigeharu and Kurahara Korehito in March 1932 marked the beginning of a Home Ministry campaign to suppress the Proletarian Cultural Federation (KOPF), four hundred of whose members were arrested or detained over the next six months, sometimes with considerable violence.[15] The Thought Police organization was upgraded to a department that year and greatly enlarged (from 70 in 1928 to 380 in 1932 in Tokyo alone).[16] In February 1933, some of their number arrested and beat to death the proletarian writer Kobayashi Takiji.[17]

Just as socialism and individualism had been the twin obsessions of the Katsura regime, communism and "modernism" (later, "libertarianism") were what the police and educational officials sought to expunge after the Manchurian Incident. Like Confucian reformers brooding over the colorful lifestyle of the Edo townsmen, they took aim at the long hair and the dance halls.[18] In 1934 the Minister of Education wanted elementary school teachers to discourage the use of the foreign words "mama" and "papa" among their pupils.[19] The Publication Law was revised in 1934 to control the production of phonograph records, which immediately led to the large-scale banning of popular records.* And the movies came under increasing pressure.

In 1934, Prime Minister Saitō Makoto appointed the Chief of the Police

---

* At first this included popular music and humor; six months before Pearl Harbor, "unwhole-

Bureau, Matsumoto Gaku, to investigate the film policies of other countries and to draft legislation to bring the movie industry under centralized government control. Matsumoto chose Fascist Italy for his model, and his draft led to the creation in March 1934 of the Committee on Film Control (Eiga Tōsei Iinkai), which was placed under the jurisdiction of the Home Minister, who was always its chairman. The committee's policy was to move away from crude suppression of movies as an evil influence to which children should not be exposed, and instead to encourage the production of wholesome, uplifting films that could exploit the medium's potential for indoctrination.[20]

This Matsumoto Gaku seems to have been a man with a mission. Not only was he involved in the control of films but the control of education and religion as well. He published his own books calling for a return to the union of administration and ceremony characteristic of ancient imperial rule, and his brand of "Japanism" included a theory that the study of foreign languages was to be discouraged.[21] Even after he had left the Police Bureau (becoming a member of the House of Peers) upon the fall of the Saitō cabinet in July 1934, he displayed an astonishing ability to maintain cultural organizations and publishing enterprises designed to promote awareness of and appreciation for the unique Japanese spirit. He had some eighteen different groups organized under his umbrella association, the Nippon Cultural Federation (Nippon Bunka Renmei), which he created to counter the Proletarian Cultural Federation. Ironically (considering his view of foreign language study), one such organization, the International Cultural Federation, published an English language quarterly called *Cultural Nippon* and sponsored groups such as the Asian Students Association (for Asians studying in Japan) and the Foreign Women's Flower Arrangement Society. Matsumoto went so far as to publish a pamphlet in English proposing the formation of a Cultural League of Nations aimed at "the eventual realization of world familyism as bequeathed by the First Tenno [Emperor] Jimmu, in accordance with the Divine Universal Way that remains, we believe, infallible for all ages and true in all places."*

One of Matsumoto's organizations, founded amid the post-Manchurian Incident thrust toward increasing cultural control, was the legitimate heir to Komatsubara Eitarō's Committee on Literature. Called the Literary Chat Society (Bungei Konwakai) when it was finally organized, it grew out of circum-

---

some jazz" was banned, and during the war the only works of Western music that could be played in public were those by German and Italian composers. OPC, pp. 81–82.

*Matsumoto Gaku, "The Cultural League of Nations / Proposition," *Nippon Bunka Renmei* (June 1936): 4. Matsumoto goes on to explain that Japan had participated in the League of Nations and the Naval Disarmament Conference in hopes of creating "a happy world family, which is the lofty national ideal of Japan," as set forth 2596 years before by Jimmu upon his founding of the Empire, but "had to withdraw" from these organizations in order to "uphold our national ideal." (ibid., pp. 7, 8)

stances almost identical to those surrounding the Committee on Literature, when the government was moving in several directions to suppress what it perceived as growing social decadence. As before, there was a period of debate for and against the founding of a rumored academy, with much speculation as to the government's true motives—whether "control" or "encouragement" was the final purpose. Both the literary scene and Japanese society were vastly more complex than they had been at the time of the Katsura government, however. Mainstream serious writers now had a fully developed proletarian literary movement and a popular mass literary establishment to take into account, which makes their influence on the formation and operation of the Literary Chat Society all the more noteworthy.

From its inception, the society was the joint product of Matsumoto Gaku and "fascist" writers of popular literature—men like Naoki Sanjūgo (for whom the present-day Naoki Prize in popular literature is named), Kume Masao, Mikami Otokichi, Yoshikawa Eiji, Shirai Kyōji, and Satō Hachirō.[22] Some of these writers had not only proclaimed themselves fascists but in February 1932, just six months after the Manchurian Incident had begun filling the newspapers with reports of rising fascism, they organized a society composed of popular writers and some dynamic young officers of the Army General Staff, several of whom were also members of the ultra-rightist Cherry Blossom Society (Sakura Kai). This precursor to the Literary Chat Society was called the Society of the Fifth (Itsuka Kai), since it regularly met on the fifth of each month.

The first meeting of the Society of the Fifth was apparently spent viewing 16-mm films that one of the officers had shot in Manchuria and listening to detailed commentary on these scenes, on various military operations and modern weaponry, on Chinese life, and on diplomatic struggles on the Chinese mainland. In November 1932, several of the literary members were invited by one of the officers to observe military exercises. And while there was little agreement among the members as to the precise meaning of "fascism," they seem to have been charmed by this kind of attention from the military and to have shared with their hosts—and each other—a typically mystical view of the unique Japanese spirit and the great anti-individualistic racial heritage of the Japanese people which was thought to shine forth with special brilliance in times of international crisis.[23]

Liberal intellectuals were by no means indifferent to the rise of fascism. When the Nazis committed their notorious book burning on May 10, 1933, seventeen prominent Japanese liberals, including the philosopher Miki Kiyoshi and the head of *Chūō Kōron*, Shimanaka Yūsaku, met to frame a note of protest to Hitler. Later that month, the Takigawa Incident erupted, marking a new wave of suppression of old liberal thought (see above, p. 232). To counter this, Miki and the others invited a broadly representative group of intellectuals, including several writers, to join them in an association they called the League for Academic and Artistic Freedom (Gakugei Jiyū Dōmei). At the July 10, 1933, inaugural meeting, Tokuda Shūsei was elected president. Unfortunately, this group seems to have been no more effective at stemming the tide than were the universities at challenging the ouster of Professor Takigawa. (Miki himself would die in prison as a thought criminal in 1945.)[24]

By New Year's 1934, the Society of the Fifth had all but ceased to function owing to the military members' inability to participate on a regular basis. Witnessing the demise of his pet project, Naoki Sanjūgo sought to establish ties instead with the bureaucracy. He met privately with Matsumoto Gaku, who at that time was still head of the Police Bureau, and together they announced a gathering to be held on January 29 for popular writers and government representatives. The topic for discussion would be "raising the Japanese spirit," an area badly neglected in literature, according to Matsumoto. Naoki agreed that the question of spirit was crucial, but he felt that it would have to be preceded by an improvement in the social status of writers, which could best be accomplished by the establishment of a literary academy.[25]

Even before this first meeting could take place, antiacademy criticism began to pour forth much as it had in 1911. Miki Kiyoshi pointed out the anomaly of having the Police Bureau, which was the headquarters for censorship and the Thought Police, as the sponsor of a literary academy: surely, the bureau would try to use the academy for the "improvement" or "guidance" of thought.[26]

The meeting itself included some discussion of censorship problems but focused on the creation of an academy and the establishment of official prizes to encourage the production of literature that would benefit the state. A decision was reached to establish a semiofficial literary club as a first step toward creating an academy. Naoki was given the task of inviting some thirty likely members in Matsumoto's name, Matsumoto himself stipulating only that "antistate" (i.e., leftist) writers be excluded. The press described the meeting as most cordial and both sides as "extraordinarily eager" to get the club started. Things were not to go so smoothly, however, when the serious writers on Naoki's list became involved. For while "fascist" authors may have enjoyed being stroked by the military and hobnobbing with the police, writers of "pure" literature would insist that they had a tradition of independence to uphold that had been established in the Meiji era. Prominent among such spokesmen were the Meiji naturalists Masamune Hakuchō and Tokuda Shūsei.

A few days after the above exploratory meeting between popular writers and bureaucrats, Hakuchō contributed a two-part article to the *Asahi* (February 2–3, 1934) tracing earlier government efforts to control literature and voicing his anxiety over this new move. "If today's authors are going to satisfy themselves with the kind of writings that can be used for the 'guidance of thought,' then everything their predecessors struggled through poverty to build up since the Meiji period will have gone for nothing." He could not conceive of any benefit that such an academy could bestow upon literature, Hakuchō concluded, but he was willing to give the participants the benefit of the doubt: perhaps they would think of something.[27]

A similar wait-and-see attitude was adopted by Tokuda Shūsei in a lengthy article he contributed to the following month's *Kaizō* (March 1934). Like Hakuchō, Shūsei said he would be receptive to a genuinely independent academy that could improve the lot of writers, but he could not believe there were officials who understood the aims of art well enough to make this a reality. He was particularly suspicious of the ties between popular writers and the military, and in any event he saw no need to promote the interests of popular literature, "which has a tendency to fall in with the cheapest grade of journalism in pandering to the tastes of the masses."[28]

Behind Shūsei's warning lay a fear of crass commercialization in the publishing world, which he perceived as fostering popular literature to the disadvantage—including the very real financial disadvantage—of serious writers. Both he and Hakuchō recognized the need for serious writers to influence the new academy, if only out of sheer self-interest, and they were among the twenty who accepted Matsumoto Gaku's invitation to an organizational meeting on March 29.*

Speaking at this meeting, Matsumoto said that he, as an individual, wanted to establish what he called a "private academy of literature" to lay the groundwork for a government-sponsored one, because he felt the government had been "cold" to literature in the past. Sitting directly opposite Matsumoto, Shūsei is reported to have said in his characteristic dry tone, "Japanese literature was born among the common people and has grown up without the least 'protection' from the government. Now you tell us that you want to protect us. I find that hard to believe. . . . What we would really like is for you to leave us alone."[29]

But Matsumoto proceeded with the meeting, and Shūsei stayed to see to the interests of the serious writers. He was opposed, he said, to glorifying the group as an "academy," and after some discussion, they settled on the name Literary Chat Society. The serious writers backed Shūsei completely.[30]

From the society's inauspicious beginning until its dissolution in July 1937, Matsumoto almost seems to have been searching for a graceful oppor-

---

*Enomoto [3], p. 629. Those who refused included Ihara Seiseien and Kōda Rohan, who had been on the Committee on Literature in 1911–1913, Tsubouchi Shōyō, Tanizaki Jun'ichirō, Shiga Naoya, Kobayashi Hideo, Izumi Kyōka, Osaragi Jirō, Kikuchi Yūhō, Kume Masao, and Hirayama Roko. Those who accepted were Kawabata Yasunari, Yokomitsu Riichi, Shimazaki Tōson, Satō Haruo, Satomi Ton, Kishida Kunio, Kikuchi Kan, Yoshikawa Eiji, Yamamoto Yūzō, Uno Kōji, Katō Takeo, Kamitsukasa Shōken, Shirai Kyōji, Chikamatsu Shūkō, Nakamura Murao, Hirotsu Kazuo, and Mikami Otokichi.

tunity to rid himself of the monster he had created. The sudden death of Naoki Sanjūgo on February 24, 1934, a month *before* the organizational meeting, considerably diluted the popular "fascist" element in the society that Matsumoto had initially hoped to support. It had been Naoki's plan to have the organization grant two literary prizes each year, one for serious and one for popular literature. As it turned out, however, both prizes were granted to serious writers as long as the society existed.* Beginning in January 1936, the society also published a small journal called *Literary Chat Society*, each issue of which was to be edited by a different member, but only six of the eighteen issues published were edited by popular writers.†

Matsumoto had insisted from the beginning that his own personal interest in literature had prompted him to organize and maintain the society, which would have made it awkward for him to disband the group when he lost his post at the Police Bureau in July 1934 with the fall of the Saitō government. And in fact, the money for the prizes and the society's monthly banquets seems to have come not from the Home Ministry but from donations privately solicited by Matsumoto from the Mitsui and Mitsubishi *zaibatsu* conglomerates. Matsumoto did confess to the writer Hirotsu Kazuo, however, that he had discussed establishing the society with Prime Minister Saitō as a method of controlling literature, just as he had worked on the control of education and religion in the past. He also admitted to Hirotsu after three or four meetings that he was finding the control of literature an impossibility.[31]

There was constant tension between Matsumoto and the serious writers, whose wariness set the tone of the society. When Matsumoto guaranteed them "absolute literary freedom except for anti-state things," someone offered to put his words into writing in order that he not forget them.[32]

Of course, the writers themselves came in for a good deal of outside criticism for their willingness to compromise on Matsumoto's exclusion of leftists. When the society held services for the souls of dead writers in September 1934, it was noted with some bitterness that the name of the murdered Kobayashi Takiji was conspicuously absent.[33] One of the two awards made by the society in 1935 should have gone to the leftist writer Shimaki Kensaku for his collection *Prison* (*Goku*) had the results of the balloting been followed, but Matsumoto refused to allow this. As a result, Murō Saisei received the award

---

*The prizewinning authors and their works were as follows: (1935) Yokomitsu Riichi, *Monshō*; Murō Saisei, *Ani-imōto* [translated in Morris, *Modern Japanese Stories*]; (1936) Tokuda Shūsei, *Kunshō* [translated in Morris, *Modern Japanese Stories*]; Sekine Hideo, Montaigne translations; (1937) Kawabata Yasunari, *Yukiguni* [the renowned *Snow Country*, translated by Edward Seidensticker in 1956]; Ozaki Shirō, *Jinsei gekijō*. NKBD 4:470.

†Enomoto [3], p. 633. The journal varied from sixty-four to ninety-eight pages in length. Enomoto [1], pp. 16–17.

for another collection, *Brother and Sister* (*Ani-imōto*).* Angry denunciations were written both by outside critics and by members, at least one of whom, Satō Haruo, resigned (although he was later persuaded to rejoin). Much of the criticism was published anonymously, a not entirely unwarranted precaution in view of the detailed records the Police Bureau was keeping of the situation.[34] A new leftist magazine, *Jinmin Bunko* (The People's Library) was actually founded by Takeda Rintarō in part to counter the journal of the Literary Chat Society.[35]

One member who responded to charges that the society was a mechanism for controlling literature was Kawabata Yasunari. "It is not Matsumoto who is controlling the writers, but the writers who are controlling Matsumoto," he insisted.[36] And the liberal editorial policy of the society's journal would seem to bear him out. Not only were the magazine's contents too varied to represent any single school of thought, its pages were opened to some of the society's fiercest leftist critics, Aono Suekichi and Takeda Rintarō. While it is true that prizes never went to leftists, their opinions were represented in the magazine.

Thus, it was probably with considerable relief that Matsumoto greeted the establishment of the Imperial Arts Academy (Teikoku Geijutsu In) in June 1937 as the signal to disband the Literary Chat Society. The society had fulfilled its stated function by somehow "laying the groundwork" for an official institution, and now Japan had a comprehensive academy for all the arts, including literature. Once again, the writers had managed to stave off a bid for the control of literature, but this new academy was established less than three weeks before the China Incident exploded on July 7, 1937, and it was only one of innumerable new organizations and policies designed to unify the populace in what was now a full-scale war effort that would continue through August 15, 1945.[37]

---

*The title work of this collection has been translated by Edward Seidensticker in Ivan Morris, ed., *Modern Japanese Stories* (Rutland and Tokyo: C. E. Tuttle, 1962), pp. 144–61. On Shimaki and *Prison*, see Donald Keene, "Japanese Literature and Politics in the 1930s," p. 231.

16

The Military and the
Thought Police Take Over

COMMITTEES, BUREAUS, AND SOCIETIES

The establishment of the Cabinet Information Committee (Naikaku Jōhō Iinkai) in July 1936 as an agency devoted to "positive" propaganda marked the beginning of the truly fanatical suppression of any but the most worshipful references to the imperial house. Now a magazine was likely to be suppressed for "desecration of the dignity of the Imperial House" if the typesetter inadvertently set up "His Majesty the Emperor" as *Tennō kaika* instead of *Tennō heika*, confusing two nearly identical characters.[1]

The committee was upgraded to a division (*bu*) the following year when the China Incident, which included the Rape of Nanking, reopened the hostilities that would lead directly into the Pacific War. The division issued a series of fundamental guidelines for newspaper editors that were remarkable as an attempt to instill precisely that attitude in the populace which had been so indispensable to the decade of devotion between the Sino- and Russo-Japanese Wars (1895–1905): "Take care not to give readers too optimistic an impression about the current Incident or the current world situation," editors were advised. "Inspire an enduring, untiring spirit in the mind of the people."[2]

The guiding force of the Cabinet Information Division came from participating officers of the Army and Navy Information Divisions, under whom negative "control" (*torishimari*, i.e., censorship) gave way to positive "guidance" (*shidō*, i.e., conversion to propaganda functions) of the publishing industry. It was also in imitation of military practice that the division ordered executives and editorial representatives from the newspapers and magazines to attend once- or twice-monthly "friendly get-togethers" (*kondankai*) for the purpose of receiving news embargoes, requests for specific editorial content, and general guidance with regard to desirable editorial policy. The services also continued their monthly get-togethers independently, which meant that for a time editors found themselves required to attend not only meetings held by the cabinet, the army, and the navy, but also by the information bureau of the Foreign Ministry, the Police Bureau, and even some semiofficial right-wing organizations such as the Imperial Rule Assistance Association and the Headquarters for National Spiritual Mobilization.[3] Editors were also frequently ordered to appear in any of these offices for individual consultation—which usually meant criticism for having carried specific articles. This was an especially vexing situation when a story or essay that had been passed by the Police Bureau censors impressed the service officers as being "antimilitary" or otherwise ill-suited to the war effort.[4]

The exhausting arrangements described here were eased somewhat on December 5, 1940, when the Konoe cabinet, employing an imperial ordinance, upgraded the division to a bureau (*kyoku*). The Cabinet Information Bureau had over six hundred employees representing the various information bureaus mentioned above, with army and navy officials holding the key posts. There ensued a power struggle between the military men and the Home Ministry bureaucrats, in the course of which the censorship authority moved from the Home Ministry to the new bureau, making it the ultimate authority for both censorship and propaganda during the war.[5]

Hatanaka Shigeo, editor-in-chief of *Chūō Kōron* from 1941 to 1947 (except for a period when he was forced by the army to resign), has described some of his experiences in dealing with the Army Information Division, which continued to be the agency in charge of magazines even after it was incorporated into the Cabinet Information Bureau.

As early as 1937, the military perceived the great potential of the four liberal "general magazines," *Chūō Kōron*, *Kaizō*, *Nihon Hyōron*, and *Bungei Shunjū*, for influencing the intelligentsia. The military organized these magazines into the so-called Four Company Society (Yonsha Kai), which was required to meet with the Army and Navy Information Divisions—separately—each month.[6] In addition to these meetings, just after Pearl Harbor the army organized meetings for *all* magazines to be held on the sixth of each month, calling this the Society of the Sixth (Muika Kai). Through these organizations, the military sought to overcome the general magazines' galling tendency toward "detached observation" of the war (*senso bōkan*).

Chūō Kōron had an especially bad reputation with the military, having served as the sounding board for, among others, the great Taishō democratic theoretician Yoshino Sakuzō, who contributed at least thirty-five pieces to *Chūō Kōron* between 1916 and 1930 warning against imperialism and the growing intrusion of military power into the political sphere. Time and again at friendly get-togethers, *Chūō Kōron* was criticized for clinging to its "foreign" tradition of "libertarianism" (*jiyūshugi*) despite the wartime need for total national unity.*

Shimanaka Yūsaku, the head of *Chūō Kōron* and a firm believer in the company's liberal tradition (but a man whom the police saw in 1930 as responsible for a leftward swing by the magazine),† had a set reply to this objection. "You military men think that all you have to do is give orders and the nation will follow, but 'journalistic guidance' is not such a simpleminded matter. When it comes to national policy, our goals are exactly the same as yours. But don't forget that we are professionals in the 'journalistic guidance' of the intelligentsia. I wish you would just leave it to us. These things take time." He would also point out that "complex intellectuals" could only be induced into genuine cooperation with the war effort by means of rational argument, and it was this that was so time consuming.[7]

Not even military bureaucrats were taken in by this, however, and the usual response was threats and shouting, followed by further erosions of editorial autonomy. (An especially egregious invasion of the "noncooperative" companies' autonomy in another area came in February 1941 when the Cabinet Information Bureau demanded that the magazines surrender their subscription lists, as a result of which local police in certain areas actually did investigate the activities of some readers; soldiers on active duty discovered to be among the subscribers were punished.)[8]

Much of the censorship that took place during the war years, then, moved out of the area of bureaucratic application of law by the Home Ministry into the less clearly defined region of pressure exerted by the military through personal contacts of various kinds, some formalized (if not always official), others highly informal. One particularly amorphous example can be seen in the publication by the *Chūō Kōron* company of Tanizaki Jun'ichirō's translation into modern Japanese of the eleventh-century classic, *The Tale of Genji*.

Tanizaki began working on his first translation of *Genji* (there were three all together) in 1935 at the "enthusiastic urging" of Shimanaka Yūsaku. It appeared in twenty-six volumes between January 1939 and July 1941. Upon commencing publication, Tanizaki wrote that he was not entirely satisfied

---

*Jiyūshugi is the standard term for "liberalism" but in these contexts it is used primarily as a term of opprobrium. SSDS pp. 25, 26–28, 60, 83–85, 114.

†See above, p. 251, for Shimanaka's anti-fascist stance, and see chap. 12, footnote p. 218, for his involvement in the early Taishō women's movement. Hatanaka admired Shimanaka for his steadfast support of the *Chūō Kōron* editorial staff (SSDS, pp. 91–93), and Tanizaki Jun'ichirō was convinced that the psychological strain of resisting the militarists helped send Shimanaka to an early grave. (TJZ 22:370 and TJZ 23:235) For the censors' remarks on Shimanaka, see Naimushō Keihokyoku Toshoka, ed., *Shimbun Keisatsu gaikan* (January 1930), p. 240, in Japan Naimushō, Reel No. 1.

with the results and hoped to spend his declining years—if he were fortunate enough to have any—polishing the style. He also noted "quite honestly"—if vaguely—that he had freely cut "one very small part of the plot" which "did not seem suitable for direct transplanting to the present day," but he assured readers that this had "virtually no effect on the development of the story as a whole."[9]

After the war, Tanizaki revealed that his dissatisfactions had not been limited to matters of style, but that he had actually been forced to make distortions in order not to infringe upon the taboos of the "hard-headed militarists." Knowing that Meiji and Taishō had been much freer periods, he had felt certain that such a "dark age" could not last forever and had looked forward to the return of liberty. "Then our country took its reckless plunge into the Greater East Asia War, and as a result of the bitter experience of defeat, the freedom I had hoped for returned to us with unexpected speed, enabling me to fulfill my long-cherished dream of perfecting the translation of *Genji*. Should I now feel joy or sorrow? I cannot say."[10]

Tanizaki wrote this in the preface to his second translation, which appeared between May 1951 and October 1954. But even earlier, in a special issue of *Chūō Kōron* (October 1949), he had taken the opportunity to publish the longest of several passages he had expurgated (without using *fuseji* to indicate this) "lest they arouse the ire of the military."* According to Hatanaka Shigeo, the publication of the translation was "forcibly postponed" for six months while "considerable revising" was done.[11] Neither he nor Tanizaki is clear on the form in which this force was applied, and a later piece by Tanizaki raises questions as to just how directly the military was involved.

Tanizaki's prefaces never fail to mention the debt he owed to Yamada Yoshio (1873–1958), the renowned classical scholar, for his meticulous revision of the manuscripts of the first two *Genji* translations. Indeed, Yamada's name appeared alongside Tanizaki's on the title page. A memorial piece Tanizaki wrote in 1959 goes so far as to say that Yamada's willingness to aid him was the clinching factor in his deciding to undertake the project. He records that he first went to pay his respects to the old professor in the spring of 1935 after having done a few months of preliminary work. The first thing Yamada did was to state, with the utmost gravity and forcefulness, the conditions under which he would agree to assist Tanizaki. There were three incidents in the story, he said, that made *The Tale of Genji* unsuitable for a faithful modern

---

*"Fujitsubo," TJZ 23:241. The suppressed passage corresponds to the passage from page 195 line 29 to 198 line 20 (ending ". . . distasteful.") in volume 1 of the Edward Seidensticker translation (New York: Alfred A. Knopf, 1976). Here are portrayed Fujitsubo's mental and physical anguish arising from her liaison with Genji, who is bustled off into a closetlike room by the ladies-in-waiting.

translation: the love affair between an imperial consort and a commoner (i.e., Genji and his stepmother, Fujitsubo); the enthronement of the offspring of that illicit liaison (i.e., the Emperor Reizei); and the elevation of a commoner to the rank equivalent to a Retired Emperor (i.e., Genji in his last years). According to Yamada, these incidents were *not* essential to the plot, and even if they were totally expunged, this would have little effect on the overall development of the story. He would participate in the project, he said, only if Tanizaki understood that these elements must be eliminated.

Tanizaki remarks that he had already resigned himself to the need for such obfuscation, given the dominance of the military. He does not point out, however, that the first two objectionable incidents, far from being inessential to the plot, are—as any reader of *Genji* will immediately recognize—*the* most decisive elements determining the cyclical structure of the novel and its theme of retribution. Tanizaki goes on to defend Yamada against the many enemies he had made during the war for his radical right-wing stance. He notes that the old scholar graciously consented to edit the unexpurgated postwar version, which indicated that "he understood that the times had changed. He was no pig-headed imitation patriot."[12]

Tanizaki's resentment was reserved for "the military," not the notorious upholder of the "national essence," with whom he seems to have worked quite compatibly. Another well-known classicist, Okazaki Yoshie, who was a Tōhoku University colleague of Yamada's, laid the blame in Tanizaki's lap. In a four-part critique of the translation printed in the *Asahi Shimbun*, May 23–26, 1939, Okazaki wrote of his "inexpressible sorrow" at the extensive surgery which had removed the "spinal cord of the story," the absence of which rendered a modern translation almost pointless. Tanizaki's smoothing over of the cut places without *fuseji*, as though nothing had occurred, was "a great atrocity" that called into question his integrity as an artist. Edo-period critics had been able to cope with the disturbing Fujitsubo story by interpreting, not by cutting; surely a Shōwa-period writer did not have to do such a shabby job. Of course, no reader who did not already know the Fujitsubo story could have guessed what it was from Okazaki, who obscured the issue by saying that the cuts had been done in the interest of making the translation more acceptable to a modern popular audience. As angry as he was, he still knew how far he could go in 1939.*

Let us turn now to more characteristic examples of pressure exerted by the military through the mechanism of the friendly get-together. At the May 16, 1941, meeting of editors held by the Cabinet Information Bureau, all maga-

---

*Okazaki Yoshie, *Genji monogatari no bi* (Hōbunkan, 1960), pp. 465–71. After the war, Okazaki said he had been criticized for lack of sympathy toward Tanizaki, but he insisted that an attitude like Tanizaki's could only encourage censorship.

zines were ordered to submit a complete table of contents by the tenth of each month, indicating titles and authors planned for the upcoming issue. The bureau would freely order the elimination of undesirable material and black-listed authors and would force the magazines to accept manuscripts by "officially approved" authors—a step that had seemed an impossibility to Asada Kōson in 1910 when he sardonically proposed an improved "intellectual coup d'etat" to the Katsura regime (see above, p. 147). Far from resisting all such approved material, however, liberal magazines consciously sought out rabidly nationalistic pieces, calling them "magic manuscripts" (*omajinai genkō*) in the hopes that their presence would cast a protective spell over the more controversial contents.[13]

Another technique for having a table of contents approved was to make it appear more bellicose than necessary. When he received an innocuous essay on the American frontier spirit entitled "Americanism," Hatanaka Shigeo himself changed the title to "Americanism as the Enemy" ("Teki to-shite no Amerikanizumu"), which earned him a sharp rebuke from both the Army Information Division and the Cabinet Information Bureau after the magazine appeared, even though it had been passed by the Police Bureau.*

At a typical meeting of the Society of the Sixth (November 6, 1942), an army major offered his critiques of the magazines' issues of the previous month. He praised Kōdansha's *Gendai* for its criticism of the philosophy of Nishida Kitarō as too individualistic and lacking in military elements.† He was deeply appreciative of another right-wing magazine's special issue, "Revere the Emperor, Expel the Barbarian" (*Sonnō-jōi*, the rallying cry of those opposed to opening the country at the end of the Tokugawa period). Concerning the nationalistic rhetoric that appeared in these journals, Hatanaka remarks: "*Chūō Kōron* simply had nothing to do with this kind of 'lofty' thinking, which probably could not be understood by the people of any other nation in the world, even in translation (if, indeed, translation of such 'ideas' is possible), and which cannot be understood by us Japanese, either."[14]

In contrast to the major's praise for the other magazines, the three liberal journals received mostly criticism. He was not entirely pleased, he said, with Niwa Fumio's "Naval Engagement" ("Kaisen"), a documentary account of the Battle of the Solomons printed in *Chūō Kōron*. He thought it was too long and

---

*SSDS, pp. 79–83. The author of this piece was Shimizu Ikutarō, an important liberal critic, the first Sōseki commentator to recognize the importance of the lecture "My Individualism," but also author of later conservative tracts.

†The "Kyoto School" of Nishida philosophy was *not* antiwar, but their justification of the war was based on "European-style reasoning" rather than the orthodox dogma, and so it was unacceptable. To hear the rhetoric employed by their critics, however—especially the fascistic Mitsui Kōshi, critic of both Natsume Sōseki (in 1910) and Minobe Tatsukichi (in 1940)—one would think the "school" and *Chūō Kōron* were out-and-out turncoats. SSDS, pp. 61–66.

contained too much extraneous material concerning Niwa's own activities as a war correspondent. Donald Keene has described the piece as perhaps the finest such account to appear during the war, with its descriptions of "the tension of an approaching battle, the brief but seemingly immensely long period of contact with the enemy fleet, the half-unbelieving sensations of joy when the Japanese realized they had won a major victory." Like the major, Keene, too, finds the piece overlong, but for different reasons. Niwa, he says, "dwells a bit too extensively on the incomparable spirit (*seishin*) of the naval officers, and the camaraderie (which arouses his envy as a mere civilian) of men who had been classmates at the Naval Academy, but his account of the battle itself is exceptionally vivid, and the moment when he is hit by shrapnel is described with an authority that marks Niwa unmistakably as a novelist." [15] Perhaps the major felt there was not enough "spirit" to offset the narrator's personal reactions.

Next *Kaizō* was criticized as lacking in emotional appeal. The major did recognize a sincere note of conversion (*tenkō*) following the magazine's "blunder" of August and September 1942 (the printing of a controversial piece, to be discussed below), but *Kaizō* was still "quite cold" toward "the great themes now demanded by the nation." The major reminded the representative of *Nihon Hyōron* that the magazine had been repeatedly cautioned against printing the fiction of Masamune Hakuchō, Satomi Ton, and others, but still it persisted in this same tendency. The October issue's story by Okamoto Ippei,[16] "Record of a Second Marriage" ("Saikonki") was guilty of "clinging to purely personal problems," and as such was not fit wartime reading matter.[17]

Already by this time (in fact, by late 1941), *Bungei Shunjū* had changed its editorial policy "one hundred eighty degrees" and had joined the chorus of antilibertarian critics at the Society of the Sixth meetings.[18] The military's campaign against the remaining three liberal magazines would develop out of the kind of objections raised at the November 1942 meeting described here. *Kaizō* was allowed to survive after its blunder of August and September on condition that it undergo a complete editorial restaffing.[19] *Chūō Kōron* experienced a similar fate in July 1943. Despite subsequent painful months of 100 percent cooperation with the military, *Chūō Kōron* and *Kaizō* were forced by the Cabinet Information Bureau to undergo "voluntary dissolution" (*jihatsuteki haigyō*) on July 10, 1944. *Nihon Hyōron* had been forced to turn itself into an economics journal in March 1944 and was no longer a threat.[20]

THE DEATH THROES OF *CHŪŌ KŌRON* AND *KAIZŌ*

The demise of these two magazines ended the last vestige of independent thought to be published commercially in Japan before the surrender.[21] Their dying struggles are worth describing in some detail as notable examples of that parallel between objectionable literary and political material so much in evidence since Narushima Ryūhoku fell victim to the censors in 1876: *Chūō Kōron* exemplifies the dangers inherent in a prescriptive, doctrinaire view of literature that would rob it of its independence; and *Kaizō* illustrates thought control in its narrowest, most vicious form.

We will look first at the dissolution of *Chūō Kōron*. As the officer at the November 1942 meeting of the Society of the Sixth made clear, the last thing that the military wanted to see in literature was a concern for "personal problems." By continuing to publish such writing, *Chūō Kōron* was demonstrating persistence in its "detached observation" of the war. It was by attempting to publish a novel that has since become one of the monuments of modern Japanese literature, Tanizaki Jun'ichirō's *The Makioka Sisters* (*Sasameyuki*), that *Chūō Kōron* helped to speed its own downfall.

Readers of *The Makioka Sisters* are usually amazed to learn that the novel was "banned," especially if they are familiar with Tanizaki's other writing. Of all his novels, this is the one that would seem least likely to offend. Gone are the demonic women, the masochistic lovers, the foot fetishes, the self-conscious pursuit of the bizarrely erotic and scatological. Instead, we find a nostalgic, slow-moving panorama of upper-middle-class life in the Osaka suburb of Ashiya, draped over a plot that hinges on nothing more controversial than a family's attempts to find a suitable husband for the third of its four daughters. Tanizaki later wrote that he had originally intended to do an even longer novel than the one he finally wrote, making it a study of the decadent life in well-to-do Ashiya, but that such material would have been too "dangerous" at the time.[22]

Toward the end of the book, some scenes describe the dissolute life of the youngest daughter, but these contain only the slightest hint of Tanizaki's shadowed eroticism. Furthermore, serialization of the novel was suspended after only two installments, bringing the action to a halt at the end of chapter 13. Readers had seen the sisters applying cosmetics and administering vitamin B injections to each other to help them through the summer of 1936; had learned of the newspaper scandal that had threatened Yukiko's chances of making a marriage worthy of the Makioka name; had met the rather ordinary first suitor; had agonized with the Makiokas over the facial spot that came and went with Yukiko's periods; and had witnessed the meticulous care with which the families investigated each other's backgrounds. But just as the Makiokas seemed on the verge of making a decision, the serialization stopped. There were still eighty-seven chapters and four more suitors to go.[*]

*Translated by Edward Seidensticker as *The Makioka Sisters* (New York: Alfred A. Knopf, 1957).

The original plan was for *Chūō Kōron* to carry an installment every other month, beginning in January 1943. The January issue also contained the first installment (there were to be four per year) of Shimazaki Tōson's final novel, *The Eastern Gate* (*Tōhō no mon*), which made it a literary bonanza for readers sick of "dessicated military pieces," and they waited in line at a downtown Tokyo bookstore for the first issues to go on sale.[23] The great response to the issue caught the attention of the army and the Cabinet Information Bureau, which began "advising" the magazine to stop publishing "novels that fail to comprehend the nature of the times." (This description did not include *The Eastern Gate*, four installments of which appeared through October 1943 before it was cut short by Tōson's death. The book's long historical perspective seems to have been leading toward a justification of Japan's role as the leader of Asia and perhaps the light of the world. Some have suggested its interruption was by no means fortunate for Tōson's postwar reputation.)[24]

After the second installment of *The Makioka Sisters* appeared in March 1943, Hatanaka Shigeo was summoned to appear at the Army Information Division, where he was sat down amid a room full of officers and blasted by one Major Sugimoto: "This novel goes on and on detailing the very thing we are most supposed to be on our guard against during this period of wartime emergency: the soft, effeminate, and grossly individualistic lives of women. Its continued serialization cannot be permitted. What are we to make of the attitude of a magazine that prints such a novel? This is more than a simple case of poor judgment: it is the rankest indifference to the war effort, the attitude of a detached observer."[25]

Major Sugimoto also unleashed a torrent of abuse for their having printed "Americanism as the Enemy," which he called "a Fifth Column essay." "Perhaps Major Sugimoto and the others were expecting me to offer cringing apologies," writes Hatanaka, "but instead I tried to make some sort of defense. Not that I was attempting any 'conscious resistance': far from a bold stance, it was more like the distant howls of a beaten dog."[26]

Four days later at the April Society of the Sixth meeting, Major Sugimoto repeated his blast at *Chūō Kōron* before the other magazines' representatives. In the May meeting, he praised the other magazines for understanding the times and cooperating sincerely with the needs of the military, but he accused *Chūō Kōron* of "antimilitary action" for having been the only magazine not to honor the army's request to emblazon its March 1943 cover with a militaristic slogan for Army Remembrance Day.[27] Turning to *The Makioka Sisters* and other objectionable content, he concluded that "we intend to put an immediate stop to the publication of any magazine that continues shamelessly to print such novels and essays at a time like this."

The decision to discontinue *The Makioka Sisters* was not made until the reading of proof for the June issue was nearly complete.[28] Readers had been notified at the end of the March installment that they would have to wait until June to see if Yukiko would marry Segoshi, but instead of the promised episode, they found this notice: "Having taken into consideration the possibility that this novel might exert an undesirable influence, in view of present exigencies at this decisive stage of the war, we have regretfully decided from the standpoint of self-discipline to discontinue further publication."[29]

In this classic example of the most strained sort of between-the-lines wartime Japanese (given here in Donald Keene's impeccable translation), the editors felt some consolation at the tentative tone they had worked into the first clause (by insertion of the single dubative particle "*ya*"), but Tanizaki was by no means pleased at the suggestion that his writing might have an undesirable influence, and he called *Chūō Kōron* to say so.[30] He would have preferred the editors to use the apology to readers he had written himself in which he had observed that the book was "not wartime reading matter" and had promised to keep the remainder of the manuscript until some day in the distant future when its complete publication could be realized.[31] Surely this would have been too blatant a suggestion that the age of the militarists was fated to end. Tanizaki later wrote that he had felt oppressed less by the loss of his creative freedom and the impossibility of protest than the tone of the age itself in which such events were taken for granted. "I felt first-hand the crushing gloom" the Edo writers must have experienced when they were jailed or shackled for venturing into forbidden territory.[32]

Tanizaki printed 248 copies of a private edition of book 1 of *The Makioka Sisters* in July 1944 with *Chūō Kōron* money.[33] He distributed them "as unobtrusively as possible" to friends, especially people outside the literary world.[34] The government did not attempt to punish him for this, but the Special Higher Police did visit his Ashiya home to learn the names of the recipients and the source of his paper. They also wanted him to sign a pledge that he would not publish further volumes. At the time, however, Tanizaki himself was several hundred miles away in Atami, and although the police never came to see him there as promised, the message had its effect. He did not attempt to publish any more.[35] In the subsequent chaos of fleeing from air raids, Tanizaki found himself unable to proceed much past the beginning of book 3.[36] All three books were finally published after the war.

Hearing Major Sugimoto's threat at the May meeting to crush *Chūō Kōron* out of existence, Hatanaka felt that his life as an editor had come to an end. Shortly after this meeting, he was formally excluded from membership in the Society of the Sixth. He submitted his resignation to *Chūō Kōron* on the grounds that he could no longer be of service to the company, but it was refused by Shimanaka Yūsaku. When new difficulties arose over a piece that Hatanaka had included in the June issue, however, he found that he was not even allowed to enter the offices of the Army Information Division to explain.

And indeed, just as he had finished proofreading what he assumed to be his last issue, formal notice arrived to the effect that no one from the magazine would be allowed into the division. This time Hatanaka's resignation was accepted (although Shimanaka insisted on making it a "leave"), Hatanaka's immediate subordinate was announced to have been censured, and the rest of the editorial staff was dispersed to different parts of the company, to be replaced by a supposedly more malleable group. Because the July issue had been produced by the original staff, however, the army did not want it printed, and so *Chūō Kōron* missed an issue for the first time in its fifty-eight-year history. From August 1943 to July 1944, when the army forced the magazine's "voluntary dissolution," *Chūō Kōron* served as an ultra-nationalistic propaganda sheet, having been cured once and for all of its annoying penchant for detached observation.[37]

Hatanaka would be reinstated as editor-in-chief after the war, but first he would be swept up in the Yokohama Incident, a conspiracy by the police and the courts to rid Tokyo of its independent journalists which was associated with the last days of *Kaizō*.

Kaizō's great blunder, alluded to above, was the publication of an essay in its August and September 1942 issues entitled "The Trends of World History and Japan" ("Sekaishi no dōkō to Nihon") by the Marxist scholar Hosokawa Karoku.* The Police Bureau allowed both issues to pass without a murmur, but the September 1942 meeting of the Society of the Sixth was quite a different matter. Major Hiragushi (Major Sugimoto's predecessor) told how shocked and appalled he had been to read the essay. "What the writer is trying to say here boils down to one thing only: that in our racial policy in the South Pacific, Japan should follow the Soviet pattern. He tells the Japanese Race to cooperate with South Seas natives on an equal footing! This is nothing less than the self-determination of peoples! A case of blatant defeatism! He all but says that we should adopt the Soviet Union's communistic racial policy *in toto*. His essay is antiwar propaganda, an ingenious piece of Communist agitation that negates the leadership position of Japan across the board." Note that Hosokawa did not anger him by speaking out against imperialism but by recommending humane treatment for captured peoples. Indeed, the essay was perfectly compatible with official slogans coined in the creation of the Manchukuo puppet state.†

A week after this friendly get-together, Hosokawa Karoku was arrested by

---

*Hosokawa had belonged to the Ōhara Social Problems Research Institute (Ōhara Shakai Mondai Kenkyūjo) and was an authority on ethnic studies and colonial policy. See Mimasaka Tarō et al., *Yokohama jiken*, p. 94.

†SSDS, p. 89; Mimasaka Tarō et al., *Yokohama jiken*, pp. 91–92. Shimaki Kensaku had successfully published a work on a similar theme in 1939, *Journey to Manchuria* (*Manshū kikō*),

the Tokyo Metropolitan Police on suspicion of having violated the Peace Preservation Law with his essay. *Kaizō*'s editor-in-chief, Ōmori Naomichi, and the editor who had handled Hosokawa's essay, Aikawa Hiroshi, both resigned four days later to take the responsibility on themselves, and eventually both of them joined Hosokawa in jail as victims of the spreading Yokohama Incident. *Kaizō* was allowed to continue publishing on condition that it undergo a complete changeover in editorial staff, thus "descending to the ranks of the stooge magazines," as Hatanaka Shigeo so unsparingly states it.[38]

THE YOKOHAMA INCIDENT

Hosokawa Karoku was not the first to be arrested in the Yokohama Incident. Three days before his arrest in Tokyo on September 14, 1942, the Kanagawa Prefectural Special Higher Police Division, headquartered in Yokohama, had decided to arrest Kawada Hiroshi and his wife Sadako, who had aroused their suspicions in January 1941 when Yokohama customs officials found Socialist materials in their luggage. It was learned that they had been studying labor problems in America. The police became convinced that Kawada, head of the Marxist-oriented World Economic Study Group (Sekai Keizai Chōsa Kai), was planning to reintroduce communism from the West, and from there it was a short step to rounding up everyone connected in any way with the "plot."[39]

All of the detention orders were issued by two procurators in the Yokohama District Court. They began with other members of the study group and some of the members' friends. When one such friend was arrested on May 26, 1943, found among his personal effects was a piece of "evidence" that must have seemed too good to be true—a photograph of this man in a group surrounding Hosokawa Karoku himself; plus the *Kaizō* editor who had been in charge of Hosokawa's controversial essay, Aikawa Hiroshi; another *Kaizō* editor; a member of the *Chūō Kōron* publications staff; and two others.[40] Clearly, this was a record of a preliminary meeting in the conspiracy to reestablish the Communist party. They arrested all the men in the picture who were not already in jail, and when they learned the identity of the cameraman, they arrested him, too.

In fact, the photograph of seven men in identical lounging kimono (*yukata*) had been taken as a souvenir of a dinner given by Hosokawa Karoku at a resort on July 5, 1942, to celebrate his having been paid some royalties for a *Kaizō* article and a book. The police chose, instead, to view this typically Japanese bit of memorabilia as a piece of evidence graciously fashioned for them by an

---

by which time he had "converted" and was considered to be "essentially friendly to the regime." Donald Keene, "Japanese Literature and Politics in the 1930s," pp. 232–33.

underground Communist cell. They arrested several dozen people who could be construed as having some connection with Hosokawa Karoku and the photograph.

In all, forty-nine "conspirators" were arrested between September 11, 1942, and May 9, 1945, and were held in various detention centers in Kanagawa Prefecture until after the war. Most of them, including Hosokawa, had to be brought from Tokyo, where they worked as journalists or functioned in other intellectually oriented capacities, although four employees of the Manchuria Railway Company were brought from Shanghai. The net spread to the *Asahi Shimbun*, the Iwanami publishers, the Shōwa Academy (a wing of the Shōwa Research Association),* and, most pertinent to our purposes, to the editorial staffs of *Chūō Kōron* (eight members), *Kaizō* (seven members), and *Nihon Hyōron* (five members). In effect, the case provided a perfect opportunity for a clean sweep from the Tokyo area of a large number of intellectuals who were viewed as uncooperative with the war effort.† What made the case symbolic not only of the times but of the government's long struggle against subversive foreign influences was that the incident ballooned from a customs seizure in Yokohama, Japan's most important window to the world.

Once the Special Higher Police had their suspects in custody, their problem was to prove the existence of a conspiracy. Since they had no evidence, they demanded written depositions and freely resorted to torture to get them. Of the forty-nine victims, thirteen were tortured severely enough to lose consciousness. Thirty-two were wounded severely enough to bleed. Two (both were former members of the *Chūō Kōron* editorial staff who had lost their positions with Hatanaka) died in prison as a direct result of torture and prison conditions, and one died shortly after his release. Some of the group were held from one to three years without even a preliminary hearing, and after Japan's defeat came on August 15, 1945, the procurators rushed them through trials. Even at the September 4, 1945, trial of the *Chūō Kōron* people, the procurator was still trying hard to obtain three-year prison terms for them. All were given

---

*The association (Shōwa Kenkyū Kai) was founded in November 1936 to act as Prince Konoe's "brain trust on domestic and foreign affairs," its mission being to formulate a policy that could mold a national consensus. The group has been called *both* Communist and fascist! See James B. Crowley, "Intellectuals as Visionaries of the New Asian Order," in James W. Morley, ed., *Dilemmas of Growth in Prewar Japan* (Princeton: Princeton University Press, 1971), pp. 319–73.

†One of those imprisoned, Ono Yasuhito (*Kaizō* editor and Hosokawa "disciple"), later wrote that far from being a communist or uncooperative with the war effort, "I was the compleat patriot, full of naive hope that by giving my utmost to my work I could turn the Greater East Asia War, which was being driven ahead by the whims of the military and bureaucracy, into a genuine holy war of popular liberation." Mimasaka Tarō et al., *Yokohama jiken*, p. 99.

two-year suspended sentences and released that day. (Hatanaka and several other prominent editors had been arrested on January 29, 1944.)[41]

A sickeningly detailed record of torture and maltreatment was assembled after the war when thirty-three of the victims brought a criminal suit against more than thirty of the Special Higher Police officers who had engaged in acts of brutality. Suspects under questioning were usually made to sit on the floor on their heels in formal Japanese fashion while several officers continually beat their thighs with bamboo staves until the flesh swelled from internal hemorrhaging and they were left with suppurating wounds. Kawada Sadako had to endure this with nothing on below the waist and was otherwise sexually molested. One *Kaizō* man had cigarettes burned on his forehead. Of the two *Chūō Kōron* editors who died, one literally drowned in his own blood and the other froze to death in his cell. Sometimes the police would not even bother to ask questions but would simply torture them for a while and throw them back in their cells.

The physical abuse would usually be accompanied by verbal abuse. Time and again the torturers would threaten them with a reminder of how Kobayashi Takiji, the proletarian author, had been tortured to death in 1933. Often the police would say, "We're allowed to kill you Commies," or would boast, "I've killed plenty of skinny eggheads like you." One man was told that his wife had committed suicide and his children were in the hospital, but that he could not see them until he confessed.

Hatanaka writes of learning to become indifferent to fleas, of becoming so numb to filth that he could go on eating while a fellow prisoner with diarrhea was moving his bowels a few feet away. The police wanted a confession from him that he was a Communist exploiting *Chūō Kōron* as a weapon in the class struggle, that everything the magazine did was designed to aid the Comintern and the Japanese Communist party. They also wanted a signed statement from him that the head of *Chūō Kōron*, Shimanaka, was a Communist. When he resisted, they beat his thighs with bamboo staves. When he fell forward in pain, they yanked him back and beat his face bloody. Finally, he says, they had to settle for a statement that Shimanaka was a "communistic libertarianist."[42]

Not surprisingly, all forty-nine signed confessions, consoling themselves with the vain hope of repudiating them in court. Equally vain were their hopes for legal redress after the war. All but three cases were dismissed for lack of evidence, and the three men when convicted received sentences of only twelve or eighteen months. Police Inspector Matsushita Eitarō, the officer in charge of left-wing investigations, received the longer sentence. It is especially shocking that Assistant Police Inspector Morikawa Seizō, whose sadistic behavior was attested to ad nauseam in the victims' depositions, should have had to serve only one year in prison.[43]

Hatanaka ascribes the despicable behavior of the policemen, and the procurators they served, to an intense desire for commendation that aroused in
them a fanatically sycophantic psychology with regard to the war policies.[44]
They were willing to go to any lengths to prove what loyal subjects they were,
including the torture of "Communists" who chose to remain detached observers of the war.

THE PUBLISHING INDUSTRY POLICES ITSELF

Much of the suffocating, redundant mechanism that flourished during the war
to control the printed word came to verge on irrelevance as Japan's declining
fortunes began to rob it of paper on which to print. If the Shōwa publishing
boom threatened to overwhelm the limited resources of the Police Bureau, the
Pacific War served to reduce the industry to manageable limits. Indeed, so
crippled was the publishing world that the situation was less reminiscent of
pre-Shōwa than pre-Meiji Japan, when Edo officials put the power (and obligation) to control written expression into the hands of the publishers themselves.

Two weeks after the Cabinet Information Division was upgraded to a bureau, an organization was founded on December 19, 1940, calling itself the
Japan Publishing Culture Association (Nippon Shuppan Bunka Kyōkai). Ostensibly an autonomous body dedicated to the "establishment of a wholesome
new Japanese culture" through service to the nation, the association had its
officers chosen for it and its policies set for it by the Cabinet Information
Bureau.[45] From its inception, the association was given the authority to create
a plan for the rationing of printing paper, and after it had been reestablished as
the Japan Publishing Association (Nippon Shuppan Kai) on March 26, 1943,
it possessed the power to carry out the rationing itself.[46]

As early as August 1938, the control of paper consumption had been begun
by the Ministry of Commerce and Industry, which ordered a 20 percent
reduction over the previous year. A further reduction of 25 percent was ordered
by an interministerial committee in August 1939, and the rationing plan
evolved by this and a subsequently formed official body was finally inherited in
1943 by the Japan Publishing Association.

Between the second quarter of 1941 and the first quarter of 1944, the paper
available for allotment by the association shrank by 84 percent. The first
criterion by which companies were ranked for the distribution of paper was the
degree of their cooperation with the war effort. Refusal to accept "official"
manuscript, for example, marked a company as uncooperative. It would be
threatened with a ration cut, which led to the ugly spectacle of companies
fighting over these manuscripts to survive. While the association's supplies
shrank by 84 percent, the allotment given to *Chūō Kōron* shrank by 92 percent.

Fujin Kōron, the company's women's magazine, was down by 97 percent late in 1943, after which it was ordered discontinued as "non-essential and non-emergency."[47]

With regard to books, the Japan Publishing Culture Association inaugurated a prior approval system (*hakkō shōnin sei*) on March 21, 1942. Beginning in April, publishers were required to submit a detailed plan to receive the paper needed to print a book. This had to include the author or editor's curriculum vitae, a description of contents and binding style, the proposed publication date and amount of paper needed. If the plan were approved, the publisher would be issued an approval number to be printed on the colophon along with the publisher's association membership number.*

Under such stringent circumstances, Japan's enormous publishing industry could not continue to function as it had with unlimited raw materials, and the Japan Publishing Association was given the task known as "industrial readjustment" (*kigyō seibi*). This meant in practice the forced merger and/or liquidation of many companies. In 1943 the number of publishing companies was reduced from 2,241 to a mere 172. Of 2,017 magazines being printed, 1,027 were picked for elimination. It was as part of this ongoing process that, on March 11, 1944, the six general magazines were cut to three, leaving only the fanatically militaristic *Kōron*, the old-fashioned emperor-worshipping *Gendai*, and the (by then) emasculated *Chūō Kōron*. *Kaizō* was ordered to restrict itself to current topics with no commentary or criticism, thus losing its status as a general magazine, as did *Bungei Shunjū*, which was restricted to belles lettres, and *Nihon Hyōron*, which was limited to economics. The *Chūō Kōron* and *Kaizō* companies, as we have seen, were dissolved four months later, and the same fate was being planned for *Nihon Hyōron* and the Iwanami publishers when the defeat intervened.[48]

Representatives of the publishing industry chosen to make these life-and-death decisions over their colleagues may well be imagined to have experienced a good deal of pain, but Hatanaka has left an unflattering account of these men. Many of the unemployed editors who took "advisory" positions with the government control agencies and the Japan Publishing Association seemed embarrassed at first but soon took to their roles with enthusiasm. Many obviously enjoyed the power their newfound status gave them to summon editors with a single phone call and blast them for having printed some

*SSDS, pp. 53–55. For example, Mori Junzaburō's biography of his brother, *Ōgai Mori Rintarō*, published on April 1, 1942, carried approval number A-11018 and membership number 135013. The fourth volume of Fujiwara Kiyozō, *Meiji Taishō Shōwa*, was printed after the company's forced merger: hence the two publishers. Most wartime (and early Occupation) publications are immediately recognizable by their paper, which was pitifully crude material surviving today as brittle, yellowed pages in flimsy books.

"uncooperative" piece of commentary or some "purely personal" work of fiction that was "too narrow for the times." Others in the industry took it upon themselves to form patriotic organizations such as the Japan Editors Association (Nippon Henshūsha Kyōkai, founded June 1941) which issued critiques of such companies as *Chūō Kōron* for "asserting the modern Western philosophy of individual freedom," and sponsored Shintō "purification retreats" for editors or "deeply moving" lectures on such topics as "A Condemnation of Christianity as Viewed from the *Kokutai*."[49]

"This was not sane behavior for men of intelligence," remarks Hatanaka of the editors' religious fervor. He is hard put to explain the publishing industry's eagerness to cast off all remnants of freedom and conscience in its frantic struggle to survive amid the paper shortage. Although many companies wore the guise of modern enterprise, he says, at heart they were traditional small businesses all too ready to engage in internecine commercial warfare. *Not one publisher* took the initiative to close its own doors during wartime in the name of editorial autonomy and freedom of the press. "We took the 'smart' option of furling the banner of progressivism and cringing at the feet of the military."[50]

WRITERS PATRIOTIC AT LAST

Drawing upon the work of Odagiri Susumu, Hirano Ken, and others, Donald Keene has amply demonstrated the lack of a literary resistance to the war in Japan.[51] Indeed, far from resisting, most writers "exulted in the triumphs of the first year, and urged redoubled efforts when the ominous signs of reverses appeared." Although in America or England few authors of the first rank lent their talents to patriotic writing, "in Japan, many excellent writers of prose and poetry were to publish vituperation. . . . Once the war began, the Japanese writers, with extremely few exceptions, became Japanese first and men of letters second." There was, as Keene abundantly illustrates, an "unmistakable ring of sincerity" to many of the writers' patriotic effusions.[52] Even employing broad definitions of what constituted both active and passive resistance, the historian Ienaga Saburō must conclude that the sporadic wartime resistance in Japan was an "abysmal failure." He notes, however, that "even in this period, when all Japanese seemed to have lost their critical faculties and lapsed into a psychotic frenzy, there were some perceptive persons with a firm grasp on reality."[53]

At this point, I would like to note a few such perceptive persons among the writers and to suggest that the military victory over literature was both incomplete and enormously costly. Only two writers emerge from Keene's study with their artistic integrity more or less uncompromised. Both of them were "well-established authors who could live on the royalties from reprints of

old works (or on the generosity of their publishers),"[54] and both were Meiji
men who have appeared repeatedly in these pages as persona non grata to the
authorities: Tanizaki Jun'ichirō and Nagai Kafū. We have seen how Tanizaki
continued writing *The Makioka Sisters* after it was dropped from *Chūō Kōron* in
1943; but he wrote little else for publication through the remainder of the war.
Kafū also continued to write (in fact, on Pearl Harbor day he began his first
piece of fiction since 1938). But after *Chūō Kōron* was prohibited from publishing his story "The Decoration" ("Kunshō") in December 1942,* Kafū stopped
submitting his manuscripts for publication. Kafū's diary, however, contains
scathing denunciations of the military.[55] Both men chose the only form of
resistance they saw open to them: silence—and even this was not absolute in
Tanizaki's case.

These two aging writers (Kafū was 65, Tanizaki was 55 in December 1941)
had had a long, cordial relationship ever since Kafū's "discovery" of Tanizaki in
an influential essay he wrote in 1911. Their diaries record gifts sent to each
other and occasional dinners with their publisher, Shimanaka Yūsaku of *Chūō
Kōron*. Kafū records on March 4, 1944, that Tanizaki stopped by on his way to
Atami, where he was taking his daughter, whose Tokyo house seemed particularly vulnerable to American air raids. They discussed Kafū's request, made at
their December dinner with Shimanaka, that Tanizaki handle certain matters
with regard to Kafū's complete works and posthumous manuscripts.[56] Tanizaki was anxious to leave Tokyo before the rumored air raids started in earnest.
After a visit with Shimanaka at *Chūō Kōron* and a flurry of telephone calls, he
managed to gather his family together at Tokyo Station and board the 6:40
P.M. train to Atami with a great sense of relief.[57]

By the time Kafū's house and library went up in flames in the devastating
raid of March 10, 1945, Tanizaki had moved several hundred miles west to a
town in the mountains behind Okayama. Kafū escaped with only his diary and
manuscripts in a briefcase, was burnt out from two more places of refuge, and
eventually made his way to Okayama. From there, he went to visit Tanizaki on
August 13. The first thing he did was to entrust Tanizaki with the manuscripts of three pieces of fiction. The next day they strolled around the town
and Kafū indicated that he would like to come to live there. Tanizaki told him
quite frankly that he could only guarantee him a room and fuel: there would be
no daily food rations as in Okayama. He agreed to send for Kafū as soon as a
food supply could be secured for him.

That day, however, they managed to obtain beef and enjoyed a sukiyaki
dinner, over which they discussed rumors that the latest air raids on Osaka and
Amagasaki had employed the "new bomb." Before Kafū returned to Okayama

*The story was published in 1946 and has been translated by Edward Seidensticker in *Kafū
the Scribbler*, pp. 329–35.

the next morning, news arrived that practically the entire Osaka-Amagasaki-Kobe area had indeed been destroyed, but with conventional bombs. Tanizaki saw Kafū off on the 11:26 A.M. train and, returning home from the station, heard the emperor's noon broadcast announcing the surrender. Owing to poor reception, however, no one could be certain what had been said until a clearer 3:00 P.M. broadcast. There were tears and enormous excitement. Kafū heard the news when he arrived in Okayama, and he went to sleep drunk that night.[58]

Tanizaki and Kafū thus came through the war with a minimum of involvement. They were too old to be drafted into the army or sent abroad to conquered territories for propaganda purposes, as many writers were. And Kafū, at least, was past the sixty-year-old cutoff point for working in the civilian labor corps.[59] Ienaga Saburō has noted that there were a few writers who took other employment rather than cooperate.[60] For the most part, however, the image of the profession as a whole is rather similar to that of the publishing industry, with writers scrambling to do whatever was needed to make ends meet. After May 1942, that usually meant joining the Meiji state's last—and most successful—"academy."

This was the Japanese Literature Patriotic Association (Nihon Bungaku Hōkoku Kai), a corporate body founded on May 26, 1942, under the direct control of the Cabinet Information Bureau.* So much did the government expect of this organization that the gala inaugural meeting in June was addressed by the head of the Information Bureau, Tani Masayuki; by the Minister of Education, Hashida Kunihiko; and by the Prime Minister himself, Tōjō Hideki, each of whom spoke in person rather than sending the usual stand-in to read a written statement.

The association's great goal, as spelled out in its charter, was to awaken the people to a new world view; specifically, to "establish our world view as writers of the Empire."[61] When one converted leftist member, Kubokawa Tsurujirō, circumspectly wrote of his misgivings concerning Premier Tōjō's remarks that all writers now had to work in close harmony, voicing doubts about the existence of a ready-made world view, an association colleague raged in response, "Nazi Germany drove out the Jews. A Jew may be recognized at a glance, but it is not easy to detect an American, Englishman, or other foreigner who wears the skin of a Japanese."[62]

If one hoped to function at all as a writer during these years, when the Cabinet Information Bureau kept a blacklist of undesirable authors, one had to be a member of the association.[63] It was well known that the qualifications of

---

*The Arts Academy (see above, chap. 15, p. 255) continued to function, but according to Masamune Hakuchō it was far less influential than the Patriotic Association during the war. GNBZ 97:421.

applicants for admission were checked, and the fact that one had been admitted was like a stamp of innocence. Nakano Shigeharu, one of several leftist writers arrested the day after Pearl Harbor and subsequently released, wrote that he had gone to great lengths to be admitted, but he, Miyamoto Yuriko, and several other blacklisted leftists did in fact join in hopes of being allowed to publish. Later criticized by her husband, who had been imprisoned from 1933 to 1945, for having thus collaborated with the enemy, Miyamoto confessed that "she was not strong enough to bear the terrible isolation to which resistance would have condemned her."[64]

No doubt such feelings were widespread, for the membership climbed to something over 2,500. These were not all writers of modern fiction, however. Novelists comprised only one division of the association. Of the 2,623 members on the rolls (as of August 1, 1942), 569 were in the haiku division and 552 specialized in tanka, the traditional poetic form most closely associated with the "Japanese spirit" during the war. Writers of fiction numbered 357, and even foreign literature was well represented at 329. Modern poetry (262), Japanese literary history (192), theater (189), and criticism (173) comprised the remainder.*

There is always the question, too, of the degree of an individual's involvement. The pure-turned-popular writer/publisher, Kikuchi Kan, who was an organizer of many writers' associations through the 1930s and 1940s and even after the war, was clearly a central figure here.[65] At the opposite extreme were the popular novelist Nakazato Kaizan, who flatly refused to join, and Nagai Kafū, who recorded angrily in his diary that "Kikuchi Kan's so-called Japanese Literature Patriotic Association has put my name on its roster without so much as a word to me. And the president of the thing is none other than Tokutomi Sohō, a man I absolutely loathe!"† Meanwhile Sohō, whom we saw as an always-absent member of the Committee on Literature, was described after the war as having been a purely honorary president of both this and the Great Japan Journalism Patriotic Association (Dai-Nippon Genron Hōkoku Kai). The novelist Ozaki Shirō says he never saw Sohō at a meeting (which is probably true: he was a very sick man at the time), that Sohō had been wheedled into the post by Kume Masao (a member of the "fascist" Society of

---

*Kubota Masafumi, *"Nihon Gakugei Shimbun* o yomu," p. 117. The autonomous Writers' Society (Bungeika Kyōkai), founded in 1926 but forced to disband upon formation of the Patriotic Association, had only 245 members in 1934. Its postwar successor, the Japan Writers' Society, had a membership of 476 in 1950, 945 in July 1975. GNBD, pp. 993–94; NKBD 4:418.

†Diary entry for May 17, 1943, in KZ 23:346. Kafū himself may have been partly to blame. He wrote to a friend that he had received several letters from the association but had never answered them. See July 13, 1942, letter to Nakagawa Yoichi, in KZ 25:351.

the Fifth; see above, pp. 251–52), but that his presidency of the two associations was the first thing he was charged with as a war criminal.*

Surely there must have been many members who were thrilled to participate in the association's activities—attending the Greater East Asia Writers Congresses with representatives from other nations in the Co-Prosperity Sphere; appearing in group lecture tours or public readings; raising funds for battleship construction; writing glorifications of Japanese motherhood; hunting for the hundred best patriotic tanka to substitute for those on love and the seasons used in the traditional New Year's card game; donating their labor in groups moving baggage at railway stations, building memorials for fallen soldiers, or weeding the imperial palace grounds.[66]

The overwhelming impression that emerges from postwar studies and recollections of those years, however, is one of tedium, of killing time until the nonsense would end. The critic Hirano Ken, who oversaw the functions of the Patriotic Association as literary advisor to the Cabinet Information Bureau from its founding through May 1943, said that he based his influential 1961 study of the association less on memory than on materials he later gleaned from the association's newspaper, mainly because he had had so little interest in the work at the time that he *had* few memories to draw upon. He simply wasted one day after another, his mind always on something else.[67]

A colleague of his, the critic Ōi Hirosuke, joined the association on Hirano's advice to avoid being shut out of publishing. He paid his dues once but never attended a meeting or participated in any activities. When Hirano tried unsuccessfully to bring him to a sparsely attended meeting of the critics' division, Ōi tried—also unsuccessfully—to lure Hirano to a baseball game instead. The division chairman agreed that the game would have been far more interesting. Ōi also went to work for a mining company in hopes of escaping the civilian labor draft. Just about the time the association began asking for a second dues payment, the mining company was designated as a military supplier, which made it a far more dependable shield, and so he never paid.

*Ozaki Shirō, "Bungaku Hōkokukai," *Bungaku* (May 1961): 85, 87. Ozaki also notes admiringly that Sohō made no excuses as he was brought to Sugamo Prison, which perhaps calls his testimony into question. Old (83 years) and sick, Sohō was kept under house arrest in Atami. See John D. Pierson, *Tokutomi Sohō, 1863–1957, a Journalist for Modern Japan* (Princeton: Princeton University Press, 1980), p. 382. The question of the degree of individuals' involvement in the war effort has often occasioned ugly bickering. Tanizaki said in 1946 that he believed there had been no genuine warmongers among Japan's writers, but "whether through weakness of character, or whatever, they just found themselves being dragged in. We were part of it, too, so we can't start blaming others," he said to Shiga Naoya. See Shiga Naoya, *Shiga Naoya taiwa shū*, p. 19. See also Ōi Hirosuke, "Bungaku Hōkoku Kai wa mui," *Bungaku* (May 1961):91, for a squabble involving Hirano Ken, Nakano Shigeharu, and Ara Masahito.

Besides, there were so few magazines left to write for that membership had become meaningless.[68]

Masamune Hakuchō, who inherited the largely honorary post of head of the novelists' division when Tokuda Shūsei died in November 1943, wrote that it was "a great convenience for most of us to have the sycophants take the initiative and form an organization that would please the military."[69] Almost as if to substantiate this, in a 1961 study of the association's newspaper, Kubota Masafumi surmises that the editors' guiding principle must have been laziness. There was nothing of value in the paper, nothing to indicate that they took the slightest interest in what they were printing, he says. They were glad to let their pages fill up with dull transcriptions of patriotic pep talks and the more enthusiastic members' bellicose tanka and haiku. "I for one feel a certain comfort in the very fact that my reading of this newspaper has been a waste of time," he concludes.[70] Perhaps, if we cannot hope for signs of resistance, this is the one cheering gleam that can be cast upon the writers' compromises.

As a literary organization, the Patriotic Association did engage in some publishing activities. One (see the preceding page) was the production of a new set of the famous *One Hundred Poems by One Hundred Poets* (*Hyakunin-isshu*) card game, with patriotic tanka replacing the verses that had been familiar to the Japanese since the thirteenth century. It was precisely this familiarity that was lacking in the wartime product, said Masamune Hakuchō; the ponderous poems in praise of god-emperors were simply unsuited to the lighthearted New Year's card game. The association compilers seriously believed it could convince people to use them, and the Cabinet Information Bureau arranged for a supply of high-quality paper—all, he suggests, to no avail.[71]

In another publishing venture, however, the association was more successful—if not in attracting readers, at least in creating tangible evidence that a significant number of Japan's most important writers (several with leftist backgrounds, some with banned works to their credit) had been moved to contribute to the war effort *as* writers. This was a 227-page volume titled *Streetcorner Stories* (*Tsuji shōsetsu shū*) which sold for one and one-half yen, the proceeds going to the battleship construction fund. Published on July 18, 1943, it contained stories and exhortatory statements by 207 contributors, each piece just one manuscript sheet in length and thus presumably suited to providing inspiration at any moment—on any streetcorner—as the reader was going about his patriotic duty. Among the writers and critics represented were Abe Tomoji, Itō Sei, Ishizaka Yōjirō, Ishikawa Tatsuzō, Uno Chiyo, Eguchi Kiyoshi, Oda Sakunosuke, Kikuchi Kan, Kishida Kunio, Sakaguchi Ango, Serizawa Kōjirō, Dazai Osamu, Tsuboi Sakae, Hayama Yoshiki, Fujimori Seikichi, Mushanokōji Saneatsu—and Tanizaki Jun'ichirō.[72]

I would like to close this study with a translation of Tanizaki's contribution to *Streetcorner Stories*, because it illustrates so vividly what Japan's wartime leaders thought they wanted from the writers for the people. We have seen the verve and insight of which Tanizaki was capable, and for which his readers turned to him over the years despite the censors' best efforts. But here from his pen, at last, was a work sufficiently barren and trivial that it could please a Katsura Tarō, a Komatsubara Eitarō, or any of their successors—from Hiranuma Kiichirō and Tanaka Giichi to Matsumoto Gaku and Tōjō Hideki. In order to induce a writer like Tanizaki to compose this feeble page of print, successive governments had invested countless man-hours and millions of yen in decades of legislation, committee work, police and administrative actions, trials, and schemes for indoctrinating, coddling, and brutally coercing the Japanese people.

Tanizaki's "story" consists of eight lines of dialogue. It begins when a boy asks his elder brother the meaning of the obscure Sino-Japanese phrase that entitles the piece:

> "What does '*Baku-mōsō*' mean?"
>
> "'Beware delusion.' When the Mongols tried to invade Japan in the thirteenth century, a great Zen priest said this to the Regent Hōjō Tokimune to strengthen his resolve."
>
> "I'll bet that priest would get mad if he saw someone frightened by Roosevelt's big talk or worrying that their stupid planes were going to come over here."
>
> "I'll bet he would."
>
> "Do you think the Divine Winds [Kamikaze] will blow this time the way they did against the Mongols?"
>
> "Absolutely—but only *after* the Sun Goddess sees us doing the best we can to arm ourselves. When she sees us turning out battleships and planes to crush the enemy in the Pacific, then she'll be sure to send the Divine Winds."
>
> "That's true: the Kamakura warriors didn't just fold their arms and wait for the winds to whip the Mongols."
>
> "Now you've got it. You *are* a clever little fellow!" [73]

Chronology

Most works listed were prohibited from sale and distribution by the Home Ministry. Parentheses indicate that a work discussed in the text was not banned. Untranslated titles have not been discussed in the text. Foreign titles were banned in Japanese translation. The listing of works is intended to be broadly inclusive through 1916 to provide context for early Taishō works discussed in the text, far more selective thereafter.

The Police Bureau's Book (Censorship) Section began to keep comprehensive records when its budget was doubled as part of the national expansion of the thought-control system carried out by the Tanaka regime (1927–1929). Precise censorship figures are available for 1921–1935 in SKG 1(1930):34, 39; and SKG 3(1935):210. For figures through 1944, see Naimushō Keihokyoku, ed., *Shuppan Keisatsu hō*; and Yui Masaomi, Kitagawa Kenzō, Akazawa Shirō, and Toyosawa Hajime, *Shuppan Keisatsu kankei shiryō: kaisetsu, sōmokuji* (Fuji shuppan, 1983). Earlier official censorship records are incomplete and unreliable. Books banned after 1888 are listed in Naimushō Keihokyoku, ed., *Kinshi tankōbon mokuroku*. Professor Wada Kingo has kindly shared with me a copy of a rare early list of banned books, magazines, and pamphlets between 1888 and 1919: Naimushō Keihokyoku, ed., *Shuppan Keisatsu shiryō: kinshi shuppanbutsu mokuroku / Dai-ippen* (1920?). Somewhat inconsistent figures for the 1918–1920 period are available in Japan Naimushō, *Shuppan Keisatsu shiryō, 1923–1938*, Reel No. 1: "Shuppanbutsu no keikō oyobi sono torishimari jōkyō gairyaku" (December 1923 and February 1924).

1868	Rebel government proclaims beginning of Meiji era. First press and book publication edicts issued, requiring "official permission" to publish.
1875	Censorship authority transferred from Ministry of Education to Home Ministry; thereafter becomes police function. New Press and Libel Regulations institute Reign of Terror. New Publication

Regulations require "occasional" submission of book manuscript prior to publication.

1876   Special ordinance gives Home Minister authority to prohibit publication of periodicals deemed disruptive to national peace. Narushima Ryūhoku, *New Chronicle of Yanagibashi* refused license to
publish.

1878–   "Poison women" boom.
1880

1883   New Press Regulations require posting of bond; empower Home
Minister to prohibit or suspend publication of any periodical
"which he deems to be disruptive of public peace and order or
injurious to public morals."

1887   New Press and Publication Regulations promulgated together; so-
lidify foundation of prewar censorship system. Finished books
to be submitted prior to sale.

1889   Constitution promulgated; guarantees free speech "within the limits
of the law."

1893   Diet passes Publication Law.

1896   Oguri Fūyō, "Making Up for Bed."

1897   Press Regulations revised by Diet; shifts emphasis toward prohibition
of sale and distribution.

1900   November *Myōjō*, French nudes. Aoyagi Yūbi, *Ren'ai bungaku*.

1901   Uchida Roan, "Broken Fence." Masaoka Geiyō, *0 Land of Prostitution!*
Aoyagi Yūbi, *Shin ren'ai bungaku*. Dumas, *La Dame aux
Camélias*.

1902   Shimazaki Tōson, *The Former Master*. (Kosugi Tengai, *Popular Song*.)

1904   Outbreak of Russo-Japanese War. (Yosano Akiko, "I Beg You: Do
Not Die.")

1905   War ends. Discontent over treaty brings down first Katsura cabinet.
Taoka Reiun, *Kochūkan*.

1906   Naturalist revolution begins. (Shimazaki Tōson, *The Broken Commandment*. Hasegawa Tenkei, "Art for an Age of Disillusionment.")
Ikuta Kizan, *Princess Fumiko*. Taoka Reiun, *Kochū gakan*.

1907   Naturalism booms. Sōseki joins *Asahi*. (Tayama Katai, *The Quilt*.
Futabatei Shimei, *Mediocrity*.) Ikuta Kizan, *Vanity*. Taoka Reiun, *Hekirekiben*. *Saikaku zenshū*. *Saikaku kōshokubun*. Fujimura
Misao (fraud), *Hanmonki*. Arahata Kanson, *Yanaka-mura met-
subō shi*.

1908   Naturalism explodes in press. Second Katsura cabinet inaugurated in
July. Ikuta Kizan, "The City." Oguri Fūyō, *Shattered Love*.
Shirayanagi Shūko, *Tekka sekka*. Molière, *Collected Works*. Zola,

Paris. (Masamune Hakuchō, "Where?" Oguri Fūyō, "Lazy Woman." Tayama Katai, *Life*.)

1909   Diet passes Press Law. Nagai Kafū, *French Stories, Pleaure*, ("The River Sumida," "Behind the Prison," "A Toast"). Oguri Fūyō, "Big Sister's Little Sister." Mori Ōgai, *Vita Sexualis*. Morita Sōhei, *Sooty Smoke* (publication delayed; expurgated). Tokuda Shūsei, "The Go-Between." Miyazaki Koshoshi, *Saikun no jihaku*. Gotō Chūgai, *Reirui*. Maupassant, *Collected Short Stories* (dedicated to Minister of Education Komatsubara). Sienkiewicz, *Bez Dogmatu*. Works of Gorki and Andreev.

1910   Naturalist movement disintegrating, Taishō literature beginning. High Treason case breaks in June; continues into January. September purge of socialist books said to take 91 titles. (Mori Ōgai, "Fasces," "The Tower of Silence," "The Lunchroom." Ishikawa Takuboku, "The Impasse of Our Age," *A Handful of Sand*. Tanizaki Jun'ichirō, "Tattoo." Masamune Hakuchō, "Faint Light.") Kinoshita Naoe, *Hi no hashira* (translated as *Pillar of Fire*), *Ryōjin no jihaku*, *Kojiki*, *Kikatsu*, *Rei ka niku ka*. Mizuno Yōshū, "The Inn," *Omiyo*, "Kage." Osanai Kaoru, *Fue*, "Hogo." Taoka Reiun, *Byōchū hōrō*.

1911   Twelve "anarchists" executed in January. Sōseki rejects doctorate in February. Committee on Literature established in May. Second Saionji cabinet inaugurated in August: censors relax for a year. Tanizaki Jun'ichirō, "Blizzards." Mizuno Yōshū, *Hekiga*. Aoyagi Yūbi, *Yūbi zenshū*. Satō Kōroku, *Sanjūhachinen*. Honma Hisashi, "Igai." (Masamune Hakuchō, "A Dangerous Character." Tokutomi Roka, "On Rebellion." Kinoshita Mokutarō, "Izumiya Dyers." Natsume Sōseki, *The Gate*, "What Will the Members of the Literary Academy Be Doing?" Shimazaki Tōson, *The Family*.)

1912   Meiji emperor dies in July; buried in September; "followed" by General Nogi Maresuke. Meiji 45 becomes Taishō 1. Third Katsura cabinet inaugurated in December. (Hiraide Shū, "The Plan.") Iwano Hōmei, *Hatten*.

1913   Third Katsura cabinet falls in February. Committee on Literature dissolved during Yamamoto cabinet's fiscal retrenchment in June. Hiratsuka Raichō founds women's magazine, *Seitō*. Women's movement takes off; immediately struck by censors. Hiraide Shū, "The Rebels." Tanizaki Jun'ichirō, *The Age to Learn of Love* refused stage license. Aoyagi Yūbi, "Kaku arubeki onna," *Seiyoku tetsugaku*. Fukuda Hideko, "Fujin mondai no kaiketsu," in February *Seitō*. Hiratsuka Raichō, "Yo no fujintachi ni," in April *Seitō*; *Marumado yori*. Zola, *Nana*. Flaubert, *Madame Bovary*. Works of Tolstoy. Nagai Kafū, *Koigoromo hana no kasamori* cut, (*Death of a Scribbler*. Arahata Kanson, "Escapists").

1914   (Tayama Katai, "Perpetual Calendar.") Flaubert, *Madame Bovary*. Maupassant, *Bel-Ami*, *Une Vie* (twice each), stories. Tolstoy, *The Power of Darkness*.

1915   Nagai Kafū, "Summer Dress" ("Natsusugata;" see Seidensticker, p. 75). Tanizaki Jun'ichirō, "Oiran." Harada Satsuki, "Goku-chū no onna yori otoko e," in June *Seitō*. Yosano Akiko, "Teisō ni tai-suru utagai."

1916   Tanizaki Jun'ichirō, "My Late Friend," "A Handsome Man," *The Age of Terror*, "Sorrow of the Heretic" (delayed). Yoshida Genjirō, "Fuku-bokushi." Nakamura Seiko, "Ningen no yoru." Various authors, "Josei no shin-kenkyū," in January *Shinkōron*. Miyajima Sukeo, *Kōfu*. Ōsugi Sakae, *Rōdō undō no tetsugaku*. Osanai Kaoru, "Utsuriyuku koi," *Berurin yawa*. Arishima Ikuma, *Nan'ō no hi*. Boccaccio, *The Decameron*. Flaubert, *Madame Bovary*.

1917   (Nagai Kafū publishes limited "secret edition" of *Udekurabe*. Not widely available uncut until 1956. Current translation, *Geisha in Rivalry* [Tokyo: Tuttle, 1963], made from colorless expurgated version.)

1918   Shiga Naoya, "Nigotta atama" (*Aru asa*). Satomi Ton, "Kanojo to seinen." Iwano Hōmei, "Irezumi-shi no ko," "Seishun no koro."

1921   (Tanizaki Jun'ichirō, "The Censor.")

1923   Great Kantō Earthquake of September 1 kills 90,000; injures 100,000; partially or totally destroys 680,000 homes; establishes permanent demarcation between "old" and "new" Japan. Home Ministry's entire collection of pre-1923 banned books lost in flames. Censorship figures for 1923 inordinately high owing to earthquake. Japan Naimushō, *Shuppan Keisatsu shiryō* (Reel no. 1, February 1924) indicates bans of 131 photographs and 101 picture postcards of corpses.

1924   Tanizaki Jun'ichirō, *A Fool's Love* forced out of *Osaka Asahi Shimbun*.

1926   Taishō emperor dies. Taishō 15 becomes Shōwa 1. Shōwa publishing boom takes off. (Tanizaki Jun'ichirō, "The Story of Tomoda and Matsunaga.") Fujimori Seikchi, *Gisei*, play based on love suicide of Arishima Takeo; September *Kaizō* responds with strong protests by Yamamoto Yūzō, Minobe Tatsukichi, etc.

1927   Censors end "consultation" system. Censorship System Reform League forms; does not survive mass arrest of suspected radicals in 1928.

1928   Tanaka cabinet carries out mass arrest of leftists on March 15. Kobayashi Takiji, "Sen-kyūhyaku-nijūhachinen sangatsu jūgonichi" (translated as "The Fifteenth of March, 1928").

1929   Kobayashi Takiji, "Kani kōsen" (translated as "The Factory Ship").

1931   "National emergency" begins with Manchurian Incident, Army's first step toward involving Japan in what will become Pacific War.

1933   Kobayashi Takiji tortured to death by Thought Police. Old liberals under fire in Takigawa Incident.

1934   Literary Chat Society founded.

1935   Movement for Clarification of the *Kokutai* begins.

1936   Cabinet Information Committee formed.

1937   China Incident involves Japan in full-scale war. Literary Chat Society disbanded in deference to new Imperial Arts Academy. Cabinet Information Committee upgraded to division. Army forms Four Company Society to control liberal magazines.

1938   Ishikawa Tatsuzō, *Ikite iru heitai*, discussed as *Living Soldiers* in Donald Keene, "The Barren Years." Ishikawa brought to trial for having depicted Japanese soldiers in China as "murdering, raping, pillaging maniacs" (Keene, p. 74).

1939   Tanizaki translation of *The Tale of Genji* begins publication.

1940   Cabinet Information Division upgraded to bureau. Japan Publishing Culture Association founded ("Culture" dropped from name in 1943).

1941   Rationing of paper begins. Niwa Fumio, *Chūnen*. Tokuda Shūsei ends serialization of *Shukuzu* when Cabinet Information Bureau consistently returns galley proofs covered with red-inked deletion orders.

1942   Japanese Literature Patriotic Association founded. Yokohama Incident begins.

1943   Japan Publishing Association carries out "industrial readjustment" of publishing industry. *Chūō Kōron* editors "voluntarily" end serialization of Tanizaki Jun'ichirō's *The Makioka Sisters*. Japanese Literature Patriotic Association publishes *Streetcorner Stories*.

1944   *Chūō Kōron* and *Kaizō* undergo "voluntary dissolution."

Abbreviations Used in the
Notes and Bibliography

AS: *Asahi Shimbun*
CK: *Chūō Kōron*
GNBD: *Gendai Nihon bungaku daijiten*
GNBZ: *Gendai Nihon bungaku zenshū*
KBHS: *Kindai bungei hikka shi*
KBHT: *Kindai bungaku hyōron taikei*
KS: *Kokumin Shimbun*
KZ: *Kafū zenshū*
MBHS: Mayabara, *Nihon bungei hakkin shi*
MBZ: *Meiji bungaku zenshū*
MGH: Midoro, *Meiji Taishō shi 1: Genronhen*
MITC: Mitchell, *Thought Control in Prewar Japan*
MN: *Monumenta Nipponica*
MOZ: *Mori Ōgai zenshū*
NBS: *Nihon bungaki shi*
NKBD: *Nihon kindai bungaku daijiten*
NKBT: *Nihon kindai bungaku taikei*
NoN: *Nihon oyobi Nihonjin*
NPBT: *Nihon puroretaria bungaku taikei*
OHSS: Odagiri, *Hakkin sakuhin shū* (1948)
OKS: Okudaira, "Ken'etsu seido"
OPC: Okudaira, "Political Censorship"
OZ: *Ōgai zenshū*
SK: *Shizenshugi no kenkyū*
SKG: *Shuppan Keisatsu Gaikan*
SSDS: *Shōwa shuppan dan'atsu shōshi*
SZ: *Sōseki zenshū*
THS: *Teihon Hiraide Shū shū*
THZ: *Teihon Hiraide Shū shū (zoku)*
TJZ: *Tanizaki Jun'ichirō zenshū*
TY: *Taiyō*
TZ: *Takuboku zenshū*

Notes

The place of publication, when Tokyo, has been omitted for books in Japanese. Titles of Japanese sources are left untranslated in the notes unless their meaning complements the discussion.

Chapter 1. INTRODUCTION

1. Richard McKeon, Robert K. Merton, and Walter Gellhorn, *The Freedom to Read*, pp. 20, 29.
2. "Taishō Democracy as the Pre-Stage for Japanese Militarism," in Bernard S. Silberman and H. D. Harootunian, eds., *Japan in Crisis*, p. 235.
3. Morris L. Ernst and Alan U. Schwartz, *Censorship*, pp. 53, 138.
4. Ibid., p. 54.
5. W. W. McLaren, "Japanese Government Documents," pp. 136, 138.
6. Masao Maruyama, *Thought and Behaviour in Modern Japanese Politics*, pp. 5, 6.

Chapter 2. THE LAW

1. OPC, p. 6. The 1887 version was somewhat less restrictive than the 1883 version, which Peter Figdor has shown to be "undoubtedly the harshest imposed upon the newspapers since the Meiji restoration." See his "Newspapers and Their Regulation in Early Meiji Japan, 1868–1883," in *Papers on Japan: Volume 6* (Cambridge: Harvard University, East Asian Research Center, 1972), p. 26. My discussion concentrates on the 1887 version as the one in effect when serious literature began to be censored. Note that "regulations" (*jōrei*) were issued by the preparliamentary Meiji government; the Diet made "laws" (*hō, hōritsu*).
2. OKS, p. 146.
3. Ibid.; NKBD 6:190, 195. The Press and Publication Laws were finally struck from the books on May 24, 1949.
4. For texts of the regulations, see MGH, pp. 407–16. Cf. W. W. McLaren, "Japanese Government Documents," pp. 543–57, and NKBD 6:133–64.

5. Naimushō Keihokyoku Toshoka (Ken'etsuka). OKS, p. 141, notes that the name change took place on December 6, 1940.

6. Keishichō.

7. Chian saibansho kenjikyoku.

8. *"Chian o bōgai shi matawa fūzoku o kairan suru mono."*

9. G. B. Sansom, *Japan*, p. 427.

10. George Sansom, *A History of Japan, 1615–1867*, p. 102.

11. Konta Yōzō, *Edo no hon'yasan*, pp. 63–66.

12. These are the approximate dates of the Genroku cultural era. The official year-period was 1688–1703.

13. Donald Keene, *World Within Walls*, p. 235.

14. Konta, *Edo no hon'yasan*, pp. 73–75.

15. Ibid., p. 75.

16. Peter F. Kornicki, "Nishiki no Ura," pp. 156-57.

17. Specifically, they were sentenced to "light banishment" (*kei-tsuihō*), which forbade the convict from entering the main populated areas of the country and included confiscation of home and property. There were two heavier degrees.

18. Kornicki, "Nishiki no Ura," pp. 158–160.

19. Konta, *Edo no hon'yasan*, p. 129.

20. Ibid., pp. 136, 142–43, 191.

21. Kornicki, "Nishiki no Ura," p. 162.

22. Ibid.

23. Keene, *World Within Walls*, pp. 430–34.

24. For the beginnings of modern journalism in Japan, see Huffman, *Politics of the Meiji Press*, pp. 47–49.

25. MGH, pp. 371-78. This section of the code included a variety of crimes, such as preaching extremist religious views and leaking government secrets.

26. Ibid., pp. 390, 413.

27. Ibid., p. 371; Huffman, *Politics of the Meiji Press*, pp. 51–60.

28. *"Minshin o dōran shi, inpū o yūdō suru."*

29. Mayabara Shigeo, *Nihon bungei hakkin shi*, p. 14.

30. MGH, pp. 43–49.

31. Ono Hideo, *Nihon shimbun shi*, pp. 25, 27. For a recent treatment of this period, see Huffman, *Politics of the Meiji Press*, pp. 104–05.

32. MGH, p. 396. OPC, p. 5.

33. OPC, p. 1.

34. The transitional ordinance appeared on October 12, 1880. MGH, pp. 127, 399. OPC, p. 6.

35. OKS, p. 156–57 n9.

36. SKG 1 (1930): 25–29. For a detailed explication of the list, see SKG 1 (1931): 9–17. On the 1926 bill, see Odagiri Hideo and Fukuoka Ikichi, eds., *Zōhoban Shōwa shoseki-shimbun-zasshi hakkin nenpyō*, 1:7–11.

37. OPC, p. 49.

38. OKS, p. 151; OPC, p. 49.

39. OKS, pp. 147–48.

40. MGH, p. 132; Figdor, "Newspapers and Their Regulation," p. 26.
41. OKS, p. 138.
42. MITC, pp. 35–36.
43. OKS, p. 180.
44. MBHS, pp. 31–32.
45. OKS, p. 138.
46. Ibid., pp. 172–73. The phrase was *"Kōshitsu no songen o bōtoku shi."*
47. *"Shakai no chitsujo matawa fūzoku o kairan suru jikō."*
48. This power was also granted to the Minister of Colonization, a post that existed from April 1896 to September 1897.
49. OKS, p. 150.
50. "Hatsubai kinshi to genkō ken'etsu," NoN (February 1, 1908), p. 202.
51. Hakubunkan is known to have done this when the sale of Nagai Kafū's *French Stories* (*Furansu monogatari*) was banned in 1909. See below, chap. 9.
52. OKS, p. 162 n28.
53. Odagiri Hideo, *Hakkin sakuhin shū* (1957), pp. 270, 273.
54. SSDS, pp. 37–38.
55. SKG 2 (1932): 25, 69–70, 142, 144, 145–46.
56. This is the term used in Harry Emerson Wildes, *Social Currents in Japan.*
57. Ibid., p. 113; OKS, pp. 180–84; OPC, p. 55.
58. OKS, pp. 184–87; OPC, p. 24.
59. SSDS, p. 176, slightly revised in accordance with SKG 2 (1932): 142, 145–46. According to the latter, SKG 2 (1932): 146, "dismemberment and restitution" was a new technique instituted on September 1, 1927. It was intended for books that had actually been banned but were given a last chance. Hatanaka Shigeo (SSDS, p. 176) says this would be done in the case of a deletion order and writes the term *bunkatsu kanpu* as *-hanpu*, but the situation he describes is clearly one involving seized publications.
60. See, for example, SKG 2 (1932): 70–146.
61. See below, chap. 9, p. 000.
62. OPC, p. 12; NKBD 6:150.
63. SSDS, pp. 182–83. See also below, chap. 9, n37. The parenthetical remarks come from author's interview of July 9, 1981.
64. SSDS, p. 181.
65. Ibid., pp. 182–83.
66. Ibid., pp. 178, 186.
67. Matsuura Sōzō, *Senryō-ka no genron dan'atsu,* pp. 69–72.

Chapter 3. TRADITIONAL IRONY AND OLD-FASHIONED TRASH

1. MBZ 4:11.
2. Several shrines in the Yanagibashi area were devoted to Katō Kiyomasa (1562–1611), a great general of the Azuchi-Momoyama period. See *Ryūkyō shinshi* in NKBT 1:227 n12.

3. NKBT 1:226–27 or MBZ 4:21–22.

4. *Tokugawa jikki* and *Nochi kagami*. MBZ 4:397.

5. NKBT 1:468.

6. Maeda Ai, *Narushima Ryūhoku* (Asahi Shimbunsha, 1976), p. 168. Nakamura Mitsuo, *Meiji bungaku shi*, pp. 62–63. Karaki Junzō sees him as part of a longer tradition in *Muyōsha no keifu* (Chikuma shobō, 1960), pp. 100–07.

7. Ono Hideo, *Nihon shimbun shi*, pp. 28, 30.

8. Kanesada Hanazono, *Journalism in Japan and Its Early Pioneers* (Osaka: Osaka Shuppan-sha, 1926), p. 41.

9. MGH, pp. 82–83; Ono, *Nihon shimbun shi*, p. 31; and James L. Huffman, *Politics of the Meiji Press*, pp. 113–14, give further details on this strange service.

10. Hanazono, *Journalism in Japan*, p. 42.

11. MBZ 4:395.

12. NBS, p. 156.

13. KS (March 1, 1908), p. 1.

14. MGH, pp. 150, 153, gives the odd pairing of *dai* and *ko*. Honma Hisao, *Meiji bungaku shi*, 1:62, gives *ō* and *ko*. Ono, *Nihon shimbun shi*, p. 21, gives *ko* but is silent on the "big." Huffman, *Politics of the Meiji Press*, p. 221 n42, gives his reasons for using *dai* and *shō*. I give up.

15. G. B. Sansom, *The Western World and Japan*, p. 419.

16. NKBT 60:213; Honma, *Meiji bungaku shi 1*, p. 62.

17. Asai Kiyoshi, "Shimbun shōsetsu no hensen," p. 87.

18. Honma, *Meiji bungaku shi 1*, p. 63.

19. Ibid., pp. 79, 86; Fujimura Tsukuru, ed., *Nihon bungaku daijiten*, 3:1055.

20. G. B. Sansom, *The Western World and Japan*, pp. 409–10.

21. Honma, *Meiji bungaku shi 1*, p. 79.

22. Ibid., p. 82.

23. Asai, "Shimbun shōsetsu no hensen," p. 87.

24. Nakamura, *Meiji bungaku shi*, pp. 73–74. The names are Kokofu Seibun, Sakigakeya Oken, and Wakokuya Minji.

25. G. B. Sansom, *The Western World and Japan*, pp. 401, 412–14.

26. Fujimura, *Nihon bungaku daijiten*, 1:725; NKBD 6:211–12; MBHS, p. 312.

27. MGH, p. 154.

Chapter 4. DEVELOPING REALISM: THE CENSORS BEGIN TO NOTICE

1. For a translation and study, see Marleigh Grayer Ryan, *Japan's First Modern Novel: Ukigumo of Futabatei Shimei* (New York: Columbia University Press, 1967).

2. Kunikida Doppo, "Kōyō Sanjin" (1902), in *Kunikida Doppo zenshū*, 1:426–35.

3. From a conversation in 1891, reported by Tayama Katai, *Tōkyō no sanjūnen*, p. 44.

4. Ibid., p. 33.

5. MBZ 18:3.

6. GNBZ 4:360.

7. Ibid., p. 366.

8. Okano Takeo, *Kindai Nihon meicho kaidai*, pp. 312–24; GNBD, pp. 995–96.

9. SK 1:171.

10. OHSS, p. 411.

11. Ibid., p. 52.

12. Ibid., p. 409; MBZ 65:415.

13. OHSS, p. 59.

14. Kyōka, most notably, turned to the mysterious, sensual world that he was to create in his unique body of writings.

15. The name is so glossed in *Myōjō*; "Hō" is the usual reading.

16. The incident is alluded to in Sanford Goldstein and Seishi Shinoda, *Tangled Hair*, p. 16.

17. I have not been able to identify these illustrations, but a colleague in the art department assures me that they are French and very ordinary.

18. *Myōjō* (November 1900): 7, 11.

19. MBHS, pp. 70–71.

20. Yamada Bimyō, "Kochō," *Kokumin no Tomo* (January 1889).

21. MBHS, pp. 71–73. The conservative magazine *Nihon oyobi Nihonjin* (NoN) became an especially active proselytizer in 1908, and the new book notices of that time frequently mentioned books on nude art.

22. "The Sino-Japanese War of 1894–95 and Its Cultural Effects in Japan," in Donald Keene, *Landscapes and Portraits*, p. 289.

23. Okano, *Kindai Nihon meicho kaidai*, p. 320.

24. See pp. 1–5 of the special December 1900 issue of *Myōjō*.

25. Shimada Hiroshi, "*Kokumin no Tomo* to junbungaku rinen," *Bungaku* 30 (October 1962): 4.

26. GNBZ 5:413; OHSS, pp. 415–16.

27. OHSS, p. 69.

28. Ibid., p. 91.

29. Ibid., pp. 413-14.

30. According to an interview with Roan, "'Yaregaki' kinshi tōji no kaisō," TY (August 1, 1909), pp. 135–36.

31. These are *Kōshoku ichidai otoko* and *Kōshoku ichidai onna*.

32. OHSS, p. 26. Masamune Hakuchō would write an almost identical critique in 1926; nothing had changed. See *Masamune Hakuchō zenshū*, 13 vols. (Shinchōsha, 1965), 7:89.

33. MBHS, pp. 171–72. Shakai mondai shiryō kenkyūkai, ed., *Shimbunshi hō narabi-ni Shuppan hō ihan jiken hanreishū*, 2 vols. (Tōyō bunka sha, 1980), 1:15–18.

34. MBZ 24:244. Loth, *The Erotic in Literature*, p. 127.

35. MBZ 24:244.

36. Uchida Roan, "'Yaregaki' ni tsuite," MBZ 24:243–45.

37. GNBD, pp. 126–27.

38. Roan, "Shakuhyō reigo" (August 1899), quoted in OHSS, pp. 417–18.

39. Kodama Kagai, *Shakaishugi shishū* (Shakaishugi toshobu, 1903). See Jō Ichirō, *Hakkinbon hyakunen*, p. 84.

40. OHSS, pp. 421–23; GNBZ 18:421. The influential acquaintance was Yamaji Aizan. On kissing, see MBHS, pp. 77–106.

Chapter 5. THE RISE OF NATURALISM

1. Kenneth B. Pyle, "The Technology of Japanese Nationalism," pp. 56–57.

2. Ishikawa Takuboku, "Bungaku to seiji," TZ 9:157.

3. F. G. Notehelfer, *Kōtoku Shūsui, Portrait of a Japanese Radical* pp. 88–108; quotation p. 105. See also Itoya Toshio, *Taigyaku jiken*, pp. 23–25.

4. NKBT 32:73. The poem is entitled "Kimi shinitamō koto nakare." For another translation, see Masao Maruyama, *Thought and Behaviour in Modern Japanese Politics*, pp. 154–56.

5. Satō Haruo, *Akiko mandara*, 31:447–52.

6. *Myōjō* (November 1904); 98–100.

7. "'Shiika no kotsuzui' to wa nani zo ya," *Myōjō* (February 1905): 10–20.

8. *Kiken naru shisō, kiken no shisō, kiken shisō*, etc.

9. Maruyama, *Thought and Behaviour in Modern Japanese Politics*, p. 147.

10. MGH, pp. 194–201.

11. Ishikawa Takuboku, "Kire-gire ni kokoro ni ukanda kanji to kaisō," TZ 9:131–32.

12. Notehelfer, *Kōtoku Shūsui*, pp. 131, 146.

13. According to Tanizaki Jun'ichirō, "Hōkan," TJZ 1:189.

14. Oka Yoshitake, "Nichiro sensō-go ni okeru atarashii sedai no seichō," *Shisō* 512 (February 1967): 137–40.

15. Special unsigned issue of *Taiyō* entitled *Bungeishi* (February 20, 1909), pp. 83–85. Takayama Chogyū is here credited with having made the remark on embarrassment.

16. Donald Keene, "Shiki and Takuboku," in *Landscapes and Portraits*, p. 164.

17. Tayama Katai, "Rokotsu naru byōsha," GNBZ 20:391.

18. KHBT 3:43–49, 476.

19. Hasegawa Tenkei, "Shizenshugi ni tai-suru gokai," TY (April 1, 1908), p. 153. Here, Tenkei is not talking about the other modern writers often lumped together as "antinaturalists" but defenders of traditional values who were opposed to naturalists and antinaturalists alike.

20. Kunikida Doppo, "Byōshōroku," *Kunikida Doppo zenshū* 9:53.

21. Nunami Keion, "Doppo ron" (1906), in *Kunikida Doppo zenshū* 10:367.

22. Kōbōshi [pseudonym], "Bungei jihyō," NoN (January 1, 1908), pp. 55–57.

23. Jirō [pseudonym], "Kenzen naru shisō to wa nani zo ya," *Teikoku Bungaku* (February 1, 1907): 282.

24. TY (January 1, 1908), p. 127.

25. Ibid., p. 139. For a similar statement, see "Nikuyoku to bungei no chōwa," *Shinchō* (January 1908): 2–3. This feature, a joint effort of Fūyō, Shun'yō, Shūkō, Chōkō, and Seika, reads like an exploiter's manifesto.

26. Takita Choin, "Teibi bundan gaikan," CK (January 1908): 220.

27. CK (October 1907): Appendix, pp. 1–40.

28. SK 2:11.

29. MBZ 68:385.

30. See Hasegawa Tenkei, "Kinji shōsetsudan no keikō," TY (February 1, 1908), p. 153.

31. *The Sun Trade Journal* (October 1, 1908), pp. 1–4. I have improved the English slightly and emended the Saga dialect *"shijenshugi"* to the standard Tokyo spelling. The April issue contains some more strong opinions by Japonicus: "By all consent, the most rotten city in the world—rotten morally and socially, is Berlin." See *The Sun Trade Journal* (April 1, 1909), p. 21.

32. NKBT 4:303; quoted from the translation by Glenn W. Shaw (Tokyo: Hokuseido Press, 1927), p. 135.

33. NKBT 4:338.

34. See translation by Shaw, p. 189, for the publisher's notice at the end of chapter 59. In the newspaper, chapter 23 was erroneously labeled 24, and all subsequent chapters followed suit. As a result, the suppressed passage originally appeared as part of chapter 60 in the December 29 *Asahi* and was missing from chapter 60 in the book. Shaw has corrected the error. NKBT 4:263 n5, 336 n3, 338 n1.

35. For an excellent study of this phase of Sōseki's career, see Matsui Sakuko, *Natsume Sōseki As a Critic of English Literature* (Tokyo: Center for East Asian Cultural Studies, 1975).

36. MBZ 65:426–27.

37. SZ 14:559–61.

38. SZ 11:493–94.

39. Uchida Roan, "Futabatei Shimei no isshō," *Omoidasu hitobito*, GNBZ 97:88.

40. Hamao Arata, "Daigaku to Sōseki," *Shibugaki* (December 1917), quoted in SK 2:32.

41. See Akutagawa's "Haguruma" (1927), translated by BeongcheonYu as "The Cogwheel," *Chicago Review* 18, no. 2 (1965); and Mishima's *Taiyō to tetsu* (1968), translated by John Bester as *Sun and Steel* (Tokyo: Kodansha International, 1970).

42. *Shinchō* (November 1908): 12–13, 16.

43. SZ 16:608–09.

44. SZ 16:626–29.

45. *Shinchō* (October 1908): 14–15.

46. "Bungei no tetsugakuteki kiso," SZ 11:94–96. Parenthetical interpretation of *kangenteki kanka* based on SZ 11:90–92.

47. "Sōsakka no taido," SZ 11:139–40. See also SZ 11:221 for a statement of Sōseki's dislike for writers who affect a superior air.

48. *Higan-sugi made*, SZ 5:7. Doi Takeo's interpretation of this preface as a satire is a brilliant stroke, but it misses the self-critical implications in Sōseki's use of the word "ordinary." See Doi Takeo, *The Psychological World of Satsume Sōseki*, trans. William J. Tyler (Cambridge: Harvard University Press, 1976), pp. 71–72.

49. Natsume Sōseki, "Dōraku to shokugyō," SZ 11:312.

50. See TY (June 1, 1907), p. 227; CK (April 1908): 76, 161–63; and CK (October 1908): 146–47.

51. SK 2:10–11.

52. In *Nijūhachinin shū* (Shinchōsha), a volume published by friends of the dying Kunikida Doppo to help defray his hospital expenses. Edited by Fūyō and Katai, it contained fiction and criticism by twenty-eight contributors, mostly of the naturalist school. The last line of Fūyō's story is deleted in this volume. See also MBZ 65:218–25.

53. MBZ 65:418.

54. Quoted in MBHS, p. 182.

55. MBZ 65:419; Jō Ichirō, *Hakkinbon hyakunen*, p. 97.

56. MBZ 65:299.

57. Hasegawa Tenkei, "Kinji shōsetsudan no keikō," TY (February 1, 1908), p. 153.

58. Ishikawa Takuboku, "Jidai heisoku no genjō," NKBT 23:473.

59. GNBD, p. 190; MBZ 65:430.

60. On the style of *The Broken Commandment*, see Hankatsū [pseudonym], "Shōsetsu no gobi," CK (October 1908): 147.

61. "Yo ga *Kusamakura*," SZ 16:543–45.

62. Letter to Suzuki Miekichi, dated October 26, 1906 in SZ 14:491–93.

63. "Takahama Kyoshi-cho *Keitō* Jo," SZ 11:550–60.

64. "Bungeikai," TY (February 1, 1907), p. 245.

65. Kōbōshi, "Bungei jihyō," NoN (January 1, 1908), p. 57.

66. Takita Choin, "Teibi bundan gaikan," CK (January 1908), p. 217.

67. "Bundan," CK (February 1908): 161.

68. "Sōseki ron," CK (March 1908): 34–56; quotations from pp. 53–54.

69. Ibid., pp. 35–36.

70. Ibid., p. 36.

71. GNBZ 84:305.

72. SZ 4:20; quoted from the translation by Jay Rubin, *Sanshiro* (Seattle, University of Washington Press, 1977), p. 14.

73. Compare Ikuta Kizan's phrase, "*ikite atsui chi o moru ningen*" (GNBZ 84:311), with this from the opening passage of *Sore kara*: "*Kono keishō o kiku koto nashi ni ikite irareta nara,—chi o moru fukuro ga, toki o moru fukuro no yō o kanenakatta nara*" (SZ 4:314). Sōseki had read—and apparently had been impressed with the newness of—a story of Kizan's in 1905 (SZ 16:452).

74. For example, see Doppo's "Gyūniku to jagaimo" (1901); "Shuchū nikki" (1902); "Shōjikimono" (1903); and "Okamoto no techō" (1906).

75. "Naturalism in Japanese Literature," *Harvard Journal of Asiatic Studies* 28 (1968): 169.

76. Letter to Kanō Kōkichi, dated October 23, 1906, in SZ 14:483.

77. According to *Vita Sexualis* (*Ita sekusuarisu*, July 1909), in MOZ 1:102. See also the translation by Kazuji Ninomiya and Sanford Goldstein, *Vita Sexualis* (Tokyo: Tuttle, 1972), p. 25.

78. "Tsuina," MOZ 1:72; quoted in Richard John Bowring, *Mori Ōgai and the Modernization of Japanese Culture* (Cambridge: Cambridge University Press, 1979), p. 155.

Chapter 6. NATURALISM EXPLODES IN THE PRESS

1. See AS (February 9, 1908), p. 6. The issue was released on February 1 and banned on February 7. For a general treatment emphasizing legal aspects, see MBHS, pp. 161–71.

2. MITC, pp. 72, 83.

3. AS (February 9, 1908), p. 6; AS (February 28, 1908), pp. 4, 6; AS (March 6, 1908), p. 6; KS (February 10, 1908), p. 2; KS (February 11, 1908), p. 4; KS (February 13, 1908), p. 5; KS (February 28, 1908), p. 4; KS (February 29, 1908), p. 4; KS (March 1, 1908), p. 1; KS (March 6, 1908), p. 4.

4. KS (February 11, 1908), p. 4.

5. "Tōdai kyōiku no ichi-heikon," NoN (March 15, 1908), p. 7.

6. "Bungeikai," TY (August 1, 1908), p. 226.

7. Jō Ichirō, *Zoku hakkinbon,* pp. 25–26.

8. SK 2:11.

9. MBHS, pp. 171–80.

10. KBHS, pp. 134–35.

11. GNBZ 84:325–26.

12. Ibid., p. 318.

13. KBHS, p. 52; MBHS, p. 161; GNBZ 84:415.

14. GNBZ 84:309, 310.

15. KS (February 10, 1908), p. 2.

16. KS (February 11, 1908), p. 4.

17. KBHS, pp. 99–104. "Hatsubai kinshi no hyōjun," TY (June 1, 1908), pp. 140–43.

18. Morris L. Ernst, and Alan U. Schwartz, *Censorship,* p. 54; Harry M. Clor, *Obscenity and Public Morality* (Chicago: University of Chicago Press, 1969), pp. 31–32.

19. Shiritsu Nihon Joshi Daigakkō, founded 1901; later renamed Nihon Joshi Daigaku.

20. Quoted in SK 1:515.

21. MBHS, pp. 160–61; KS (March 24, 1908), p. 4; KS (March 25, 1908), p. 4; KS (April 6, 1908), p. 2; KS (April 7, 1908), p. 4; KS (April 8, 1908), p. 4; AS (March 24, 1908), p. 6; AS (March 25, 1908), p. 6; AS (June 30, 1909), p. 5; NoN (July 15, 1908), p. 42; NoN (September 1, 1908), p. 6; NoN (August 1, 1910), p. 40. See also Mori Ōgai, *Vita Sexualis,* MOZ 1:103; *Vita Sexualis,* trans. by Ninomiya and Goldstein, pp. 26–27; Tanizaki Jun'ichirō, "The Affair of Two Watches," TJZ 1:54–55; Nagai Kafū, "Kawaya no mado," KZ 13:179. The name is also pronounced "Deppakame."

22. Tōseishi [pseudonym], "Bungei hachimenkan," NoN (May 1, 1908), p. 56.

23. KS (December 30, 1907), p. 6.

24. There is a noteworthy, but untranslatable, pun in chapter 55 after Okinu saves the daimyō from drowning. When she explains that she learned how to swim so well by diving for abalone as a youngster, he replies, "Nani? Awabi-tori o shite otta to? Aa, dōri de, yoku suitsuku to omotta—a ha ha ha."

25. Monoshiri-ō [pseudonym], "Kōdan to gishi," NoN (March 15, 1910), p. 109.
26. KS (December 8 and 12, 1907).
27. Teisui's biographies of the Loyal Forty-Seven followed *Okinu* in *Kokumin Shimbun*, continuing from April 23, 1908, to February 18, 1911, plus a sequel.

Chapter 7. LITERATURE AND LIFE / ART AND THE STATE

1. *Hōritsu Shimbun*, no. 482 (1908): 378.
2. See Maeda Ai, *Kindai dokusha no seiritsu* (Yūseidō, 1973), pp. 132–67.
3. For an especially dramatic—and untranslatable—statement on the value-neutrality of naturalism, see "Shizen-ha ni taisuru gokai," TY (April 1, 1908), p. 153: "Shizen-ha wa ratai no mama, chijō ni rikkyaku-shite, ganzen ni kuru genjitsu o byōsha suru nomi de, THE REST IS SILENCE."
4. "Bungei shinsa-in no hitsuyō," TY (June 1, 1908), pp. 158–60.
5. "Bungei no torishimari ni tsuite (bungeiin no setsuritsu o nozomu)," TY (November 1, 1908), pp. 153–57.
6. "Ware o-shite jiyū-ni katarishimeyo," TY (August 1, 1908), pp. 153–54. The title of the piece is misleading. It is not an appeal to the authorities for free speech but to the reader for permission to write at random.
7. KBHT 3:226–32.
8. SK 2:9.
9. SK 2:51–54.
10. Wada Kingo, "'Heimen byōsha ron' no shūhen," MBZ 67:375–82.
11. GNBZ 20:5–30.
12. MBZ 67:57–63.
13. SK 2:160.
14. GNBZ 20:130.
15. Ibid., p. 106.
16. SK 2:170.
17. Ishikawa Takuboku, "Kire-gire ni kokoro ni ukanda kanji to kaisō," *Subaru* (December 1909), in TZ 9:131–42.
18. "Hatsubai kinshi no konpon mondai," TY (June 1, 1908), in MBZ 24:270–71.

Chapter 8. THE GOVERNMENT MOVES RIGHT

1. F. G. Notehelfer, *Kōtoku Shūsui*, pp. 145–46.
2. Ara Masahito, *Sōseki kenkyū nenpyō*, p. 313. The term for "four horsemen" is *shitennō*. Notehelfer, *Kōtoku Shūsui*, pp. 146, 156–60.
3. Mori Ōgai, "Bungei no shugi," OZ 15:457–59.
4. Kenneth B. Pyle, "The Technology of Japanese Nationalism," pp. 58–61.
5. Ōtsuki Takeshi, and Matsumura Ken'ichi, *Aikokushin kyōiku no shiteki kyūmei*, p. 155.

6. Pyle, "The Technology of Japanese Nationalism," p. 61; Fujiwara Kiyozō, *Meiji Taishō Shōwa kyōiku shisō gakusetsu jinbutsu shi*, 2:825. The document was popularly known as the "Rescript on Thrift and Diligence." See Fujii Kenjirō, "Kokka, jindō, kojin," CK (January 1909):32.

7. *Teikoku Kyōiku*, no. 323 (November 1908):118−19, quoted in Ōtsuki and Matsumura, *Aikokushin kyōiku no shiteki kyūmei*, p. 154.

8. Wilbur M. Fridell, "Government Ethics Textbooks in Late Meiji Japan," p. 826.

9. Fridell, "Government Ethics Textbooks," pp. 828−32. See also Roger F. Hackett, *Yamagata Aritomo in the Rise of Modern Japan, 1838−1922*, pp. 14−15, 246, on the sources of Yoshida Shoin's pro-imperial ideas and the genuine devotion of his disciple, Yamagata, to the throne.

10. Saburō Ienaga, *The Pacific War*, p. 48.

11. Fujiwara Kiyozō, *Meiji Taishō Shōwa kyōiku shisō gakusetsu jinbutsu shi*, 2:823−26.

12. For example, see Ueda Mannen, "Bungei-jō no ni-mondai," CK (July 1908):19; "Bungeikai," TY (December 1, 1908), p. 227; "Uwasa," TY (January 1, 1909), p. 96; "Kansōroku," *Teikoku Bungaku* (January 1909):149; Ueda Mannen, "Bungeiin no setsuritsu ni tsuite," *Teikoku Bungaku* (March 1909):18−22.

13. KBHT 3:402.

14. AS (January 21, 1909), p. 5; AS (January 22, 1909), p. 4; KS (January 21, 1909), p. 4; KS (January 22, 1909), p. 4; OZ 20:397; OZ 19:528−31; TY (February 1, 1909), p. 221; NBS, p. 435; Gotō Chūgai, *Meiji bundan kaiko roku* (1933−1935), in GNBZ 97:194−97.

15. Bandō Tarō [pseudonym], "Bunkai zakki," NoN (February 11, 1909), p. 90; "Bungei zatsuji," NoN (May 1, 1909), p. 80; ibid. (August 15, 1910), p. 90; "Komatsubara Bunshō enzetsu," KS (May 24, 1911), p. 3. Imai Yasuko, "Meiji-matsu bundan no ichi-chōkanzu," p. 45 n5, suggests that the banning of Ōgai's *Vita Sexualis* might have been connected with the postponement.

16. "Bunshō no bunshi shōtai," TY (February 1, 1909), pp. 155−58.

17. "Bunshi shōtai kai ni okeru hakken," CK (February 1909):153−56.

18. See advertisements and contest results in TY (February 1, 1909), pp. 160, 227; TY (May 1, 1909), p. 226. Natsume Sōseki had 14,539 votes, followed by Shimazaki Tōson (12,115), Tokutomi Roka (10,450), Masamune Hakuchō (9,120), and Kosugi Tengai (8,385). For Sōseki's written refusal, which appeared in the lavish special issue of *Taiyō* on June 15, 1909, see SZ 11:209 and chap. 12 below.

Chapter 9. Working Under the Mature System

1. Anonymous, "Bungei," TY (January 20, 1910): Appendix, p. 241; Takita Choin, "Kiyū bundan gaikan," CK (January 1910):340; and others.

2. See below, p. 299, n4.

3. Furoku, "Dai 25-kai Teikoku Gikai shi," TY (May 15, 1909), p. 1.

4. For text, see MGH, pp. 442−49.

5. OKS, p. 151 n23.

6. MGH, pp. 231–41; Furoku, "Dai 25-kai Teikoku Gikai shi," p. 39; "Shūgiin no giji ni agaritaru honshi zengō hatsubai kinshi mondai no tenmatsu," NoN (April 1, 1910), p. 124.

7. "Shimbunshi hō no kaisei," TY (May 1, 1909), pp. 92–96.

8. AS (July 8, 1909), p. 4.

9. Referring specifically to (and reported in) NoN (April 1, 1910), pp. 123–32. The magazine had been banned for an article on sensitive military matters, "Gunji shigi," NoN (March 15, 1910), pp. 17–28.

10. Jō Ichirō has noted that page 98 of the Police Bureau's *Kinshi tankōbon mokuroku* indicates that action was taken on March 27, but he fails to observe that the year indicated is 1908, which would tend to throw suspicion on the accuracy of the rest of the date. There is no reason for us to doubt Kafū's own assertion, cited below, that the book was banned on the day the Home Ministry received it. Jō, *Hakkinbon hyakunen*, p. 102.

11. "Kakademo no ki," KZ 14:368. The company was Hakubunkan, publishers of *Taiyō*.

12. Edward Seidensticker, *Kafū the Scribbler*, p. 27.

13. KZ 3:646–47.

14. Seidensticker, *Kafū the Scribbler*, p. 27.

15. KZ 12:26–27; quoted from Seidensticker, *Kafū the Scribbler*, p. 27, except that "drunks" has been revised to "drunken gentlemen."

16. CK (December 1952) printed the play one month before the Chūō Kōron-sha publishers released this volume (24) of the Complete Works.

17. KZ 3:643.

18. Ibid., p. 629.

19. Ibid., p. 625.

20. Seidensticker, *Kafū the Scribbler*, p. 28.

21. KZ 18:272–76. For publication details of *Furansu monogatari*, see KZ 3:639–52 and KZ 12:551–52.

22. "*Furansu monogatari* no hatsubai kinshi," *Yomiuri Shimbun* (April 11, 1909); KZ 26:87–90.

23. "'Ane no imōto' no hatsubai kinshi," KZ 27:25–26.

24. "Betsu ni nan'tomo omowanakatta," TY (August 1, 1909); KZ 27:27–28.

25. Seidensticker, *Kafū the Scribbler*, p. 33.

26. The July 1909 issue of *Shinshōsetsu* was banned for the story "Kumori" by Takasaki Shungetsu. KZ 4:469.

27. KZ 4:18, 35–36.

28. KZ 4:472.

29. See note 24 above.

30. KZ 4:27, 471, 472.

31. KZ 4:27, 472. For some other examples, see ibid., pp. 470–73.

32. See note 11 above.

33. KZ 4:55–56. See also ibid., pp. 66–67.

34. "Konnen no tokuchō mittsu," *Bunshō sekai* (December 1909), in Nihon bungaku Kenkyū Shiryō Kankōkai, ed., *Nagai Kafū* (Yūseidō, 1971), pp. 259–60.

35. KZ 4:152–73; quotations from ibid., pp. 168, 173.

36. See *Nagai Kafū* (note 34 above), pp. 245–47; Mori Ōgai, "Jidan henpen," OZ 19:532.

37. CK (July 1909):1–2.

38. CK (May 1909):95; KZ 4:156.

39. CK (May 1909):103; KZ 4:163, 164. Compare CK (May 1909):109 line 16, and KZ 4:167 line 5. See also KZ 4:482–84.

40. The book must have been submitted to the Police Bureau at least three days prior to its publication date of September 20, 1909, and Bureau records show September 24 as the date it was banned. See Naimushō Keihokyoku, ed., *Kinshi tankōbon mokuroku*, p. 20. As suggested in note 10 above, however, this is not an entirely reliable source; the year indicated here is Meiji 24, an obvious error for Meiji 42 (1909).

41. See "'Suisan no ji' o meguru ronsō," in *Nagai Kafū*, pp. 256–58, 272–86; "Suisan no ji," *Waseda Bungaku* (February 1910), KBHT 3:391; Mitsui Kōshi, "Saikin no kansō," NoN (March 1, 1910), p. 84.

42. For a detailed publication history, see KZ 4:467–84. Seidensticker discusses "Fukagawa no uta" and provides a translation of "Botan no kyaku," both from *Pleasure*, in his *Kafū the Scribbler*, pp. 33–35, 219–25.

43. Reprinted in OHSS, pp. 193–226.

44. See his incredible—and very funny—"Nagoya onna ron," CK (March 1910):52–108, and his "Yukiguni bijin ron," CK (January 1911):103–23.

45. Matsui Hakken, "Ningen o egakazaru shōsetsu," CK (August 1909):12–14.

46. SSDS, pp. 26–28.

47. "*Futari gakō* no hatsubai kinshi," TY (January 1, 1910), pp. 35–36. The Sienkiewicz novel was probably *Bez dogmatu* (1891).

48. *Tokyo Nichi-nichi Shimbun* (July 1909), quoted in Mayabara Shigeo, *Nihon bungei hakkin shi*, pp. 28–29.

49. Hofūsoku Keirō [pseudonym], "Bungei torishimari no yukue," NoN (November 1, 1909), pp. 95–98. For other contemporary comments on censorship, see the *Sun Trade Journal* (January 1, 1909), p. 22; TY (July 1, 1909), p. 159; TY (September 1, 1909), p. 227; NoN (July 15, 1909), p. 70; NoN (May 1, 1910), p. 67.

50. Hasegawa Tenkei, "Goshippu," TY (August 1, 1909), p. 158; Satō Kōroku, "Kodomo ni tsukiataru jidōsha," TY (August 1, 1909), p. 140.

51. For some of the controversy surrounding this story, see "Bungei zatsuji," NoN (May 1, 1909), p. 80; Richard John Bowring, *Mori Ōgai and the Modernization of Japanese Culture*, p. 108.

52. Mori Ōgai, "Daihakken," MOZ 1:86; Tayama Katai, "Rokotsu naru byōsha," GNBZ 20:391–93.

53. MOZ 1:103, quoted from Bowring, *Mori Ōgai*, pp. 137–38. For a complete (if not entirely reliable) translation, see Kazuji Ninomiya and Sanford Goldstein, *Vita Sexualis* (Tokyo: Tuttle, 1972).

54. MOZ 1:154, quoted from Bowring, *Mori Ōgai*, p. 139.

55. MOZ 1:67.

56. This story appears mistakenly on several lists of banned materials. For details, see Hasegawa Izumi, *Ōgai "Ita sekusuarisu" kō* (Meiji shoin, 1968), pp. 15–19, 25.

57. Bowring, *Mori Ōgai*, pp. 65–67.

58. OZ 13:235, quoted from Bowring, *Mori Ōgai*, pp. 80–81.

59. Bowring, *Mori Ōgai*, p. 123.

60. "Chinmoku no tō," MOZ 1:281, quoted from Bowring, *Mori Ōgai*, p. 187.

61. "Gendai shisō," OZ 16:377, quoted from Bowring, *Mori Ōgai*, p. 180.

62. See Ōgai's diary entry, OZ 20:443–44, and his letter to Kako Tsurudo of August 1, 1909, in OZ 22:272. "Ihō," TY (September 1, 1909), p. 227, surmises that *Vita Sexualis* was the cause of the ban and also notes the banning of the July and August 1909 issues of *Shinsei*, remarking on the authorities' increasing severity.

63. "Bungei zatsuji," NoN (September 15, 1909), p. 80.

64. Diary entry, OZ 20:472; "Bungei zatsuji," NoN (September 1, 1911), p. 81.

65. Satō Kōroku, p. 140. (See note 50 above.)

66. Hofūsoku Keirō, pp. 97–98. (See note 49 above.)

67. Diary entry, OZ 20:439.

68. Takita Choin, "Kiyū bundan gaikan," CK (January 1910):338; "Bungei zatsuji," NoN (March 15, 1910), p. 78. The original price was twenty-five sen. For an example of an advertisement meant to exploit the banning of an author's previous book, see CK (March 1911):93, facing page.

69. William J. Sebald, trans., *The Criminal Code of Japan* (Kobe: The Japan Chronicle Press, 1936), p. 128. Note that the retailer was not treated under the Press or Publication Laws but under the Penal Code.

70. Quoted in Hiraide Shū, "Hatsubai kinshi ron," THS p. 175.

71. AS (January 6, 7, 8, 1910), in MBZ 24:252–55.

72. KBHS, p. 57. The first Complete Works appeared between February 1923 and October 1927.

73. "Bungei zatsuji," NoN (April 15, 1909), p. 54.

74. SZ 4:387–90. For translation, see Norma Moore Field, *And Then* (Baton Rouge: Louisiana State University Press, 1978), pp. 60–62.

75. "Bungei zatsuji," NoN (September 15, 1909), p. 80; Suzuki Miekichi, untitled segment, CK (July 1909): Appendix, pp. 10–13, quoted in MBHS, pp. 194–97; Hiraide Shū, "Hatsubai kinshi ron," THZ p. 174.

76. SZ 11:568–71.

77. GNBZ 44:198.

78. GNBZ 44:184; Morita Sōhei shū: Gendai Nihon bungaku zenshū (Kaizōsha, 1930), 42:347.

79. "Bungei zatsuji," NoN (April 15, 1910), p. 87. The author referred to was Sasa Seisetsu, later member of the Committee on Literature. The book in question was *Nihon jōshi*.

80. See note 50 above. This collection was *Hota* (April 1908).

81. "Kaisetsu," in *Fukuseiban Shinshichō*, Yoshida Seiichi, ed. (Rinsen shoten, 1967), pp. 8, 32, 33; "Real Conversation," *Shinshichō* (November 1910):71.

82. According to *"Shōnen Sekai* e ronbun" and "Sōsaku yodan: sono ni," quoted in Nomura Shōgo, *Denki: Tanizaki Jun'ichirō* (Rokkō shuppan, 1974), pp. 141–42.

83. *Shinshichō* (November 1910):68–69.

84. Most of the other early writings suffer from the kind of pedantry and triviality seen in "The Birth."

85. TJZ 1:212.

86. Nomura, *Denki*, 157–59.

87. Ibid., p. 203.

88. The banned works, discussed in chap. 14 below, were "Oiran," *Arusu* (May 1915); *Kyōfu jidai* (March 1916); "Bōyū," *Shinshōsetsu* (September 1916); and "Binan," *Shinchō* (September 1916).

89. "'Itansha no kanashimi' hashigaki," TJZ 23:22–25. I have incorporated a few sentences from *"Itansha no kanashimi* jo," TJZ 23:26.

90. TJZ 4:377–452.

91. Jō Ichirō, *Hakkinbon* (Tōgensha, 1965), pp. 26–30.

92. Bō-tōkyokusha dan, "Hikokuminteki bungaku no ryūkō," TY (July 1, 1910), pp. 105–07.

Chapter 10. Mori Ōgai and Hiraide Shū: Inside the High Treason Case

1. Notehelfer, *Kōtoku Shūsui, Portrait of a Japanese Radical*, pp. 162, 170, 174–76, 179–80, 183. For readings of the defendants' names, I have relied on Itoya Toshio, *Taigyaku jiken* (31 shobō, 1970), pp. 271–74.

2. CK (December 1910):122.

3. See TY (June 1, 1911) and *The Taiyo* (July 1, 1911) for articles on the charity organization proposed by the administration. The government wanted ¥30,000,000 from the wealthy to match a mere ¥1,500,000 in seed money in the form of an imperial gift.

4. Imai Yasuko, "Meiji-matsu bundan no ichi-chōkanzu," p. 44; Jō Ichirō, *Hakkinbon hyakunen*, pp. 105–07; Ishikawa Takuboku, "Nihon museifushugisha inbō jiken keika oyobi futai genshō," TZ 10:87.

5. GNBZ 94:104–05. *Hototogisu* was banned for the story "Onna" by Ichinomiya Takiko.

6. "Fūzoku kairan!! Kōan binran!!," TY (October 1, 1910), pp. 25–36. This piece was apparently translated, in whole or in part, in *The Japan Weekly Mail* (October 22, 1910), p. 520, as cited in Helen M. Hopper, "Mori Ōgai's Response to Suppression of Intellectual Freedom, 1909–12," MN 29, no. 4 (Winter 1974):398. Asada was no flaming liberal: for him, the emperor was still sacrosanct. See his "Tenchōsetsu ni tsuite," TY (November 1, 1910), pp. 29–35.

7. See Shiosawa Masasada, "Shakaishugi torishimari ni tsuite," and Ichiki Kitokurō, "Shuppanbutsu hatsubai kinshi shobun ni tsuite," TY (October 1, 1910), pp. 49–52, 103–05, respectively; Inoue Tetsujirō, "Gendai shisō no keikō ni tsuite,"

TY (November 1, 1910), pp. 60–67. Cf. Shimizu Sumu, "Shakaishugi to shakai seisaku," TY (February 1, 1911), pp. 93–98.

8. Asada Kōson, "Nokoreru inshō," TY (December 1, 1910), pp. 26–35; Shimamura Hōgetsu, "43-nen no bundan," ibid., pp. 91–93; "Meiji 43-nen shi: Bungaku," TY (February 15, 1911), pp. 233–34.

9. Kiso Ryūichi, "Hikka," *Nihon bungaku kōza*, 4 vols. (Kawade shobō, 1952), 1:163–64.

10. AS (March 8, 1912), p. 6.

11. "Meiji 43-nen shi: Bungaku," TY (February 15, 1911), pp. 230, 233.

12. "Bungei zatsuji," NoN (June 15, 1910), p. 68; ibid. (October 15, 1910), p. 73; ibid. (December 15, 1910), p. 72; "Tsuyoki appaku ni taeyo," NoN (November 1, 1910), pp. 14–15.

13. "Hyōron," CK (October 1910):131; "Shuto no keisatsu kairyō ron," CK (November 1910):1–4.

14. CK (December 1910):1–6, 35–40, 122–24. On Takebe, see Fujiwara Kiyozō, *Meiji Taishō Shōwa Kyōiku shisō gakusetsu jinbutsu shi*, 3:844.

15. Paraphrased from "Bungei no shugi," OZ 15:457–59. On Kōtoku and Kanno's relationship, see Notehelfer, *Kōtoku Shūsui*, p. 174.

16. TY (August 1, 1910), pp. 99–102.

17. OZ 1:679–99.

18. MOZ 1:281, quoted from Richard John Bowring, *Mori Ōgai and the Modernization of Japanese Culture*, p. 186.

19. Ibid.

20. MOZ 1:293–94.

21. Mori Junzaburō, *Ōgai Mori Rintarō*, p. 200; THZ, p. 584. Ōgai's diary does not confirm these visits recorded in the Hiraide Shū chronology, although the December 14, 1910, entry mentions dinner with Hiraide Shū and Yosano Hiroshi. OZ 20:556.

22. Not "Osamu," as the character is more commonly read, although not even his children knew why. See Hiraide Akira, "Chichi Hiraide Shū no koto," THZ, p. 597. Hiraide's rarely used pen name, Roka, should not be confused with that of Tokutomi Roka, which was written with different characters.

23. Sanford Goldstein and Seishi Shinoda, *Tangled Hair*, p. 11. Yoshii Osamu, "Yosano Tekkan ron," GNBZ 32:380.

24. Hiraide Akira, "Chichi Hiraide Shū no koto," THZ, p. 593.

25. Furukawa Kiyohiko, "Hiraide Shū, hito to sakuhin," THS, p. 430, Ishikawa Takuboku, "Nihon museifushugisha inbō jiken keika oyobi futai genshō," TZ 10:87; "A LETTER FROM PRISON," TZ 10:107–54; "Tōyō nikki," TZ 16:137.

26. Hiraide Akira, "Chichi Hiraide Shū no koto," p. 604.

27. Shiota Shōbei and Watanabe Junzō, eds., *Hiroku taigyaku jiken*, 2 vols. (Shunjūsha, 1961), 1:1–2; Itoya Toshio, *Taigyaku jiken*, pp. 278–79.

28. Hiraide Hiizu, *Senjika no genron tōsei: genron tōsei hōki no sōgōteki kenkyū* (Nakagawa shobō, 1942; reprinted in 2,000 copies, 1944).

29. Ishikawa Takuboku, "Nihon museifushugisha . . . ," p. 102; Hiraide Shū, "Taigyaku jiken ikensho," THS, p. 342.

30. William J. Sebald, trans., *The Criminal Code of Japan*, p. 64.

31. "Taigyaku jiken ikensho," THS, pp. 327–42.

32. Ibid., pp. 342–44.

33. "Shisō happyō no jiyū o ronzu," TY (February 1, 1911), in THS, pp. 368–74. Written January 4, 1911.

34. Tetsuo Najita, *Hara Kei in the Politics of Compromise 1905–15* (Harvard University Press, 1967), p. 59. In 1925, the electorate was expanded from 3,000,000 to 13,000,000.

35. "Shisō happyō no jiyū o ronzu," TY (February 1, 1911), in THS, pp. 368–74 (esp. pp. 372–73).

36. Sebald, trans., *Criminal Code of Japan*, p. 64; Hiraide Hiizu, "Taigyaku jiken o megutte," THS, pp. 440–41.

37. See "Hiraide Shū nenpu," THS, p. 403, and "Hiraide Shū sakuhin mokuroku," THS, p. 413; OZ 20:591 ff.

38. Hiraide Akira, "Chichi Hiraide Shū no koto," THZ, p. 603; TZ 10:124, 128, 133.

39. THS, pp. 293–306. Also in GNBZ 84:378–86, followed immediately by "Gyakuto," ibid., 386–98.

40. The second (and last?) did not occur until 1921, when the January issue was banned for an article called "The Military Mentality," ("Gunjin no shinri"). See Saitō Shōzō, *Gendai hikka bunken dainenpyō*, p. 259.

41. There is an irregularity in the number of *fuseji* here. Moriyama, *Taigyaku jiken*, p. 27, suggests "museifutō banzai" and "museifushugi."

42. THS, pp. 307–26. See also "Kōhan," *Subaru* (February 1913), in THS, pp. 226–37 (esp. pp. 229–30), for a bitterly sarcastic view of Japan's judges as servants of the emperor. Takuboku records an extreme conservative's rebuttal to the need for "civilized" law in "A LETTER FROM PRISON: EDITOR'S NOTES," TZ 10:128.

43. Summarized from "Hatsubai kinshi ni tsuite," THS, pp. 375–83.

44. See "Shiryō," THS, pp. 389–90; Hiraide Hiizu, THS p. 442.

45. Ishikawa Takuboku, "Tōyō nikki," TZ, p. 135.

46. Kawazu Akira, "Shakaishugi torishimari ron," TY (November 1, 1910), pp. 68–72, is a notably hysterical piece. "Joshō no mitaru gendai shakai," TY (February 15, 1911), p. 185; Asada Kōson, "Gyakuto shobun no keika o ronzu," TY (February 1, 1911), pp. 26–31.

47. Eguchi Kiyoshi, *Waga bungaku hanseiki* (1953), in NKBT 60:388; Odagiri Hideo, "Kaisetsu," in NPBT 1:406–7.

Chapter 11. OTHER WRITERS REACT

1. Tatsuo Arima, *The Failure of Freedom*, p. 82; Jansen, "Changing Japanese Attitudes Toward Modernization," in Marius B. Jansen, ed., *Changing Japanese Attitudes Toward Modernization* (Princeton: Princeton University Press, 1965), p. 80; Janet Walker, *The Japanese Novel of the Meiji Period and the Ideal of Individualism* (Princeton: Princeton University Press, 1979), p. 99.

2. Moriyama cites the standard sources on page 295 of *Taigyaku jiken* and gives his updated version of the list on pages 291–94. The list I found most helpful before Moriyama was in Itoya Toshio, *Taigyaku jiken*, pp. 288–91.

3. Nakano Yoshio, "Kaisetsu," in Tokutomi Kenjirō, *Muhon-ron* (Iwanami bunko, 1976), p. 127; MBZ 42:406–7.

4. "Tennō heika ni negai-tatematsuru," in Tokutomi Kenjirō, *Muhon-ron*, pp. 7–8.

5. Kenneth Strong, *Footprints in the Snow*, p. 37. For the pronunciation of the title of Roka's speech, I have followed the edition cited in note 3 above.

6. Nakano, "Kaisetsu," pp. 123–24.

7. Tokutomi, *Muhon-ron*, pp. 9–24. For the censored text, see *Roka zenshū*, 20 vols. (Shinchōsha, 1929) 19:39–53.

8. Strong, *Footprints in the Snow*, pp. 37–38.

9. AS (February 7, 1911), p. 3.

10. Strong, *Footprints in the Snow*, p. 32.

11. Moriyama, *Taigyaku jiken*, p. 123.

12. KBHT 3:329–32, 490.

13. NKBT 23:477, 478, 471, 479.

14. Ibid., pp. 472 n1, 478 n2, 471 n10.

15. Ibid., p. 477 n13. See also ibid., p. 560 n268.

16. Donald Keene, "Shiki and Takuboku," in *Landscapes and Portraits*, pp. 169–70.

17. In a frequently cited letter of February 6, 1911, in TZ 12:176–80.

18. "Sono mukashi shūsai no na no takakarishi / Tomo rō ni ari / Aki no kaze fuku," NKBT 23:95. Written September 9, 1910.

19. "Ware ni nishi tomo no futari yo / Hitori wa shini / Hitori wa rō o idete ima yamu" (first appeared in *A Handful of Sand?*), NKBT 23:76; translated by Carl Sesar in his *Takuboku: Poems to Eat* (Tokyo and Palo Alto: Kodansha International, 1966), p. 50.

20. "Akagami no hyōshi tezureshi / Kokukin no / Fumi o kōri no soko ni sagasu hi," NKBT 23:159. Written July 27, 1910; variant form in AS (August 7, 1910).

21. "Uru koto o sashitomerareshi / Hon no chosha ni / Michi nite aeru aki no asa kana" (September 9, 1910), NKBT 23:160.

22. "Ya to bakari / Katsura Shushō ni te torareshi yume mite samenu / Aki no yo no niji," (September 9, 1910), NKBT 23:87.

23. "Tsune higoro / Konomite iishi / Kakumei no / Go o tsutsushimite / Aki ni irerikeri," TZ 1:198.

24. "Ima omoeba / Ge-ni kare mo mata / Shūsui no / Ichimi narishi to / Shiru fushi mo ari," TZ 1:198.

25. The following discussion owes much to Imai Yasuko's fine annotations to NKBT 23. See NKBT 23:549 n236 for the textual history of the series, which is now included in *Yobiko to kuchibue*, a title contemplated by Takuboku for a volume of poetry but rendered meaningless by his own editorial decisions. For the "*yobiko*," see TZ 3:178, 183. Moriyama, *Taigyaku jiken*, pp. 56–59, does not approve of Imai's

skeptical reading of Takuboku as indulging in "mental dramas" in these poems, but his tedious catalog of active leftists who liked them is beside the point.

26. NKBT 23:406–14.

27. NKBT 23:409 n9; TZ 12:178.

28. TZ 12:166–67.

29. Iwaki Yukinori, "Kaisetsu," NKBT 23:37–39.

30. Donald Keene, "Shiki and Takuboku," in *Landscapes and Portraits*, p. 169.

31. Lionel Trilling, *The Liberal Imagination* (New York: Charles Scribner's Sons, 1976), p. vii.

32. Ibid., p. viii.

33. Ibid.

34. "Yumichō yori: kuraubeki shi," AS (November 30–December 7, 1909), in TZ 9:148; translated in Carl Sesar, *Takuboku: Poems to Eat*, p. 15.

35. "Dai to iū ji o hyaku amari / Suna ni kaki / Shinu koto o yamete kaeri kitareri," NKBT 23:59; Sesar, *Takuboku*, p. 32.

36. "Tawamure-ni haha o seoite / Sono amari karoki ni nakite / Sanpo ayumazu," NKBT 23:59; Sesar, *Takuboku*, p. 33.

37. "Yogoretaru tabi haku toki no / Kimi-waruki omoi ni nitaru / Omoide mo ari," NKBT 23:140; Sesar, *Takuboku*, p. 77.

38. "Kanashiki wa waga chichi! / Kyō mo shinbun o yomiakite / Niwa ni koari to asoberi," NKBT 23:206; Sesar, *Takuboku*, p. 130.

39. "Yoru osoku teishaba ni iri / Tachi suwari / Yagate ideyukinu bō-naki otoko," NKBT 23:163; Sesar, *Takuboku*, p. 83.

40. "Yoru osoku doko yara no heya no sawagashiki wa / Hito ya shinitaran to / Iki o hisomuru," NKBT 23:188; Sesar, *Takuboku*, p. 118.

41. Trilling, *The Liberal Imagination*, p. xv.

42. KHBT 3:391.

43. Moriyama, *Taigyaku jiken*, pp. 288–89.

44. Moriyama, *Tagyaku jiken*, p. 213, notes that Kanson's creative writing effectively ended with the demise of *Kindai Shisō*, the journal mentioned above, chap. 11 footnote p. 180.

45. Masamune Hakuchō, *Bundan gojūnen*, GNBZ 97:416; Trilling, *The Liberal Imagination*, pp. 298–99. Cf. Allain Robbe-Grillet, *For a New Novel*, trans. Richard Howard (New York: Grove Press, 1965), p. 141: "in art, nothing is ever known in advance."

46. Moriyama, *Taigyaku jiken*, p. 207, identifies these lesser figures as Kinoshita Naoe and Nishikawa Kōjirō.

47. *Gendai Nihon shōsetsu taikei*, 65 vols. (Kawade shobō, 1949), 30:67–73.

48. Ibid., p. 71.

49. CK (February 1911), pp. 117. This story is missing from the *Zenshū*.

50. Some say that to search for such connections is an error, but the timing and general subject matter are obviously linked to the case. See Moriyama, *Taigyaku jiken*, p. 141.

51. Ibid.

52. GNBZ 36:196–207.

53. The most that Moriyama can point to is a similarity between Kōtoku's final fatalism and that of the play's protagonist, Kōichi. See Moriyama, *Taigyaku jiken,* p. 143.

54. TZ 10:86–87.

55. GNBZ 21:356–66, 427.

56. Moriyama, *Taigyaku jiken,* pp. 185–98, discusses fleeting references to the High Treason Case in some of Katai's other writings during 1917–1918.

57. Edward Seidensticker, *Kafū the Scribbler,* pp. 58, 61.

58. Ibid., p. 58.

59. Donald Keene, *World Within Walls,* p. 434.

60. Ibid.

61. KZ 6:34–35; Seidensticker, *Kafū the Scribbler,* p. 61, gives a translation of this moving passage, whence the quoted phrase.

62. Keene, *World Within Walls,* p. 434.

63. KZ 15:12; translated by Seidensticker, omitting "often," in *Kafū the Scribbler,* p. 46. Moriyama, *Taigyaku jiken,* p. 114, notes Kanzaki Kiyoshi's reconstruction of Kafū's experience and his conclusion that Kafū could have seen the police wagons "often" only during the trial in December 1910.

64. KZ 15:7–17; quotation from p. 9.

65. "Modern Society As Seen Through Fiction and Drama" ("Shōsetsu kyakuhon o tsūjite mitaru gendai shakai"), TY (February 15, 1911), pp. 107–13; also in MBZ 24:255–59.

Chapter 12. A Crashing Stalemate:
The Committee on Literature

1. See Etō Jun, *Sōseki to sono jidai,* 2 vols. (Shinchōsha, 1970), 1:148.

2. SZ 4:528.

3. Ara Masahito, *Sōseki kenkyū nenpyō,* pp. 381–82, 493; SZ 15:344.

4. "Hakase mondai," SZ 16:697.

5. "Hakase mondai no nariyuki," SZ 16:699–700.

6. "Dōraku to shokugyō," SZ 11:308.

7. See Ōgai's diary entry for February 18, 1911, in OZ 20:572.

8. "Shin bungaku hakase Mori Ōgai shi dan," OZ 19:536–37.

9. See diary entry for September 28, 1911, in OZ 20:612 and January 14, 1912, in OZ 21:5. The *Bunshō Sekai* editor who brought him the news was Tayama Katai. For a photo of the bust, see Mori Oto, *Mori Ōgai* (Yōtokusha, 1946), frontispiece.

10. See chapters 6 and 7 of *Seinen.*

11. Quoted in Ōtsuki and Matsumura, *Aikokushin kyōiku,* p. 155, from *Kyōiku Jiron* (February 5, 1911). For further remarks by Komatsubara, Katsura, and Hirata, see TY (May 15, 1911), p. 45.

12. Quoted in Ōtsuki and Matsumura, *Aikokushin kyōiku,* p. 156, from *Komatsubara Eitarō kun jiryaku* (1924), pp. 111–12.

13. Ōtsuki and Matsumura, *Aikokushin kyōiku*, pp. 156–57. The ministry had formulated such policies well before the committee actually met, however. See AS (May 17, 1911), p. 2.

14. Except where indicated, the following account is based on reports in AS (May 18, 1911), pp. 3–5; AS (May 20, 1911), p. 2; AS (May 24, 1911), p. 5; and KS (May 24, 1911), p. 3. I have checked details against Insatsukyoku, ed., *Hōrei zensho* (1911), pp. 184, 185, 1304, 2274, which show that the official designation (not simply the popular appellation) of the committee was Bungei Iinkai.

15. THZ, p. 596.

16. See, e.g., KHBT 3:404–06.

17. The other appointees were Fujishiro Teisuke, Ihara Seiseien, and Adachi Hokuō.

18. Interview with Fukuhara, "Dai-bungaku dai-shisō no shinkō," NoN (June 1, 1911), p. 130.

19. Interview with Hōgetsu, "Bungei-in shōrai no konnan," NoN (June 1, 1911), p. 133.

20. Mizuno Yōshū, "Shukan sūtsū," CK (June 1911): 94; "Bungei zatsuji," NoN (June 1, 1911), p. 81; Tokuda Shūsei, "Shinsa saruru hitsuyō nashi," ibid., pp. 132–33; Higuchi Ryūkyō, "Kōjushugi no renchū," ibid., p. 134.

21. SZ 11:274–81 passim.

22. The following account is based on reports in AS (May 24, 1911), p. 5; AS (May 30, 1911), p. 4; AS (June 2, 1911), p. 4; and KS (May 24, 1911), p. 3.

23. G. B. Sansom, *Japan: A Short Cultural History*, p. 494.

24. Kaneko Chikusui, "Bungei-in no setchi," TY (June 1, 1911), p. 24; translated as "The Institutes of Literature and Art" in *The Taiyo* (July 1, 1911), p. 11.

25. Tokuda Shūsei, "Bungei iinkai ni tsuite," CK (June 1911): 100.

26. Baba Kochō, "Seifu no shigoto," ibid., p. 108.

27. Kōtōsei [pseudonym], "Bungei iinkai ni tai-suru gimon," ibid., p. 226.

28. Higuchi Ryūkyō, "Kōjushugi no renchū," NoN (June 1, 1911), p. 134.

29. Satō Kōroku, "Aru mo yoshi naki mo yoshi," CK (June 1911): 103; Baba Kochō, "Seifu no shigoto," ibid., p. 105; Tayama Katai, "Shinsa yori mo bengi o ataeyo," ibid., p. 109.

30. Mizuno Yōshū, "Shukan sūtsū," ibid., p. 98; Gotō Chūgai, "Sakka dai-danketsu no hitsuyō," NoN (June 1911), p. 135.

31. "Bungei iinkai ni tsuite," CK (June 1911): 99.

32. Togawa Shūkotsu, "Bungei iinkai shi-ken," ibid., p. 87; Kamitsukasa Shōken, "Nani mo iū hitsuyō wa nai ga," ibid., pp. 92–93; Mizuno Yōshū, "Shukan sūtsū," ibid., pp. 94–95; Satō Kōroku, "Aru mo yoshi naki mo yoshi," ibid., p. 101.

33. Shimazaki Tōson, "Bungei iin ni tai-suru yo no kibō,: ibid., pp. 91–92; Morita Sōhei, "Geijutsu ni kyōryoku nashi,: ibid., p. 105; Tayama Katai, "Shinsa yori mo bengi o ataeyo," ibid., p. 109.

34. Masamune Hakuchō, "Bungei iinkai shūgō no zenjitsu," ibid., p. 90; Gotō Chūgai, "Sodateagetara rippa ni narō," ibid., p. 110; Gotō Ghūgai, "Sakka dai-danketsu no hitsuyō," NoN (June 1, 1911), p. 135.

35. Tokuda shūsei, "Shinsa saruru hitsuyō nashi," ibid., p. 132.

36. Tokuda Shūsei, "Bungei iinkai ni tsuite," CK (June 1911): 99.

37. According to reports in AS (June 7, 1911), p. 4, and KS (June 7, 1911), p. 2.

38. Togawa Shūkotsu, "Bungei iinkai shi-ken," CK (June 1911); 88–89.

39. Mizuno Yōshū, "Shukan sūtsū," ibid., pp. 94–98.

40. The following account is based on reports in AS (June 5, 1911), p. 4; AS (June 7, 1911), p. 4; AS (June 9, 1911), p. 4; AS (June 10, 1911), p. 5; KS (June 4, 1911), p. 1; KS (June 5, 1911), p. 1; and KS (June 7, 1911), p. 2.

41. More precisely, they agreed not even to *consider* a work without the author's permission, but this must have proved impracticable.

42. See Ōgai's diary entry for June 4, 1911, in OZ 20:592.

43. KS (March 5, 1912), p. 4.

44. Cf. OZ 20:593; AS (July 5, 1911), p. 4.

45. KBHS 21, 57–58.

46. AS (July 5, 1911), p. 4; KS (July 5, 1911), p. 3; Shimamura Hōgetsu, "Kokka ga sasageru kōden," in *Hōgetsu zenshū* 2:345–48.

47. See reports in AS (September 18, 1911), p. 4, and KS (September 18, 1911), p. 1.

48. See Ōgai's diary entry for January 13, 1912, in OZ 21:5; "Bungei iinkai yosen sakubutsu ni tsuite," CK (April 1912): 243–45; AS (December 4, 1911), p. 4.

49. Mitsui Kōshi, "Bungei jihyō," NoN (July 1, 1910), p. 85. This is actually an attack against Sōseki as an admirer of Akiko's poetry.

50. Jōbari Dōji [pseudonym], "Mondai no hito: Tokotsugu to Fukuhara," NoN (April 1, 1912), p. 45.

51. AS (March 4, 1912), p. 5; AS (March 5, 1912), p. 5; KS (March 5, 1912), p. 4; Imai Yasuko, "Meiji-matsu bundan no ichi-chōkanzu," p. 48. Imai's hard-to-find essay is the only serious study I have encountered on the Committee on Literature. Imai also relies heavily on the newspaper reports that I have used, but in concentrating on the committee's antecedents (see above, chap. 8, footnote p. 112) and on Sōseki's critique, she gives far too little credit to other writers of the day.

52. "Yatto anshin," SZ 16:959.

53. "Bungei iinkai" (May 17, 1912), in *Tōson zenshū*, 18 vols. (Chikuma shobō, 1967), 6:149–50; "Geijutsu no hogo" (n.d.), in *Tōson zenshū* 6:175.

54. Nakahara Mumei, "Bungei jihyō: Bungei iinkai no senshō," TY (April 1, 1912), p. 35.

55. "Bungei zatsuji," NoN (March 15, 1912), p. 92.

56. AS (April 26, 1912), p. 4.

57. AS (May 2, 1912), p. 2.

58. AS (May 5, 1912), p. 4.

59. AS (May 29, 1912), p. 4.

60. See Ōgai's diary entry for May 2 and 6, 1913, in OZ 21:100.

61. Kaneko Chikusui, "Fuausuto no hōgoyaku," TY (May 1, 1913), p. 15.

62. AS (June 14–15, 1913), p. 2; *Kyōiku Jiron* (June 15, 1913), p. 33; ibid. (June 25, 1913), p. 55. Nothing in TY, NoN, CK.

63. *Kyōiku Jiron* (June 25, 1913), p. 35.

64. SZ 6:109, 114; from translation by Edwin McClellan (Chicago: Henry Regnery, 1957), pp. 88, 91.

65. SZ 6:285, 286; McClellan, pp. 245, 246.

66. Tenchōsetsu ni tsuite," TY (November 1, 1910), pp. 29–35.

67. John Whitney Hall, "A Monarch for Modern Japan," p. 26, explains the ritual that "links" each new emperor with the power of the sun goddess, making him a god.

68. Here I have borrowed the opening lines of the Nippon Gakujutsu Shinkōkai translation of *Man'yōshū* 2:199, remarkable more for its effect that its precision. See *The Man'yōshū* (New York: Columbia University Press, 1969), p. 39.

69. The following account is based primarily on reports in AS (September 12, 13, 14, 1912). Imperial funerals take place at night in accordance with traditional taboos.

70. In 1912 dollars, approximately $763,000. 1980 value estimated from United States Department of Labor *Handbook of Labor Statistics* (1978), p. 379. Indexes: 1967-1.000; 1977-.551; 1913-3.367.

71. AS (September 14, 1912), p. 3.

72. Robert Jay Lifton, Shūichi Katō, and Michael R. Reich, *Six Lives / Six Deaths*, p. 60.

73. AS (September 14, 1912), p. 4. The author of this editorial was Sakaino Kōyō (1871–1933), Buddhist scholar and occasional *Asahi* contributor. This piece is quoted in Ōhama Tetsuya, *Nogi Maresuke* (Yūzankaku, 1967), pp. 207–08. See also pp. 204–69 of this remarkable book (the primary source for Lifton et al.) for a survey of contemporary reactions.

Chapter 13.
OVERVIEW: THOUGHT CONTROL AND CENSORSHIP AFTER MEIJI

1. MITC, pp. 139, 134.

2. Ibid., p. 168.

3. Ibid., p. 146.

4. Ibid., p. 127, 170.

5. Ibid., p. 135.

6. Ibid., p. 139.

7. Ibid., n48.

8. Ibid., p. 98.

9. See ibid., pp. 190–92 for comparisons of Japan's thought control with that of other countries.

10. Robert B. Radin, "Law and the Control of Popular Violence in Japan," unpublished paper (Harvard University, 1979).

11. MITC, p. 58.

12. Ibid., p. 28.

13. Ibid., pp. 39–68; quotation from p. 66.

14. John K. Fairbank et al., *East Asia*, pp. 581–82.

15. Yui Masaomi, Kitagawa Kenzō, Akazawa Shirō, and Toyosawa Hajime, *Shuppan Keisatsu kankei shiryō: kaisetsu, sōmokuji* (Fuji shuppan, 1983), pp. 14–15.

16. MITC, pp. 195–96; OPC, p. 38.
17. SSDS, pp. 15–17.
18. NKBD 4:280–82; Edward Seidensticker, *Kafū the Scribbler*, p. 79.

Chapter 14. TANIZAKI IN TAISHŌ

1. TJZ 3:27–39; *Geppō* 3:12.
2. The former is a slightly fictionalized literary and sexual history of one of the young men who founded the journal *Shinshichō* with Tanizaki in 1910, but who died young. It is of little value except as a memorial portrait of a particular associate of Tanizaki's and perhaps as a glimpse at the literary life of the time. Tanizaki did not bother to restore the deleted passages after the war. "A Handsome Man" is a similar portrait of a friend. Tanizaki appears in the piece under his own name, and the story has the looseness of a factual chronicle. Concerned as it is with the suffering the hero caused a vast array of women he seduced, complete with graphic descriptions of their fighting over him, we can imagine the censors' uneasiness—especially since one victim is the daughter of a high official. TJZ 4:93–153; *Geppō* 4:12.
3. The volume *Ningyo no nageki* was banned in 1917, but this was apparently due to one overly graphic illustration. TJZ *Geppō* 4:3, 12. The volume *Ningyo no nageki, Majutsushi* (Shun'yōdō, 1919) was apparently not suppressed despite several boldly bare-breasted views of a particularly fulsome mermaid.
4. TJZ 10:3.
5. "*Chijin no ai* no sakusha yori dokusha e," TJZ 23:80; quoted in Nomura Shōgo, *Denki*, p. 297. See also ibid., pp. 295–99.
6. TJZ 10:471–72.
7. Compare the elided passages in *Meiji Taishō bungaku zenshū: Tanizaki Jun'ichirō shū* (Shun'yōdō, 1928), 35:550, 549, 529, 532, with the corresponding passages in TJZ 10:480–81, 479, 448, 453.
8. "*Manji* ni tsuite," TJZ 23:197.
9. Odagiri Hideo, *Zoku hakkin sakuhin shū*, pp. 283–84.
10. TJZ 2:23–74.
11. TJZ 4:76.
12. "Meiji Taishō bungaku zenshū Tanizaki Jun'ichirō hen kaisetsu," TJZ 23:107.
13. Cf. TJZ 4:70; *Meiji Taishō bungaku zenshū* 35:320.
14. TJZ 4:43.
15. "Hatsubai kinshi ni tsuite," TJZ 22:32–33.
16. Morris L. Ernst and Alan U. Schwartz, *Censorship*, p. 107.
17. TJZ 7:483–518.
18. "*Eien no gūzō* no jōen kinshi," TJZ 22:135–41.
19. "Kyakuhon ken'etsu ni tsuite no chūmon," TJZ 22:142–44.
20. Fujimura Tsukuru, ed., *Nihon bungaku daijiten*, 2:982.

Chapter 15.
THE SHŌWA PUBLISHING BOOM AND THE LITERARY CHAT SOCIETY

1. Ichiko Teiji et al., *Nihon bungaku zenshi*, 5:585–86; *Nihon bungaku no rekishi*, 11:364–65, 417–18.

2. *Nihon bungaku no rekishi*, 12:11. The series was not without its predecessors; see GNBZ Bekkan 2:443; NKBD 6:11–68.

3. Kōno Toshirō et al., eds., *Shōwa no bungaku* (Yūhikaku, 1972), p. 51; Hirano Ken, *Gendai Nihon bungaku shi: Shōwa*, in GNBZ Bekkan 1:362.

4. Senuma Shigeki, *Hon no hyaku-nen shi* (Shuppan nyūsu sha, 1965), pp. 172, 175; SKG 3 (1935):2–3 shows the number of nonperiodical publications submitted for inspection going from 47,529 in 1924 to 126,733 in 1934; the number of periodicals registered going from 2,127 in 1912 to 6,899 in 1925 (after dipping to 3,854 following the earthquake) to 11,915 in 1934.

5. *Nihon bungaku no rekishi*, 12:65.

6. Senuma, *Hon no hyaku-nen shi*, p. 187.

7. GNBZ 97:411.

8. Yamada Seizaburō, *Puroretaria bungaku shi*, 2:269.

9. Saegusa Shigeo, *Genron Shōwa shi*, p. 22.

10. AS (January 11, 1928), p. 5; AS (January 27, 1928), p. 6.

11. Odagiri Hideo, *Hakkin sakuhin shū* (1957), pp. 270, 290–91, 315–16; for the complete text of the pamphlet, "Ware-ware wa ika-naru ken'etsu seido no moto ni sarasarete iru ka?," see ibid., pp. 269–93.

12. OPC, p. 68.

13. Odagiri, *Hakkin sakuhin shū* (1957), pp. 270–73, 278, 284, 286–89. The censorship fee was ¥.05 per three meters of film.

14. *Nihon no rekishi*, 24:451–59, 462–3; John K. Fairbank et al., *East Asia*, p. 522.

15. *Iwanami kōza Nihon rekishi*, 23 vols. (Iwanami shoten, 1972), 20:327–28; G. T. Shea, *Leftwing Literature in Japan* (Tokyo: Hōsei University Press, 1965), pp. 229–30; AS (June 20, 1932), p. 7, reports the arrest of 198 participants in a KOPF rally by 300 policemen whose violent actions provoked a free-for-all and much bloodshed.

16. MITC, p. 119.

17. Yamada, *Puroretaria bungaku shi*, 2:348.

18. Tosaka Jun, "Ken'etsu-ka no shisō to fūzoku" (1936), in *Tosaka Jun zenshū*, 5 vols. (Keisō shobō, 1966), 5:77–80.

19. AS (August 30, 1934), p. 11. The report ridiculed him.

20. Matsumoto Gaku, *Bunka to seiji*, pp. 61–63.

21. Matsumoto, *Bunka to seiji*, pp. 155–59. NKBD 4:113.

22. The following discussion is based primarily on four overlapping studies written by Enomoto Takashi: {1} "Bungei Konwakai: bungei tōsei e no ichi-katei," pp. 15–33; {2} "Bungei Konwakai: sono seiritsu jijō to mondaiten," pp. 227–35; {3} "Bungei Konwakai to taishū sakka no ugoki," pp. 628–33; {4} "Bunka no taishūka

mondai to kokkashugiteki henkō," pp. 1–32. Hereafter referred to as "Enomoto [1]," etc. Here, see Enomoto [4], pp. 17–18.

23. Enomoto [4], p. 20. A report on the writers' viewing maneuvers is in AS (November 2, 1932), p. 7. For a variety of views on fascism in literature, see the *zadankai* with Tokuda Shūsei, Chikamatsu Shūkō, Nii Itaru, Shirai Kyōji, Yoshikawa Eiji, Mikami Otokichi, Chiba Kameo et al., "Fuassho to fuasshizumu bungei ni tsuite," *Shinchō* (October 1932):125–46.

24. *Nihon no rekishi* 24:365–67; NKBD 4:25.

25. Enomoto [2], p. 227.

26. "Teikoku bungei in no keikaku hihan," *Yomiuri Shimbun* (January 27, 1934), cited in Enomoto [2], p. 227.

27. "Bungei in ni tsuite," AS (February 2, 3, 1934), p. 9.

28. "Ika-naru bungei in zo," in *Shūsei zenshū*, 15 vols. (Hibonkaku, 1936), 15:232.

29. Hirotsu Kazuo, "Zoku nengetsu no ashioto," *Gunzō* (November 1964):192.

30. Ibid., p. 193.

31. Enomoto [2], p. 233; Hirotsu, "Zoku nengetsu," p. 193.

32. Enomoto [2], p. 231.

33. Nakano Shigeharu, "Bungei tōsei no mondai ni tsuite," *Nakano Shigeharu zenshū*, 20 vols. (Chikuma shobō, 1959), 7:242.

34. Naimushō Keihokyoku, ed., *Shuppan Keisatsu shiryō*, no. 3 (August 1935): 1–30, in Japan Naimushō, *Shuppan Keisatsu shiryō, 1923–38*, 4 reels (Library of Congress Microfilm, Orien Japan 0107), Reel no. 2. Summarized in SKG 3 (1935): 176–78.

35. Enomoto [2], p. 235.

36. "Bungei Konwakai," *Bungei Shunjū* (October 1935), in *Kawabata Yasunari zenshū*, 19 vols. (Shinchōsha, 1969), 18:317.

37. See Izumi Aki, ed., "Sensō-ka no bunka / bungaku kankei tōsei to sono hannō," *Bungaku* (April 1958):516–38, which is a chronology consisting of twenty-two solidly packed pages of small type listing cultural control measures taken between 1937 and 1945.

Chapter 16.
THE MILITARY AND THOUGHT POLICE TAKE OVER

1. Saegusa Shigeo, *Genron Shōwa shi*, pp. 4–5; OKS, p. 187.
2. OPC, p. 25.
3. Taisei Yokusan Kai and Kokumin Seishin Sōdōin Honbu.
4. The primary source for this section is SSDS (esp. pp. 22–23).
5. SSDS, p. 23; OPC, p. 27.
6. In 1942, two right-wing journals were added, and the name was changed to Six Company Society (Rokusha Kai), which continued until *Nihon Hyōron, Kaizō*, and *Bungei Shunjū* were forced out of the general magazine category in 1944. SSDS, p. 84.
7. SSDS, pp. 24–25, 29.
8. SSDS, p. 36.
9. "Genji monogatari jo," TJZ 23:166–67.

10. "Genji monogatari shin'yaku jo," TJZ 23:253.

11. SSDS, p. 47.

12. "Ano koro no koto (Yamada Yoshio tsuitō)," TJZ 23:356−58.

13. SSDS, p. 187.

14. Ibid., p. 126.

15. Donald Keene, "The Barren Years," MN 33 no. 1 (Spring 1978):94−95.

16. Okamoto Ippei, better known as a cartoonist, was the husband of the writer Okamoto Kanoko.

17. SSDS, p. 87.

18. Ibid., p. 66.

19. Ibid., p. 89.

20. Ibid., pp. 46, 98, 130.

21. On privately published journals, see Saburō Ienaga, *The Pacific War,* p. 209.

22. "*Sasameyuki* o kaita koro," TJZ 23:364−65.

23. Ibid., p. 365.

24. SK 2:773−77.

25. SSDS, p. 166.

26. Ibid., p. 168.

27. Ibid., pp. 90, 166.

28. Hatanaka Shigeo (ibid., p. 168) mistakenly says this was the May issue, which confuses the sequence of events. Major Sugimoto would not have known at the May meeting of the magazine's decision to suspend serialization.

29. Donald Keene, "Japanese Writers and the Greater East Asia War," p. 313. For the complete original text, see *Nihon no rekishi* 25:324.

30. SSDS, pp. 168−69.

31. "Sasameyuki jōkan genkō dai jūku-shō atogaki," TJZ 23:191.

32. "*Sasameyuki* kaiko," TJZ 22:362.

33. Tanizaki, "Shimanaka kun to watakushi," TJZ 22:369; Keene, "Japanese Writers and the Greater East Asia War," p. 314. For details on Tanizaki's rather liberal financial arrangements at this time, see Nomura Shōgo, *Denki,* p. 419.

34. Tanizaki letter of July 29, 1944, in TJZ 24:417.

35. Shiga Naoya, *Shiga Naoya taiwa shū,* pp. 14−15.

36. Tanizaki, "*Sasameyuki* sadan," TJZ 23:239.

37. SSDS, pp. 91−98.

38. SSDS, p. 89.

39. The following account is based primarily on SSDS, pp. 189−285.

40. The photograph can be found in *Nihon no rekishi* 25:325.

41. SSDS, pp. 199−201. 274−78, 196−97.

42. Ibid., p. 246.

43. Ibid., pp. 279−80.

44. Ibid., p. 279.

45. Ibid., pp. 40−41.

46. Ibid., p. 43.

47. Ibid., pp. 44, 79.

48. OPC, p. 36; SSDS, pp. 45−46, 132.

49. SSDS, pp. 102–03, 41–42.

50. Ibid., pp. 122, 134.

51. Particularly in his earlier-cited "Japanese Writers and the Greater East Asia War."

52. Ibid., pp. 300, 301–02.

53. Ienaga, *The Pacific War*, pp. 208, 223.

54. Keene, "Japanese Writers and the Greater East Asia War," p. 301.

55. Ibid., p. 315.

56. Kafū's diary entry for March 4, 1944, in KZ 23:434.

57. Tanizaki, "Sokai nikki," TJZ 16:319–23. Written 1946 to 1950.

58. Ibid., pp. 389–91; Kafū's diary entry for August 15, 1945, in KZ 24:64.

59. Shiga Naoya, *Shiga Naoya taiwa shū*, p. 22; Keene, "Japanese Writers and the Greater East Asia War," p. 313.

60. Ienaga, *The Pacific War*, p. 204.

61. Hirano Ken, "Nihon Bungaku Hōkoku Kai no seiritsu," p. 4.

62. Ibid., p. 5; quoted by Keene, "Japanese Writers and the Greater East Asia War," p. 308, with source confused.

63. SSDS, pp. 56–60; Hirano, "Nihon Bungaku Hōkoku," p. 7. For a view of the difficulties involved in documenting the extralegal blacklisting process, see Nakajima Kenzō, *Kaisō no bungaku* (Heibonsha, 1977), pp. 287–95. Thanks to Professor Odagiri Hideo for bringing this article to my attention and commenting at length on the problem. Clearly, embargoes were issued to editors against certain writers at times of high international tension and removed when the crises were past.

64. Keene, "The Barren Years," p. 103.

65. Hirano, "Nihon Bungaku Hōkoku," p. 1; NKBD 4:418.

66. Kubota Masafumi, "*Nihon Gakugei Shimbun* o yomu," *Bungaku* (August 1961):120; Kubota, "*Bungaku Hōkoku* o yomu," *Bungaku* (December 1961):85; Ōi Hirosuke, "Bungaku Hōkoku Kai wa mui," *Bungaku* (May 1961):90.

67. Hirano, "Nihon Bungaku Hōkoku," p. 3.

68. Ōi, "Bungaku Hōkoku Kai," pp. 87, 90.

69. GNBZ 97:416.

70. Kubota, "*Nihon Gakugei Shimbun* o yomu," pp. 118, 121. See also Iwaya Daishi, *Hijōji Nihon bundan shi* (Chūō Kōron sha, 1958), pp. 20, 70–75.

71. GNBZ 97:421.

72. NKBD 6:127. Ten thousand copies were printed.

73. TJZ 23:188.

Bibliography

Most works cited only once, and translations cited mainly for reader convenience, have been excluded from this list. Some sparsely cited sources have been retained to reflect a larger, if less tangible, influence. More weight has been given to sources on the relatively unfamiliar topic of censorship.

Individual articles and works appearing in the periodicals and series listed here are given in the Index under the author's name.

As in the notes, the place of publication, when Tokyo, has been omitted for books in Japanese. A comma separating the surname and given name of a Japanese author indicates the use of Western name order in the cited work.

Works cited by abbreviation in the notes are cross-referenced by author and title.

Ara Masahito. *Sōseki kenkyū nenpyō*. Shūeisha, 1974.

Arima, Tatsuo. *The Failure of Freedom*. Cambridge: Harvard University Press, 1969.

AS. *Asahi Shimbun*.

Asai Kiyoshi. "Shimbun shōsetsu no hensen." *Kokubungaku: kaishaku to kanshō*, 28, no. 11 (September 1963): 86–90.

Banned Japanese Publications, 1923–1943. 57 reels. Library of Congress Microfilm, Orien Japan 74.

Bowring, Richard John. *Mori Ōgai and the Modernization of Japanese Culture*. Cambridge: Cambridge University Press, 1979.

CK. *Chūō Kōron*.

Enomoto Takashi. [1] "Bungei Konwakai: bungei tōsei e no ichikatei." *Waseda Daigaku Kōtō Gakuin kenkyū nenshi*, 6 (1961): 15–33.

———. [2] "Bungei Konwakai: sono seiritsu jijō to mondaiten." *Kokubungaku kenkyū*, 25 (Waseda Daigaku, March 1962): 227–35.

———. [3] "Bungei Konwakai to taishū sakka no ugoki." *Nihon bungaku* 11 no. 6 (Nihon bungaku kyōkai, June 1962): 628–33.

Bibliography

———. [4] "Bunka no taishūka mondai to kokkashugi henkō." *Shakai kagaku tōkyū*, 40 (Waseda Daigaku, March 1969): 1–32.

Ernst, Morris L., and Schwartz, Alan U. *Censorship: The Search for the Obscene.* New York: Macmillan, 1964.

Fairbank, John K.; Reischauer, Edwin O.; and Craig, Albert M. *East Asia: The Modern Transformation.* Boston: Houghton Mifflin Company, 1965.

Fridell, Wilbur M. "Government Ethics Textbooks in Late Meiji Japan." *Journal of Asian Studies*, 24, no. 4 (August 1970): 823–33.

Fujimura Tsukuru, ed. *Nihon bungaku daijiten.* 4 vols. Shinchōsha, 1934.

Fujiwara Kiyozō. *Meiji Taishō Shōwa kyōiku shisō gakusetsu jinbutsu shi.* 4 vols. Tōa seikeisha/Nippon keikokusha, 1942–1944.

Gendai Nihon bungaku daijiten. See GNBD.

Gendai Nihon bungaku zenshū. See GNBZ.

Gendai Nihon shōsetsu taikei. 65 vols. Kawade shobō, 1949.

GNBD. Hisamatsu Sen'ichi, Kimata Osamu, Naruse Masakatsu, Kawazoe Kunimoto, and Hasegawa Izumi, eds. *Gendai Nihon bungaku daijiten.* Meiji shoin, 1965.

GNBZ. *Gendai Nihon bungaku zenshū.* 100 vols. Chikuma shobō, 1967.

Goldstein, Sanford, and Shinoda, Seishi. *Tangled Hair.* Lafayette, Indiana: Purdue University Studies, 1971.

Hackett, Roger F. *Yamagata Aritomo in the Rise of Modern Japan, 1838–1922.* Cambridge: Harvard University Press, 1968.

Hall, John Whitney. "A Monarch for Modern Japan." *Political Development in Modern Japan.* Edited by Robert E. Ward. Princeton: Princeton University Press, 1968.

Hatanaka Shigeo. See SSDS.

Henderson, Dan Fenno. "Law and Political Modernization in Japan." *Political Development in Modern Japan.* Edited by Robert E. Ward. Princeton: Princeton University Press, 1968.

Hiraide Akira. See THZ.

Hiraide Shū. See THS; THZ.

Hirano Ken. "Nihon Bungaku Hōkoku Kai no seiritsu." *Bungaku* 29, no. 5 (May 1961): 1–8.

Hisamatsu Sen'ichi. See NBS.

Hōgetsu zenshū. 8 vols. Ten'yūsha, 1919.

Honma Hisao. *Meiji bungaku shi.* 2 vols. Tōkyōdō shuppan, 1964.

Huffman, James L. *Politics of the Meiji Press.* Honolulu: University Press of Hawaii, 1980.

Ienaga, Saburō. *The Pacific War.* New York: Pantheon Books, 1978.

Ichiko Teiji, Akiyama Ken, Ōkubo Tadashi, Kubota Jun, Tsutsumi Seiji, and Miyoshi Yukio, eds. *Nihon bungaku zenshi.* 6 vols. Gakutōsha, 1978.

Imai Yasuko. "Meiji-matsu bundan no ichi-chōkanzu." *Gakuen ronshū*, 16 (Hokkai Gakuen Daigaku, March 1970): 27–53.

Ishikawa Takuboku. *See* TZ.

Itoya Toshio. *Taigyaku jiken.* 31 shobō, 1970.

Japan Naimushō. *Shuppan Keisatsu shiryō, 1923–1938.* 4 Reels. Library of Congress Microfilm, Orien Japan 0107.

Jō Ichirō. *Hakkinbon hyakunen.* Tōgensha, 1969.

———. *Zoku hakkinbon.* Tōgensha, 1965.

Kafū zenshū. See KZ.

KBHS. Saitō Shōzō. *Kindai bungei hikka shi.* Sūbundō, 1924.

KBHT. *Kindai bungaku hyōron taikei.* 10 vols. Kadokawa shoten, 1971.

Keene, Donald. "The Barren Years." *Monumenta Nipponica* 33, no. 1 (Spring 1978): 67–112.

———. "Japanese Literature and Politics in the 1930s." *Journal of Japanese Studies* 2, no. 2 (Spring 1976): 225–48.

———. "Japanese Writers and the Greater East Asia War." *Landscapes and Portraits.* Tokyo: Kodansha International, 1971.

———. *Landscapes and Portraits.* Tokyo: Kodansha International, 1971.

———. *World Within Walls.* New York: Holt, Rinehart and Winston, 1976.

Kindai bungaku hyōron taikei. See KBHT.

Kindai bungei hikka shi. See KBHS.

Kokumin Shimbun. See KS.

Konta Yōzō. *Edo non hon'yasan.* Nippon Hōsō shuppan kyōkai, 1977.

Kornicki, Peter F. "Nishiki no Ura: An Instance of Censorship and the Structure of a *Sharebon.*" *Monumenta Nipponica* 32, no. 2 (Summer 1977): 153–88.

Kōtoku Shūsui zenshū henshū iinkai, ed. *Taigyaku jiken arubamu.* Meiji bunken, 1972.

Kōza: Nihon kindai hō hattatsu shi. See OKS.

KS. *Kokumin Shimbun.*

Kubota Masafumi. "*Bungaku Hōkoku* o yomu." *Bungaku* 29, no. 12 (December 1961): 78–85.

———. "*Nihon Gakugei Shimbun* o yomu." *Bungaku* 29, no. 8 (August 1961): 114–21.

Kunikida Doppo zenshū. 10 vols. Gakushū kenkyūsha, 1964.

KZ. *Kafū zenshū.* 28 vols. Iwanami shoten, 1962.

Lifton, Robert Jay; Katō, Shūichi; and Reich, Michael R. *Six Lives / Six Deaths.* New Haven: Yale University Press, 1979.

McKeon, Richard; Merton, Robert K.; and Gellhorn, Walter. *The Freedom to Read.* New York: R. R. Bowker Company, 1957.

McLaren, W. W. "Japanese Government Documents." *Transactions of the Asiatic Society of Japan* 42, no. 1 (1914).

Maruyama, Masao. *Thought and Behaviour in Modern Japanese Politics.* London: Oxford University Press, 1969.

Matsumoto Gaku. *Bunka to seiji.* Tōkō shoin, 1939.

————. "The Cultural League of Nations / Proposition." Pamphlet. Nippon Bunka Renmei, June 1936.

Matsuura Sōzō. *Senryō-ka no genron dan'atsu.* Gendai jānarizumu shuppan kai, 1977.

Mayabara Shigeo. See MBHS.

MBHS. Mayabara Shigeo. *Nihon bungei hakkin shi.* Sōgensha, 1952.

MBZ. *Meiji bungaku zenshū.* 100 vols. Chikuma shobō, 1965.

Meiji bungaku zenshū. See MBZ.

MGH. Midoro Masaichi. *Meiji Taishō shi 1: Genronhen.* Asahi Shimbun sha, 1930.

Midoro Masaichi. See MGH.

Mimasaka Tarō, Fujita Chikamasa, and Watanabe Kiyoshi. *Yokohama jiken.* Nihon editā sukūru shuppanbu, 1977.

MITC. Mitchell, Richard H. *Thought Control in Prewar Japan.* Ithaca: Cornell University Press, 1976.

Mori Junzaburō. *Ōgai Mori Rintarō.* Morikita shoten, 1942.

Mori Ōgai. See MOZ; OZ.

Moriyama Shigeo. *Taigyaku jiken: bungaku sakka ron.* 31 shobō, 1980.

MOZ. *Mori Ōgai zenshū.* 9 vols. Chikuma shobō, 1971.

Myōjō.

Nagai Kafū. See KZ

Naimushō Keihokyoku, ed. *Kinshi tankōbon mokuroku.* 1935. Reprint (vol. 1 of series). *Hakkinbon kankei shiryō shūsei.* 4 vols. Kohokusha, 1976.

————. *Shuppan Keisatsu gaikan.* See SKG.

————. *Shuppan Keisatsu hō.* 1928–1933. Reprint (15 vols.). Ryūkei shosha, 1981.

————. *Shuppan Keisatsu shiryō.* See Japan Naimushō.

Nakamura Mitsuo. *Meiji bungaku shi.* Chikuma shobō, 1963.

Natsume Sōseki. See SZ.

NBS. Hisamatsu Sen'ichi, ed. *Nihon bungaku shi: kindai.* Shibundō, 1966.

Nihon bungaku no rekishi. 12 vols. Kadokawa shoten, 1967.

Nihon bungaku shi: kindai. See NBS.

Nihon kindai bungaku daijiten. See NKBD.

Nihon kindai bungaku taikei. See NKBT.

Nihon no rekishi. 26 vols. Chūō kōron-sha, 1967.

Nihon oyobi Nihonjin. See NoN.

Nihon puroretaria bungaku taikei. See NPBT.

NKBD. Nihon Kindai Bungakkan, ed. *Nihon kindai bungaku daijiten.* 6 vols. Kōdansha, 1977.

NKBT. *Nihon kindai bungaku taikei.* 61 vols. Kadokawa shoten, 1968.

Nomura Shōgo. *Denki: Tanizaki Jun'ichirō.* Rokkō shuppan, 1974.

NoN. *Nihon oyobi Nihonjin.*

Notehelfer, F. G. *Kōtoku Shūsui, Portrait of a Japanese Radical.* Cambridge: Cambridge University Press, 1971.

NPBT. *Nihon puroretaria bungaku taikei.* 9 vols. 31 shobō, 1955–1976.

Odagiri Hideo, ed. *Hakkin sakuhin shū*. Hokushindō, 1957. See also OHSS.

————. *Zoku hakkin sakuhin shū*. Hokushindō, 1957.

Odagiri Hideo, and Fukuoka Ikichi, eds. *Zōhoban Shōwa shoseki-shimbun-zasshi hakkin nenpyō*. 3 vols. Kawasaki: Meiji bunken shiryō kankōkai, 1981.

Ōgai zenshū. *See* OZ.

OHSS. Odagiri Hideo, ed. *Hakkin sakuhin shū*. Yakumo shoten, 1948.

Ōi Hirosuke. "Bungaku Hōkoku Kai wa mui." *Bungaku* 29, no. 5 (May 1961): 87–91.

Oka Yoshitake, "Nichiro senso-go ni okeru atarashii sedai no seichō." 2 parts. *Shisō* 512 (February 1967): 137–49. *Shisō* 513 (March 1967): 361–76.

Okano Takeo. *Kindai Nihon meicho kaidai*. Yūmei shobō, 1962.

Okazaki Yoshie. *Genji monogatari no bi*. Hōbunkan, 1960.

OKS. Okudaira Yasuhiro. "Ken'etsu seido." In *Kōza: Nihon kindai hō hattatsu shi*. Edited by Ukai Nobushige, Fukushima Masao, Kawashima Takenori, and Tsuji Kiyoaki. Keisō shobō, 1967.

Okudaira Yasuhiro. *See* OKS; OPC.

Ono Hideo. *Nihon shimbun shi*. Ryōsho fukyūkai, 1948.

OPC. Okudaira, Yasuhiro. "Political Censorship in Japan from 1931 to 1945." Mimeographed paper distributed by the Institute of Legal Research, Law School, University of Pennsylvania (1962).

Ōtsuki Takeshi, and Matsumura Ken'ichi. *Aikokushin kyōiku no shiteki kyūmei*. Aoki shoten, 1970.

OZ. *Ōgai zenshū*. 35 vols. Iwanami shoten, 1936.

Pyle, Kenneth B. "The Technology of Japanese Nationalism: The Local Improvement Movement, 1900–1918." *Journal of Asian Studies* 33, no. 1 (November 1973): 51–65.

Rubin, Jay. "Sōseki on Individualism: '*Watakushi no Kojinshugi*.'" *Monumenta Nipponica* 34, no. 1 (Spring 1979): 21–48.

Saegusa Shigeo. *Genron Shōwa shi*. Nihon hyōron shinsha, 1958.

Saitō Shōzō. *Gendai hikka bunken dai-nenpyō*. Suikodō shoten, 1932.

————. *See* KBHS.

Sansom, G. B. *Japan: A Short Cultural History*. New York: Appleton-Century Crofts, 1943.

————. *The Western World and Japan*. New York: Alfred A. Knopf, 1958.

Sansom, George. *A History of Japan, 1615–1867*. London: Cresset Press, 1964.

Sebald, William J., trans. *The Criminal Code of Japan*. Kobe: Japan Chronicle Press, 1936.

Seidensticker, Edward. *Kafū the Scribbler*. Stanford: Stanford University Press, 1965.

Sesar, Carl. *Takuboku: Poems to Eat*. Tokyo and Palo Alto: Kodansha International, 1966.

Shiga Naoya. *Shiga Naoya taiwa shū*. Daiwa shobō, 1969.

Shimamura Hōgetsu. *See Hōgetsu zenshū*.

Shinchō.

Shinshichō: Fukuseiban Shinshichō. Rinsen shoten, 1967.

Shiota Shōbei, and Watanabe Junzō, eds. *Hiroku taigyaku jiken.* 2 vols. Shunjūsha, 1961.

Shizenshugi no kenkyū. See SK.

Shuppan Keisatsu Gaikan. See SKG.

Sibley, William F. "Naturalism in Japanese Literature." *Harvard Journal of Asiatic Studies* 28 (1968): 157–69.

Silberman, Bernard S., and Harootunian, H. D., eds. *Japan in Crisis.* Princeton: Princeton University Press, 1974.

SK: Yoshida Seiichi. *Shizenshugi no kenkyū.* 2 vols. Tōkyōdō shuppan, 1955–1958.

SKG. Naimushō Keihokyoku, ed. *Shuppan Keisatsu Gaikan.* 1930–1935. Reprint (3 vols.). Ryūkei shosha, 1981.

Sōseki zenshū. See SZ.

SSDS. Hatanaka Shigeo. *Oboegaki: Shōwa shuppan dan'atsu shōshi.* Tosho shimbun, 1965.

Strong, Kenneth, trans. *Footprints in the Snow,* by Tokutomi Kenjirō. New York: Pegasus, 1970.

Sun Trade Journal, The. See TY.

SZ. *Sōseki zenshū.* 17 vols. Iwanami shoten, 1974.

Taigyaku jiken arubamu. See Kōtoku Shūsui.

Taiyō. See TY.

Taiyo, The. See TY.

Takuboku zenshū. See TZ.

Tanizaki Jun'ichirō. *See* TJZ.

Tayama Katai. *Tokyo no sanjūnen.* Edited by Maeda Akira. Kadokawa bunko, 1955.

Teihon Hiraide Shū shū. See THS.

Teihon Hiraide Shū shū (zoku). See THZ.

Teikoku Bungaku.

THS. *Teihon Hiraide Shū shū.* Shunjūsha, 1965.

THZ. *Teihon Hiraide Shū shū (zoku).* Shunjūsha, 1969.

TJZ. *Tanizaki Jun'ichirō zenshū.* 28 vols. Chūō Kōron sha, 1966.

Tokutomi Kenjirō. *Muhon ron.* Iwanami bunko, 1976.

————. *Footprints in the Snow.* Translated by Kenneth Strong. New York: Pegasus, 1970.

Trilling, Lionel. *The Liberal Imagination.* New York: Charles Scribner's Sons, 1976.

TY. *Taiyō.* Also contains *The Sun Trade Journal* and *The Taiyo.*

TZ. *Takuboku zenshū.* 17 vols. Iwanami shoten, 1953.

Wildes, Harry Emerson. *Social Currents in Japan.* Chicago: University of Chicago Press, 1927.

Yamada Seizaburō. *Puroretaria bungaku shi.* 2 vols. Rironsha, 1954.

Yoshida Seiichi. *See* SK.

Index

Kokumin Shimbun, 83–86 *passim*, 92, 170n,
    200, 214
Kokutai (national polity): defined, 6; and
    art, free thought, 6; and Christianity, 98,
    158, 272; propagation of, 106; and the
    irrational, 137; and democracy, 219; and
    individualism, liberalism, and Marxism,
    229; in law, 231; Movement for the
    Clarification of (*Kokutai meichō undō*),
    232, 283; mentioned, 76, 150, 159, 227
Komatsubara Eitarō: wants reform of litera-
    ture, 9, 199; conservative indoctrination
    by, 109–10; hosts writers, 112–13,
    198; need for wholesome literature, 199,
    205; and Committee on Literature,
    205–7, 210; leaves office, 213; policies
    prevail, 278; mentioned, 166n, 232, 250
Konoe Fumimaro, 257, 268n
Kornicki, Peter F., 19
Kōroku. *See* Satō Kōroku
Kōron, 271
Koshimaki Jiken (Waistcloth Incident), 44
Kōshokubon, 18
Kosugi Tengai: *Popular Song* (*Hayariuta*),
    51; compared with Katai, 100, 111;
    Demon Winds of Love (*Makaze koikaze*), 129
Kōtoku Incident. *See* High Treason case
Kōtoku Shūsui: as pacifist, 55, 57; as seen
    by Hiraide Shū, 162–63; as seen by
    Tokutomi Roka, 172–74; mentioned,
    145–48 *passim*, 152, 157, 159–60,
    167, 168, 179, 180n, 185, 186, 195,
    230
Koyama Matsukichi, 83, 84, 85
Kōyō. *See* Ozaki Kōyō
Kropotkin, Pëtr, 179, 186n, 230
Kubokawa Tsurujirō, 274
Kubota Masafumi, 277
Kume Masao, 246, 251, 253n, 275
Kunikida Doppo: "Byōshōroku," 61–62;
    "The Bamboo Gate" ("Take no kido"),
    65; mentioned, 76, 78, 216
Kurahara Korehito, 249
Kuroda Seiki, 44

Lady Chatterley's Lover, 233
Law. *See* Censorship: laws; Constitution;
    Criminal Code; Peace Preservation Law
League for Academic and Artistic Freedom
    (Gakugei Jiyū Dōmei), 251–52
Lèse majesté, 160n, 162
Liberalism/libertarianism (*jiyūshugi*), 249,
    258

Literary Chat Society (Bungei Konwakai),
    232, 250–55
Literary Society (Bungei Kyōkai), 215–18
Literature: developed in spite of govern-
    ment, 203, 208–9, 253
"Literature and Zeit-Geist," 66
Local Improvement Movement (*Chihō kairyō
    undō*), 108–9

McKeon, Richard, 4
Maeda Akira, 95
Maeterlinck, Maurice, 127
Magazines: general, 257; "voluntary dis-
    solution" of liberal magazines, 262. *See
    also Arusu*; *Bungei Kurabu*; *Bungei Sekai*;
    Bungei Sensen; *Bungei Shunjū*; *Chūō Kōron*;
    Cultural Nippon; *Fujin Kōron*; *Hototogisu*;
    Jinmin Bunko; *Josei*; *Kaizō*; *Kindai Shisō*;
    King; *Kokumin no Tomo*; *Kōron*; *Myōjō*;
    Nihon Hyōron; *Nihon oyobi Nihonjin*; *Seika-
    tsu to Geijutsu*; *Senki*; *Shinchō*; *Shinsei*;
    Shinshichō; *Shinshōsetsu*; *Shirakaba*; *Sōmō
    Zasshi*; *Subaru*; *The Sun Trade Journal*;
    Taiyō; *The Taiyo*; *Teikoku Bungaku*; *Tōa
    Bungei*; *Waseda Bungaku*
Magic manuscripts (*omajinai genkō*), 261
Makino Shinken, 63, 203n
"Mama" and "papa" subversive, 249
Manchukuo, 266
Manchurian Incident, 10, 230, 232, 249,
    250, 251
Manchuria Railway Company, 268
Man'yōshū, 217, 220
"Marseillaise," 123, 186
Masamune Hakuchō: on Fūyō, 77n; "life
    unresolved," 185; on Committee on Lit-
    erature, 206, 208; and *enbon* boom, 247;
    on academy (1934), 252–53; militarists
    disapprove of, 262; and Japanese Litera-
    ture Patriotic Association, 274n, 277
—works: "Pool Parlor" ("Tamatsukiya"),
    65; "Where?" ("Doko e"), 65, 81; "A
    Dangerous Character" ("Kiken jin-
    butsu"), 187–88; "Faint Light"
    ("Bikō"), 213, 214
Masaoka Geiyō: *O Land of Prostitution!* (*Aa
    baiinkoku*), 47n
Masaoka Shiki, 60
Matsudaira Sadanobu, 18, 19, 206
Matsui Sumako, 218
Matsumoto Gaku, 250–55, 278
Matsushita Eitarō, 269
Matsuzaki Tenmin, 84

Niwa Fumio: "Naval Engagement" ("Kaisen"), 261–62
Nogi Maresuke: in Russo-Japanese War, 56; suicide, 218, 222–24; with Peers' School Swim Club, 223n
Nogi Shizuko, 222–24
Notehelfer, F. G., 56
Nude art, 43–45, 57, 67

Odagiri Susumu, 272
Oda Sakunosuke, 277
Oden, 37–38
Ōgai. *See* Mori Ōgai
Oguri Fūyō: and "distressing fiction," 41; defends fiction, 63–64; and writer's social role, 70–82 *passim*; as scribbler, 72, 79–80; compared with Tenkei, 98; compared with Katai, 99, 100
—works: "Making Up for Bed" ("Neoshiroi"), 42–43, 64, 70; "Cold and Flaming" ("Ryōen"), 74; "Lazy Woman" ("Gūtara onna"), 74–76; *Shattered Love (Koizame)*, 74, 96; "Big Sister's Little Sister" ("Ane no imōto"), 120, 124, 126–27
Ōhara Social Problems Research Institute (Ōhara Shakai Mondai Kenkyūjo), 266n
Ōi Hirosuke, 276
Ōishi Seinosuke, 157–58, 159–60, 172
Okada Ryōhei, 113, 199, 210, 211
Okami, 189
Okamoto Ippei: "Record of a Second Marriage" ("Saikonki"), 262
Okazaki Yoshie, 260
Okinu, 37, 92–93, 199
Okudaira Yasuhiro, 21
Ōkuma Shigenobu, 92
Ōmachi Keigetsu, 57, 58, 134, 156, 200, 211
Omatsu, 37, 42
Ōmori Naomichi, 267
One Hundred Poems by One Hundred Poets (Hyakunin-isshu), 277
One-yen books, 246–47, 249
Ono Yasuhito, 268n
Osanai Kaoru, 281
Osaragi Jirō, 253n
Ōsugi Sakae, 180, 184–86, 282
Ozaki Kōyō: "The Erotic Confessions of Two Nuns" ("Ninin Bikuni: Irozange"), 40–41; *The Golden Demon (Konjiki yasha)*, 77; mentioned, 42, 60, 63, 74, 76, 131
Ozaki Saburō, 35
Ozaki Shirō, 254n, 275

Paper rationing, 10, 233, 270–71
Peace Preservation Law (Chian iji hō), 228, 231, 249, 267
Pearl Harbor, 10, 257, 273, 275
Penal Code, 134, 158, 162
Pitt, William, the Younger, 144
Poison women (*dokufu*), 37–38, 92
Police. *See* Special Higher Police
Police brutality, 228, 249, 268–70
Police Bureau: Chief on naturalism, 94. *See also* Censorship: agencies
Political novel, 38–39
Popular literature, 246, 251–54
Press Law, 4–5, 8, 15, 26, 115–17, 145
Press Regulations, 4, 15–16, 23–26, 55
Proletarian Cultural Federation (KOPF), 249, 250
Proletarian literature, 184–86, 247, 251
Publication Law, 4–5, 15, 27, 117, 249
Publication Regulations. *See* Censorship: laws
Publishing companies merged, 271

Radio, 248
Raichō. *See* Hiratsuka Haruko
The Ramayana, 212
Red Flag Incident, 108, 166n
Reign of Terror, 21, 148
Revere the Emperor, Expel the Barbarian (*Sonnō-jōi*), 261
Roan. *See* Uchida Roan
Roka. *See* Tokutomi Roka
Rokkaku: "The Committee on Literature: A Tragedy in One Act," 205, 207
Romeo and Juliet, 215
Roosevelt, Franklin D., 278
Roth case, 89
Russell, Bertrand, 230n
Russian literature, 39, 60
Ryūhoku. *See* Narushima Ryūhoku
Ryūtei Tanehiko: *The False Murasaki and the Rustic Genji (Nise-Murasaki inaka-Genji)*, 19, 190–91

Saigō Takamori, 21, 173, 174
Saikaku, 18, 48, 280
Saionji Kinmochi: "liberal," 59, 63, 111; and Zola, 96n; and writers, 112; and Katsura, 145, 149; and Hara Kei, 167; second cabinet of, 213, 214, 219, 281
Saitō Makoto, 83, 249, 250, 254
Saitō Ryokuu, 76
Sakaguchi Ango, 277
Sakaino Kōyō, 307n73